Eli M. Bower

March 1964

Essays on

EGO PSYCHOLOGY

Selected Problems in Psychoanalytic Theory

HEINZ HARTMANN

By the Same Author

EGO PSYCHOLOGY AND THE PROBLEM OF ADAPTATION

PSYCHOANALYSIS AND MORAL VALUES

Essays on

EGO PSYCHOLOGY

Selected Problems in Psychoanalytic Theory

HEINZ HARTMANN

INTERNATIONAL UNIVERSITIES PRESS, INC.

NEW YORK

Contents

Preface   vii

Introduction   ix

Part I

1. Psychoanalysis and the Concept of Health   1
✓2. Psychoanalysis and Sociology   19
3. On Rational and Irrational Action   37
4. Comments on the Psychoanalytic Theory of
   Instinctual Drives   69
5. The Application of Psychoanalytic Concepts to
   Social Science   90
6. Psychoanalysis and Developmental Psychology   99
7. Comments on the Psychoanalytic Theory of the Ego   113
8. Technical Implications of Ego Psychology   142
9. The Mutual Influences in the Development of Ego and Id   155
10. Contribution to the Metapsychology of Schizophrenia   182
11. Problems of Infantile Neurosis   207
12. Notes on the Theory of Sublimation   215
13. Notes on the Reality Principle   241
14. The Development of the Ego Concept in Freud's Work   268
15. Comments on the Scientific Aspects of Psychoanalysis   297
16. Psychoanalysis as a Scientific Theory   318

Part II

17. On Parapraxes in the Korsakoff Psychosis   353
18. Understanding and Explanation   369
19. An Experimental Contribution to the Psychology of Obsessive-Compulsive Neurosis: On Remembering Completed and Uncompleted Tasks   404
20. Psychiatric Studies of Twins   419

Bibliography   446
Bibliographical Notes   464
Author Index   467
Subject Index   473

Preface

THE first part of this volume consists of a selection of essays on psychoanalytic theory written and published between 1939 and 1959. The second part contains some earlier publications whose primary concern was not with the development of analytic theories, but which still, in one way or another, seem to me to contribute to it. The papers contained in Part I are reproduced in chronological order and have hardly been changed. Thus a certain number of repetitions has become unavoidable. As the essays—even those which form the first part of this volume—present the development of my thought over a comparatively long period, formulations on the same subjects occasionally differ in earlier and later papers. Finally, I want to mention that references to work done after the first appearance of the individual articles have been added in only very few instances.

I want to thank Dr. Stefan Betlheim for his permission to publish in this volume the paper written in collaboration with me (Chapter 17).

I want to thank the translators for undertaking the arduous task of providing an English rendition of those papers which were originally written and published in German. The late Dr. David Rapaport translated Chapter 17. Prof. Jacob Needleman, Dept. of Philosophy, San Francisco State College, undertook the translation of Chapter 18; Dr. Lewis W. Brandt, Dept. of Psychology, Farleigh Dickinson University, translated Chapters 19 and 20.

I am particularly grateful to Mrs. Lottie Maury Newman both for her many valuable editorial suggestions and for her review of the translations. I appreciate above all the comprehensive knowledge of the field she brings to bear on her work, her steady helpfulness, and her clear-sighted judgment.

Introduction

THE papers included in this volume deal with various aspects of psychoanalytic theory, the large majority of them more specifically with the topic indicated by the main title of this book. This is not the place to determine in detail their position with respect to various trends in the development of psychoanalytic psychology, but in some of them this point is referred to more extensively. The history of Freud's later thought, particularly on ego psychology, has repeatedly been traced by myself, E. Kris, and Rapaport. These historical studies describe in part Freud's own work and in part that of later contributors. Here it must suffice to state that as a consequence of Freud's work on the ego in the twenties and thirties, we now attribute greater importance to the ego in the total human personality, and gradually have come to emphasize the ego's partial independence as to its structural, dynamic, and economic aspects.

Freud's structural point of view, and above all his later hypotheses on the functions and development of the ego, added a new dimension to psychoanalytic psychology. They indicated an inherent potential for growth, and their actual fruitfulness was soon realized. While in his later papers he gave a very comprehensive outline of the field, he could no longer give it the same kind of systematic elaboration he had given to other chapters of psychoanalysis. However, an important step in this direction was made during his lifetime by Anna Freud in her subtle classification of the mechanisms the ego uses in its defenses against the instinctual drives and against outer reality. The stimulating effect of these works on the clinical, theoretical, and technical developments of psychoanalysis was broad and incisive.

My first approach to some of the questions that had been asked or could be asked in the new area of research were laid down in *Ego Psychology and the Problem of Adaptation* (1939). In some instances, the papers collected in this volume represent an unfolding of points of view and hypotheses I introduced in that essay.

The consistent study of the ego and its functions promised to bring analysis closer to the aim Freud had set for it long ago—to become a general psychology in the broadest sense of the word. The thorough investigation of the drives and their development had for a long time been at the core of psychoanalytic psychology; to it was later added a close scrutiny of the defensive activities of the ego. A next step pointed to extending the analytic approach to the manifold activities of the ego which can be subsumed under the concept of the "conflict-free sphere." However, the ego functions so described can under circumstances become secondarily involved in conflicts of various kinds. On the other hand, they often do exert an influence on the conditions and outcomes of conflicts. This means that our attempts to explain concrete situations of conflict will often have to consider also the nonconflictual elements. These observations and considerations can lead us to a better understanding of health and achievement, aside from the understanding of impairment and distortion of function—the area which strictly speaking had never been the sole subject matter of psychoanalysis, though it is still the one to which analysis has made the essential contributions. The broadening of the psychoanalytic approach I have in mind here has so far probably been most fruitful in the direct observation of child development by analysts. This clearly presupposes a theory of adaptation (and of integration), which in turn means also a theory of object relationships and social relationships in general. Such a theory of adaptation will be more useful for our purposes the more clearly it shows the interplay between adaptive functions and the synthetic (or organizing) functions—in which ways the former facilitate, or interfere with, the latter, and vice versa.

In one of his latest papers (1937) Freud suggested that not only the instinctual drives but also the ego might have a hereditary core.

I think we have the right to assume that there are, in man, inborn apparatuses which I have called primary autonomy, and that these primary autonomous apparatuses of the ego and their maturation constitute one foundation for the relations to external reality. Among these factors originating in the hereditary core of the ego, there are also those which serve postponement of discharge, that is, which are of an inhibitory nature. They may well serve as models for later defenses.

On the other hand, many, though not all, ego activities can be traced genetically to determinants in the id or to conflicts between ego and id. In the course of development, however, they normally acquire a certain amount of autonomy from these genetic factors. The ego's achievements may under some circumstances be reversible, but it is important to know that in normal conditions many of them are not. The degree to which its activities have become functionally independent from their origins is essential for the undisturbed functioning of the ego, and so is the degree to which they are protected against regression and instinctualization. We speak of the degrees of this independence of the ego as the degrees of secondary autonomy.

This view—and I mention it here because the point has sometimes not been fully understood—certainly does not imply any neglect of the genetic point of view, which is fundamental in psychoanalysis. But it means a differentiation in our approach to the processes of mental development; and it means a clearer differentiation between the concepts of function and of genesis which is particularly necessary in the psychology of the ego. Even in the same individual different ego functions may show different degrees of secondary autonomy. This is one of several reasons why not only the differences between ego and id, and between ego and superego, are relevant, but also differences in the ego itself and the cooperation and antagonisms between its various functions (the concept of intrasystemic conflicts belongs in this context). Both in a general way, or in studying concrete situations in mental life, we may speak of a hierarchy of functions and of layers of motivation. Ego psychology is im-

portant for a general psychology not only because it adds certain
layers of motivations to others long since known in psychoanalysis.
It is important also because only on this level has analysis come to
a fuller understanding of the ways in which the various layers inter-
relate. Freud's later theory of anxiety may be the best example of
this. Comparable multidimensional structural considerations, and especially again the knowledge of the human ego, lead also to a neater
definition not of the psychoanalytic field but of the psychoanalytic
approach as against the "biological," and allow the understanding
of a significant distinction between man and lower animals: the
sharper differentiation between ego and id functions in the human
precludes the functional equation of "animal instincts" with what in
analysis is called "instinctual drives."

The differential study of the ego suggests also a broadening of
the concept of structure, and it has become meaningful to speak of
"structures in the ego" and of "structures in the superego." This
refers, in contrast to "flexibility," to a "relative stability" of functions,
as it is clearly observable, e.g., in the automatisms.

All these problems have to be considered also from the economic
point of view. Many of the activities of the ego are object-directed.
A further clarifying distinction is that between the cathexes of functions and the cathexes of contents. And the concept of cathexis of
the ego (as against cathexis of id or superego) does not coincide
with cathexis of the "self" (as against object cathexis). I have
therefore proposed that we differentiate libidinal cathexis of the
"self," or the "self-image" ("self-representation"), from the cathexis
of the ego functions, and reserve the term narcissism for the former.

Freud has repeatedly stated that the ego works with desexualized
energy. It seemed reasonable, to me as to other analysts, to broaden
this statement to include also energies derived from aggression
which, through the mediation of the ego, can be modified in a way
analogous to desexualization. The term neutralization refers, then,
to the process by which both libidinal and aggressive energies are
changed away from the instinctual and toward a noninstinctual

mode—or to the results of this change. (I want to mention here, for the sake of clarification, that the term neutralized energy, as used here, is not fully synonymous with the term *"indifferente Energie,"* rendered in the *Standard Edition* by "neutral energy," which Freud used in a passage of *The Ego and the Id.*) With the help of this conceptualization we can unambiguously describe the clinically important distinction of sexualization (or instinctualization in general) and neutralization. Secondary autonomy and neutralization are closely related to each other and to the reality principle. Their development allows the ego to perform reality-syntonic tasks beyond the pressures of need fulfillment. They are biologically essential, if we accept Freud's thesis that in the human it is mainly the ego to which self-preservation is entrusted. Moreover, neutralization of aggression is of particular importance in that it provides man with a way out of the dire dilemma of destroying either the objects or himself.

It is justified and useful to posit different stages or degrees of neutralization, that is, transitional states between instinctual and fully neutralized energy. We may also assume that the optimal functioning of different ego activities (e.g., defenses on the one hand and thought processes on the other) is dependent on different shades of neutralization. These degrees seem correlated with transitional states in the replacement of primary by secondary processes; but this point is clearly in need of further investigation.

As I just said, or implied, it would be wrong to expect that all successful activities of the ego invariably work necessarily best with the maximum of neutralization. It is also evident, e.g., in the case of adaptional processes, that, functionally speaking, the use of the most highly differentiated ego activities alone does not necessarily guarantee an optimum of adaptation; more primitive functions may be needed to supplement them. It even happens that the ego itself, for its own purposes, puts some of its highly differentiated functions temporarily out of action. This leads back to the problem of a hierarchical organization of ego functions.

Once the ego has developed into a separate system of personality, it has also accumulated a reservoir of neutralized energy, which means that the energies required for its functions need not depend entirely on *ad hoc* neutralization. This is part of its relative independence from immediate inside or outside pressures, and this relative independence is part of a general trend in human development. It is likely that part of the energy which the ego uses is not derived (by way of neutralization) from the drives but belongs from the very first to the ego, or to the inborn precursors of what will later be specific ego functions. We may speak of it as primary ego energy.

These brief notes, having the character of a summary, must of course waive all claim to completeness. But I also want to say that all the problems discussed and the thoughts advanced in these papers do not amount to a systematic presentation of ego psychology, much less to a systematic presentation of the theories of psychoanalysis in general. The textbook on ego psychology remains to be written.

But a tendency toward an at least partial integration, or "architectural adjustment," of the theories with which I am dealing is obvious in a considerable number of the chapters of this book. There is a sufficient inner coherence between them, a thematic relationship and continuity of approach, to make me feel that their publication as a unit is justified and, I hope, useful.

I might at this point state explicitly that the prevalent concern with theory does not mean a neglect of the clinical foundations of psychoanalysis, nor does the emphasis on ego psychology imply an underrating of other aspects of analytic theory. The development and clarification of theory have proved essential to the progress of clinical analysis; moreover, a certain degree of specialization in matters of research has had a salutary effect in psychoanalysis, as in other fields. Of course, the "theories by reduction," frequent in various writings today, which base their explanatory attempts on only a very few of the many factors I consider essential, can hardly avoid the danger of sterility. I have consistently aimed at solving the problems of ego psychology by studying them in the framework of the general tenets of psychoanalytic theory, and I hope that in this

I have succeeded. Some authors have suggested that one develop a theory of the ego which disregards the basic insights we owe to Freud into the psychology of instinctual drives and into their interactions with ego functions. I would consider such an attempt as definitely unpromising.

The approach to the developmental, integrative, adaptive, economic aspects of the ego which I propose in these papers may well facilitate the interchange between knowledge gained in analysis and knowledge gained by other methods of psychology. Some of the concepts I use were introduced also with the aim in mind to allow an easier correlation of analytic data with data obtained by the direct observation of children. It could be anticipated too that the trend in analysis I am writing about contains possibilities for developing propositions which may become the starting point for psychological experimentation. Recent research appears to confirm this expectation.

PART I

CHAPTER I

Psychoanalysis
and the Concept of Health

(1939)

PERHAPS it would be true to say that we attach less importance in analytic circles to differentiating between healthy and pathological behavior than is often done outside those circles. But the concepts of "health" and "illness" always exert a "latent" influence, so to say, on our analytic habits of thought, and it cannot but serve a useful purpose to clarify the implications of these terms. Moreover, it would be a mistake to suppose that the subject possesses no more than a theoretical interest, that it lacks any practical significance. For, when all is said and done, it often depends upon the analytic concept of health whether we recommend a course of analytic treatment—so that the matter is important as a factor in our judgment of the indications present—or what changes we should like to see effected in a patient, or when we may consider that an analysis is ripe for termination. Differences of outlook in this sphere must ultimately lead to corresponding differences in our therapeutic technique, as was clearly foreseen by Ernest Jones (1913) many years ago.

While psychoanalysis was still in its infancy, it seemed a relatively simple matter to define mental health and mental illness. During this period we became acquainted for the first time with the conflicts which give rise to neuroses and believed that we had thereby acquired the right to differentiate between health and illness. Subsequently the discovery was made that conflicts such as those we had come to regard as pathogenic could be shown to exist also in healthy people; it became apparent that the choice between health and illness was determined rather by temporal and quantitative factors. To a greater extent than any theoretical considerations our therapeutic experience has compelled us to recognize this truth. It has been found that our efforts have met with very variable success, and we are not always able to accept the familiar explanations of the responsibility for this state of affairs. We are finally forced to the conclusion that the quantitative factor of the strength of the instinctual drives and a quantitative factor residing in the ego function have here acquired, side by side with other factors of course, an importance of their own. Moreover, mechanisms are evidently not as such pathogenic but only in virtue of their topographical value in space and their dynamic value in action, if I may so express myself. The process of modifying the original analytic conception of health has been advanced a stage further by the contributions to the psychology of the ego which have now been in the forefront of psychoanalytic interest for nearly twenty years. But the more we begin to understand the ego and its maneuvers and achievements in dealing with the external world, the more do we tend to make these functions of adaptation, achievement, etc., the touchstone of the concept of health.

However, a psychoanalytic definition of health presents certain difficulties which we shall now proceed to examine. As is well known, it is never at any time an easy matter to say what we really mean by "health" and "illness" and perhaps the difficulty of differentiating between them is even greater when we are concerned with the so-called "psychological illnesses" than it is with physical maladies. Health is certainly not a purely statistical average. If it were, we should have to look upon the exceptional achievements of single individuals as pathological, which would be contrary to the ordinary usage of speech; and besides this, a majority of people exhibit characteristics which are generally regarded as pathological (the example

4 ·

most frequently given being caries of the teeth). "Abnormal" then, in the sense of a deviation from the average, is not synonymous with "pathological."

In the conceptions of health most widely prevalent, subjective valuations play a considerable part, whether explicitly or implicitly, and that is the chief reason why such conceptions, especially when they relate to mental health and mental illness, may vary considerably at different periods and among different peoples. Here judgment is influenced by a subjective factor depending on cultural and social conditions and even personal values. Within a uniform society these judgments will exhibit a far-reaching similarity, but that does not deprive them in the least of their subjective character. "Health" is generally one expression of the idea of vital perfection; and this itself implies the subjectivity of the judgments concerning it. A logical analysis of the concept of health would have to devote especial attention to the valuations embodied in the different conceptions of health.[1]

But these are not the only difficulties inherent in a psychoanalytic definition of health. So long as we make freedom from symptoms, for instance, the criterion of mental health, it is comparatively easy in practice to arrive at a decision. Even by this standard there exists no absolutely objective basis for our judgment; for a simple answer is not readily forthcoming to the question whether a given mental manifestation is in the nature of a symptom or whether on the contrary it is to be regarded as an "achievement." It is often a difficult matter to decide whether the pedantry or ambition of an individual or the nature of his object choice are symptoms in a neurotic sense or character traits possessing a positive value for health. Nevertheless this standard does provide us, if not with a basis for objective judgment, at all events with a consensus of opinion which is usually sufficient for all practical purposes. But health as it is understood in psychoanalysis is something which means far more than this. In our

[1] For a further elaboration of this problem, see Hartmann (1960a, 1960b).

view, freedom from symptoms is not enough for health; and we cherish higher expectations of the therapeutic effects of psychoanalysis. But over and above this, psychoanalysis has witnessed the development of a number of theoretical conceptions of health which often lay down very severe standards. We have accordingly to ask ourselves what health signifies in a psychoanalytic sense.

By way of preamble I would remark that man's relation to health and illness itself often presents features of a distinctly neurotic order. When these problems are very much in the foreground one is sometimes actually tempted to speak of a "health neurosis." This idea is made the basis of a paper recently published by Melitta Schmideberg (1938).[2] A conspicuous characteristic in certain well-marked types is their conviction that they themselves enjoy superior health, accompanied by a compulsive urge to detect in others deviations, mainly of a neurotic or psychotic kind, from their ideal of health. In certain circumstances such people are capable of fulfilling a useful function in society by very reason of their particular form of neurosis, which may mark them out for the role of eternal sick nurse to their fellow men. In the simplest form of this behavior the operative mechanism is commonly projection; by constantly seeing others as patients in need of one's help one avoids recognition of one's own neurosis. In the same way Freud once expressed the opinion that many analysts probably learn to absolve themselves from personal compliance with the obligations of analysis by exacting it from others. We know too that a like tendency to overestimate the neurotic and psychotic reactions of one's fellow men belongs to the growing pains of many analysts. It is a common feature of "health neuroses" that those afflicted by them cannot allow themselves to suffer or to feel ill or depressed (Schmideberg, 1938). But a healthy person must have the capacity to suffer and to be depressed. Our clinical experience has taught us the consequences of glossing over illness and suffering, of being unable to admit to oneself the possi-

[2] See also the observation made by Glover in the ensuing discussion, quoted on p. 141.

bility of illness and suffering. It is even probable that a limited amount of suffering and illness forms an integral part of the scheme of health, as it were, or rather that health is only reached by indirect ways. We know that successful adaptation can lead to maladaptation—the development of the superego is a case in point, and many other examples could be cited. But conversely, maladaptation may become successful adaptation. Typical conflicts are a part and parcel of "normal" development, and disturbances in adaptation are included in its scope. We discover a similar state of affairs in relation to the therapeutic process of analysis. Here health clearly includes pathological reactions as a means toward its attainment.

But we must return to the concept of health and ask ourselves once more what criteria we possess in analysis for gauging mental health and illness. I have already mentioned that we do not identify health with freedom from symptoms. And we still find ourselves on ground which is comparatively accessible, from an empirical though not, of course, from a prognostic point of view, if we take into consideration the extent to which this immunity from symptoms is durable and capable of withstanding shocks. But the wider implications which the term health assumes for us and what analysis aims at in this sense cannot readily be reduced to a scientific formula. At the same time we find a number of useful theoretical formulations concerning the attributes of that state of health to which we are anxious to bring our patients with the help of the methods available to analysis. Of these the most general is Freud's "Where id was, there shall ego be" (1923a); or there is Nunberg's "the energies of the id become more mobile, the superego becomes more tolerant, the ego is freer from anxiety and its synthetic function is restored" (1932, p. 360). But the distance between such necessarily schematic formulations and the measurement of actual states of mental health, of the actual degree of mental health enjoyed by a given individual, is far greater than one would like to suppose. It is not at all a simple matter to bring these theoretical conceptions of health into line with what we in actual fact call "healthy." Moreover, one gains an impression that

· 7

individual conceptions of health differ widely among analysts themselves, varying with the aims which each has set for himself on the basis of his views concerning human development, and also of course with his philosophy, political sympathies, etc. Perhaps for the time being it will be advisable to proceed with caution before attempting to arrive at a precise theoretical formulation of the concept of health —otherwise we shall be in danger of allowing our standards of health to become dependent on our moral preoccupations and other subjective aspirations. It is clearly essential to proceed on purely empirical lines, i.e., to examine from the point of view of their structure and development the personalities of those who are actually considered healthy instead of allowing our theoretical speculations to dictate to us what we "ought" to regard as healthy. This is precisely the attitude that psychoanalysis adopts toward the normative disciplines. It does not ask whether these norms are justified but concentrates on a totally different problem, namely that of the genesis and structure of behavior which has, in fact, for whatever reason, been assigned a place in a scale of positive and negative values. And besides, theoretical standards of health are usually too narrow in so far as they underestimate the great diversity of types which in practice pass as healthy. Needless to say analysis itself possesses criteria intended to serve as a purely practical guide, such as the tests so frequently applied of a capacity for achievement or enjoyment.

But I propose here to examine in greater detail those theoretical schemes for the classification of mental health and illness which one finds contained, either expressly or by implication, in psychoanalytic literature; and for this purpose we may ask ourselves what conceptions of health have in fact been advanced and not whether certain conceptions "ought" to be advanced. These descriptions of a healthy or "biologically adjusted" individual, if we confine ourselves entirely to their broadest general outlines, reveal a pronounced development in two directions. In neither direction, it need scarcely be said, is it merely a question of some subjective factor, some personal predilection achieving expression; they are the results of a rich harvest of clinical experience, and of much valuable experience of the analytic process of cure. These two directions emphasize as the goal of development and health on the one hand rational behavior and on the other hand instinctual life. This twofold orientation already commands our interest because it reflects the twofold origin of psychoanalysis in the history of thought—the rationalism of the age of enlightenment and the irrationalism of the romantics. The circumstance that these two aspects are emphasized in Freud's work certainly reflects a genuine insight into the dualism which does in fact inform the problem. Now the analytic conceptions of health which have developed on the basis of Freud's suggestions often proceed to assign undue prominence to one of these standpoints at the expense of the other.

When one makes the mistake in analysis of contrasting the id as the biological part of the personality with the ego as its nonbiological component, one naturally encourages the tendency to make "life" and "mind" into absolutes. When in addition all biological values are acknowledged as supreme, one has approached dangerously near to that malady of the times whose nature it is to worship instinct and pour scorn on reason. To be sure, these tendencies, which lead to a glorification of instinctual man and which at the present time have widely assumed a highly aggressive and political complexion, play a less conspicuous part in the literature pertaining to psychoanalysis or subject to its influence than they do elsewhere.

At the other end of the scale we find the ideal of a rational attitude, and the "perfectly rational" man is here held up as a model of health and as an ideal figure generally. This conception of mental health deserves closer consideration. That some connection exists between reason and successful adaptation seems clear enough, but it is not such a simple one as is assumed in many psychoanalytic writings. We should not take it for granted that recognition of reality is the equivalent of adaptation to reality. The most rational attitude does not necessarily constitute an optimum for the purposes of adaptation. When we say that an idea or system of ideas is "in accordance with reality," this may mean that the theoretical content of the system is true, but it can also signify that the translation of these ideas into action results in conduct appropriate to the occasion. A correct view of reality is not the sole criterion of whether a particular action is in accordance with reality. We must also reflect that a healthy ego should be able to make use of the system of rational control and at the same time take into account the fact of the irrational nature of other mental activities. (This is a part of its coordinating or organizing function; see Chapter 3.) The rational must incorporate the irrational as an element in its design. Moreover, we shall have to admit that the advance of the "rational attitude" is not an even one along a single front, as it were. One often has the impression that a partial progression in this respect may entail a partial regression in other directions. It is evidently very much the same with the process of civilization as a whole. Technological progress may very well be accompanied by mental regression or may actually bring it about by way of mass methods (Mannheim, 1935). Here I can only present these ideas in brief outline but I have developed them at greater length elsewhere (1939a). They show us the need to revise those analytic conceptions which maintain that the individual who is most rational (in the ordinary sense of the word) is also psychologically the most completely healthy.

Another fundamental criterion of mental health available to psychology has a somewhat less general character, one more firmly rooted in the structural conceptions of analysis: I refer to the criterion of freedom. By freedom is meant not the philosophical problem of free will but rather freedom from anxiety and affects, or freedom to perform a task. The credit for introducing this criterion into analysis belongs to Waelder (1936b). I believe that at the root of this conception there lies a well-founded idea; yet I would rather have avoided the term freedom because it is so equivocal in meaning and has been so heavily overtasked by successive philosophers. In the present context it means no more than control exercised by means of the conscious and preconscious ego and might well be replaced

freedom to perform a task includes freedom to be non rational

by that description. The mobility or plasticity of the ego is certainly one of the prerequisites of mental health, whereas a rigid ego may interfere with the process of adaptation. But I would add that a healthy ego is not only and at all times plastic. Important as is this quality, it seems to be subordinated to another of the ego's functions. A clinical example will make this clear. We are all familiar with the obsessional neurotic's fear of losing his self-control—a factor which makes it so very difficult for him to associate freely. The phenomenon which I am thinking of is even more clearly marked in those persons who, for fear of losing their ego, are unable to achieve orgasm. These pathological manifestations teach us that a healthy ego must evidently be in a position to allow some of its most essential functions, including its "freedom," to be put out of action occasionally, so that it may abandon itself to "compulsion" (central control). This brings us to the problem, hitherto almost entirely neglected, of a biological hierarchy of the ego's functions and to the notion of the integration of opposites, which we have already met in connection with the problem of rational conduct. I believe that these considerations relative to the mobility of the ego and the automatic disconnecting of vital ego functions have enabled us to make very considerable progress toward discovering an important condition of mental health. The threads which lead us from this point to the concept of ego strength are clearly visible. But I do not now wish to discuss this well-worn theme.[3]

I shall now develop this critical exposition of analytic conceptions of health in a direction which will enable us to penetrate more deeply into the realm of ego theory. For obvious reasons psychoanalysis has hitherto been concerned principally with situations in which the ego finds itself in conflict with the id and the superego and, more recently, with the external world. Now one sometimes meets with the idea that the contrast between a conflict-ridden and a peaceful development can automatically be correlated with that afforded by

[3] For this and the topics discussed in the following paragraphs, see also Hartmann (1939a).

mental health and mental illness. This is a quite mistaken view: conflicts are a part and parcel of human development, for which they provide the necessary stimulus. Nor does the distinction between healthy and pathological reactions correspond to that between behavior originating or not originating in defense. Nevertheless it is by no means an uncommon thing to discover passages in psychoanalytic literature in which it is maintained that whatever is prompted by the needs of defense, or else results from unsuccessful defense, must somehow be accounted as pathological. Yet it is perfectly clear that a measure which is successful in relation to defensive needs may be a failure from the standpoint of positive achievement, and vice versa. We are really concerned here with two distinct approaches to the classification of the same facts and not with two different sets of facts. This consideration does not invalidate our experience that pathological function offers the most fruitful approach to the problems of mental conflict. Similarly we first became familiar with the mechanisms of defense in their pathogenic aspect, and it is only now that we are gradually coming to recognize the part they play in normal development. It would seem that we cannot adequately assess the positive or negative value which such processes possess for mental health so long as we only think of the problems of mental conflict and fail to consider these matters from the standpoint of adaptation as well.

If we examine these situations more attentively, we very often make the interesting discovery that the shortest way to reality is not always the most promising from the standpoint of adaptation. We often learn to find our bearings in relation to reality by devious ways, and it is inevitable and not merely "accidental" that this should be the case. There is evidently a typical sequence here—withdrawal from reality leading to an increased mastery over it. (In its essential features this pattern is already realized in the process of our thinking; the same remark applies to the activity of imagination, the avoidance of unsatisfactory situations, etc.) The theory of the neuroses has always presented the mechanism of turning away from reality solely in terms of pathological processes: but an approach from the standpoint of the problems of adaptation teaches us that such mechanisms have a positive value for health (see also A. Freud, 1936).

In this connection a further problem has a claim upon our interest: I allude to the way in which we use the terms "regression" and "regressive" within the analytic system of criteria for measuring mental health. We are generally accustomed to think of regressive behavior as the antithesis of conduct adapted to reality. We are all familiar with the part which regression plays in pathogenesis, and for that very reason I shall not need to consider that aspect of the problem. But in actual fact we have to distinguish between progressive and regressive forms of adaptation. We shall have no difficulty in defining a progressive adaptation: it means an adaptation in the direction of development. But we also find instances of successful adaptation achieved by way of regression. These comprise many examples of the activity of the imagination; a further illustration is afforded by artistic activity as well as by those symbolic devices for facilitating thought which are found even in science, where it is most strictly rational.

We do not readily perceive at a first glance why it is so comparatively often the case that adaptation can only be achieved in these regressive detours. Probably the true position is that in his ego, especially as expressed in rational thought and action, in its synthetic and differentiating function (Fuchs, 1936), man is equipped with a very highly differentiated organ of adaptation, but this highly differentiated organ is evidently by itself incapable of guaranteeing an optimum of adaptation. A system of regulation operating at the highest level of development is not sufficient to maintain a stable equilibrium; a more primitive system is needed to supplement it.

The objections which I felt obliged to raise against the definitions of mental health and illness last mentioned (in connection with the problems of defense, regression, etc.) may be summarized as follows: these conceptions of health approach the problem too exclusively from the angle of the neuroses, or rather they are formulated in terms of contrast with the neuroses. Mechanisms, developmental stages, modes of reaction, with which we have become familiar for the part they play in the development of the neuroses, are automatically relegated to the realm of the pathological—health is characterized as a condition in which these elements are absent. But the contrast thus established with the neuroses can have no meaning so long as we fail to appreciate how much of these mechanisms, developmental stages, and modes of reaction is active in healthy individuals or in the development of those who later become so, i.e., so long as an analytic "normal psychology" is still very largely nonexistent. This is one of the reasons why it is precisely the analysis of conduct adapted to reality which is today considered of such importance.

I should add that the arbitrary nature of such definitions of mental health and illness is very much less evident in the literature of psychoanalysis itself than in many of its applications to social conditions, artistic activity, scientific production, etc. Where ethical, aesthetic, and political valuations enter very clearly into play and proceed to make use of the concept of health for their special purposes, a considerably wider latitude is allowed to such arbitrary judgment. By skillful conjuring with these kinds of standards it becomes easy enough to prove that those who do not share our political or general outlook on life are neurotic or psychotic or that social conditions to which we are for some reason opposed are to be accounted as pathological. I believe that we are all clear in our own minds that such judgments—whether we personally share them or not—have no right to speak in the name of psychoanalytic science.

It will now have become quite obvious to us where many of the conceptions of health and illness discussed in this paper stand most in need of amplification, namely, in the direction of the subject's relations with and adaptation to reality. I do not mean to suggest that in these attempts to formulate a definition, to arrive at a theoretical concept of health, the factor of adaptation has been neglected; this is very far from being the case. But in the form in which it is expressed the concept of adaptation itself is in many respects too ill defined—and, as I have already remarked, "conduct adapted to reality" has hitherto offered little opportunity for a psychoanalytic approach.

It is obvious that what we designate as health or illness is intimately bound up with the individual's adaptation to reality (or, in the terms of an oft-repeated formula, with his sense of self-preservation). I have recently made an attempt to probe more deeply into the problems which confront psychoanalysis at this juncture (1939a). Here I shall confine myself to a few suggestions which may seem worth considering in framing a definition of health. The individual's adjustment to reality may be opposed to that of the race. Now it is true that we are accustomed, from the standpoint of our therapeutic aims, to allow a substantial margin of priority to the claims of individual adaptation over those of the race. But if we are to insist that some connection exists between mental health and adaptation, we are bound to admit in the light of our previous remarks that the concept of health may bear inconsistent meanings according to whether we think of it in relation to the individual or to the community. Moreover, we shall deem it expedient to distinguish between the state of being adapted and the process by which it is achieved. And lastly I must point out that adaptation is only capable of definition in relation to something else, with reference to specific environmental settings. The actual state of equilibrium achieved in a given individual tells us nothing of his capacity for adaptation so long as we have not investigated his relations with the external world. Thus an unhampered "capacity for achievement and enjoyment," simply considered in isolation, has nothing decisive to tell us concerning the capacity for adapting oneself to reality. On the other hand disturbances in one's capacity for achievement and enjoyment (for the sake of simplicity I will keep to these familiar criteria) are not to be evaluated simply as a sign of failure in adaptation. This really goes without saying and I only mention it because it is occasionally overlooked when attempts are made to formulate a definition. As an indispensable factor in assessing an individual's powers of adaptation we would single out his relation to a "typical average environment." We must take account of all these aspects of the concept of adaptation if we are to establish criteria of health based on adaptation or the capacity for it. We would insist that the processes of adaptation are always appropriate only to a limited range of environmental conditions; and that successful efforts at adaptation toward specific external situations may in indirect ways lead at the same time to inhibitions in adaptation affecting the organism.

Freud (1937a) recently characterized this state of affairs by quoting Goethe's "Reason becomes unreason, benefits a torment." Conversely, when viewed from this angle, the proposition that the nature of the environment may be such that a pathological development of the psyche offers a more satisfactory solution than would a normal one loses its paradoxical character.

This necessarily condensed presentation must inevitably make the considerations here adumbrated appear somewhat arid; but I am convinced that no analyst would have any difficulty in illustrating them from his clinical experience. In this connection I should like to insist once more that we shall obviously be in a better position to correlate all these definitions with concrete, clinically manifest conditions and thus to apply the concept of health in an unequivocal and trustworthy manner, when we have been able to advance further in the sphere of analytic "normal psychology," in the analysis of adapted behavior. I believe that a more attentive examination of the phenomena of adaptation may also help us to escape from the opposition between "biological" and "sociological" conceptions of mental development which plays a certain part in analysis but is fundamentally sterile. It is only when we consider the social phenomena of adaptation in their biological aspect that we can really start "getting psychology rightfully placed in the hierarchy of science, namely as one of the biological sciences" (Jones, 1936).

It is important that we should clearly realize both that there exists a close connection between adaptation and synthesis, and the extent of this. An "organization of the organism," the specific representative of which in the mental sphere we bring into relation with the synthetic function (and also with the differentiating function which has, however, been less fully explored), is a prerequisite of successful adaptation; on the other hand its efficacy is doubtless dependent on the measure of adaptation achieved. A process when viewed "from within" may often present itself as a disturbance of mental harmony; when viewed "from without" we should have to characterize the same process as a disturbance of adaptation. So, too, instinctual conflicts are very frequently bound up with a disturbed relation to the environment. It is also significant in this connection that the same process of defense quite commonly serves the twofold purpose of acquiring mastery over the instincts and of reaching an accommodation with the external world.

By thus seeking to make adaptation, and especially synthesis, the basis of our concept of health, we seem to have arrived at an "evolutionary" concept of health. And in point of fact this does represent a psychoanalytic contribution to the concept of mental health which should not be underestimated. But on the other hand a conception which relates the degree of mental health to the degree of development actually attained (compare the factor of rational control and, on the instinctual plane, the attainment of the genital stage as a prerequisite of health) suffers from certain limitations, at least as regards the ego, to which I have briefly alluded.

In summary: I have endeavored to explain and discuss a number of standpoints which psychoanalysis has in fact adopted toward the concept of health, either expressly or by implication. In a one-sided fashion I proceeded to single out for almost exclusive attention those conditions of mental health which are seen to be related to the ego. I purposely restricted myself in this way. It seemed to me that there were good reasons why the psychology of the id had failed to provide us with a key to the problems of mental health. Moreover, by conducting my survey from the standpoint of the ego I found myself in a position to discuss certain problems of ego theory which are decidedly no less important than the question of our criteria of health. The contribution that I myself have been able to make toward the further development and criticism of these views certainly does not yet enable us to formulate a concept of mental health in simple, unequivocal, definitive terms. But I believe that it will have helped us to discern quite clearly in which direction these prolegomena to a future analytic theory of health must be developed.

CHAPTER 2

Psychoanalysis and Sociology

(1944)

IT IS evident today that many problems which belong to the social sciences not only can but must be considered from the psychological standpoint. The results of psychoanalysis and of nonanalytic psychiatry and psychology are being consulted to an increasing degree by workers in sociology. Similarly, psychologists and psychiatrists, particularly the psychoanalysts, have encroached on the field of sociology. The psychological worker is also called upon when practical problems, such as education, criminology, morale, propaganda, and similar subjects are under discussion.

It could be expected that any psychology which is not limited to isolated expressions of the human personality, or to its superficial layers, as were some of the older schools, would eventually find itself faced with the task of explaining the relation of the individual to his social environment; on the other hand, every sociological approach must be based upon certain assumptions concerning the structure and behavior of the human personality. Sociology is actually a study of human behavior, even though it is limited to only one aspect. It is therefore perfectly plausible that sociology should find its base in the laws of psychology. The earlier concepts of society as used by the psychologist, and of human personality as used by the sociologist, were highly schematic and, on this account, not particularly fruitful. These concepts rarely went beyond that point which would be arrived at by common sense under the conditions of an average education. Several sociologists, disappointed by the methods of scientific psychology current at that time, created a psychology of their own which better suited their needs. In this they followed the path taken by the pedagogues, criminologists, and aestheticians who were handicapped by the absence of a body of systematic empirical knowledge of those personality functions which were relevant to them.

Not every psychology, not even one which can produce correct and verifiable results, is qualified to answer the questions of social science. Many schools of psychology have completely disregarded the individual's social relationships. They speak of laws governing thought processes without taking into account the world to which thought refers; they speak of laws of affectivity, neglecting the objects of the emotions and the situations which provoked them. In other words, they do not take into account the concrete objects in relation to which the behavior occurred, or the roots of the behavior in concrete life situations. This is due to their studying the individual as if he were completely isolated from the world of social phenomena. The phenomena of group psychology are, therefore, completely inaccessible to this type of psychological approach. Such a separation of the individual from the world in which he lives is totally artificial. This tendency served as a severe handicap in the development of psychology not only in its social applications but in many other contexts as well.

Freud and psychoanalysis gave the science a decisive change of direction. Surely, at the end of the last century, few students would have anticipated that the basis for a psychology of relationships between human beings would have come from a study of the neuroses. As it actually occurred, through the new approach to the problem of neurosis, an approach completely foreign to the atmosphere of the psychological laboratory, the entire complexity of an individual's relations to his fellow men as objects of love, hate, fear, and rivalry suddenly became the main focus of psychological interest, probably without Freud's having anticipated the direction which his work would take. As mentioned before, the approach to this field was through pathology and, beyond this, through the study of human instinctual drives, their development, their transformations, and their inhibitions. Since then, analysis has developed into a general psychology that includes also the analysis of normal behavior and of the other psychic structures. The fact, however, that psychoanalysis had this origin, that it began as a psychology of the "irrational" mental phenomena and of the unconscious, or rather of the id, was, on the whole, decisive for its development, as well as for that of social psychology. It is evident that a psychology which analyzes only an individual's conscious interests in power, social position, money-making, etc., ignoring the roots of these interests in the id, is bound to be too narrow to do justice to the extraordinary variety of social phenomena which require elucidation. Even many forms of behavior, which appear "rational," assume a different aspect when seen not as isolated phenomena but in the light of an individual's total behavior. In psychoanalytic terminology we would say, they appear in a different light when we observe not only the ego aspect but also the id and superego aspects.

We may ask: in what form does the relation of an individual to his fellow man and to "Society" come within the sphere of psychoanalysis? In the first place, man's love relationships in the widest meaning of the word, that is, from the sensual to the sublimated manifestations (friendship, for instance), and society's protest against many forms of sexual expression captured the interest of the workers in this field. Later, psychoanalysis dealt also with other types of relationships, such as the aggressive tendencies and the identifications, which became equally important in group psychology. The essential approach to the understanding of these phenomena, here as elsewhere in psychoanalysis, was the genetic. The study of the development of human object relations has been one of the most important parts of analysis since the beginning. The way in which the child learns to choose and recognize objects, and the way in which these infantile object relations, through repetitions, displacements, reversions and so on, influence decisively the love relations of the adult as well as his social relationships in professional and political life, constitute one of the major themes of analytic experience, which up to this time has not yet been fully exhausted. Here, I choose only one group of problems which appears to be a suitable basis for certain reflections.

The infant, from the moment of its birth (actually even earlier), is in constant contact with its social surroundings and for a long period of time its life depends upon these early contacts. But in the beginning the infant does not know any object in the psychological sense. The process of actually crystallizing objects follows a period in which there was a remarkable lack of differentiation in all reactions. The process occurs in close connection to the needs of the instinctual drives on the one hand and to the development of the ego on the other. The recognition of the world of objects is partly based on the replacement (or modification) of the pleasure principle by the reality principle and is dependent upon the growing maturity and strength of the ego. Freud has found that the prolonged helplessness of the infant and his protracted dependence upon the adult world have two main consequences, which are important from the point of view of his development. This early dependence promotes a far-reaching differentiation between the id and the ego, and it furthers the possibilities of ego maturation and the processes of learning. But this dependence also increases the importance of external danger as well as that of those objects who offer protection, to a degree unknown among the lower animals. Considering this complete dependence upon the care and protection of others, it is natural that man's need for love and his fear of losing the love of the object are especially strongly developed.

It is evident that analytic findings of this kind are of great importance for sociology. At the same time when viewed from the angle of adaptation, maturation, and learning, they present an essential field in the biology of man. The relationship of the infant to his mother, the institution of the reality principle, the changes in the types of instinctual gratification, may all be described "biologically" as well as "sociologically." There are of course elements to which this does not apply, such as the instinctual endowment, ego constitution, maturation, etc. As a matter of fact, psychoanalysis is particularly interested in the psychological study of such "social" factors which are of "biological" importance as well. I am well aware of the vague character of these terms, and it might be best simply to state that these different fields can find their place in the framework of sociology as well as biology. If I concentrate here solely on the sociological approach, it is because my subject calls for it. I do not underrate the biological implications of these subjects.

The dependency and helplessness which are of such long duration in the child are phenomena which we see in all human beings regardless of their culture and civilization, even though when rigidly compared they may not be identical. The way in which the adult world deals with these facts, however, differ in different civilizations. Furthermore, given one civilization, the problem is not handled in the same way in all families, and in the same family there will be a variation from one child to the next. Among these factors, then, there are some which are constant and some which are variable. They do not at all coincide with the biological and sociological factors. One can arrive at average values, characteristic of any specific civilization in regard to the boundary between the two, or the manner, the degree, and the time in which the impulses of the very young child are controlled by cultural influences, or the gratifications and frustrations which the child experiences during the process and the particular development of his ego, which reconciles with greater or less success the demands of the external world with his infantile needs. (This is true even though in each case other factors, such as constitutional and developmental, play a part.) As Freud made the results of psychoanalysis available to anthropology (this will be discussed later), one can in this context use anthropology in order to resolve analytic problems. Under the influence of psychoanalysis,

· 23

anthropologists began to take into consideration the above factors and others belonging in the same sphere. It happened that, as in other social sciences, concepts based on analytic experience brought to light new facts and new relationships in the material, and that the new manner of asking questions evoked new answers, which in turn became relevant in the psychoanalytic framework. The plasticity of the infantile situation and its limits, the degree to which it can or cannot be influenced by cultural factors, are best delimited by anthropological studies rather than by analyzing individuals of the same culture. In such problems anthropology has a certain experimental value and can, in certain cases, contribute material which will verify or negate psychoanalytic assumptions.

The historic aspect of psychoanalytic thinking prevents analysis from being nothing else but a doctrine of "the nature of man" in the sense in which, for instance, the philosophers of the eighteenth century envisaged this problem. Psychoanalysis concerns itself with the modifications which changing conditions exert on generally human situations and attributes. Among these conditions, social factors play a unique role. Although we anticipate the presence of aggressive instinctual impulses in all people, we cannot conclude that one completely delineated expression of these impulses, making war, for example, should be inevitable in the history of man. The expression of basic aggressive tendencies is determined by factors which can change during the course of generations. On the other hand, a negation of all constant elements among those which can be demonstrated to have an influence on the process of becoming man is, of course, contradicted by experience. Psychoanalysis can go further and demonstrate that the id, the ego, and the superego offer resistances of different degrees to the influences of the external world, and particularly to those of cultural factors. Psychoanalysis gives us an impression of the manner in which ego and superego can be modified, and similarly it gives us a strong indication of the obstinacy with which the id opposes the influences from the external world. (I do not wish to discuss, at this point, the typical transformations of the id during the individual's development and the possibility of influencing the id by the therapeutic process of analysis.) In any case, I wish to emphasize not only that Freud fully recognized the importance of social factors in the development of character and neurosis but that he was the first to give them a scientifically comprehensible place in the diverse realms of psychology and psychopathology.

It might perhaps be useful to group the great variety of ways in which the conduct of the individual can be affected by cultural factors, from at least two different viewpoints, starting with the layers of the personality on which these factors exert an influence. They can, along with other influences, codetermine the central structure of the personality, by provoking, for example, the early establishment of specific reaction formations, or they can codetermine the degree of severity of the superego or the degree of mobility of the ego. On the other hand, their effect can take place a little further away from the nucleus of the personality. Individuals with the same (or more correctly, with a similar) constitution and childhood history will, nevertheless, be driven into different developmental channels according to whether they belong to a society of one social structure or another, and in this society to one or another social level, inasmuch as the frustrations and possibilities of sublimation, etc., are characteristic of the society and the social level. (It is to be taken for granted that I leave out of consideration factors which are not psychological.) There are, then, cultural factors which do not influence a person's mental structure or the way in which he resolves conflicts, but only influence the superficial layers of the personality, e.g., the choice of rationalizations, the conceptual language, certain mental contents, and so on. This distinction serves merely to make our problem concrete and to militate against a tendency to consider social factors equivalent in the face of completely dissimilar psychological connotations. There are, of course, transitions between the three groups of factors which I have mentioned. Another equally indispensable contribution to the organization of social facts according to their psychological significance consists of noting their specific effects on the id, the ego, and the superego.

If we are, for example, confronted with the question: what are the cultural factors which exert an influence on the frequency and type of neuroses? one must take many of the above-mentioned groups of factors into account, according to their individual importance. The fact that neurosis is the specific result of a conflict between the instinctual drives and the ego and superego remains the basic psychological characteristic of the neurosis, when it is considered etiologically. There are, however, transformations of the type of neurotic phenomena. Changes in the forms of neuroses, in occidental civilization during the last generation, for example, suggest that the deep structure of the personality was modified by cultural conditions. Moreover, different social factors play a part. This is proven by the fact that the same type of neurosis will have different implications for people living in different social and economic situations. Finally, there is a difference in the symptomatology of the neuroses in different civilizations, which has to do exclusively with the content (the choice of the object of anxiety in the phobias, for example). The relative importance of social elements, when compared with the other factors which exert an influence on the genesis and form of neurosis, is a problem which I do not wish to approach at this time. I have brought up this example only to show in what way one must break down concepts such as "culture," "civilization," and "forms of society," which are primarily defined not by the conceptual system of psychology but by that of other sciences, when one studies the interrelations between man and society.

I do not wish to continue in the direction of becoming increasingly specific in this respect, but I would like to focus on one general characteristic of these mutual relationships. Let us introduce this problem by a comparison with certain instructive observations which have to do with the theory of neurosis. We know that in hysteria the choice of the affected organ is partly determined by the particular physical characteristics of the organ. Freud described this as *somatic compliance.* There is an analogous relationship between the individual's mental structure and his social environment. This gives us the right to speak of *social compliance,* by which we understand the fact that social factors must also be described psychologically in such a way as to demonstrate their selective effects; they operate in the direction of the selection and the effectuation of certain tendencies and their expression, and of certain developmental trends, among those which, at any given moment, are potentially demonstrable in the structure of the individual. These selective processes are present at every stage of human development.

We are, therefore, primarily concerned with the question: in what manner and to what degree does a given social structure bring to the surface, provoke, or reinforce certain instinctual tendencies or certain sublimations, for instance? On the other hand, the way in which different social structures facilitate the solution of certain psychic conflicts by a participation—by action or in fantasy—of the given social realities, merits special investigation. Let us take an example which encroaches on pathology. Freud (1924b) described a type of person (moral masochists) in whom morality is sexualized and in whom the usual conflicts between the ego and the superego are expressed regressively in social relations and against institutions in the outside world. Such people expect and invite suffering and punishment from parental representatives, from personal or impersonal authorities and from fate. Existing in an absolute authoritarian system—one which would be intolerable for other personality types—makes it possible for such a person to find a solution of his conflicts by utilizing reality.

There is then a large number of people in whom active social conduct represents not a rational action but an "acting out," which is more or less neurotic, in relation to social reality. In this "acting out," they repeat infantile situations and seek to utilize their social conduct to resolve intrapsychic conflicts. A strong reliance on reality can also be used to overcome fear. It can, but it does not need to have, the character of a symptom. It also depends on the peculiarities of the social milieu, what conflicts and anxiety tensions are overcome by the social behavior. On the other hand, sometimes a modification of the social structure which limits this activity or which, for example, makes certain sublimated activities more difficult leads to a reappearance of those conflicts which were temporarily overcome and serves to precipitate a neurosis. (Naturally, this is true only where there were situations in childhood which predisposed the person to developing such a neurosis.)

The possibilities of adaptation of the same (or about the same) psychic structure can be different in different types of society, and among different social classes. A grade of the compulsive character, for example, which in a certain group or in the presence of certain institutions manifests itself as a disturbance of adaptation, producing what we might call a social failure, can, under other social conditions, not only not interfere with the accomplishment of essential social duties but can actually be responsible for them. Visualizing the problem along the lines which I have discussed up to this point, we can consider the different possibilities for resolving the conflict, and the different degrees of psychic stability which the social structure offers the individual. On the other hand, one can completely ignore the question of what is the contribution of the social environment to the elaboration of the specific behavior pattern, the resolution of conflicts, and the degree of equilibrium achieved, and ask another question: what are the social functions which are accessible, either easily so, with difficulty, or not accessible at all, in any given social setting for any given personality structure, independent of the manner in which the personality structure was developed? (I limit myself here to the psychological side of the problem.) It is hardly necessary to point out that this question can only be answered *ceteris paribus,* as a large number of nonpsychological factors, economic and others, participate in this process. Thus we can say: the relation between the individual and society can be characterized for specific types of people and for specific systems and strata of society, not only as to the effect which the system exerts on the individual, but also as to the social functions which the system requires of him. The former consists of a coming-to-the-fore, suppression, and displacement of psychological impulses of the individual, in so far as these are being conditioned by society's influence. In the latter case one could speak of a kind of social selection and understand this as the displacements in the social environment which are accessible or forbidden to a given type of individual. This also could be considered under the heading of social compliance if one broadens this concept. Not only the first, but both questions must be answered, so that psychoanalysis can contribute something essential to such problems as, for example, how in a given social system the selection of political leaders is likely to take place.

We are now at a point where one can consider the sociological application of the findings and points of view of psychoanalytic research. I shall attempt to sketch some of the premises, possibilities, and difficulties of the analytic approach in relation to this scientific field. One can draw one conclusion from that which has already been said. A common argument against the application of psychology to sociology is that psychology can only understand the individual whereas sociology concerns itself with collective behavior. But this argument is valid only to the extent to which psychology excludes from consideration the relations between the individual and his environment, particularly his social environment. It is not valid when the mutual relations between man and his fellows in all their variations and shadings form the core of the observations and of the theoretical deductions as is the case in psychoanalysis. Moreover, sociologists today also use in increasing measure life-history documents in their studies.

Another argument states that one cannot understand or, at least, fully understand social behavior if one does not take into account the social reality around which the behavior is oriented. But a brief consideration shows that what I have said about the position of psychoanalysis in relation to interpersonal relations has a more general significance. This was only a special case of the way in which psychoanalysis understands the relation between man and reality in general. Human conduct is oriented to its environment, and the psychoanalytic approach includes the structure of reality in its description. This is especially clear in Freud's last version (1926a) of his theory of anxiety which relates the internal danger to the external one, and in Anna Freud's description (1936) of types of defense which the child develops against the discomforts and dangers which threaten him from the outside world. We do not believe that one can completely explain the total behavior of an individual from his instinctual drives and his fantasies. If we, as analysts, ask ourselves what are the causes of war and peace, or of a religious movement, if we ask ourselves why certain political leaders achieve power and why certain specific groups behave in one manner rather than in another in relation to the leader, we believe that we can contribute to the solution of these problems through our understanding of the reactions of individuals and types in concrete situations. But one cannot under any circumstances ignore or neglect the part played by the economic or social structure as partially independent factors. In applied psychoanalysis they take the place of "reality" in the sense which I have outlined, and it would be completely senseless to deny their autonomy. This would be as if we were to overlook in our analytic practice the fact that the patient orients his specific behavior around his particular environment.

The contributions which psychoanalysis can make to social science differ in significance and importance in the varying branches of this science. Scattered throughout Freud's papers we find many comments on this subject, some of which are very penetrating. In his paper, " 'Civilized' Sexual Morality and Modern Nervous Illness" (1908b), however, he presented for the first time explicitly and systematically his views on the relation of psychoanalysis to a sociological problem. The subject of the study concerned itself with the influence of cultural factors on the instinctual life and its significance in neuroses and perversions. Several years later he followed this paper with *Totem and Taboo* (1913-14). This book represents a more far-reaching attempt to apply psychoanalytic results to anthropology. The subject has to do with primitive man's fear of incest and the relation between taboos and ambivalence. The point of comparison here, in the first place, is the analytic psychology of obsessive-compulsive neurosis. In relation to the problem of totemism he also finds in empirically well-consolidated analytic experience an approach to anthropological problems. This time it is the animal phobias in children and the oedipus complex in general. His interpretation introduces a hypothesis about the very early history of men which centers around the killing of the father. Freud's second decisive contribution to sociology is presented in his book *Group Psychology and the Analysis of the Ego* (1921). The phenomena of group psychology are described here with the underlying hypothesis that, in the transitory formation of the group, members of the group replace the ego ideal with the leader and, on this account identify their own egos with those of the others. On the other hand, the new viewpoints arrived at during this work are utilized for an elaboration of the analytic psychology of the ego. Another series of Freud's studies also serves this double purpose, simultaneously explaining social phenomena and assisting in a broader development of psychoanalytic psychology. We see this in his later work, *Civilization and Its Discontents* (1930), which concerns itself primarily with relations between the aggressive instincts and civilization, yet at the same time gives a completely new insight into guilt feelings and into the fate of aggressions during the development of the superego. It would be impractical as well as unnecessary for me to go into greater detail to show the extraordinary fertility of ideas which appear in these works of Freud's. Suffice it to say that these ideas represent the first major invasion on a wide front of the psychology of the core of personality into the realm of the social sciences.[1] At this point I merely wish to emphasize that it was certainly not by chance that

[1] Here, as in other instances, I speak of social science in general, instead of confining myself to sociology, because in applying pychoanalysis to sociology we are confronted with problems that are of equal importance in its applications to history, anthropology, etc. Some such general problems may even be better elucidated in choosing examples from these other branches of social science.

Freud, in these most important works, selected topics which can be clarified only through the fructification of a psychology of unconscious psychic impulses and "irrational" behavior. Furthermore, in the majority of situations which Freud described, he deals with events which occurred not only once in history. These events are of a kind which repeat themselves with essential elements remaining unchanged.

Many other sociological problems, such as market research, advertising, political statistics, etc., will probably not gain as much from psychoanalysis. In these situations the human behavior under investigation stems in large measure from those layers of the personality which are not in the center of analytic interest and research. I shall come back to this. In the meantime, however, I wish to consider at what points, actually, one can interpret analytically the more complex social occurrences, and what are the prerequisites which make these analytic interpretations possible.

In theory, one should be able to utilize the results of personal analyses of which a large number are now available, in order to study many of the current sociological problems. Each of these analyses gives us an unparalleled insight into the intimate relations between the personality structure and the social structure. But the experiences of psychoanalysts in this respect up to this time have not been used in a systematic manner. There is another approach which psychoanalysis discovered very early and with which it could study civilizations of diverse epochs. This involves a study of the myths, collective symbols, and ideologies of a people which are accessible to analytic interpretation. Such analyses have advanced our understanding considerably in some situations, but in others it is difficult to visualize sufficiently clearly the actual social significance, distribution, and function of these collective phenomena. Analytic study of social institutions frequently permits us in a sufficiently reliable manner to state what instinctual impulses, ego interests, or types of guilt feelings are satisfied by this type of institution. It is not infrequent that such an analytic interpretation contributes also to an understanding of the genesis of these phenomena. By means of such analyses one can throw more or less light on the psychic tendencies and the reaction types of members of the society to which these institutions belong. As a rule, a sociological investigation is necessary for a reliable answer to the question: to what degree do institutions express the psychic tendencies of the individual members of a given society and what strata of society are represented in this way? An institution will sometimes satisfy the needs of the majority, but it can also be imposed by a minority group; or, on the other hand, it may be part of a tradition which itself is maintained for psychological reasons, etc. But in this context we must also think of the phenomenon "change of function," inasmuch as certain social phenomena which originated as expressions of definite psychological tendencies can become the expressions of different tendencies during their historical development. Institutions which are built on tradition, even when they can be historically traced entirely or in part to the psychological trends of preceding generations, impose themselves on the individuals of the following generations as realities in the sense in which I have described it above. Frequently they continue to satisfy along broad lines the same psychological needs to which they originally owed their creation. But, as I have said, this does not always follow. It also goes without saying that the conclusions which one can draw from the overt political behavior of an individual concerning his motives or his personality structure will be different in a democratic system from what it would be in a totalitarian one; and similarly, they are different in a modern dictatorship from what they would have been in one of earlier days. Something similar is true in relation to everything which we include under the heading of technical equipment, whose use characterizes a society. Psychoanalysis as applied to an individual makes it possible for us to understand the psychological significance of his utilizing one technical means rather than another to reach his goals. If one applies psychoanalysis to sociology, this direct source of information is lacking. Certainly even in this situation, it is frequently possible to draw

· 33

conclusions concerning the underlying psychological tendencies from the means utilized. It goes without saying, however, that it is impossible to conclude that the magnitude of the destructive force of war implements used in any one epoch will in itself be a direct indication of the relative aggressivity of the participating individuals. The relations between these two factors are not univocal. On the other hand, it may be entirely possible to draw the conclusion on the basis of a preceding analysis of the historical situation, of the social structure, and of the stage of technological development. This means that one must set up patterns which are as specific as possible in relation to both their psychological and their sociological aspects. These patterns then will permit us to apply to them our psychoanalytic findings concerning the forces and mechanisms acting under given circumstances.

The foregoing discussion was aimed at elucidating the premises which in certain sociological spheres make an analytic interpretation possible. I now return for a moment to the differentiation mentioned above between sociological problems which are more and those which are less accessible to psychoanalysis. In each situation in which human behavior is preponderantly rational, one can predict the average person's response with a certain degree of accuracy without having to draw on psychoanalytic concepts. This applies to such situations in which the behavior is largely determined by the conscious or preconscious ego. Naturally one must here too explain the behavior psychologically. Nevertheless there are situations in which one can rather accurately predict the behavior, putting the deeper layers of the personality in parentheses, as it were. Apart from this, in all situations in which the id, the superego, or the unconscious part of the ego play an important role, statements will be reliable only if they are based on psychoanalytic findings.

At the core of the analytic investigation one always found, and one still finds today, those psychological areas which have to do with human conflicts, such as the conflicts between conscience and instinctual drives, the conflicts with the external world and so on. It was late in our analytic experience that we came to studying the nonconflictual development and the entire nonconflictual spheres of the ego; and when we did so, it was with some special points in mind. Psychoanalysis, for instance, studies the way in which the process of maturation, talents, and also such ego interests which correspond to these factors, influence conflicts and their resolution. Accordingly, in applying psychoanalysis to sociological problems, the theory of human conflicts is its most important contribution to this science. Furthermore, as we have found that conflicts and the resolution of conflicts can be thoroughly understood only if one includes the history of the individual's development—the genetic point of view must be an integral part of the psychoanalytic investigation. The question of stability of character traits, for example, or the question of whether or not one can expect a certain specific behavior from an individual, cannot, in many instances, be answered without a knowledge of his development. Frequently a cross-section does not permit a prognosis, yet the sociologist must ordinarily content himself with this state of affairs. Generally speaking, he cannot take conflicts and their resolution into account and will often limit himself in this investigation to a study of the individual's overt behavior. For many sociologists nothing but the actual social behavior seems relevant. Rather than consider the complex determinants of human behavior which have been demonstrated by psychoanalysis and which frequently go beyond consciousness, the sociologist is mostly limited to the knowledge of conscious motivation. I have already shown under what circumstances this can produce reliable results and under what circumstances it cannot. Many phases of human conduct which are relevant in psychoanalysis are peripheral in sociology and vice versa. Even if we want to state as a principle that sociology is based on psychology, we have to admit that the two realms have different centers. Despite this, recent work wherein sociologists and psychoanalysts collaborated in a common investigation, studying the same phenomena from both angles, has brought about gradual beginnings of a common scientific language.

Some anthropologists who are analytically trained have begun to concern themselves in their field work and in their conclusions with aspects of primitive behavior which previously would have escaped their notice. Certain characteristics, which they probably would have ignored at an earlier time, now appear to them important in their descriptions. This is true also of historical research. Analysis can be applied to its fullest extent only after the historian has collected data in those spheres of life which appear to the analyst to be of greatest import in the development of the personality. The questions which the analyst asks the historian have to do with a mass of details concerning customs, habits, or fashions which guide the private lives of members of an occupational group, a social class, a nation of a specific historical era. It goes without saying that the psychoanalyst is interested in the various ways in which infants are handled. Up to this time historical research has brought us much too few data on the question of how, in the Middle Ages, the Renaissance, or the eighteenth century, etc., the feeding, weaning, and toilet training of the infant was managed, or in what way the parents and parent representatives handled the child's sexual and aggressive drives. Yet the analyst must rely on just this type of information, along with a great deal of other data, when he answers the historian's question. On the other hand, a whole series of correlations, which the sociologist meets in his work, such as those between the social status and the vocational choice or the sexual life, or the distribution curves of certain social attitudes in different nationalities, and many other sociological findings have an effect on psychoanalysis in that they clarify its conceptual system and stimulate it to revise and broaden its factual material. Seen from this point of view, the relation between psychoanalysis and sociology (and the social sciences in general) appears to be not merely an exchange of findings but rather a dynamic process of mutual inspiration aiming toward new investigations which can prove fertile for both sides.

CHAPTER 3

On Rational
and Irrational Action

(1947)

S INCE its beginnings psychoanalysis has made important contributions to the psychology of action that clearly reflect the consecutive levels of analytic experience and thought. The approach became more explicit once a solid foundation was laid in analytic ego theory. However, we still have no systematic presentation of an analytic *theory of action,* to which I could refer here as to an accepted or at least generally known body of facts and hypotheses. This paper is primarily concerned with certain aspects of rational and irrational behavior. However, it will also have to deal with a number of topics that would be parts of such a general theory.

From the standpoint of an older concept of psychoanalysis, which had limited its scope to an auxiliary science of psychiatry, questions like those I want to present here seem peripheral. However, in an implicit way from its beginnings, and quite explicitly in the last two or three decades, psychoanalysis has set out to lay the groundwork for a general psychology, including normal as well as pathological behavior. Psychoanalysis has its origin in the clinical investigation of what one generally calls "irrational" behavior, of the instinctual drives and their development, and of the role they play mainly in pathological phenomena. As long as it was centered around the psychology of the id, it dealt with a field of observation neglected by nonanalytic psychology. By developing ego psychology, analysis has more and more come to include in its scope phenomena that previously had been studied by other methods. However, in this broad field of encounter of the analytic method with others, it is the specific nature of this method, and the insight into the unconscious processes, that frequently lets the common object of observation appear in a different light; and, above all, analytic knowledge allows one to assign the observed facts their proper place in the structure of personality.

The problems of rational and irrational behavior are located on a crossroad of various branches of science. Not only psychology, but also history, sociology, and economics have their share in it. It is when faced with the borderline questions of analysis and social science, that the necessity of extending and clarifying our knowledge of these problems most definitely appears. One has not yet succeeded in giving the various sociological and economic studies of human action the psychological basis they need. Many theories of action, as introduced, for instance, by economists, tend to reduce the motivations of action, and the rather complex relationships of action with other aspects of behavior, to a few isolated cases considered as typical; but as a rule they neglect the basic facts of the personality structure, of the driving forces, and of the adaptive capacities of man. However, in limiting the psychological foundations to those model situations one may endanger a full comprehension even of those few behavior patterns these theories take into consideration. I have delineated the possible influence of psychoanalysis on the social sciences in Chapters 2 and 5. Here I shall simply state that it seems probable that a theory of action based upon the knowledge of the structural aspects of personality and of its motivations is the most important contribution psychoanalysis will one day be able to make in this field.

What, then, to begin with this side of the multiform problem, is the position of action in the *structure of personality,* as described by psychoanalysis? The systems of personality (ego, id, superego) are defined in analysis on the basis of their functions, the concept formation here being somewhat similar to that used in biology and, more especially, in physiology. Normal action in all of its varieties, even instinctual or emotional action, is formed by the ego. But between action and the ego there exist manifold relationships. In action we have an intention toward a goal; and the motor and other phenomena used to reach this goal are controlled and organized accordingly (the presence of the goals and this control and organization may be more or less complete and may take place on a great variety of different levels, as we shall see later). Freud has shown how the partial replacement of merely reactive motor outlet, and of instinctual breakthrough, by directed and organized action is an important part of ego development and an essential step in replacing the pleasure principle by the reality principle. Objectivation, another function we attribute to the ego, in helping to develop our knowledge of the outside world, is also instrumental in the organization of action. Or rather, there is an interdependent relationship between the two processes: insight into the structure of reality guides action, but action is also one of our most efficient instruments for the development of insight, or knowledge.

A few sketchy remarks about the *developmental aspects* of at least some of the factors involved may prove useful. If the wants of a child exceed a certain degree without being satisfied, and if they can no longer be satisfied by fantasy either, the child feels himself driven toward the outer world, in perception and in activity, in order to search it for pleasure and to avoid pain. This behavior may also mean a protection against fantastic fears; it can serve the mastering of anxiety. In both cases the turning to the outer world comes under the pleasure principle; it is its continuation by other means. There is, however, another decisive factor involved in establishing the reality principle: "A momentary pleasure, uncertain in its results, is given up, but only in order to gain along the new path an assured pleasure at a later time" (Freud, 1911a, p. 223). This step cannot, as I have shown elsewhere (1939a; see also Chapter 12), be derived from the pleasure principle alone. The *anticipation of the future,* one of the most important achievements of early ego development, enters the process as an independent variable. Now, anticipation is also another prerequisite for the development of action and participates in every action to some degree. We know of many anticipating activities of the ego, the one that has been most thoroughly studied by analysts being the anxiety signal, which from a certain level of development on is used by the individual in danger situations. I think there can be no doubt that this special form of anticipation, because it safeguards the stability of the mental apparatus, is also paramount among those forms of anticipation that make organized action possible.

In the psychoanalytic literature of the last years there has been a tendency to consider a partly *autonomous development of the ego,* which cannot entirely be traced to manifestations of the instinctual drives (see, e.g., Freud, 1937a). Here I only want to mention that this area of ego development is partly based on the function of somatic or mental apparatus which, as a consequence of maturation, become available to the ego. This is a close parallel to the libido development, the consecutive levels of which we partly link with anatomical and physiological growth (of the teeth, of the sphincter muscles, and so forth). Now, the functions of the ego area just touched upon, including those underlying controlled and directed action, often have the character of inhibiting the immediate gratification of the instinctual drives; postponement or displacement of gratification is frequently the consequence of their activity. On the other hand, the development of new ego functions, like, for instance, that of acting in the outer world, may open up new avenues for direct and indirect (sublimated) gratifications of instinctual tendencies. Changes in the distribution of psychic energy, in the direction of a stronger investment of the ego functions, go parallel with these developments.

In stressing the importance of such factors as anticipation, postponement of gratification, and the like, in the development of action, we at the same time give action its place in a general trend of human development, the trend toward a growing independence from the immediate impact of present stimuli, the independence from the *hic et nunc*. This trend can also be described as one toward "internalization" (Hartmann, 1939a). The danger signal is an example in question. The signal helps in many cases to master "inner" danger before it can become danger threatening from outside. Directed and organized action (organized as to its motivations and as to the way it is brought about) is gradually substituted for the immediate reactions of motor discharge, as mentioned above. Trial activities with whose help we attempt to master a situation, to solve a problem, are gradually internalized: thinking is, in this sense, trial action with small quantities of psychic energy (Freud, 1911a). Finally, the internalizations that are essential to the formation of the superego lead to a growing independence from the outside world in so far as a process of inner regulation replaces the reactions and actions due to fear of the social environment (social anxiety).

As to the use of psychic energy in action, a few words may suffice. We work in psychoanalysis with the hypothesis that once the three mental systems are formed, each of them disposes of psychic energy (see Chapters 7 and 12). Action certainly uses energies of the ego. This, however, does not imply that it might not also find energies of the id or the superego at its disposal. The separation of the ego from the other systems is as a rule not complete. Thus action will frequently draw on the energy reservoir of the other functioning units of personality.

Analytical observation has taught us that human behavior is essentially overdetermined; and that in every cross-section of behavior (upward of a certain age) we can trace the influence of all three psychic systems. We call this the *principle of multiple function* (Waelder, 1930). According to this principle, the result of the activation of, let us say, an ego function will be codetermined by the state of affairs in the id and the superego; we have learned to realize the multiplicity of interdependent factors that every analysis of actual behavior has to take into consideration. However, this complexity does not make it unnecessary or impossible to correlate functions with systems, in a way that in some instances might be more, in others less definite. If in this sense I have called action an ego function, I have to add now that it is possible to describe a variety of types of action, first of all from the point of view of the influence the other systems exert upon it. While the formation of the action is normally accomplished by the ego, other of its characteristics may derive from the id or the superego. The stimulus that sets action going may be found in one of the other systems as well, and the driving force of action may be supplied by any one of the systems. The configuration of action is different in instinctual from what it is in rational action. Action may predominantly serve the ego; or it may predominantly serve the gratification of instinctual needs; it may also be mainly in the service of the superego, for instance when it is promoted by a strong unconscious guilt feeling. These types of action as a rule differ also in respect to the clarity of motivation, the degree of explicitness in the presentation of the object, and the somatic phenomena that accompany them.

From the point of view of the participation of a variety of ego functions in the action and of the degree to which they participate, we may say: differences in the type of action correspond to differences in the ego level (level of integration, of differentiation, and so forth) that directs it; to differences in the organization of the motives, in the type of goals, in the organization of the means; differences are determined by whether these factors act on a conscious level or not, by the degree of automatization, and so forth. Action may satisfy certain tendencies of the ego while it is rejected by others. Action may be more or less under the influence of the rational elements of behavior. Thus one point of view from which action has to be described is also the one I am mainly concerned with in this paper, i.e., its rational or irrational character[1] (about definitions see later).

About what we call the *aims, goals, or ends of action,* a few unsystematic remarks will have to suffice here.[2] There is a distinction to be made between them and what we call the aim of an instinctual tendency. In speaking of the latter having an aim, we point to nothing else but the fact that these tendencies, if not inhibited, will take their course toward satisfaction. However, we speak of the aim, or goal, of action in the sense that the anticipation of the action's outcome plays a role in its setup.

The goals of an individual's actions mirror his relationships with the outer world, but also his instinctual drives, his interests, his moral demands, the state of his mental equilibrium, and so forth. To the many questions involved here, every analysis gives us a rich material of answers, but these answers have never been made the object of a special study in analysis. We emphasize the complex nature of these goals, the fact that they are overdetermined, and also that in the goal structure contradictions frequently occur. However, normally a mutual adjustment of the different sets of aims takes place in the ego, so that the aims connected with moral demands are compatible with those connected with adaptation to the environment, or with those representing the ego interests, and so forth. The basic goals of human action have been described by Aristotle as "profit, pleasure, morality." This classification is somewhat similar to, while not exactly coinciding with, an analytic one based on the distinction of the ego, id, and superego functions that influence the formation of the goals.

[1] It has been suggested, that the concept of irrational action be dropped completely (von Mises, 1944). The argument runs as follows: since psychoanalysis has shown that the behavior of neurotics, and even of psychotics, is meaningful, can be understood, and that mentally ill people no less than the normal basically strive toward satisfaction (though by using other means), what previously was thought to be irrational action is proved to be not irrational at all, and the term, therefore, is misleading. However, for us, neither the statement that pathological as well as normal action strive toward satisfaction, nor that both can be understood and explained by analysis, implies that they are, or in how far they are, rational. We refer to rational and irrational as to empirical psychological characteristics of action that may be present or absent. In this sense the terms are meaningful and useful.

[2] For one important aspect of the problem see French (1941).

We realize that there is a close interrelationship between these three sets of goals. Goals that are formed under the influence of the superego may at the same time be goals of the ego and of the id. The value systems originating in the superego are something the individual shares with many others, and their acceptance facilitates the ego's task of social adaptation; and we know that the superego functions, in an indirect way, often also gratify instinctual tendencies. I may add that, for instance, the aim of the superego to repress instinctual demands leads to changes of the ego and of the ego's aims in relation with the environment. Also, as in the case of intellectualization, we see that a function that has (partly) been developed as defense against the instincts may become an independent aim of the ego (A. Freud, 1936). We must indeed realize that a great many of the ego's aims originate in such a way. This is a special case of *change of function,* a term familiar to biology. On the other hand, aims of the ego actually influence the superego demands. This happens normally in the course of the elaboration and unification of these demands, a process which takes place in the latency period and in adolescence. Special conditions in the formation of the superego, a high tension of unconscious guilt feelings, weakness of the ego traceable to a variety of factors, are often responsible for the ego's failure in elaborating the aims of the superego. These, then, ask for rigid compliance and are considered as "absolute ends." However, this is a question of degrees, since even in the average person who has developed a superego, its demands, or some of them, tend to be considered as more absolute than other aims; other goals are supposed to be sacrificed to them, and they are kept more independent from practical considerations. Dewey (1922, 1939) has frequently stressed the points that the ends only function within action, that they are merely turning points in activity, and that the acceptance of "fixed ends" is just an aspect of man's devotion to an ideal of certainty. I will not discuss his theory of ends, means, and values. I merely want to emphasize one point: that human beings actually do set more or less fixed aims, or "absolute aims," beyond their actions, and that action is partly determined by factors of this kind, can, in analysis, actually be traced to the functioning of the superego.

In his clinical work, the analyst is constantly confronted with rational as opposed to irrational action, but also with other phenomena commonly classified as rational or irrational. He learns about the factors that may handicap the development of rationality, or inhibit the rational functions. He sees irrational elements of behavior first of all as they interfere with healthy behavior, with adjustment, with progression, and in a more or less definite positive correlation with pathology, maladjustment, and regression. This clinical experience has found its classical expression in Freud's theory of neurosis and psychosis. There is, of course, also a wealth of observations that point to the positive role that irrational, for instance, affective, behavior may actually play in normal adjustment. But this side of the problem, being part of an analytic psychology of the normal person, has so far been formulated less explicitly and less completely than the theory of neurosis. Difficulties also arise from the fact that the terms "rational" and "irrational," while being widely used by analysts, are used inside as well as outside analysis in a rather loose way.

A few words about *use and abuse of these terms* are necessary here. The word "rational" is frequently used as a synonym of "guided by reason," or of "reasonable." As far as "reason" is meant to be just another word for "intellect," and "reasonable behavior" another word for behavior based on insight and thinking, this terminology comes close to the one I shall introduce later. However, "reason" and "reasonable" have also many other meanings and are generally rather poorly defined concepts. Of course, we all use these words frequently in evaluating a person's behavior; still, we should not forget that they are equivocal, unless we add further specifications as to the points of view from which such evaluations are derived. What is called reasonable is actually frequently based in part on a set of implicit or explicit value judgments, the validity of which is taken for granted, and its meaning varies accordingly. If it is considered a legitimate aim of the individual to place certain personal interests above other considerations, an activity that serves this aim will no doubt be called reasonable; while, looked at from the viewpoint of a different system of values, to sacrifice those interests will be considered the very essence of reasonable behavior. Obviously, in these cases the statement that behavior is reasonable is not a purely psychological statement, but there is an element of moral judgment inextricably merged with it. This subjective element, implied in the formation of the concept, makes it inadvisable to use the word "rational" in this sense, if we want to consider it as a psychological term.

In the history of philosophy many attempts have been made to link the concept of *reason* with definite mental functions. However, the rationalistic approach did not get very far in this direction because of various reasons, for instance, because rationalism, at least in some of its implications, is opposed to empiricism. Also, the high evaluation of "reason" led many philosophers to believe in the actual near omnipotence of intellect and to scotomize the true strength of the irrational factors. On the other hand, romantic irrationalism shed some light on unconscious mental functions and on the dynamic importance of irrational forces. But romanticism, even more than enlightenment, fell short of developing our empirical knowledge of personality structure to a point where it might become possible to assign places to rational as well as irrational functions and to understand their mutual relationships. Today "reason," "unreason," "reasonable," "unreasonable" are less used as scientific terms.

However, if there is still so much confusion about meaning and function of rationality, this is at least partly due to the fact that this concept has so many connotations whose origin leads back to the philosophical schools of the past. But other factors have their share in this obvious lack of clarity. It may be worth while to digress here in order to see how implied value judgments, of which I spoke before, influence concept formation and our insight into the connection of facts. There is a strong tendency to equate rational behavior with healthy behavior and with behavior we judge to be "good" or "right," and irrational behavior with the opposites. Even analytic authors find it difficult to realize that rational behavior may be put into the service of destructive or self-destructive aims. There is no doubt a positive correlation, for instance, between rational behavior and adapted behavior, between rational behavior and healthy behavior, and these correlations have long been recognized. However, the value factor implied makes it difficult to realize the fact that the interrelationship of rational and irrational behavior is actually far more complex than these simple correlations make it appear. In studying the effects of those implied value judgments we find that there exists a rather general tendency which I propose to call a tendency toward *agglutination of values.* If, for example, we attach to an element of behavior a positive value accent, our thinking will tend to have other elements valued in a positive way more easily identified with it, considered part of it, or in causal relation to it, than elements that have a negative value accent. The same agglutination takes place in the realm of behavior elements that are negatively valued. Thus, connections according to the common evaluation of facts will be substituted for their real connections, and insight into the structure of reality will be interfered with. There is a second tendency which I shall call *irradiation of values.* It follows the laws of affect irradiation. If an element has a positive value accent, those other elements we know to be somehow or other in contact with it may come to participate in this value accent (the case in which means derive value from the ends is more complex and cannot be included here). According to the first principle, we put together what we value in the same way; according to the second, we value in the same way what we know somehow to belong together. Both tendencies point to regressive elements in our thought (and child observation shows us somewhat similar phenomena to an even more impressive degree). Still, they do influence our psychological thinking, they are frequently found at the base of errors in judgment in political thought, and generally wherever highly invested value judgments come into play. Their character of shifting accents, of establishing and severing connections of facts with disregard of the object structure makes us think of the primary process. While the irradiation of values takes place according to what we know about emotional thinking in general, in the case of the agglutination of values also other factors may come into play. Here we may sometimes be confronted with the interference of a superego function with an ego function: reality testing (other instances of such an interference have been described in analysis; see Freud, 1936); it is a mixing up of superego schemes with ego schemes. It is well known that the superego, the source of at least part of our value judgments, has its roots in layers of the personality governed by the primary process. The common fact that reality testing is impaired when the objects have a strong value accent (moral, aesthetic, and the like) may be partly accounted for along these lines. I should like to add that I do not consider my explanation in terms of value agglutination to be complete. Other factors will have to be taken into consideration, for instance, a tendency toward isolation ("good" things must not be contaminated with "bad" things—as a consequence of which the causal nexus between the facts may be disrupted, may not appear, and so forth). Furthermore, it would be worth while to describe the influence of ambivalence on value agglutination.

After this long digression I shall define the *strictly psychological meaning of the terms "rational" and "irrational"*: irrational behavior, to start with, can be defined in a negative way, in the sense of absence of rational control, or of being governed by principles different from those that govern rational behavior. In a positive characterization, we designate as irrational behavior that is predominantly emotional or instinctual. There is also an attempt toward a more definite positive characterization of the laws governing at least a considerable part of irrational behavior: part of it certainly follows the laws of the primary process. The instinctual drives are irrational in the first and in the second sense; and so are all unconscious functions in general. It is just a statement about the actual usage of the word and does not imply any addition to these definitions (or characterizations), when I mention that in analysis the word is preferably used to describe behavior that allows also of a rational alternative. Cases in question are irrational (instinctual or emotional) action as opposed to rational action, and irrational as opposed to rational thinking.

The term rational, when applied to thinking, means logically correct thinking. But it does not only mean that (except in the case of logic and mathematics). It also implies the consideration of available facts, and the checking on these facts and their connections according to commonly accepted rules.

As to *rational action,* I start with a definition by the sociologist M. Weber (1921): "a man's action is purposively rational if he considers the goals, the means, and the side effects, and weighs rationally means against goals, goals against side effects [consequences], and also various possible goals against each other." I add that this process of calculation can be on a conscious, but also on a preconscious level. Obviously here, as in rational thinking, a consideration of reality (in many cases inner as well as outer reality) is implied. A thorough insight into the reality structure may be found together with a strong tendency toward balancing the ends against the means; but these factors vary partly independently from each other. Thus, a variety of types can be observed. For the sake of clarification it might also be useful to introduce here a distinction between two forms of reality-syntonic behavior. Behavior may fit into the reality conditions in the sense that it actually furthers the attainment of a certain aim though it may not have been calculated to do so; in this case we may call it *objectively reality syntonic*. Or behavior may attain a given aim as a consequence of being calculated to reach it; we call this form *subjectively reality syntonic* (Hartmann, 1939a). "Instinctual" or emotional behavior frequently fits a reality situation in the former sense (objectively). The highest degree to which behavior can be subjectively reality syntonic is represented by purposive rational action.

I hope that from what I have said here it is quite clear that I do not think of rational and irrational action as always rigidly separated from each other in real behavior; also, between the extreme cases described, a series of transitions can actually be observed.

I have discussed the psychological meaning of the term rational action. But I have made no attempt to define as rational any set of goals. Actually, the setting of an aim may or may not be based on rational thinking; but the goals themselves—that is to say, as long as we consider them as goals and as distinct from the other elements of action—cannot be called rational or irrational in the sense of psychological description (while we may, of course, say that they agree or disagree with a person's value system, mental equilibrium, chances of adaptation in a given situation, and so forth). On the other hand, if we consider the goals in a larger complex of ends and means in which the goal in question might be regarded as a means to further ends, the terms rational and irrational may apply. If to be socially successful is from one point of view a goal but from another a means to gain wealth, its use for that purpose may or may not be rational; but here again it is not its function as a goal that may correctly be called rational. I mention this fact mainly in order to stress again the necessary distinction between "rational" and "reasonable"; actually, when the words rational aims or goals are used, what is really meant, as a rule, is that the goals are reasonable in one of the various meanings of the word. However, in making my point, I am also aware of the fact that there are no doubt psychological connections between the aims of a person and the means he chooses in order to reach them; also, looked at from an objective viewpoint, certain goals will be reached easier than other by rational means.

I said before that our insight into the interrelationship of rational and irrational behavior is rather incomplete and obscured by simplifying dichotomies. Our understanding of the actual complexity of the problem may be helped by discussing an example which I choose from the borderland between psychoanalysis and sociology. Freud's theory of *group formation* (1921) is so widely known that I shall point to only those elements which are of special interest in this connection. In describing and trying to explain group-psychological phenomena, Freud thought of a type of behavior that is not limited to definite epochs of history, but that under certain conditions will repeat itself, so to say, over and over again in the history of mankind, with essential elements remaining unchanged. The irrational character of the individual's behavior in a group is contrasted with the comparatively rational behavior of the same individual outside the group situation. The changes we observe in an individual who is a group member can partly be described as regressive phenomena. Furthermore, a splitting of the superego takes place, and as a member of the group the individual accepts moral standards that as a private person he would reject; killing, prohibited by his private superego, may be required by his group superego. This feature of the "superego cleavage" is characteristic enough to be considered by Waelder (1929) as a basis for defining the groups just dealt with (as against what may be called "associations," that is, stable and more or less lasting social organizations). Where the group has a personal leader, the member of the group substitutes him for his superego; and on this basis a mutual identification of the group members takes place.

In elaborating on these premises, I may briefly comment on an example from the history of our times, namely, group formation in totalitarian societies. Obviously, a variety of types can be observed. In some of them we see as a decisive factor a definite tendency to regress, to abandon individual freedom for dependence on the leader, and moral autonomy for the group's moral precepts. Violent aggressive outbreaks and extraordinary cruelties which have an entirely irrational character occur. These forms come close to the scheme outlined above. Analysts as well as social scientists have repeatedly given a correct account of them. However, there are more complex forms that disclose other aspects of totalitarian group formation. If we look at the factors that actually bring about these complex forms, which frequently are no less virulent than the others, we clearly realize the importance of purposive rational tendencies (in the sense defined above) among the determining factors of group formation. We also see that totalitarian groups—and I have emphasized their regressive character—have at the same time increased the "rationalization" of the individual's life, including the details of daily routine, beyond the limits of what we know of any other social system; however, I will not discuss the relationships that exist between "rationalization" in this sense, a term widely used in sociology, and "rational behavior." Here I am interested in the fact that in the formation of collective mythologies planning can participate; and that the break-through of instinctual drives can also be the result of planning. Of course, I do not, by any means, want to assert that regressive phenomena are not involved; what I want to state is that the threshold for their manifestation can be lowered, and in the cases in question is actually lowered partly by purposive calculation. The members of that part of society that does the planning may accept those mythologies for themselves; but not all of them do.

To begin with, there appears a certain degree of rationally calculated action in the organization and development of that subgroup that actually does the planning; but, in some instances, it also appears in the selection of the group members who are supposed freely to act out their aggression. The tendency toward "rationalizing" and controlling of ever more fields of everybody's life also includes purposive attempts to perpetuate in the group members, even when they are not in immediate contact with the group, certain characteristics which according to the classical description of group psychology manifest themselves only in the group situation; for instance, the superego split and the attitude toward the leader, as mentioned above, the aim, in this special case, being clearly twofold: to have these individuals stick to certain values of social cohesion so far as the maintenance of the system in power is concerned, and on the other hand to have them freely live out their aggression against the out-siders—as a consequence of the induced changes in ideal formation.

In an extremely elucidating contribution to this subject Kris (1941) emphasized that totalitarian propaganda much more than democratic propaganda uses broadcasts from mass meetings for its purpose; the listener "is made to share the emotions of the many who react to the spell of the mass-situation." In other cases, social reality is made to provoke or to strengthen certain characteristics of "mass-psychological behavior," even in the physically isolated indi-vidual, by putting a premium on it, as we shall see later. In these cases the distinction between mass psychology and the psychology of stable organizations is more or less obliterated.

Somewhat similar conditions may well be found in many political parties and also in some cases of religious group "fanatization." How-ever, there are also striking differences. In the case of totalitarian systems, an infinitely more intense and more direct expression of aggression than in political parties is generally expected. Also, the purposive factors are more predominant here than in the formation of religious groups. There is a difference in the structure of the goals, in so far as in totalitarian societies, at least vis-à-vis the outsider, a nearly complete sacrifice of human values to a very poorly structured political end is demanded. In the case of religious systems, a set of values, characteristics of the system, is included into the structure of the goals which under no condition must be sacrificed to ulterior ends.

Emotional regimentation for the purpose of subordinating a vast field of other goals to the one that at a particular moment appears most important can also be observed in nontotalitarian systems, for instance, in time of war. Still, the narrowing of the goal structure and the debasement of all other values to means calculated to serve that single end go so much further in the totalitarian set-up that they might be considered a characteristic of these systems. Besides, this sacrifice of values is not a temporary measure but intended to become a constant feature of man. This, too, presupposes deep changes in the structure of the superego.

To what degree all these changes could be achieved, and what subsidiary psychological consequences this would imply, I do not want to discuss here. I shall merely mention one characteristic feature that can be described as a vicious circle: in reducing the structure of the individual's aims, in decreasing his moral autonomy, an appeal is made to regressive tendencies which then, on their part, intensify the individual's readiness for cooperation with the groups in question and for letting his behavior be planned according to the aims of the leaders.

I here want to emphasize a third factor which appears in this type of group in addition to the planned break-through of instinctual drives and the intended changes in the formation of the superego. Social institutions and a psychological climate develop, or are created, in such a way that when action takes place in agreement with the changed attitudes toward the instinctual drives and the superego, it will simultaneously tend to gratify interests of the ego (for social status, influence, wealth, and so forth). Rewards and punishment are distributed accordingly. Now an appeal is made no longer only to the regressive tendencies but also to the ego interests and the rational behavior of the individual. Acting according to the lowered threshold of aggression and the changes in the structure of the superego may fit into this social reality and be expedient (objectively); obviously it would not fit as well into another type of society. But the individual will also use this type of behavior in a purposive rational way, in order to conform to the reality that is to fit into the social situation (according to the distinction I introduced before, acting in this case is subjectively reality syntonic). Looked at from this point of view, this is another case of what could be called social compliance (see Chapter 2). The synergism of ego interests with the two other factors, described first, is consequential also because it introduces into the picture an element comparable to what in neuroses we call the secondary gain. However, it is obvious that the appeal these systems make to the ego is not limited to what we call the "interests"; real or imaginary danger situations are used as an appeal to the ego's more basic reactions of self-protection (Kris and Speier, 1944).

This presentation of the problem of group psychology in totalitarian systems is obviously incomplete in regard to many of its sociological as well as psychological aspects. I have not attempted to formulate the arguments which on analytic grounds could be raised against the possible psychological durability of this set-up: that the aims are partly incompatible, that the planning relies in part on factors of low stability, that the conditions are unfavorable for synthesis, and so forth; nor do I want to decide in how far psychological factors of this kind might have contributed to an actual weakening of systems of that order. I have intentionally emphasized only those viewpoints which I feel add to the presentation of the problem as we find it in most analytic writings; I believe the scheme evolved here comes closer to elucidating the relationships between rationality, superego formation, and instinctual drives that we see in the cases in question. There are many other social phenomena which clearly show the interrelationship of rational and irrational factors, in the sense that one set of factors may actually provoke or strengthen another one, and vice versa. Also how "rationalization" in the social field affects the rational or irrational behavior of the individual has been frequently described, one of the best studied examples being the psychological changes that accompany the process of industrialization (Mannheim, 1935). Leaving the subject of group formation, I shall now turn to a study of these interrelationships in fields closer to clinical analytic observation.

I have mentioned the fact that in analytic literature the distinction of rational and irrational behavior is most frequently put side by side with that of adjusted versus nonadjusted, and normal versus pathological behavior. We now ask: what actually are the *relations between rationality,* as I have defined it, *and adaptation?* We take it for granted that rational thinking and action have a positive value for the individual's adjustment to the environment. This is a matter of common psychological knowledge and as a result of analytic experience has rightly received new emphasis; Freud's attitude toward the adaptive value of rationality was that of a cautious optimism. I shall not try to contribute toward a better understanding of this side of the problem. Still, there is evidence to support the thesis that the relations between rational behavior and adaptation are often more complex than we expect them to be. In discussing some special illustrations, I shall take into consideration what the structural approach of psychoanalysis has taught us about this subject.

First of all, there are activities that can adequately be performed only if the higher ego functions, rational thinking and action among them, are temporarily kept in abeyance. The impossibility of transitorily switching off these functions may have the character of a neurotic symptom and interfere with successful adaptation. Some clinically well-known examples are certain sexual disturbances, and also difficulties in falling asleep, both due to a pathological fear of loss of ego control.

So far as our problem is concerned, things are somewhat similar, though not identical, in the case of what we call the preconscious automatized activities. It is no doubt true that this type of behavior, as has been stressed by analysts, does in many cases serve a tendency away from reality; also that difficulties with deautomatizing might interfere with adjustment. This is clearly seen in personalities of the obsessional type. On the other hand, automatized behavior does actually serve adaptation in a wide range of activities (by providing standardized methods for the solution of problems, and for the switching of psychic energy; also, if we look at the economic side of the question, by saving psychic energy). In some instances, it may even be more useful if each intermediary phase of behavior does not have to be calculated anew in each case, as is done in rational action. Moreover, it is generally accepted that the adaptive value of automatized activities may be impaired when rational action impinges upon them. Of course, this is not to deny that the opposite case is probably of even greater importance: the rigidity of automatized action is in need of frequent readjustments by rational thinking and action; however, in this connection the former case deserves our special interest. It reminds us of the fact that the various ways of adaptation are generally appropriate only for a limited range of situations; and that successful adaptation to one set of situations may lead to an impairment of adaptation to another one. Also, achievements of adjustment in respect to one function may be disturbances of adjustment in respect to other functions. "Each of the mental differentiations that we have become acquainted with represents a fresh aggravation of the difficulties of mental functioning, increases its instability, and may become the starting-point for its breakdown, that is, for the onset of a disease (Freud, 1921, p. 130). On the other hand, disturbances in adaptation may well develop into adaptative achievements. It is not merely pathological development that comes about through conflict but also development culminating in a state of successful adaptation—and it does so not merely occasionally but rather generally.

The fact that the fixation of outdated ways of problem solving frequently interferes with successful adaptation is familiar to all analysts; increased rational insight and rationality of action will often be helpful in overcoming such a lag in adaptation. In certain historical epochs we often see, as a typical phenomenon, that failure in adaptation is due to the increasing demands made on the ego from the side of the rapidly changing structure of the environment. I will briefly mention a situation, rather widely discussed in our days (e.g., by Lowenfeld, 1944): I am thinking of the individual in a world in which traditional goal structures and standards of conduct have collapsed. He is confronted with the task of substituting purposive rational calculations and a new organization of his aims for behavior built on traditional patterns. In this situation, the demands on the integrating function of the ego to secure stable forms of adaptation grow; and the ego is not always able to cope with them. As a consequence, a kind of ataxia may develop between different tendencies as expressed in the goal structure; and also in the distribution of purposive rational and irrational behavior in the variety of adaptive processes. In the transitory phase of increased trial and error in the use of rationality, before the ego can re-establish a balance among the goals, and between the ends and means, adaptation may suffer. However, the final outcome may be a strengthening of the ego and a widening of its field of action: the ego may be enabled to integrate not only a higher degree of rationality but also directing tendencies that had previously been active in the superego.

My next example concerns the means-ends calculation, the very characteristic of purposive rational action. As long as the child values momentary pleasure gains more highly than future gains, rational planning of his actions will be impossible or incomplete. This stage is normally overcome in the course of development and if we find it in an adult, we know it to be pathognomonic. However, the extreme opposite is also to be considered as pathological. We find it in people who immediately withdraw the character of a goal from the aim as soon as they have reached it, or even before they have reached it, and shift it on to ulterior ends. Thus they postpone to an ever more remote future the gratification normally connected with the reaching of a goal. Each step in this unending sequence is experienced as incomplete and provisional. The difference between the real and the possible is lost. On the other hand, the process of rational calculation may have become an aim in itself. The instinctual elements and the defenses involved in this picture are rather well known from the analytic study of neuroses and need not be elaborated upon. What matters here is that we realize how the calculation of means and ends, given certain conditions, may, as it were, run wild.

In summarizing much of what has been said, and collating it with experiences from other fields of observation, we may say that highly differentiated functions, for instance rational behavior, do not by themselves guarantee the optimum of adjustment, though their value for adaptation is obvious; they need to be coordinated with and supplemented by other systems of regulation, some of which may even function on a much more primitive level of organization (see Chapter 1). Therefore, the picture of a "totally rational" human being is a caricature; it certainly does not represent the highest degree of adaptation accessible to man. Freud seems to have pointed in the same direction when, in one of his last papers (1937a), he said that we could not expect the result of even the most complete analysis to be an individual who "shall never again feel the stirrings of passion."

Another aspect of the problem has a claim upon our interest. Every progress of growth and development in man can be viewed from the angle of changing the conditions under which adaptation takes place and of changing the methods used in complying with the demands of reality. Even those defenses which are not primarily directed against the outside world but rather toward checking instinctual drives will at the same time modify the individual's attitude toward reality. Psychoanalysis has particularly emphasized the developmental aspect of adaptation. Thus, in the realm of the instinctual drives, the attainment of the latest stage of libidinal evolution, the genital stage, has been recognized to be one of the most important prerequisites for the adult person's adaptation; and we are familiar with the fact that the mature ego is more adjustable than the infantile ego. Also, clinical experience has taught us in a most impressive way the role regression plays in pathogenesis. However, I want to stress here that, apart from this much more general parallelism between progression and adaptation, there exist phenomena that have the character of *regressive adaptation.* These are the cases in which adapted, and normal, behavior of adult persons is actually achieved by way of regression. I am not thinking here so much of such observations which are well known to every analyst, e.g., that pregenital sublimations may supplement or be substituted for sublimations on the genital level, in order to provide adjustment to reality. I rather stress the fact that even in productive scientific thinking the detour over irrational elements, the use of visual imagery in general and of symbolic elements, far from being a handicap, may actually be helpful. In every form of artistic activity this regressive detour has been recognized as an important prerequisite for achievement. To label these phenomena, we may adopt the term "regression in the service of the ego," introduced by Kris (1936). These phenomena too must be looked at from the viewpoint that to achieve optimal adaptation more primitive functions may be needed to supplement the highly differentiated ones.

There is still another fact we must take into consideration when we try to check on what relations actually exist between developmental level and adaptation. The idea of a disharmonious precocity in the development of certain tendencies is familiar to us from the pathogenesis of neurosis. Reaching forward, ahead of ego development, of instinctual drives, as a result of maturation or of developmental sequences, is known to us as a factor which is frequently pathogenic. But there is also the possibility that precocious development of certain ego functions, among them rational thought processes, might be a causative element in the genesis of obsessional neurosis. Facts like these and some others mentioned before make me inclined to formulate conditions of health in terms of the equilibrium that exists between the substructures of personality on the one hand, and between these and the environment on the other hand.

I hope that as a result of the foregoing remarks we have gained a better understanding not only of the paramount role rational behavior plays in human adaptation but also of some less obvious ways in which rationality and adaptation are actually interrelated. If we look at the problem from a biological viewpoint, which is in accordance with at least one basic trend of psychoanalytic thinking, we may say that the term "rational" should not be used as a magic word above and beyond consideration of the conditions under which the various forms of rationality have adaptive value; the general criteria of adaptation must be applied to them. It is equally misleading to call "rational" all behavior that serves self-preservation, and "irrational" that which runs contrary to it. It is, of course, true that rationality is typically used for the purpose of self-preservation, but it can also be used in the service of, for instance, self-destruction. Moreover, self-preservation in man is based on the interaction of rational and irrational ego functions, but also on that of ego apparatus, instinctual drives, and so forth. If we call this whole ensemble rational, we again obscure the specific psychological meaning of the term.

From our discussion of some typical situations it also became evident that the adaptive value of rationality is partly determined by whether it fits into the state of balance that at a given time exists between the functions of the different psychic systems. I have mentioned that an adaptive achievement in the mastering of one set of situations may very well impair adaptation in the mastering of another. This fact plays a considerable role in biological thinking and has been thoroughly studied also in analysis. Acceptance of reality demands beyond a certain individual threshold may lead to conflicts with the instinctual drives and consequently, given certain conditions, to the development of phenomena that will interfere with successful adaptation. To comply with the outer world, as required by the ego, is favorable for the individual in so far as in doing so he does not overtax the situation in the other systems. The way in which incongruities that may arise are prevented or settled is analogous to the processes that in biology have been described under different headings, for instance, "organization of the organism." This coordination of the parts of the organism and of their functions differs on the various levels of development: and in the adult several layers of it can be distinguished. In psychoanalysis, one expression of the coordinating tendencies is known to us as the synthetic function. It is not the most primitive regulating function we know from analytic experience; it develops only gradually, parallel to the development of the ego. In the course of its development as a specialized form of ego activity, the synthetic function partly replaces more primitive regulations. Freud found that the element of synthesis enters the formation of psychic structure itself, as is clearly seen in the development of the superego. Once the superego has developed and psychic structure can be described in terms of three centers of functioning, the constant balancing of these three systems against each other as well as the checking of demands of the outer world against those of the psychic systems are carried out by the synthetic function.

Though, as a matter of nomenclature, it is not too important, I should like to mention that I wonder whether the use of another term instead of synthetic function, the one commonly used in analysis, might not be preferable. In the phenomena under consideration, what might be called synthesis no doubt plays an important role. However, an element of differentiation and something that could be compared to a "division of labor" are frequently part of the picture. Nunberg (1930) correctly described the elements of synthesis in the development of causal thinking and of the tendency toward generalization. But both phenomena are at the same time clear indications of differentiation taking place in the development of thinking. The superego formation, one of the most portentous results of synthesis, also includes differentiation, in the sense of specialization of function. Therefore, the term *organizing function* may fit the facts better than *synthetic function,* because in the concept of organization we include elements of differentiation as well as of integration. Nunberg also advanced the hypothesis that the synthetic function of the ego is linked to the "uniting" characteristics of the libido. This hypothesis would have to be widened to include not only libidinal but also nonlibidinal tendencies, stemming from the aggressive drives, as the ultimate basis of the integrating and differentiating aspects of organization.

In adding these remarks about the organizing function, my aim still remains to describe the relation of action to the setup, the conditions existing in the psychic structure. I have said that action develops on the basis of, and parallel with, the child's acceptance of the reality principle. It means a definite further step in development, beyond the acceptance of the reality principle, when the more complex regulations of the psychic systems and of their relations with reality (and also the ways in which they may react to the intended action) can be included in the plan of action. In his attempt to master reality in an alloplastic way, the older child's ego also learns to consider, to utilize, and to develop autoplastically the state of affairs in his psychic systems.

Concepts of organization, of equilibrium, of harmony have been used in explaining human behavior since Socrates, Aristotle, and the Stoics. Some of these concepts seem to come rather close to those of analysis. However, the relevance of the psychoanalytic concept of organization is due to the fact that it is neither a philosophical principle nor a moral demand, but that it refers only to empirical findings. The analytic concept of organization actually covers part of what philosophers refer to when they speak of "reason"; and, in speaking of reasonable behavior, one often refers to phenomena that in analysis we should describe as behavior guided by the organizing function. This psychic function is closer than rationality to what is commonly called reason; still, because of what I have said before, I prefer not to use "reason" as a psychological term.

Basing the theory of action on the structural concepts of analysis, I will sketch one type of action that is widely held to dominate man and that is of paramount importance in the "utilitarian" schools of social science. It is actually normal and adaptive in a wide range of situations. I am discussing it in order to show that despite this fact it cannot be judged without insight into its structural position. The form of action I have in mind is another one of those that have been indiscriminately called rational. Its aims are what is commonly called usefulness. Striving toward what is "useful," however, does not delineate the goal in an unequivocal way. From the point of view of psychological description we can characterize these strivings as a certain group of what in psychoanalysis we call *ego interests,* for instance, those concerned with social status, influence, professional success, wealth, comfort, and so forth. Genetically we can trace the origin of many ego interests more or less completely to tendencies of the id. However, once structuralization has taken place, they become partly independent in the service of the ego and this development is, under normal conditions, not wholly reversible;[3] therefore psychoanalysis has to describe them as a separate group of phenomena. The weight that this group of ego interests carries in the dynamics of individual behavior, and in social life, is a matter of common knowledge. However, they represent only one part of the ego, and to make a distinction between these and other tendencies of the ego becomes important when we try to characterize various types of action. Here I should like to refer to but one point on which our clinical experience can shed some light.

We often see the form of behavior under discussion exaggerated to a kind of caricature in some of our patients. I am thinking of that well-known type of person who constantly emphasizes the matter-of-fact view he has of life, his realistic attitude, and the high degree of so-called rationality he has reached. Every piece of behavior that does not visibly serve a "useful" purpose is discarded as archaic, as based on superstition or on prejudice; where activities do not serve a useful end, they are unmasked as hypocrisy. Such patients force themselves to regard sexual behavior as an expedient for ulterior purposes (for instance: mental hygiene), and they try to act accordingly. Their characteristic reaction to death is to suppress mourning.

The origin and structure of such attitudes are obviously rather complex. For my purpose I want to stress the preferred type of action that is contingent upon these attitudes. That action, moreover, is correlated with a specific relation to reality, in the sense that while

---

[3] For the development of the concept of secondary autonomy, see Hartmann (1939a) and Chapters 7 and 9.

parts of reality are emphasized, other parts, mainly of inner reality, are scotomized. We soon discover that this type of behavior is full of self-deception. It starts from a highly limited concept of "reality," as a policy that takes pride in calling itself realistic often does. We understand this behavior to be an attempt to deny inner conflicts and to protect oneself from fear; its defensive character is obvious. Of course, this does not imply that it is invariably pathological. In some individuals we find it as a more or less central element of their neurosis. But in many others, a lesser degree of it is obviously part of normal behavior and proves very valuable for adjustment in a large number of situations; but even in these persons, it often serves the purpose of defense. The adaptive value of such behavior varies with the social setup in which it occurs.

From the point of view of the various systems of valuation which develop on the basis of the superego demands, the type of action in question is evaluated in different ways. Frequently it is found to be in conflict with the moral demands of the individual. This may be worth while mentioning, since the psychoanalytic approach has investigated mainly that side of the moral demands which forms a barrier against the instinctual drives. But ego tendencies of various kinds—action according to the ego interests, also the very element of calculation in purposive rational action—are actually in many situations evaluated in a negative way by various ethical systems; and by no means only as a consequence of possible instinctual implications. I think that these evaluations as well as those condemning instinctual behavior can in the last instance be traced to the conditions under which the superego is formed. But this is a special matter which I have pursued further elsewhere (see Hartman, 1960; Hartmann and Loewenstein, 1962).

Analysis clearly reveals the manifold genetic and structural interrelationships of the ego interests with other driving forces. No analyst doubts that the picture of man guided exclusively by this or that group of ego interests falls short of psychic reality. However, it still plays a role where standards of health, aims of therapy, and pedagogical problems are discussed. Thus it is often maintained that the freedom of the individual to subordinate other tendencies to what is useful for him makes the difference between healthy and neurotic behavior. Actually this is too small a basis on which to build a definition of health. The ego interests are only one set of ego functions among others; and they do not coincide with the ego function that considers also the demands of the other psychic systems and that I have described as the ego's organizing function; their prevalence in an individual does not warrant the assumption that the drives are harmoniously included in the ego, or that the superego demands have been integrated into it.

Obviously, even a type of action commonly judged as "normal" cannot be properly evaluated without structural analysis. There is no reliable correlation with health if the three systems and their interrelationships are not considered. If we speak of subordination of other psychic tendencies not under the ego interests but under ego control, and particularly under the ego's organizing function, this will better describe what we call healthy behavior; though even this characterization remains incomplete.

These considerations also make it clear why the many attempts to plan human existence that have been based on an appeal to a certain group of ego interests are doomed to failure; from the psychological viewpoint they are likely to prove defective, and eventually to lead to unforeseen conflicts, particularly when these attempts are aimed at a structurally central and complex sector of human behavior.

What changes the psychic systems of a patient undergo during a psychoanalytic treatment, and the role the organizing function plays in it, have been often described. In this connection I want to point to the fact that the psychoanalytic process itself can be considered as a model of how purposive rational action can, often successfully, use irrational elements of behavior. Here, obviously, in the plan of a rational technique, devised to alter the patient's behavior, the fact of irrationality is included (see also Chapter 8). Rational means are used even in order to mobilize irrational forces which, as we know from experience, will finally become integrated into a new state of balance. The ego is strengthened, and a synthesis of the tasks set by itself, by the instinctual drives, by the claims of moral conscience, and by reality is made possible; the individual learns to coordinate his aims. In the psychoanlytic procedure, rational insight takes itself into account as a partial function besides and in relation to other psychic functions. Thus, this method of "planning" intentionally leaves a certain degree of freedom to the instinctual and emotional forces. The possibilities and limitations of rationality are empirically tested in every analysis. In this approach, "rationalism" and "irrationalism" have both been integrated.

Freud's sentence, "Where id was, there shall ego be," indicates in a general way the aims of psychoanalytic therapy. It certainly does not mean that the rational functions, or the ego interests, and so forth, could or should ever totally replace the functions of the other systems. He thought mainly of guidance by the ego, of supremacy of its organizing function, as I have described it. However, there is no doubt that the strengthening of the ego, one consequence of analysis if it has been successful, may also result in the ego's taking over in its own organization certain functions that had previously been executed by the other substructures of personality. This case is very different from that discussed above, in which an attempt is made to substitute certain ego interests for the functions of the other systems, often as an act of defense against the latter. What I have in mind here is the successful integration of these functions into the ego; this presupposes ego strength, relative freedom from anxiety, and intactness of the organizing function. How far one may have the right to hope that this degree of reorganization could be achieved by any methods other than psychoanalysis, I shall not discuss here. However, we do hope that what analysis, and also what more particularly our insight into the analytical procedure itself, have taught us about the dialectics of rational and irrational behavior can be useful as a model for the understanding and the handling of social phenomena on a larger scale.

CHAPTER 4

Comments on the Psychoanalytic Theory of Instinctual Drives

(1948)

THE field that the psychoanalytic theory of instincts, or drives, is meant to cover is not too well defined. It may well be true, as Freud himself felt, that some aspects of this theory do not show the same degree of lucidity we find in many other tenets of analysis. It seems, therefore, advisable to review, from time to time, the place of this theory in the whole of psychoanalysis, particularly in view of the ways in which analysis has developed so far. Progress in one direction has frequently implied changes—at least changes in emphasis—which often have not been explicitly stated. The empirical foundations of analysis are manifold, its theories are complex, verification is difficult and time consuming; therefore the actual interrelation of its various parts on (chronologically speaking) the same level has not always been clearly realized. Despite incomplete attempts toward a more or less systematic presentation, we may say that even at present an understanding of analysis is hardly possible without a detailed knowledge of its history. When working on some analytic proposition without such knowledge, one is likely to find one's way encumbered by hypotheses which actually belong in quite

Many of the questions discussed in this paper are taken up again in Chapter 9.

different stages of its development. This state of affairs is troublesome for the understanding and, of course, for the teaching of analysis. The endeavor to promote architectonic adjustments, a better coordination of factual and theoretical aspects, may also help us gain some new insight into certain problems which are either neglected or incompletely understood.

As this sounds like a rather ambitious program, I hasten to state that my aim is limited to the discussion of a few aspects of the theory of instincts. I shall try to find a point of view from which various concepts of what is called an instinct, or a drive, can be properly evaluated in human psychology. Following this I shall submit to your consideration some thoughts about the much discussed, but still, maybe, insufficiently discussed, relationships between the instincts of biology and the instinctual drives or instinctual urges of psychoanalysis, and the light our insight into psychic structure may shed on this problem. This leads then to the question of the probable difference in the function of the pleasure principle in relation to instincts and drives. I also want to discuss briefly what analysis can contribute toward our understanding of the tendencies of self-preservation in man, and of self-regulating systems in general. Finally, I want to cast at least a glance at the way in which the specific approach of analysis can be helpful vis-à-vis some problems of general biology, and how the differences in approach reflect on one problem of the classification of instincts.

It has been said repeatedly that the definition of instinct is, after all, just a matter of convention, which is, of course, true in a sense; still, not all actual or possible concepts of instinct are equally helpful. Also, it may well be that for different fields of observation and for different methods of approach, the use of somewhat different concepts of instincts or drives may prove expedient. If what we call instinctual drive in analysis actually differs in some respects from most definitions of instinct used by biologists, this is no doubt partly due to the fact that Freud's immediate and main interest was in human psychology, while the observational data of the biologists pertain mainly to other species, particularly lower animals, and their findings and hypotheses are from there extrapolated to human beings. A second reason for such differences, closely related to this first one, we find in the specific methods of approach used here and there. Of course, all hypotheses about instincts must be checked the same way every scientific proposition is: as to consistency and conformity with whatever factual knowledge we have in the field with which we are dealing. Besides this, looked at from the point of view of analysis as a branch of human psychology, hypotheses about instincts must be evaluated according to whether or not in human psychology they are actually or potentially useful.

It would be naïve to underestimate the positive contribution which the concept of instinctual drive, as defined by Freud, made to the development of analysis. Obviously, this concept is the residue of detailed and prolonged study of human behavior under controlled conditions, and of the use of an observational technique yielding data which are, at least in part, not directly accessible to any other approach. Let us not forget that although scientific concepts are intended to facilitate, they may also handicap the coordination and explanation of facts; and not only the formulation of hypotheses, but the process of fact finding itself. In both, it makes a decisive difference whether the concept of drives is based on that plasticity and variety of needs we find in sexuality, or only on that lesser plasticity and lesser variety of needs we find, for instance, in the case of intake of food, or in the case of respiration. The history of analysis shows in a particularly conclusive way a mutual promotion of observation and theoretical formulation. While there are quite a few questions in the minds of some analysts and others as to the consistency of Freud's theory of instinctual drives, and as to some of its broader implications, there is hardly a doubt as to the fitness of his concept with respect to the methods he used and the field of observation for which it was devised and which it helped to develop.

To avoid misunderstanding, I add that here and in the following considerations I am referring to the concept of drives which we actually encounter in clinical psychoanalytic psychology, omitting Freud's other, mainly biologically oriented set of hypotheses of the "life" and "death" instincts whose interplay is meant to explain "the phenomena of life" (Freud, 1930). These concepts are of a different order, as Freud clearly realized, and the corresponding hypotheses have to be proved or disproved biologically; also they could account for only one aspect of the psychological problems under consideration here, and so far have not added much to our understanding of the specific functions of drives (in the psychological sense) in contradistinction to other psychic functions.

Freud defined an instinctual drive in the former sense as having an impetus, an aim, an object, and a source. He speaks of an instinct as a demand made on the mental apparatus by the body; however, even at the comparatively early stage of theory formation in which he introduced this formulation (1915a), he occasionally looked upon drives not only as factors acting on the mental apparatus "from without," but also in a sense as working in the mental apparatus itself. Later he defined their position more closely by including their mental aspect in the functions of the id. Bibring (1936) clearly traced the steps by which Freud came to develop his theory of drives and of their relationships to mental functions, and also to the principles which regulate these functions; but here I wish to discuss Freud's concept of instinct from a different angle. It may be useful at this point to summarize briefly some of the specific features of this theory which have been instrumental in that advancement of human psychology which is due to analysis. I need hardly mention here that for developing the greater part of these features it was the study of the sexual drives which actually proved decisive.

In the field of psychology, the importance of the aims and objects of the drives soon outdistanced by far the importance of their sources, although the sources remain relevant because of their developmental aspects and because insight into the sources may be helpful in classifying the drives. This part of Freud's concept also presents a hope—not the only one—for a future meeting of psychoanalysis with physiology. The interest in the aims became predominant, particularly because of their wide variability, characteristic of the human species. Looked at from this point of view (with all its implications for substitute gratification and aim-inhibited expression), it became possible to draw a rather comprehensive picture of the correlations between a person's needs on various levels, his emotions, his ways of solving problems, etc.; and a wealth of concrete features, heterogeneous as they might have appeared from another approach, fell into line. This, of course, also emphasizes the comparative freedom from reactive rigidity, the comparative independence from, and variety of, possible responses to outer and to inner stimuli that we attribute to man to a greater extent than to other species. The study of the objects of the drives was the first, and still is one basic approach of analysis to the interdependence of individual and environment. It led to a detailed investigation of manifold typical and individual "situations" in which the person finds himself confronted with reality. Genetically, Freud traced the interrelation of the child's demands on the one hand, and of object formation and object relationships on the other hand, through the successive stages of instinctual development. This study, too, yielded significant insights into some more or less specific features of human nature. Thus the protracted helplessness and dependence of the young of the human species on the objects were found to be responsible for the fact that "the influence of the real external world . . . is intensified and an early differentiation between the ego and the id is promoted. Moreover, the dangers of the external world have a greater importance for it [the infant], so that the value of the object which can alone protect it against them . . . is enormously enhanced" (Freud, 1926a, p. 154f.). Because of the actual predominance of the human objects over all other categories of objects, the detailed investigation of object relationships opened the way for analysis to become one fundamental approach to the social sciences. But in gathering a wealth of material on the ways in which a person's needs have a bearing on his relationships with the object world and vice versa, and in thus gaining insight into the mutual influence of outer and inner stimuli, a field was entered that is equally important today for the biologist's study of instincts. Furthermore, the distinction of typical stages of instinctual development, best studied in the case of sexual drives, and of their impact on aims, attitudes toward the objects, modes of action, etc., facilitated the task of finding a frame of reference for many data on growth as well as development, that is, for the ever more fruitful genetic aspect of general psychology. It became possible to envisage the genetic aspect of human behavior in terms of a typical succession of instinctual organizations, of the conflicts among the drives, and between drives and ego and superego which correspond to these stages. Freud's emphasis on the energic aspect of mental functions, which he soon came to tie up at least partly with the drives because they appeared to be an unexpectedly strong moving power in the background of human behavior, was frequently criticized by psychologists and biologists. In analysis, however, this energy is nothing like a metaphysical *élan vital;* it is rather an operational concept, devised to coordinate observational data. The concept of a continuity of this "driving force" and the consideration from this angle of a great variety of mental acts make these acts comparable, and their connections often traceable, at least as to this one aspect. The hypothesis that there may be different forms or conditions of that energy, and that they may be transformed into each other, has proved helpful also in describing the energic aspect of the psychic systems. I conclude this enumeration by mentioning what should, because of its importance, perhaps have been mentioned first: that Freud's approach to the position of the drives in human personality included from the outset the consideration of conflict (between the drives themselves, or between drives and other psychic tendencies), and that this element has remained central in psychoanalytic psychology through all its stages.

Though it may already be implied in what I have said, I still want to add explicitly that in order to meet the needs of a dynamic and genetic psychology, it has proved necessary to extend the concept of drives in at least three respects. First, it has to extend beyond the physiological substratum traceable today. Second, it cannot be limited to the data of external behavior. We must go to the "sources of inner instability," as Gardner Murphy, (1947, p. 90) has it, who rightly emphasizes that to classify motivation according to external conduct is not too satisfactory, because observable behavior frequently gives no reliable information on what is going on inside. Also, in analysis we are accustomed to basing our conclusions on the inter-relation of both internal and external factors. Third, the concept of drives, which in analysis is necessary not so much to describe as to explain phenomena, has to transcend the phenomenological aspect, which here means the aspect of inner or subjective experience; that is, the conscious phenomena of need, desire, compulsion, etc. Such extensions, though they may seem arbitrary from a more limited approach, are indicated for correlating the variety of aspects psycho-analysis has to take into consideration.

While stressing as essential these points of actual fruitfulness in the analytic approach to the problem of drives, I certainly do not wish to imply anything like a belief in the immutability or complete-ness of this theory. But I think that what I have said so far gives us some points of orientation in evaluating the potential significance of various approaches. To mention briefly two contrasting examples: there are quite a few psychologists who favor a very broad concept of drives, sometimes even broader than the one we use in psycho-analysis today. But as those concepts are not specific enough and lack an intimate relationship with clinical data, they appear some-what thin, and fail if one applies them to our empirical findings. In contrast, many psychologists have attempted to narrow the concept, to center it more or less around only one or another of the aspects it comprises in psychoanalysis—either the sources of the instincts, or the "needs," or the patterns of "instinctual behavior"; either the maturative or the cultural aspects, etc. There is no doubt that these avenues of approach have yielded a wealth of empirical data and worth-while theoretical contributions in dealing with some circumscribed situations in limited fields of observation. Much of it—experimental and theoretical—may also help to clarify and to develop some phases of analytic theory. However, when confronted with more complex interrelationships of aims, objects, and sources, as encountered in clinical work, these attempts prove not too helpful, especially for the genetic approach. Most likely it will become necessary and feasible to integrate what is valid in these various approaches to our problem on a more comprehensive psychological level. While many of them started, historically speaking, with rejecting the scope and the concepts of analytic theory, this integration may after all prove to be not too dissimilar to the one that has and still is being developed in analysis.[1]

In turning to what biologists call an instinct, I limit myself to a few points. In biology too the views on instincts vary rather widely, even among workers in the same field. There are still some controversial issues as to the relations between reflexes, tropisms, and instincts; also as to the respective roles of "outer" and "inner" factors in instinctual behavior; needs, appetites, and instincts are correlated in a kaleidoscopic variety of conceptual patterns. There is no complete agreement on hereditary factors, the degree of rigidity of the instincts, or the role of learning. A glance at the concepts of Lloyd Morgan, Drever, Lashley, Myers, and Wheeler—to name only a few among the great number of well-known authors—will bear out this point.

Many observers of animal behavior like to emphasize the almost complete rigidity of the instincts. They are most impressed by what Forel called the primary or hereditary automatisms, an expression of this inflexibility being that slight changes in the situation "throw the whole instinctive series out of gear." Others have modified these views to a certain extent. They observe that "intelligence" enters instinctual behavior to a certain degree that varies with the species;

[1] For a psychoanalyst's view of recent research in ethology, see M. Schur (1961).

also, to a slight degree, from one individual to another. There is also some variability according to the nature of the environment; furthermore, a more systematic knowledge has been gained of instinctual behavior in higher animals, particularly the mammals, and of the role of learning, and has contributed toward modifying the views held by the older school of biologists. These discoveries have acted as an added stimulus to formulations about instinct which include human behavior as well as the behavior of lower animals. These few barren sentences do not do justice to what is one of the most fascinating chapters of biology.

At this point we meet again a great many diverging opinions. No longer satisfied with the sweeping generalizations encountered in the older literature, it is difficult to find a definition applicable to both lower animals and man. What in man can be compared to "instincts," one author states, consists ". . . far less essentially in the release of appropriate, inborn, mechanized reflexes, far less essentially in any stereotyped means of achieving certain 'ends,' than in the awareness . . . of those 'ends,' in the interests in and the desires . . . for them, in the 'innate determining tendencies' evoked . . . and in the use of intelligence brought to bear in their achievement. . . . In man, indeed, intelligence has largely usurped the functions of specific inherited behavior" (Myers, 1945). With this clear and suggestive statement we may easily agree. It is noteworthy that it uses psychological terms; and indeed the use also of psychological methods of investigation has been advocated by many who have studied the problem of the equivalents of instincts in man. Here and there even a few elements of the psychoanalytic theory of drives have been accepted, but to describe the specific position of the drives in human psychology it is not enough to say that there is a difference of degree between instincts and drives; structural concepts are called for.

Some of the characteristics of human behavior, which are often difficult to account for by the biological concept of instincts, coincide rather neatly with those phenomena which the analytic theory of drives was developed to cover: the relative independence from outer stimuli which makes for a greater plasticity of adaptive behavior; the greater variability of responses to inner stimuli; the continuity of the driving forces; the fact that there is constant transformation of the energies we relate to the drives—therefore the relaxation of tension in one system must always be considered in connection with the tensions in other systems, etc. I choose these examples at random; many others come to mind. To account even better for the more specific correlations of these and other phenomena, which we consider to be characteristic of human behavior, the psychoanalytic theory of drives had to be supplemented by still another set of concepts and hypotheses.

With respect to the point in question, the work on instincts done by biologists has for us a twofold interest: while pointing to elements common to lower animal and human behavior, it also challenges us to gain a clearer and more complete understanding of the differences. Analogous situations and questions arise in the research of biologists and analysts, though in a different factual and conceptual setup. One author (Brun), who is a biologist and a psychoanalyst, studied the behavior of lower animals in terms of psychoanalytic concepts such as the pleasure principle, conflict, displacement, etc.[2] But even where the biologist's approach and terminology differ widely from ours, we still can greatly profit from his findings and conclusions. To give one example: Lashley, in his brilliant study on the experimental analysis of instinctual behavior (1938), has no use for a general concept of drives, relying entirely upon "very specific sensory-motor mechanisms." But his paper abounds in suggestions which can bear fruit also in analysis; however, in such cases, assigning them their place in our own experience has to be preceded by some careful work of translation and of scrutiny to find out whether, or how far, seemingly similar problems are really homologous.

[2] In his book (1946) Brun proposes a general theory of instincts which partly differs from the propositions in this paper.

Even if one could devise a definition which covers everything that biologists, physiologists, psychologists, psychoanalysts, and philosophers call an instinct, the expectation that this most general concept would be the one best suited, let us say, for the biological or for the analytic approach would have to be proved. Some degree of differentiation, according to the field, might be found useful. An over-all definition would stress the continuity of the phenomena from animal to human behavior, which has in many respects proved helpful in biology. But, then, this continuity is after all a genetic one, and what degree of actual homology of the phenomena exists on different levels would require much further empirical study. Equating instinct and drive, though stimulating in some respects, has proved misleading in others.

As to terminology, Freud used the word *Trieb,* in contradistinction to the word *Instinkt,* used in biology. Freud's translators did not deem it important to make an analogous distinction. However, it was often said by analysts, as well as by others, that it would help toward clarification if the acceptance of the respective factual and conceptual differences were followed by a terminological differentiation, and it was suggested to speak in analysis of drives, or of instinctual drives or instinctual urges. Accustomed to the older term, we all sometimes use "instinct" where "instinctual drive" would be more appropriate. Of course, this terminological habit would have no importance if it were not for its possible theoretical implications. In any case, to do away with the conceptual ambiguities will enable us better to deal with the very real problem of what are the actual relationships between the two sets of facts, which the terms instinct and drive are meant to cover.

Let us view the problem this time from the angle of structural psychology. Psychoanalytic psychology has frequently been considered a psychology of drives only. This opinion, held by many, is incorrect, even more so in the later than it was in the earlier stage of psychoanalytic development. It does not correspond to the psychological theory of analysis to include all aspects of mental functions in the psychology of drives, not even, strictly speaking, in a genetic sense—and in this connection I refer the reader to some statements about an autonomous aspect of ego development in Freud's last writings (1937a).[3] This portion of his work is still partly in that phase of latency through which many of his important discoveries had to pass before being generally recognized, even among analysts. Energically, we may well say that the id, the realm of the drives, is the most important reservoir of psychic energy; still, we assume that once the differentiation into three mental systems has taken place, each one of these systems dispenses psychic energy. We describe the systems also as to the forms and conditions of energy they use. Of the forms and conditions of the energy used, of their origin, and their interchange, suffice it to say that the momentum to activity, the dynamic and energic aspects apply to all systems of personality, but that we find differences among the id and the ego and the superego not only with respect to their organization but also with respect to this momentum.

Certainly no thorough insight into psychic structure and into psychic conflicts could have been gained without knowledge of the psychology of the drives. But today we may add the reverse statement: we cannot really understand the functions of these drives without looking at their position in the framework of the psychic structure. Furthermore, the differences between the instincts of lower animals and the drives of man become quite clear only if we take into account what insight into the formation of psychic structure psychoanalysis has developed.

In the first, the undifferentiated phase of mental development (Hartmann, 1939a; Hartmann, Kris, and Loewenstein, 1946), we find in the child a certain number of needs, impulses, and behavior patterns which can hardly be attributed either to an ego or to an id in the sense we apply these terms to later development. With the

[3] See also Hartmann (1939a).

differentiation of the ego functions the picture changes. The ego grows and develops into a specific organ of adaptation and organization, and the id becomes a partly separate system with its specific characteristics. This process of differentiation is in part traceable to a characteristic feature of human development, the "protracted helplessness and dependence of the young of the human species" (Freud, 1926a). Some years ago (1939a) I suggested that it is this very process of structural differentiation to which the differences mentioned between the instinctual behavior of lower animals and the behavior of human beings are mainly due. Obviously many functions, which are taken care of by instincts in the former, are in man functions of the ego. The characteristic plasticity of man's adaptive behavior, in contradistinction to the relative rigidity of that of lower animals, and his greater learning capacity are outstanding examples of the resulting differences. The freeing of many abilities from close connection with one definite instinctual tendency, we could describe analytically as the emergence of the ego as a definable psychic system. To speak of greater or lesser plasticity, of more or less intelligence involved, as was frequently done, is to give a rather poor account of the facts; hence we need a model of psychic structure which shows the interrelations of drive, intellect, adaptation, integration, etc., by assigning them their place in relation to those centers of mental functioning which in analysis we call systems.

We assume that there is a continuity in the evolution of the mind from the functioning of lower animals to the human mind, and that there is a genetic connection between the instincts of the former and the determinants of human conduct. Today it is quite obvious, however, that it is a one-sided approach to consider only the genetic relations between animal instinct and human drive; it means an overlooking of the no less important relations between animal instinct and human ego functions. That mistake is suggested by formulations which stress the identity of instincts and drives.

I consider it rather likely that the differentiation of which I spoke provides us not only with a specific organ of adaptation, the ego;

some characteristics of the drives, of the id itself, as we know them in man, may be the result of changes traceable to the same differentiating process. The id, too, does not appear to be a simple extension of the instincts of lower animals. While the ego develops in the direction of an ever closer adjustment to reality, clinical experience shows the drives, the id tendencies, to be far more estranged from reality than the so-called animal instincts generally are (Hartmann, 1939a), although the instinctual reactions of lower animals are by no means always adaptive. This is a second point where the description of drives in terms of instincts has, I think, considerably delayed the progress of psychology.

A certain degree of structural differentiation might also be found in other higher animals, though not to the same extent to which it is developed in man; here, then, we may expect to find something more or less similar to the drives of man. On the other hand, even in man, especially in very young children, vestiges of instincts in the sense of biology may be traceable.

As for the relation of the pleasure principle to self-preservation, one may assume that Freud's statement, ". . . there is a long way from pleasure principle to self-preservation," is probably not valid to the same extent in lower animals as it is in human beings. The famous thesis of Malebranche and many others on this subject describes the situation in man rather incompletely. This thesis says that God has attached pleasure to certain objects which man ought to seek, and pain to other objects which he ought to avoid in the interest of self-preservation. What Malebranche means here comes rather close in a sense to what modern authors say about instincts, but it can be applied to the drives of man only with major modifications. To account more fully for the facts, we would have to consider the changes of pleasure conditions which follow growth and learning, and to trace the differences between pleasure offered by the ego and pleasure due to the id functions.

The most plausible way to coordinate this with psychoanalytic experience seems to be to trace it again to the process of structure formation; however, a reciprocal influence is not out of the question. While structural differentiation probably complicates the relations between pleasure and preservation of the self—which, of course, is not to say that they are absent in man—this factor actually makes the development of a specific system for learning and for the adaptation to reality even more necessary, if, for a moment, you allow me to think teleologically.

What, then, can we say from our point of view about those psychic functions which actually do serve self-preservation in man? Here we certainly have to mention the drives, sexual as well as aggressive, as they obviously contribute to self-preservation, though it appears that they are much less directly connected with it (and also with preservation of the species) than are the instincts of biology. But I should hesitate to speak of whatever such contributions toward self-preservation there are as constituting an independent and definite drive. Freud at one time made such an attempt and tried to identify this assumed drive with what he called the ego drives, or ego instincts, while later he included the drives toward self-preservation with the libidinal ones. Actually, in the course of the development of psychoanalytic theory, they gradually more or less lost their status as an independent unit. The tendencies whose aim it is to master the environment and which show a definite relation to self-preservation had a rather indefinite position in the system; today we rather tend to stress the aggressive elements we find in them and the role ego tendencies play in their setup.

This may be the place to say a few words about what psychologists call pleasure in functioning (*Funktionslust*), the pleasure in activities themselves, or in overcoming difficulties, the child's enjoyment in the exercise of a recently learned function (Bühler, 1930), etc., as contrasted with the pleasure we get from the effect of an activity. Its developmentally important role can be traced partly to the fact that through maturation and learning a series of apparatus in the nonconflictual sphere of the ego, and the corresponding activities, become available to the child (Hartmann, 1939a). What is pleasure and what is not parallels at least to some extent the development of the ego, and the potentialities of pleasure gain offered by the evolution of the ego functions play a paramount role in the acceptance of the reality principle (see Chapter 13). Somewhat similar ideas are expressed in a paper by Hendrick (1942), but I am not convinced that the introduction of what he calls a basic "instinct to master" is really unavoidable.

Of Freud's "principles," the reality principle, of course, contributes directly to self-preservation.[4] The other principles (the pleasure principle, the nirvana principle, and I may mention here the repetition compulsion also) do not aim at self-preservation in any direct way, but they may, in collaboration with and under the influence of other factors, be made indirectly to serve its purpose. Factually, there is even in man a broad field of coincidence of pleasure gain with self-preservation, about which I said a few words before. However, what I want to stress here is that it is the functions of the ego, developed by learning and by maturation—the ego's aspect of regulating the relations with the environment and its organizing capacity in finding solutions, fitting the environmental situation and the psychic systems at the same time—which become of primary importance for self-preservation in man. In a different and less specific way, the superego partly contributes to it too, as in the case of social adjustment.

It is mainly the ego functions, but also the other factors mentioned, and their interaction with situations the individual has to meet, which we consider when in analysis we speak of self-preservation. To throw all these factors together and to call the sum total a drive for self-preservation does not agree with our concept of drives and obscures rather than clarifies the problem. Whatever the part played

---

[4] The relation of this principle to other forms of regulation is not always clear. Freud's other "principles" are tendencies serving the aim of dealing with the quantities of excitation in the mental apparatus, in modifying them as to quantity, quality, or rhythm; but the reality principle rather points to the ways in which such tendencies are changed as a consequence of the individual's adaptation to the outer world; therefore, it is difficult to consider it on the same plane as the other principles.

Child's ego seeks self preservation in the real world & some pain reduction — conflict resolution

by the drives in this setup, there can be no doubt that other important elements participate in it. It is certainly not easy to evaluate the respective strength of the many factors involved. But I should rather agree to what Freud says in his *Outline of Psychoanalysis,* published after his death (1940, p. 111): "The ego has set itself the task of self-preservation, which the id appears to neglect."

Freud's principles represent several kinds of regulating processes, tending toward different types of equilibrium. To accept this plurality instead of adopting a monistic theory of regulation, Freud was led by factual observation and not only by some implications of his theory. Actually, these tendencies overlap; also, a process establishing a state of balance in regard to one such self-regulating mechanism often induces a state of unbalance in another. This is especially clear in the case of the pleasure and reality principles. To compare these principles to homeostasis is certainly a tempting undertaking. Hendrick (1946), Orr (1942), Kubie (1948), and recently K. Menninger (1954), among others, approached the problem from this angle; however, it may be necessary to make a distinction between the principles with respect to the degree to which they lend themselves to such comparison. Only of the reality principle can we say that it directly serves self-preservation and tends toward something that could rightly be described as "adaptive stabilization" (Cannon, 1932). As to the other principles, this criterion of homeostasis does not apply. The tendency, attributed by Fechner and Freud to the psychic apparatus, to keep excitation at a constant level, makes for a type of equilibrium which is not directly adaptive; and the nirvana principle which we may distinguish from that tendency, as it attempts a minimization of excitation, is even further removed from adaptation. On the other hand, we may add that these self-regulating mechanisms introduced by Freud have another characteristic of homeostasis (the achievement of a greater independence from actual stimulation).

Self-regulation can be described on different levels; at least in the adult different layers can be distinguished. Apart from the principles, there is one level of self-regulation which corresponds to what we usually call the synthetic function of the ego or, as I would prefer to call it, its organizing function (see Chapter 3): it balances the psychic systems against each other and regulates the relationships between the individual and his environment. In the course of development this form of regulation is partly added to less specialized mechanisms and partly substituted for them. The development of this organizing function seems to be part of a general biological trend toward internalization; it also helps toward a growing independence from the immediate impact of stimuli. On the other hand, when this highly differentiated form of regulation is interfered with, more general and primitive ones may take its place. A suggestive parallel to this psychoanalytic insight is found in experimental physiology (Richter, 1941).

It is obvious that Freud's approach to the problem of drives has paralleled the growth of psychoanalytic insight and refinement of the method. In the beginning, Freud applied to his material the conventional dichotomy of drives that serve the preservation of the individual (at one time they were identified with the "ego drives"), and drives that serve the preservation of the species—while being quite aware that this proposition "is merely a working hypothesis, to be retained only so long as it proves useful" (Freud, 1915a, p. 124). Later, much of what had been called "ego drives" was ascribed to functioning of the system "ego," and all drives were attributed to the system "id"; also the earlier dualistic theory was gradually abandoned and after some tentative, intermediary, theoretical steps, Freud's main interest was finally centered around another dualism of primary drives, sexuality and aggression.[5]

Structurally, aggression in the sense used here has the same position as sexuality; it is nothing like an "ego drive" but part of the id. This structural position, by the way, also distinguishes it from the

[5] For a historical presentation see, besides the paper by Bibring (1936), Jones (1936) and Hitschmann (1947).

older concept of aggression as used by Alfred Adler. Of the psychology of aggression, I will mention only one point which stresses a parallel with libido.[6] While the two drives differ as to the contributions they make to the formation of ego and superego, I think it is true of both drives that their energy can be neutralized in the service of ego and superego. Aggressive energy participates in the development of psychic structure, but the psychic systems, once they are formed, also provide it with specific modes of expression. Reality situations, in man, appeal sometimes to the unmitigated expression of aggression, but in many more cases to its sublimation (K. Menninger, 1942). Both obviously may be useful for the maintenance of life, but it is of course even more true of aggression than it is of sexuality that its aims often run counter to self-preservation, specifically in the case of that typical expression of aggression, self-destruction. However, if we accept the hypothesis of a neutralized form of aggressive energy working in the ego (which does not represent self-destruction), we can question that far-reaching idea of Freud's which in its strictest sense means that self-destruction is the only alternative to destruction (1932, p. 144). One may say of this idea that, while it occurs historically in the later phases of his thought, it belongs systematically to the prestructural stage of psychoanalytic psychology.

May I repeat what I said before: neither the aims of sexuality nor of aggression, as we use these terms today, suffice to account for the mental mechanisms which serve self-preservation in man. But it also has long been recognized that the aims of sexuality are by no means limited to the aim of preserving the species either. We may ask ourselves what this detachment of our theory of drives from the problems of the preservation of the individual and of the species actually means. In part, as mentioned before, it is certainly due to a more complete understanding of the place of drives in psychic structure; from here, the contribution of other factors than drives can

[6] For a more extensive treatment of aggression, see Hartmann, Kris, and Loewenstein (1949).

more clearly be seen and described; but I think that this detachment also reflects a better insight into the analytic approach in contrast to the biological one. I am speaking only of a difference in approach, because in a systematic sense we may very well maintain that analysis is also a biological science. We find in the psychoanalytic literature of the past, sometimes even in current writings, the discussion on one plane of drives toward self-preservation, and of sexual and aggressive drives. It may well be that such a juxtaposition is altogether misleading; one cannot put them one beside another if they reflect different principles of classification. How the biological, the "outside" approach came to distinguish between self-preservation and preservation of the species does not need any comment. How far does the analytic approach differ from it, and how can it still be put into the service of answering questions on the biological level? I think the role of analysis with respect to such problems is approximately as follows: we find out what the drives in our sense (in interdependence with ego and other tendencies) contribute toward forming those reactions which then—looked at from outside or "biologically"—manifest themselves as self-preservation or as preservation of the species. Analysis shows along which ways, when, and by using what psychic material, behavior, as characterized by biology, is actually brought about and under what conditions it manifests itself. I may add that in proceeding along these lines the specific advantages of the psychoanalytic method with respect to biological problems can be fully utilized and at least one danger of equivocation is avoided. If what I have said is true, then that juxtaposition of which I spoke is really ambiguous as I have purported it to be.

Assuming that the analytic study of drives can make the contribution to biology just outlined, it might interest us to know whether the analytic approach may perform an analogous function in regard to other problems on the biological level. To give you an example: as many other psychologists do, Freud (1926a, p. 93) regarded the anxiety signal as a "biological necessity." Taking this for granted, what he actually studied was which way this biological necessity is dealt with in man, how it has been contrived in man, what are the preconditions of anxiety, what is its structural position, and what are the typical sequences of its developmental stages.

As a second example I choose the psychoanalytic theory of play as compared to other theories. There is a biological theory of play whose clearest formulation views it as a kind of exercise with the function of preparing the child for situations it will have to meet in its future life (Groos, 1901). The analytic theory considers play according to its content, the experience the child may master in this way, the roles of the pleasure principle and repetition compulsion in it, and how, according to the developmental level, the contributions of these factors vary. Here again, the theories are not on the same plane. The role of analysis in explaining the play of children is analogous to the one it performs in explaining anxiety. In both, analysis tends to substitute a dynamic-genetic explanation for a teleological one.

CHAPTER 5

The Application of Psychoanalytic Concepts to Social Science

(1950)

ANY theories and findings of sociology appear ambiguous if viewed from the angle of psychoanalytic interpretation, and similarly some aspects of psychoanalytic findings and theories, important as they may be in the study of the individual, seem irrelevant to the sociologist. For mutual understanding it would be desirable to create a common conceptual language, or to define sociological problems in terms of their psychological meaning and, as Parsons (1950), has stated, formulate psychological problems in direct relation to the social structure.

Certainly when what appears to be the same "subject" is approached by both sciences, the relevant factors may not be the same, the centers of fruitful interest do not necessarily coincide. The psychoanalyst, for his purposes, may put certain features that interest sociologists into parentheses; sociologists in some fields of social studies may make valid predictions with no consideration of the total personalities of individuals. Such predictions will most likely be correct where social action is predominantly determined by the conscious or preconscious ego (Waelder, 1936a), as in rational action, or in action involving such ego interests as we plausibly may assume are present in the average member of a group. An obvious example is economic theory.

But there are other social actions and functions where one cannot rely on such simple psychological models if one wishes to make valid predictions. These models will prove a source of failure for the sociologist in matters where functions of the personality other than rational or ego interests come into play in a way which is dynamically relevant and likely to differ from individual to individual. However, when we apply this rather general formulation to concrete sociological problems, we should obviously feel on safer ground if we could take into account the psychological meaning of the sociological data in a systematic way. We should, for instance, wish to know the significance of the sociological data not only for the egos of the persons in question, but for all three of the psychic systems of the personality: ego, superego, and id. And it would be most helpful if also the sociological meaning of the psychological data were known. Such systematic knowledge would assist us in determining the direction and degree and the specific problems in which those abstractions from the "total motivation of the concrete personality" have to be made, or are likely to be fruitful, whose importance for the use of analysis on the level of social structure has been stressed by Parsons.

A mutual reinterpretation of analytic data by sociology, and sociological data by psychoanalysis, presupposes some previous agreement between the two on a definite theory of social action that would make correlation possible. At the beginning of his clear and comprehensive outline, Parsons states that both sociological and analytic theory have a common ground in the frame of reference presented by the theory of social action; yet there is a disproportion or lack of symmetry: social action may be the most basic concept of sociology but it is not the most basic in psychoanalysis, nor is action in general. In psychoanalysis, structurally and genetically, action is derived from more fundamental human properties. No completely systematic analytic theory of action has been achieved or presented up to now, although analytic contributions to the theory of action are important enough to suggest that the sociological theory of action will need and include many aspects of analytic theory, even beyond those that Parsons has recognized as common to both fields.[1] It is true that often in science it proves useful to handle different problems on different levels of conceptualization, and that to reduce problems to their most general level is not necessarily the optimal approach; nevertheless, if we are to have a general theory of action, there is no alternative to basing it on the most fundamental psychological concepts.

Action, in analysis, is primarily defined by its position in the structure of the personality and the contributions made to its various aspects by the psychic systems. But action is also viewed genetically, and described in relation to the energy factor involved, its motivation, the motor (or other) means of attaining its goal, and with respect to reality. To refer to this vast field of research, without pretending to systematic presentation, what analysis has discovered about the various types of action—its structural, dynamic and reality aspects, overdetermination, and conflicts in the structure of goals—will enrich theories of action used by social scientists, who until now have oversimplified the motivations of action and their relation to other aspects of behavior (see Chapter 3). Actions in various forms (rational and irrational, utilitarian, moral, reality syntonic and reality dystonic) can all be studied by analysis in their interrelations and assigned their proper places in the structure of the personality. And the question of the mutual relevance of psychological and sociological data can be solved only by the use of a pluridimensional theory and structural concepts.

A point worth emphasizing is that most of what we know in analysis about action has been gained from a study of social action. Analysis studies human conduct in relation to an environment. In contrast to some other schools of psychology, psychoanalysis includes within its scope of interest the structure of reality. Since human beings are by far the most important of real objects, the structure

[1] See now also Parsons and Shils (1951).

of reality most interesting to analysts is the structure of society. Society is not a projection of unconscious fantasies, though it offers many possibilities for such projection and their study reveals to us the influence of unconscious factors on men's attitudes to society. We must accept social reality as a factor in its own right; certainly most analysts do not attempt to interpret human behavior exclusively in terms of unconscious drives and fantasies. This "reality aspect" is an intricate topic and has manifold connotations; we are quite aware that the same institution can be used to provide an outlet for a great variety of tendencies.

From these considerations, it appears that the intimate analytic study of an individual's interaction with his social environment can be included among the methods of sociology. Analysis has taught us as much about the various family structures as it has about biological human needs. The attention of analysts has been perforce directed to the object relationships of childhood, for these are infinitely more important to the development of personality than those of later life; the general and legitimate prevalence of the genetic point of view among analysts has reinforced this attitude. This is a second point, besides the general theory of action, where psychoanalytic data and hypotheses are indispensable to sociology but in which there has been a divergence of interest between the two fields. This statement in no way denies, indeed is far from denying, that our patients' current social environment constantly enters the analytic picture. It simply explains why this aspect has been less energetically studied, and why our knowledge about the current milieu appears less clearly in our largely genetic psychological concepts. I agree with Parsons that in this regard our descriptions of analytic work could be more explicit. If a concerted attempt in this direction were systematically made, it would probably yield a more complete insight into the psychological meaning of specific social structures than could be obtained through any other method.

The term "meaning," used here rather vaguely, refers to the fact that a given social structure selects and makes effective specific psychological tendencies and their expression, and certain developmental trends. This relation might, by analogy to Freud's term "somatic compliance," be called "social compliance"; or rather, this relation is one part of something that might receive such designation—one side of social compliance. The other part refers to the relation between an individual's psychological characteristics and the potentiality of social function, status, etc., with which a concrete social structure provides him (see Chapter 2).

To heed Parsons's warning, I repeat that between personality type and institutional structure there is no simple correspondence. I refer to his statement concerning the "structural generalization of goals." The structuralization of motive forces as a "function of the institutional situations . . . rather than of . . . particular personality structure" is familiar to analysts, though they use different words. To approach this problem at the level of the individual, we must go beyond what we are accustomed to call "personality types." In analysis we have found that most psychological typologies, especially the merely descriptive ones not based on genetic principles, though perhaps useful for certain purposes, do not account fully for the manifold dynamic interrelationships of an individual's characteristics. Thus they often fail us when we try to determine whether such characteristics are modifiable or capable of being superseded or replaced by others in keeping with internal or external situations; and just such points are the ones most relevant to the issue under discussion.

Modifiability, replaceability, and similar qualities explain why the external behavior and part of the motivation of individuals (who belong to different personality types according to one of the usual typologies) will more frequently be equal in regard to a given institutional structure than we might expect on the basis of such a typological diagnosis only—granted that the relation to reality is unimpaired. These qualities tell us more of such possible behavior and motivation than could be learned from a purely typological diagnosis. Obviously the variation in such qualities also depends on the institutional structure with which the individual is confronted. Nor does this run counter to the previous remarks concerning social compliance; the factors just mentioned must be given equal consideration. The main point is that a study of the individual's plasticity in relation to concrete reality, its degree and its conditions, must be included in the psychological approach. Psychoanalytic typologies, precisely because they are less descriptive and more genetic than others, take this element into consideration and define expectations of behavior in regard to internal and external situations. In clinical work, too, the analyst is constantly aware of this problem, with all its implications as to reality-syntonic behavior in its structural and genetic aspects and also as to the possible participation of superego functions.

Thus far, I have referred only to such contributions to sociology as may be gathered from the analyst's couch. What the analyst garners from the analytic situation in regard to conscious and unconscious motivation, psychological mechanisms, and attitudes to social reality, he may try, as many analysts have tried, to apply elsewhere in dealing with social phenomena. This "application" of analysis, as it is often called, to the interpretation of myths or other anthropological data, for example, at first served to demonstrate the presence of certain contents of the id, discovered in analysis proper, in many different ages and forms of civilization. To this same sphere was extended our gradually growing knowledge of the ego's mechanisms of defense. Reconstructions of the past of mankind dealt with prehistoric rather than with historic times (Freud, 1913-14; and others). It is not necessary to trace the development of this branch of psychoanalysis; it suffices to say that in his second decisive contribution to this field, the description and explanation of group psychology in terms of structural psychology (1921), Freud again chose for his subject a type of behavior not limited to a definite historical epoch or social organization.

From this we may see that to deal with specific social structures in specific historical situations our approach cannot only be through an understanding of the unconscious contents and mechanisms; it must be supplemented by a study of their interrelation with the reality aspects of behavior and with the institutional setup. An interpretation, for instance, of group formation in a totalitarian society of our day would not be limited to the categories used by Freud (see Chapter 3). This is not to imply that an analytic approach to such fields is doomed to failure, but the approach must be modified in the direction of that mutual interpretation of psychological and sociological problems previously discussed.

Parsons has sounded a warning also against attempting too "direct" an explanation of sociological phenomena by the use of psychological categories, and I partly agree. Undoubtedly the work in many of these fields needs a sounder methodological foundation. In approaching problems outside clinical psychoanalysis, many appear to forget what an analyst would hardly forget in his clinical work: we cannot understand human beings independently of the reality in which they live. Institutions that characterize a social system have often been interpreted solely as the direct expressions of the unconscious and conscious desires of people living in that system, as if reality were no more than a wish fulfillment. This approach avoids the problem raised by my statement that social structures are, in the first place, imposed upon the growing individual as an external reality. It overlooks the interesting role that tradition plays in the actual setup, and the different contributions that different social strata make toward the formation of institutions. It sometimes neglects entirely the variability of individual attitudes toward them, the ways in which individuals are affected by institutions, and the ways in which they manage—or do not manage—to conform. The avoidance of these issues is not a simple, wise, and operationally legitimate limitation to what is often called "the psychological side" of the problem. It leads inevitably to a misinterpretation of this "psychological side."

Another difficulty is exemplified, for example, in much of the voluminous anthropological literature currently devoted to the investigation of "national character."[2] In tackling the infinitely complex phenomena of Western civilizations, into which we have incomparably more detailed extra-anthropological insight than into any primitive culture, the application of the usual methods of anthropology often resembles somewhat a willful turning of a scientific economy of plenty into one of scarcity. From our point of view, the data actually used remain ambiguous so long as they cannot be analyzed with regard to motivational structure, dynamics, orientation to reality, to social reality itself, and to their history. Obviously a concept of "national character," as of character in general, should include much more than statements concerning actual behavior; it should, we have a right to expect, tell us about the potentialities of behavior in relevant intrapsychic and external situations. As previously stated, descriptive typologies do not sufficiently reveal such potentialities, for which we should need such dynamic and genetic typologies as are employed in analysis. Though not genetic in our sense, the studies of "national character" that are based on the investigation of typical childhood situations and emphasize such matters as differences in child rearing represent considerable progress. While not covering all aspects of the problem, Kardiner's concept (1945) of basic personality types appears to be useful in some respects.

Psychoanalysis can be helpful in the study of "national character" mainly by indicating fruitful points of approach, eliminating certain shortcomings, and insisting on a more complex view. Potentially, it could make an even more incisive contribution by using its own method in its original setup, at least in cultures where analysts and analysands are available. A comparative study based on analyses of representatives of different cultures has never been made in a systematic way, but it seems eminently possible. The method of analysis is well suited to deal with the intricate aspects of the problem.

[2] See also Hartmann, Kris, and Loewenstein (1951).

To "apply" psychoanalytic findings and theories to sociological phenomena is not sufficient. We must, rather, aim at a mutual penetration of sociological and analytic theory, the posing of new questions, and the discovery of new ways of checking against the data in both fields. This will mean that one must set up patterns which are as specific as possible in respect to both their psychological and sociological aspects (see Chapter 2).

CHAPTER 6

Psychoanalysis and Developmental Psychology

(1950)

THERE is some thematic continuity between our previous Panel Discussion on "Theories of Psychoanalysis" (1949) and the papers we shall hear today. In choosing as our topic "Psychoanalysis and Developmental Psychology," we wanted to emphasize the growing importance of this aspect of psychoanalysis; and also to give a fuller account of thoughts and experiences that were presented at last year's Convention. Some aspects of what will be said today will no doubt overlap with the field covered by the recent meeting in Stockbridge, at which Anna Freud and others discussed the present state of analytic child psychology. However, given the incompleteness of our knowledge in this field, and the tentative nature of our propositions, a repeated working through of the rather complex problems involved will, I think, be all for the good.

Years ago Freud complained that the direct observations of child psychologists are frequently questionable because they describe phenomena not really understood in their relationships and in their dynamic impact—while, on the other hand, the conclusions about childhood which we reach on the basis of analysis with adults have the disadvantage that we gain them only through a complicated system of reconstructions and through many detours of thought. This gap could be closed in part, but not completely, by child analysis. Therefore the combination of the direct longitudinal observation from early childhood on, with the reconstructive data furnished by analysis, is of paramount importance. But this twofold approach has been made possible only as a consequence of systematic analytic work on ego psychology, or of structural psychology in general, which provided us with the indispensable frame of reference and with the necessary tools for a fruitful collaboration.

It is a memorable fact that Freud, using reconstructive methods, could ascertain not only experiences of early childhood, typical or atypical, but also typical maturational sequences that had escaped the methods of direct observation, as in the case of the stages of libidinal development. Still it remains true that certain groups of facts and connections are more easily accessible to some techniques of observation than to others. Of course, methods are being adjusted to the objects of study, but what I have in mind here is rather the fact that each method implies a selection of data; and that, depending on our approach, the data are being centered in different ways. In the case of analysis, what its method has made accessible to observation, and in many instances made visible for the first time, is centered in the sphere of conflict. Although there actually is constant interaction between conflictual and nonconflictual development, so far analysts have shed less light on the nonconflictual sphere.

In stating that the analytic "method" opens the way to the developmentally central position of conflict, I should actually have referred to three factors, not only to one, although the three are obviously interrelated. There is, besides the method, in the narrower sense in which we use the word, also the analytic situation, which owes many of its possibilities to the fact that, despite its strict circumscription, it is essentially a real life situation, it is meaningful also as part of the therapeutic process. The third contributing factor is the attitude of the analyst toward the psychological data he uncovers. I have discussed this in greater detail at Stockbridge. Here I will limit myself to only a few remarks. I am thinking particularly of the correction of what in other fields is called the "personal equation," that is, of the correction of those potential handicaps of observation traceable to the personality of the observer and to his interference in the field. Because the analyst is not only an observer of the field, but also an actor in it, it has been said that analysis is actually a kind of "technosophy," and that this contradicts its claims to being a regular science. It is true that analysis introduces new factors, factors neglected by other methods of observation, not only into the analytic situation but also into the direct observation of children; and that the field of observation in this case not only is defined by the child's behavior but also includes conscious and unconscious attitudes of the observer and the interaction of both groups of factors. But all these factors are subject to constant psychological scrutiny. By acting in the field and studying action and reaction, data are made accessible that had not been accessible to other methods; and we come to understand the personal relationship which is at the basis of the observational situation. This is also what Kris (1951b) pointed to when he spoke about "action research" and "pure research." Actually in carefully studying the interaction in the field of the observer with his object, analysts have done radically and in a consistent way something that has become ever more important in some disciplines of natural science, too, or for that matter, of social science.

All three of the factors which I mentioned are characteristics of analysis, but absent in other psychological methods. Direct observation by nonanalysts of necessity missed many central developmental positions and trends, because it tends to scotomize the child's instinctual and other conflicts, and particularly their unconscious aspects. What often appears as a detail hardly understood and seemingly negligible may become all important if viewed from the angle of analysis. A great number of childhood situations of incisive significance for the formation of adult personality have a low "probability of direct manifestation," if I may borrow a term from genetics;

but in such cases analytic insight, the bulk of which is based on reconstruction, enables us to gain an understanding of the continuity of development. Gradients of growth, as established by child psychologists, mainly dealt with the maturational aspects and gave only part of the picture. The comparison and cross-checking of data revealed by the two methods promise more complete understanding. Theories of early developmental stages have to be built on data of both reconstruction and direct observation.

It is obvious that I conceive of the problem not as one to be approached by just adding reconstructive data to data of direct observation, but rather as one of meaningful interpenetration. How a conflict hardly accessible to the so-called objective methods may influence the intellectual or motor achievements of a child; how, on the other hand, maturational sequences underlying the intellectual or motor achievement may bear on a child's ego development and his ways of solving conflicts—these can best be seen on the basis of such a comparative study. There is another important aspect to this. Such studies will of necessity lead to a growing awareness of the sign- or signal-function which behavior details may have for the observer, that is, to a better or more systematic understanding of how data of direct observation can be used as indicators of structurally central and partly unconscious developments—in a sense that by far transcends the possibilities of sign interpretation accessible to the various methods of testing. You realize how decisive this may become also for analytically planned preventive measures.

To what I said about the selective nature of every approach, I may now add the fact that there is also a temporary limitation to the use of the analytic method. It does not provide us with data (memories) about the undifferentiated phase during which the demarcation lines between the ego and the id, and between the self and the objects, are not yet drawn; and it does not provide us with direct information on the preverbal stage. Direct observation here helps first of all to discard hypotheses which are not consistent with behavioral data. But it is equally relevant in giving positive cues for the formulation of our developmental propositions.

Again, the importance of this factor has to do with the genetic character of so many analytic propositions. Analytic concepts, in striking contradistinction to those of most other branches of psychology, are frequently genetic in nature (Hartmann, 1929; Hartmann and Kris, 1945). They encompass mental phenomena which have a common origin rather than being merely descriptive. For instance, our typologies, oral character, anal character, etc., are defined by the genetic predominance of certain factors but nevertheless may comprise elements that are contradictory in a descriptive sense —greediness and wastefulness, sadism and pity, and so forth. This approach proves superior because it allows us to evaluate the dynamic potentialities of such characteristics, and thus to make more reliable predictions.

It is this genetic nature of analytic thinking that finds itself handicapped by the temporary limitations set by the analytic method and which challenges us to extend our insight beyond these borders. This extension can proceed along the lines of extrapolation of analytic findings to the preverbal stage, which may be described in terms of basic concepts (Glover, 1947) derived from the study of later stages of development; or it can be done by direct but analytically informed observation. Both approaches are necessary. Because of what I said, the study of the preverbal stage is a testing ground for many of our most general assumptions, and also a prerequisite for theoretical advances in a variety of aspects. This is the reason why I thought that in the framework of our discussions on theories of analysis a special place should be assigned to its interrelations with developmental psychology.

From what I said it is clear that today we attribute a significant position to this comparatively recent direction of research in analysis. We come to the conclusion that psychoanalytic psychology is not limited to what can be gained through the use of the psychoanalytic method; and, second, that the meaning we give to analysis transcends its psychiatric aspects. Analysis is also, and has always been in Freud's work, a general psychology. Freud's aim, expressed as early as in the 90s (1887-1902), was to get insight into the entirety of mental functions and not only in the pathology of neuroses. That the study of normal behavior is an essential element of analysis is particularly clear in that aspect which we are discussing today. If a comparison to physical medicine is permissible: the narrower concept of analysis, which is the explanation of nervous diseases, gives you pathology and clinical data without "physiology," or with physiology only as a by-product. The more comprehensive one adds "physiology" with all the implications this is bound to have for our insight into both normal and pathological behavior. Strictly speaking, how sound our general statements and our predictions can be depends in the last resort here, as in other fields, on how far a general theory can be developed, and this, in the case of analysis, can only mean a theory dealing with normal as well as pathological development.

The description of several typical stages of libidinal development, and of their relations to aims, attitudes toward objects, modes of action, etc., was Freud's first approach to finding a frame of reference for a great variety of data on growth as well as development—after a short, rather "environmentalist" phase, in which Freud had considerably overemphasized the generality and developmental significance of actual seduction of children by adults. He was able to describe individual deviations in their relations to typical sequences. These stages depend to a certain extent on physiological growth; Freud mentions the development of the teeth, or of the anal sphincter muscle, as cases in point. However, while representing steps in maturation, they also show some degree of plasticity vis-à-vis environmental influences, as all Anlage factors do. And beyond this, the meaning of these biological sequences for the sphere of object relations and the importance of object relations in the biological context—that is, the mutual influence of inner and outer stimuli—have held a central position in analysis from the very first.

What we imply in speaking of these phases is actually not always really limited to libidinal positions and their derivatives, or to their interactions with the objects or other environmental factors. We are aware that one cannot describe cross-sections of development in terms of the inner and outer vicissitudes of the sexual drives only. It is important to describe them also in terms of the involvements of other, partly independent variables, one being the vicissitudes of the aggressive drives. This already constitutes a material broadening and differentiation of the developmental frame of reference we use. A further step was made possible by a more detailed and more systematic study of the ego. And again, what we find here is the closest interaction with object relations: while the development of object relations is codetermined by ego development, object relations are also one of the main factors that determine the development of the ego. Many of the papers forming part of this symposium (Hoffer, 1950; Kris, 1950b; Loewenstein, 1950; Rank and MacNaughton, 1950; Spitz, 1950) refer to the impact which the advance in ego psychology has had on our insight into growth and development. Actually, the new level of ego psychology has proved decisive for the analysts' renewed interest in problems of developmental psychology and for a more systematic correlation of reconstructive data with those of direct observation; moreover, in regard to practical questions, such as prevention or education, it has demonstrated its ability to overcome certain limitations inherent in the earlier approach.

Ego development, like libido development, is partly based on processes of maturation. And in regard to the ego aspect, too, some of us are agreed that we have to consider it as a partly primary, independent variable, not entirely traceable to the interaction of drives and environment; also that it partly can become independent from the drives in a secondary way. That is what I mean by the terms *primary* and *secondary autonomy* in ego development. The secondary autonomy of functions of the ego has a bearing on the stability of its developmental acquisitions—a problem that I cannot discuss in this context. The point I want to make here is that the ego as well as the two primary drives appear to be partly independent variables. But while we may, or even must, isolate one or the other aspect for purposes of research or of presentation, we shall not forget that only all these aspects together can provide a picture of an individual's development as we see it in analysis.

Thus, an outline of comparative studies, using both reconstructive data and data of direct observation, may in part be focused on the typical phases of growth and development so familiar to us from psychoanalytic clinical material. Certain principles of the genetic psychology of analysis can be particularly well demonstrated in studying Freud's conception of those phases; some of this I shall discuss later. But that outline must also embrace the structural aspect, the development of the mental systems, and such a comparative study may even prove especially fruitful with respect to the preliminary stages of structure formation.

Among the functions of the ego most systematically studied in relation to the drives and to reality are no doubt the mechanisms of defense (Anna Freud, 1936). Still, certain aspects of their psychology confront us with unsolved problems. A chronology of defense mechanism has been attempted, but so far only its bare outlines are visible; and we know little about the factors which determine the individual choice of defense methods. Here I only want to point to the possibility of approaching these problems by observing in children such primitive functions of the autonomous ego which we may consider the first developmental elements of what later will be used in the process of defense. I may mention what Freud calls the "protective barrier against stimuli," or the various functions of inhibition and postponement of discharge which we find even before the ego as a definite system has evolved. There may well be a correlation between observable individual differences in such primary factors and later defense mechanisms, and this is why I mention this point here.[1] It is likely that the methods by which infants deal with stimuli

[1] This question is discussed in greater detail in Chapter 7.

are later used by the ego in an active way, and especially for defense. This may add to our understanding of the choice of defense mechanisms, and maybe also of their chronology. But such autonomous factors are relevant not only for the understanding of the "negative" aspects of defense. Factors in the conflict-free sphere also codetermine other aspects of the methods by which instinctual stimuli are dealt with—their neutralization, their utilization for a variety of ego functions, and so forth—and thus influence in many ways individual modes of solving conflicts (see Loewenstein [1950] for a striking example). These are some essential points in which the direct observation of early autonomous ego development can be expected to prove helpful for the understanding of those later situations of conflict we meet with in our clinical work.

Still thinking along the lines of such comparative investigations, I want to mention that our clinically necessary and fruitful focusing on the problems of conflict between the psychic systems often leads us to confound a part for the whole; e.g., we speak of the involvements of "the ego" or of "ego development," where, for the purpose of developmental studies, a differential consideration of various ego functions would be indicated. What I say is in a sense already implied in a warning by Freud (1926a) not to conceive of the ego and the id as if they were two opposing camps. Similarly, it would often be feasible and useful to replace the global use of terms like "precocious" or "retarded ego development" by more detailed statements specifying what ego functions have actually undergone a precocious or retarded development in relation to the drives and in relation to one another. Influences acting on the ego's development do not always exert a parallel effect on all of its functions in the sense of developing or retarding them. We know that in some cases not only single ego functions but whole sectors of the ego may be retarded; an example is the influence of the mother's absence in cases described by Spitz (1945). But in other cases it is clear that where we often speak of "precocious ego development," as in the pathogeny of obsessional neuroses, actually only the intellectual or the defensive functions of the ego have prematurely developed, while, for instance, the tolerance for unpleasure is retarded. These differences are relevant and can be partly confirmed by direct observation.

Such irregularities in functional and structural development are, as you know, among the most arresting problems that analytic child psychology has to face. Cases of severe irregularities in ego development were designated by Beata Rank (1949) as "fragmented ego," and studied in their interaction with object relations. We describe such deviations in relation to what we know about typical sequences. To what I said before about developmental phases in general, I may add here that the crucial phases of maturation coincide, as a rule, to a large extent also with the crucial phases as viewed from the angle of environmental influence.[2] For the case of libido development, the crucial anal, or the crucial phallic phase has a maturational aspect, but is equally defined by the prohibitions and demands of the environment coinciding with it. The same is true of the crucial steps in ego development. The average interactions of the child's growth and development, of the psychological characteristics of the relevant figures of his environment, and of the cultural equipment they use in dealing with the child's needs, result in the features typical of the phases in question; the concept of the "phase" here being used in the broader sense I mentioned before. They are the outcome of a variety of developmental trends, of their chronology and their intensity, which on the average converge at a given time and in a specific way, and all of these aspects must be described. Their sequence, found by Freud on the basis of reconstruction, we can today take for granted; also what he said about their regular overlapping, and about the clearly traceable impact of earlier on later phases. They are indispensable for genetic research, as an average and as a model. Their simplifying interpretation, however, shifting the accent too exclusively either on maturation or on object relation, or on any other single one of the factors I mentioned, gives a one-

[2] See also E. Erikson (1940).

sided picture of development. Such seems to me to be the case in Melanie Klein's overemphasizing of the so-called "biological" factor, or in the opposite overemphasis of culturalism.

However, every one of these factors is variable, although not all to the same extent, and deviations in the timing or shaping of the typical phases may result. We should not be too surprised if features we are used to consider as characteristics of a certain phase may occasionally appear earlier; that is, before the main elements of the phase to which we are used to relate these features have become dominant. Thus phenomena may make a precocious appearance, which, as a rule, would be reserved to the influence of the phase-specific conflicts. This may be the case if some aspects of the ego have precociously developed because of some factors in the autonomous sphere, because of early and intense identifications, because of an atypical development of the body ego, or because of a number of other reasons. The particular feature that results may resemble what in other cases is the outcome of later maturational or environmental sequences. Reaction formations, like orderliness or cleanliness, displacements, generalized attitudes, which we are accustomed to find correlated with the anal phase, may then appear before problems of anality have come to dominate the child's life. Empirical evidence in this field is unfortunately scarce so far,[3] but some observations seem to suggest this interpretation. What I just said, as well as what I said previously about the preliminary stages of defense, is meant as an appeal to observation—I think this hypothesis should be accessible to direct verification. The tools analytic theory provide us with are not only a reliable key to reconstruction; I think that, if consistently used, they are well suited to inform developmental research; and allow us to indicate the points at which direct observation can be expected to be most fruitful and to give us truly new insights.

The phase concept as just outlined contains one fundamental approach of analysis to child psychology. Another one is the principle

[3] For a recent example, see M. Kris (1957).

of phase specificity. Obviously we find "phallic" experiences also on the oral level, and "oral" experiences also on the phallic level. But we see, in analysis, quite generally that the importance of factors of any kind which affect development depends to a large extent on the specific phase in which they occur. This, as you know, is also one general principle of developmental physiology or embryology. Here we find that there is a critical period for every experimental interference.

The reaction basis at a given level has also a historical aspect. It is determined by previous growth and development. To remind you of just one familiar example: the situations that provoke anxiety, and its effects, are specific of developmental stages; still, the disposition to anxiety at any given level is also historically determined. This complexity, though well known, might occasionally have created some confusion in our thinking on genetic causation, and more specifically on pathogenesis. We cannot do away with that complexity, but may try to clarify at least one point. For instance, the pathogenic vulnerability we see on a certain level—that is, vulnerability vis-à-vis inner or outer stimuli may find its expression in a way which is specific of this level, even though this vulnerability is definitely traceable to the antecedents; that is, to what we know about the factors of growth or environment which marked the earlier phases of an individual's development. We realize how often specific phallic castration anxiety in the boy is determined by his oral and anal history. On the other hand, phallic castration anxiety may be predominantly due to factors of growth or environment specific of the phase in which it occurs. Thus while the determinants of vulnerability on a given phase may differ, its symptomatic or other expressions may still be very much alike.

It appears to me desirable to note clearly the difference between these two possibilities: (1) the case in which phase-specific vulnerability (and its eventual expression in specific symptoms) is mainly determined by what happened in earlier stages; and (2) the case in which both the vulnerability in question and its main determinants are specific of the phase in which they occur. This may help us to distinguish more clearly the specific features of a given phase from its genetic determinants; it may help us to differentiate more clearly the element of genetic continuity from the element of phase specificity. It also should prevent us from describing what is actually a specific disposition of a later phase as characteristics of its genetic antecedents, as is widely done in some analytic writings; the interpretation of very early object relations in terms of specific features of the oedipal phase, or of early prohibiting functions of the ego in terms specific of the superego being cases in point.

What I said about phase specificity, from the point of view of vulnerability and potential pathological development, is equally true of positive influences on growth and development, and of potentially normal development. There are specific optimal phases for every step in adjustment, integration, overcoming conflicts, and so on. All measures of demand and prohibition, of child rearing, training, and education, and consequently also of mental prophylaxis, must in their timing and dosage be oriented toward phase specificity and its genetic determinants. Anna Freud has clearly stated the problem. This orientation can profit greatly from utilizing data of direct observation. Here we meet again the question of the sign function of behavioral data. It points to the necessity of greater refinement in the use of early developmental data as indicators of actual or potential conflict, and, which is not the same, of actual or potential pathology. The greatest practical importance of what we are discussing today lies, no doubt, in the field of prevention.

The discussion even of only the few points I chose for my introduction tends to demonstrate the complexity of developmental problems as we see them, and also the complexity of our concept formation, which is not arbitrary but in direct relation with the former. I want to mention that, in reaction to our working with many variables and with complicated causal relations, we find today in the periphery of analysis, as in certain trends in child psychology, or, for that matter, in anthropology, a growing number of rash generalizations and simplifying propositions. Out of that great variety of factors which our experience has taught us to consider, one or the other only is selected and made the basis of "new" theories. We may refer to such simplifications as "theories by reduction." They see one specific phase, or one specific measure of infant training, as the sole causative factor for a character type or for general lack of adjustment. Or they see the fact that the mother has not been constantly "good" to the infant as responsible for all the ills that can befall a human being.[4] That an infant has or has not been nursed according to certain principles is brought into direct and unilinear causal relation with the later personality type, etc. The elements of the proposition are, if you wish, "analytic," but the use made of them is certainly not. Do not misunderstand me. All those factors are relevant and may be isolated for certain purposes. However, what our approach shows us about the whole of a person's development is a rather different picture. We see a complex interdependence of a great variety of developmental factors and a branching out of many alternatives on every subsequent developmental stage.

Finally, speaking of the purpose and the rationale of Panels on Theory, may I say that psychoanalysis today has reached a stage on which it should have become obvious that theory must no longer be considered merely as a more or less occasional by-product of clinical experience, or as an intellectual hobby of some analysts.[5] Though one or another among us may feel that way, Freud most certainly never did. It has become sufficiently clear that clinical as well as technical work is severely handicapped and bound to stagnate without it. And we shall keep in mind that, as I just said, prevention, which might well become more essential than therapy, is directly dependent upon the trends of research under discussion today.

[4] See now also Anna Freud (1954a).
[5] See also Hartmann, Kris, and Loewenstein (1953) and Chapter 15.

CHAPTER 7

Comments on the Psychoanalytic Theory of the Ego

(1950)

As early as in the 90s, and even before his interest had definitely shifted from physiological to psychological theory, Freud speaks of an ego, partly in a sense that foreshadows considerably later developments of ego psychology. However, the closer elaboration of this part of his work had to be postponed during a period in which his main concern was with the development of other aspects of psychoanalysis. All the revolutionary work of those years approached personality via what today we would call the study of the id. Thus, in analysis, a broad fundament of facts and hypotheses was laid down—on the laws governing unconscious mental processes, on the characteristics and development of instinctual drives, and on some aspects of psychic conflict. The absence of these facts and hypotheses had been a severe handicap to preanalytic psychology. That Freud's investigation of the id preceded his approach to structural psychology is indeed one of the most momentous events in the history of psychology.[1]

When after a period during which his interest in the ego was comparatively latent, Freud in the early 20s explicitly constituted

[1] For a survey of the development of Freud's ego concept, see Chapter 14.

ego psychology as a chapter of analysis, this step was made possible, and as a matter of fact imperative, by the convergence of clinical and technical as well as theoretical insight he had gained in the meantime. Today this phase in the development of ego psychology is accepted by most analysts as an integral part of their theoretical and practical thinking. It had a far-reaching modifying influence also on many earlier hypotheses in other fields of analysis, e.g., technique, the theory of anxiety, or the theory of instinctual drives. Despite all this, one gets the impression that Freud himself considered his formulations of that period as a bold first inroad into a new territory rather than as a systematic presentation of ego psychology or as the last word on the structural aspects of personality. In his later papers, including his last ones, we find modifications and reformulations the importance of which has as yet not always been realized. Some of these I shall discuss later.

The term "ego" is often used in a highly ambiguous way, even among analysts. To define it negatively, in three respects, as against other ego concepts: "ego," in analysis, is not synonymous with "personality" or with "individual"; it does not coincide with the "subject" as opposed to the "object" of experience; and it is by no means only the "awareness" or the "feeling" of one's own self. In analysis, the ego is a concept of quite a different order. It is a substructure of personality and is defined by its functions.

Which functions do we attribute to the ego? A catalogue of ego functions would be rather long, longer than a catalogue of functions of either the id or the superego. No analyst has ever endeavored a complete listing of ego functions, nor is it among the aims of my presentation to do so. Here I shall mention only some of the most important ones. You know that among them Freud (1932) has always emphasized those which center around the relation to reality: "This relation to the external world is decisive for the ego" (p. 106). The ego organizes and controls motility and perception—perception of the outer world but probably also of the self (while we think that self-criticism, though based on self-perception, is a separate function which we attribute to the superego); it also serves as a protective barrier against excessive external and, in a somewhat different sense, internal stimuli. The ego tests reality. Action, too, in contradistinction to mere motor discharge, and thinking, which according to Freud (1911a) is trial action with small quantities of psychic energy, are functions of the ego. In both is implied an element of inhibition, of delay of discharge. In this sense many aspects of the ego can be described as detour activities; they promote a more specific and safer form of adjustment by introducing a factor of growing independence from the immediate impact of present stimuli. In this trend toward what we may call internalization is also included the danger signal, besides other functions that can be described as being in the nature of anticipation. I also want to remind you here of what Freud thought about the relation of the ego to time perception. From what I just said it already appears that a large sector of the ego's functions can also be described from the angle of its inhibiting nature. You know that A. Freud (1936) speaks of a primary enmity of the ego vis-à-vis the instinctual drives; and the ego function most extensively and intensively studied in analysis, namely, defense, is a specific expression of its inhibiting nature. Another set of functions which we attribute to the ego is what we call a person's character. And still another one that we can conceptually distinguish from those mentioned so far are the coordinating or integrating tendencies known as the synthetic function. These, together with the differentiating factors, we can comprise in the concept of an organizing function; they represent one level (not the only or the earliest one) of mental self-regulation in man. While speaking of the reality aspects of the ego, or of its inhibiting, or its organizing nature, etc., I am, of course, aware of the fact that its specific activities may and actually do express many of these characteristics at the same time.

With all these functions of the ego we are in continuous contact in our clinical as well as in our theoretical thinking. But it also appears that while analysts have thoroughly investigated some of these functions, others have attracted only casual attention. As Freud

(1932) writes: "psycho-analysis could not study every part of the field at once" (p. 82). Thus Freud's outline of the ego is richer in motifs and dimensions than its elaboration so far in psychoanalytic literature. Of course, there is the obvious reason that certain aspects of the ego are more specifically accessible to the psychoanalytic method than others. We have only to think of the psychology of conflict or of the psychology of defense. On the other hand, there are fields of ego functions of which one is used to think as the exclusive domain of direct observation, or of experimental methods, though we should realize that these fields too will have to be reconsidered from the angle of psychoanalytic psychology. It is also true that certain aspects of ego psychology appear to be of greater or lesser relevance according to the context in which one views them: whether we look at them from the clinical or technical points of view, or from that of a general psychological theory—the angle from which I have chosen to view the field today. Historically the study of the ego had different meanings at different times, according, for instance, to the preponderance of certain technical over certain theoretical questions or vice versa. On the other hand, though it appears from his writings that he was rather opposed to considering analysis as a psychological "system," at least in its present state, Freud unquestionably had all these aspects in mind, and one of his aims, particularly in his ego-psychological work, was to constitute analysis as the basis of a general psychology. Also, the trend toward developing psychoanalytic psychology beyond its medical origin, including in its scope a growing number of aspects of normal as well as pathological behavior, is clearly inherent in ego psychology today. The techniques of adjustment to reality and of achievement emerge in a more explicit way (Anna Freud, 1936; French, 1936, 1937; Hartmann, 1939a; Hendrick, 1943; and others), and some errors in perspective that are bound to occur in viewing them only from the pathological angle can be corrected. This broader approach is also indicated, and indeed essential, wherever we use psychoanalytic propositions in so-called applied psychoanalysis, as in the vast field of encounter between analysis and the social sciences. But even the field of psychopathology proper, its clinical and technical aspects, has already greatly profited from that trend in the work of Freud and many of his followers which aims at the more comprehensive conception of analysis as a general psychology. While we know how much psychology owes to pathology, especially to the pathology of neuroses, here by means of a detour the reverse takes place.

This trend should not be interpreted as a tendency away from the medical aspects of analysis or, for that matter, from its biological or physiological aspects. This point deserves emphasis, because in its beginnings Freud's ego psychology was misunderstood by many, analysts and nonanalysts, as a parting with his original ideas on the biological foundation of analysis. Actually, the opposite comes closer to the truth: it is, in certain respects, rather a rapprochement. No doubt, the continuity with biology has, in analysis, first been established in the study of the instinctual drives. But ego psychology, by investigating more closely not only the ego's adaptive capacities but also its "synthetic," "integrating," or "organizing" functions (Nunberg, 1930; French, 1941, 1945; and Chapter 3)—that is the centralization of functional control—has extended the sphere in which a meeting of analytic with physiological, especially brain-physiological, concepts may one day become possible.

In what follows I do not aspire after a systematic presentation of ego psychology. I shall select for discussion a few aspects only, and what I am aiming at is a better mutual adjustment of some hypotheses in the field, which sometimes implies their elaboration or modification, and also their synchronization according to one level of theory formation.

Let us start with problems of ego development. Part of our hypotheses in this field rests on the solid grounds of manifold and verifiable findings of psychoanalytic clinical data. However, this is unfortunately not true of the earliest stages, of the undifferentiated phase; nor is it true of those somewhat later developments that occur up to the end of the nonverbal stage. Hypotheses on these early stages can be tested as to their agreement or disagreement with the basic concepts of analytic theory, a point recently emphasized by Glover (1947). Any reconstructions of this period have to beware of two dangers: of the "adultomorphic" (Spitz) and of the "psychosomorphic" (Hartmann) errors. Direct observation of the growing infant, especially if directed by analytically experienced observers, can prove helpful in this respect and will prove even more helpful in the future, not only by eliminating propositions which are contradicted by behavioral data (Hartmann, Glover), but also by directing the formation of hypotheses in a more positive way. I do not share the extreme skepticism of some analysts with regard to such a possibility. We shall not forget that in developing his ideas on the earliest stages of infantile development, Freud was in many instances guided, though not in a systematical way, by knowledge gained from other than analytic sources.

Leaving questions of methodology aside for the moment, we may say that today we possess a considerable wealth of reliable and more or less systematic information, gained from many sources, about questions such as the following: how the ego is being molded under the impact of reality on the one hand and the instinctual drives on the other hand; in which way it learns to defend itself in both directions; and about how its development is interrelated with the development of object relationships. We also at least try to account for the development of the ego as a definite system in terms of metapsychological concepts; and, more particularly, I here want to point to the role which we think the establishment of the secondary process plays in it. We say that the ego extends from the preconscious memory traces. Glover (1935) has tried to bridge the gap between systems of memory traces and the ego as a structural unit by introducing a hypothesis according to which a synthesization of such psychic elements as are associated with drive components takes place in nuclear ego formation. One other possible origin of ego nuclei I shall discuss later.

Most attempts to explain the origin of the infant's relation with reality have relied heavily on the drive for self-preservation. I should prefer a formulation which does not speak of self-preservation as a result of an independent set of drives (see Chapter 4), but rather stresses the roles which libidinal and aggressive tendencies play in it, in addition to physiological mechanisms, and above all the role of the ego and of those autonomous preparatory stages of the ego which I shall soon discuss. We all agree that, in his development toward reality, the child has to learn to postpone gratification; the recognition, by the child, of constant and independent objects in the outside world already presupposes a certain degree of this capacity. But for the acceptance of reality also the pleasure possibilities offered by the developing ego functions are essential as well as love and other rewards from the side of the objects and, in a later stage, gratifications due to the renunciation of instinctual satisfaction (Freud, 1937-39).

One approach to ego development has been somewhat neglected in psychoanalytic theory, though it might hold out a promise for a more consistent integration of the analytic findings and hypotheses with the data of direct observation. Some aspects of early ego development appear in a different light if we familiarize ourselves with the thought that the ego may be more—and very likely is more—than a developmental by-product of the influence of reality on instinctual drives; that it has a partly independent origin—apart from those formative influences which, of course, no analyst would want to underestimate; and that we may speak of an autonomous factor in ego development (Hartmann, 1939a) in the same way as we consider the instinctual drives autonomous agents of development. Of course, this is not to say that the ego as a definite psychic system is inborn; it rather stresses the point that the development of this system is traceable not only to the impact of reality and of the instinctual drives but also to a set of factors that cannot be identified with either one of them. This statement also implies that not all the factors of mental development present at birth can be considered part of the id—which is, by the way, included in what I have said elsewhere in introducing the concept of an undifferentiated phase. What, in the history of psychoanalytic theory, had for a long time militated against the acceptance of this position is, above all, the fact that we were so much used to thinking in terms of "the id being older than the ego." The latter hypothesis also has an aspect which refers to phylogenesis. However, I should like to suggest that we try to reformulate it even as to this implication. I should rather say that both the ego and the id have developed, as products of differentiation, out of the matrix of animal instinct. From here, by way of differentiation, not only man's special "organ" of adaptation, the ego, has developed, but also the id; and the estrangement with reality, so characteristic of the id of the human, is an outcome of this differentiation, but by no means a direct continuation of what we know about the instincts of lower animals (see Chapter 4). As to the ontogenetic aspect, more important for the problems under discussion here, there is no doubt, though it has not been generally realized, that Freud has come to develop his theory in a direction which modifies his previous stand, at least in one essential aspect. I am quoting from his "Analysis Terminable and Interminable" (1937a) which might prove to be the most far-sighted of his last papers: "We have no reason to dispute the existence and importance of primary congenital variations in the ego. . . . When we speak of 'archaic heritage' we are generally thinking only of the id and we apparently assume that no ego is yet in existence at the beginning of the individual's life. But we must not overlook the fact that id and ego are originally one, and it does not imply a mystical over-valuation of heredity if we think it credible that, even before the ego exists, its subsequent lines of development, tendencies and reactions are already determined" (p. 343f.).

We come to see ego development as a result of three sets of factors: inherited ego characteristics (and their interaction), influences of the instinctual drives, and influences of outer reality. Concerning the development and the growth of the autonomous characteristics of the ego we may make the assumption that they take place as a result of experience (learning), but partly also of maturation— parallel to the assumption more familiar in analysis that processes of maturation intervene in the development of the sexual drives (for instance, in the sequence of libidinal organizations), and in a somewhat different way also in the development of aggression (Hartmann, Kris, and Loewenstein, 1949). Keeping in mind the role of maturation in ego development may also help us to avoid one pitfall of the reconstruction of mental life in early infancy: that is, the interpretation of early mental processes in terms of mechanisms known from much later maturational stages.

The problem of maturation has a physiological aspect. Speaking of this aspect we may refer to the growth of whatever we assume to be the physiological basis of those functions which, looked at from the angle of psychology, we call the ego; or we may refer to the growth of such apparatus which sooner or later come to be specifically used by the ego (e.g., the motor apparatus used in action). However, the role of these apparatus for the ego is not limited to their function as tools which the ego at a given time finds at its disposal. We have to assume that differences in the timing or intensity of their growth enter into the picture of ego development as a partly independent variable; e.g., the timing of the appearance of grasping, of walking, of the motor aspect of speech (see also Hendrick, 1943). Neither does it seem unlikely that the congenital motor equipment is among the factors which right from birth on tend to modify certain attitudes of the developing ego (Fries and Lewi, 1938). The presence of such factors in all aspects of the child's behavior makes them also an essential element in the development of his self-experience. We can assume that from the earliest stages on the corresponding experiences are preserved in his system of memory traces. We have also reasons to think that the reproduction of environmental data is very generally fused with and formed by elements of that kind, e.g., the reproduction of motor experiences.

Freud has repeatedly stressed the importance of the body ego in ego development. This points, on the one hand, to the influence of the body image, particularly on the differentiation of the self from the object world; but it also points to the fact that the functions of those organs which establish the contact with the world outside gradually come under the control of the ego. The way in which the infant learns about his own body and its functions has been described as a process similar to identification (Müller-Braunschweig, 1925). However, it is doubtful whether this process, though leading to an integration in the ego, is actually the same as the one we have in mind when, in analysis, we are referring to identification as a specific mechanism.

The autonomous factors of ego development as introduced above may or may not, in the course of development, remain in the non-conflictual sphere of the ego. Concerning their relation with the drives—which does not necessarily coincide with their relation with conflict—we know from clinical experience that they may secondarily come under the influence of the drives, as is the case in sexualization or aggressivization. To give only one example: in analysis we observe how the function of perception, which has certainly an autonomous aspect, may be influenced—and frequently handicapped —by becoming the expression of oral-libidinal or oral-aggressive strivings. But in the context of developmental psychology, this relation with the drives has a more universal importance. In the earliest stages of development the dependence of, let us again say, perception upon situations of "need"—and upon the drives these needs represent —is quite obvious. In these stages, then, it is clear that perception, rather generally, must be described not only in its autonomous aspect but also as to the ways it is used by sexual and aggressive tendencies. However, the reality ego gradually evolves precisely by freeing itself from the encroachment of such instinctual tendencies. Thus what we later call sexualization (or aggressivization) may also be a problem of regression. This addition was necessary in order to make it quite clear that the autonomous nuclei, while traceable to an independent origin, constantly interact with the vicissitudes of the drives.

The autonomous factors may also come to be involved in the ego's defense against instinctual tendencies, against reality, and against the superego. So far we have in analysis mainly been dealing with the intervention of conflict in their development. But it is of considerable interest not only for developmental psychology but also for clinical problems to study the converse influence too: that is, the influences which a child's intelligence, his perceptual and motor equipment, his special gifts, and the development of all these factors have on the timing, intensity, and mode of expression of these conflicts. We know infinitely more, in a systematic way, about the other aspect, the ego's development in consequence of its conflicts with the instinctual drives and with reality. I have only to remind you of the classical contribution of A. Freud (1936) in this field. Here I want to touch upon only one side of this complex problem. Through what one could call a "change of function," what started in a situation of conflict may secondarily become part of the non-conflictual sphere (Hartmann, 1939a). Many aims, attitudes, interests, structures of the ego have originated in this way (see also G. Allport, 1937). What developed as a result of defense against an instinctual drive may grow into a more or less independent and more or less structured function. It may come to serve different functions, like adjustment, organization, and so on. To give one example: every reactive character formation, originating in defense against the drives, will gradually take over a wealth of other functions in the framework of the ego. Because we know that the results of this development may be rather stable, or even irreversible in most normal conditions, we may call such functions autonomous, though in a secondary way (in contradistinction to the primary autonomy of the ego I discussed before).

It should hardly be necessary to mention that my stressing here, and in later passages, the independent aspects of ego functions does not imply any undervaluation of other aspects, earlier known and more systematically studied in analysis. No doubt, if this presentation were intended to give an over-all picture of the ego, in which the space allocated to each chapter could be expected to be proportionate to its importance, the structure of my paper would have to be very different indeed. However, as I said at the beginning, I want to focus only on certain aspects of ego theory rather than on its system.

There are many points concerning the origin of defense mechanisms that we have not yet come to understand. Some elements, according to Freud, may be inherited; but he, of course, does not consider heredity the only factor relevant for their choice or for their development. It seems reasonable to assume that these mechanisms do not originate as defenses in the sense we use the term once the ego as a definable system has evolved (Hartmann, 1939a; Helene Deutsch, 1944). They may originate in other areas, and in some cases these primitive processes may have served different functions, before they are secondarily used for what we specifically call defense in analysis. The problem is to trace the genetic connections between those primordial functions and the defense mechanisms of the ego. Some of these may be modeled after some form of instinctual behavior: introjection, to give but one example, probably exists as a form of instinct gratification before it is used in the service of defense. We will also think of how the ego can use, for defense, characteristics of the primary process, as in displacement (Anna Freud, 1936). But neither the first nor the second case covers all the defense mechanisms. Others may be patterned after some autonomous preliminary stages of ego functions and after processes characteristic of the ego apparatus. I am, for instance, thinking of the fact that these ego apparatus, while in the long run guaranteeing to the child more highly differentiated and safer forms of gratification, have often also a definitely inhibitory aspect so far as the discharge of instinctual energy is concerned. This we may correlate to what A. Freud has called the primary enmity of the ego against the drives, and it may be one genetic basis of later defensive actions against them. May I suggest another example. Freud (1926a) has drawn a parallel between the mechanism of isolation and the normal process of attention; from the point of view I am stressing here, we will be interested in the question whether there exists a genetic—not necessarily direct or simple—connection between the often precocious development of certain ego functions in obsessional neurosis and the choice of this defense mechanism characteristic of it. On the other hand, Freud has often pointed to the analogy between defense actions against the drives and the means by which the ego avoids danger from without, that is, flight and fight, about which more will be said later. Here I want to emphasize that it is indeed tempting to consider very early processes in the autonomous area as forestages of later defense against both inner and outer dangers. Some aspects of what may be transitional steps are well known in child psychology; e.g., the neonate's closing of the eyelids when exposed to light; definite flight reactions of no longer a merely diffuse character at the age of about four months; and other later and more specific phenomena of that kind. These reactions impress us like models of later defense. Also, in this connection, I want to point to Freud's statements concerning what he calls protective barrier against stimuli, in its possible relation to later ego development. Glover (1947) is right in stating that strictly speaking we cannot reduce the concept of a mechanism to simpler elements. Still, he continues, "we must postulate certain innate tendencies, conveyed through the id which lead to the development of mechanisms." With this, too, I can agree, as is implied in what I have said before. But I should like to draw attention not only to those "innate tendencies conveyed through the id" but also to the at least equal importance of those tendencies that do not originate in the id but in the autonomous preliminary stages of ego formation. It might well be that the ways in which infants deal with stimuli—also those functions of delaying, of postponing discharge mentioned before—are later used by the ego in an active way. We consider this active use for its own purposes of primordial forms of reaction a rather general characteristic of the developed ego. This hypothesis of a genetic correlation between individual differences in primary factors of this kind and the later defense mechanisms (apart from those correlations that we think exist of defense mechanisms with other developmental factors, with the nature of the drives involved, with the danger situation, etc.) is intended as an appeal to those analysts who have the opportunities for conducting longitudinal developmental studies on children. I think that this hypothesis will prove to be accessible to direct verification or refutation.

In turning now to questions of ego cathexis, the second point I have singled out for presentation today, we are confronted with the many-faceted and still puzzling problem of narcissism. Many analysts do not find it altogether easy to define the place which the concept of narcissism holds in present analytic theory. This, I think, is due mainly to the fact that this concept has not been explicitly redefined in terms of Freud's later structural psychology. I shall limit my remarks to those points only that are essential if we want to avoid possible misunderstandings of what I want to say about ego cathexis. Many aspects of narcissism have been reformulated by Federn in a series of searching papers (1929, 1936). I shall not discuss this reformulation because in the course of his studies Federn came to modify the concept of the ego in a way which seems to me not altogether convincing. I would prefer to integrate Freud's early formulations on narcissism into his later views on mental structure, rather than to change any of the main aspects of the latter.

We speak of a narcissistic type of personality, of narcissistic object choice, of a narcissistic attitude toward reality, of narcissism as a topographical problem, and so on. The aspects of topography and cathexis are fundamental in analytic theory. In his paper "On Narcissism" (1914a), speaking of the relation of narcissism to autoerotism, Freud says that, while autoerotism is primordial, the ego has to develop, does not exist from the start, and therefore something must be added to autoerotism—some new operation in the mind—in order that narcissism may come into being. A few years later (1916-17, p. 360) he stated that "narcissism is the universal original condition, out of which object-love develops later," while even then "the greatest volume of libido may yet remain within the ego." At the time when Freud wrote his paper "On Narcissism," just the bare outlines of structural psychology had become visible. In the following decade during which the principles of ego psychology were laid down, we find a variety of formulations that I cannot all quote in detail. In some, reference is still made to the ego as the original reservoir of libido, but in *The Ego and the Id* (1923a) Freud made it quite explicitly clear that it was not the ego but the id he had in mind when speaking of this "original reservoir"; the libido accrued to the ego by identification was termed "secondary narcissism." The equivalence of narcissism and libidinal cathexes of the ego was and still is widely used in psychoanalytic literature, but in some passages Freud also refers to it as cathexis of one's own person, of the body, or of the self. In analysis a clear distinction between the terms ego, self, and personality is not always made. But a differentiation of these concepts is essential if we try to look consistently at the problems involved in the light of Freud's structural psychology. But actually, in using the term narcissism, two different sets of opposites often seem to be fused into one. The one refers to the self (one's own person) in contradistinction to the object, the second to the ego (as a psychic system) in contradistinction to other substructures of personality. However, the opposite of object cathexis is not ego cathexis, but cathexis of one's own person, that is, self-cathexis; in speaking of self-cathexis we do not imply whether this cathexis is situated in the id, ego, or superego. This formulation takes into account that we actually do find "narcissism" in all three psychic systems; but in all of these cases there is opposition to (and reciprocity with) object cathexis. It therefore will be clarifying if we define narcissism as the libidinal cathexis not of the ego but of the self. (It might also be useful to apply the term self-representation as opposed to object representation.) Often, in speaking of ego libido, what we do mean is not that this form of energy cathects the ego, but that it cathects one's own person rather than an object representation. Also in many cases where we are used to saying "libido has been withdrawn into the ego" or "object cathexis has been replaced by ego cathexis," what we actually should say is "withdrawal onto the self" in the first, and either "by self-love" or "by a neutralized form of self-cathexis" in the second case. If we want to point to the theoretically and practically important part of self-cathexis being localized in the system ego, I would prefer not just to speak of "narcissism" but of narcissistic ego cathexis.

These differences are obviously important for our insight into many aspects of structural psychology, and their consideration may help to clarify questions of cathexes and their topography. Is it the turning back of the libido from the objects upon the system ego which is the source of delusions of grandeur? Or is it not rather the turning back upon the self—a process of which the accumulation of libido in the (regressed) ego is only one aspect? Here I can discuss neither this question nor some of its manifold implications.[2] In what follows I shall briefly mention only one more aspect of withdrawal of libido from the objects, namely, the energic quality of the libido involved.

In the course of that development of analytic theory which led Freud on the one hand to reformulate his ideas on the relations between anxiety and libido, and on the other hand to constitute the ego as a system in its own rights, he also came to formulate the thesis that the ego works with desexualized libido. It has been suggested (see, for instance, Menninger, 1938; or Hartmann, Kris, and Loewenstein, 1949) that it is reasonable and fruitful to broaden this hypothesis to include besides desexualized also desaggressivized energy in the energic aspect of ego functions. Aggressive as well as sexual energy may be neutralized,[3] and in both cases this process of neutralization takes place through mediation of the ego (and probably already through its autonomous forestages too). We assume that these neutralized energies are closer to one another than the strictly instinc-

---

[2] Some of its implications are taken up in Chapter 10.

[3] I use this term, also used by K. Menninger, rather than "sublimated," because the latter Freud has expressly reserved for desexualized libido.

tual energies of the two drives. However, they may retain some of the latters' properties. Theoretical as well as clinical considerations speak in favor of assuming that there are gradations in the neutralization of these energies; that is to say, not all of them are neutral to the same degree. We ought to distinguish them according to their greater or lesser closeness to drive energy, which means according to whether or not, and to what extent, they still retain characteristics of sexuality (object-libidinal or narcissistic) or of aggression (object- or self-directed). (Freud thinks of the possibility that, in the process of sublimation, object libido is first transformed into narcissistic libido, in order to be then directed toward new aims. One aspect of this hypothesis is that sublimation takes place through mediation of the ego, which I just mentioned. Another aspect is discussed in Chapter 12.)

To be able to neutralize considerable amounts of instinctual energy may well be an indication of ego strength. I also want to mention, at least, the clinically well-established fact that the ego's capacity for neutralization is partly dependent on the degree of a more instinctual cathexis being vested in the self. The degree of neutralization is another point we have to consider—besides those mentioned before—if we are to describe adequately the transition from the "narcissistic" state of the ego to its later reality-syntonic functioning. Furthermore, the ego energies' relative closeness to the drives may also become a decisive factor in pathology. To take again an example from the field of "narcissism": it is of paramount importance for our understanding of the various forms of "withdrawal of libido from reality," in terms of their effects on ego functions, to see clearly whether the part of the resulting self-cathexes localized in the ego is still close to sexuality or has undergone a thorough process of neutralization. An increase in the ego's neutralized cathexes is not likely to cause pathological phenomena; but its being swamped by insufficiently neutralized instinctual energy may have this effect (under certain conditions). In this connection, the ego's capacity for neutralization becomes relevant and, in the case of pathological development, the degree to which this capacity has been interfered with as a consequence of ego regression. What I just said about the bearing of neutralization on the outcome of libido withdrawal is equally true where not libidinal but aggressive cathexes are being turned back from the objects upon the self and in part upon the ego. In the case in which aggression is turned back we will, of course, likewise always have to consider the superego's proclivity to use certain gradations of aggressive energy. These instances of the role of neutralization in the functioning of the ego I choose at random out of many. Another one I shall discuss in greater detail below.

The question whether all energy at the disposal of the ego originates in the instinctual drives, I am not prepared to answer. Freud thinks that "nearly all of the energy" active in the psychic apparatus comes from the drives, thus pointing to the possibility that part of it may have a different origin. But what other sources of mental energy may there be? Several possible answers come to mind, but obviously this question is hard to decide in the present state of our knowledge. It may be that some of the energy originates in what I described before as the autonomous ego. However, all these questions referring to the primordial origin of mental energy lead ultimately back to physiology—as they do in the case of instinctual energy. Our factual insight and conceptual tools make a positive answer to the question of possible noninstinctual sources as difficult to ascertain as a negative one.[4]

We return to the ego. Regardless of whether its energic aspect be wholly or only partly traceable to the instinctual drives, we assume that once it is formed it disposes of independent psychic energy, which is just to restate in other terms the character of the ego as a separate psychic system. This is not meant to imply that at any given time the process of transformation of instinctual into neutralized energy comes to an end; this is a continuous process. The ego's energy is available for the great variety of ego functions I mentioned before.

[4] For a more definite statement, see Chapter 12.

In this connection I want to add that many of the ego's tendencies which express these functions are object directed—i.e., not "narcissistic" in the sense that they take the self as their object; nor do all of them only work with the different gradations of self-cathexis.

In speaking of various shades of desexualization or desaggressivization one has to think of two different aspects. One may refer to different modes or conditions of energy, and this energic aspect of neutralization may partly coincide with the replacement of the primary by the secondary process, which allows of any number of transitional states. We are used to consider the secondary process as a specific characteristic of the ego, but this excludes neither the use, by the ego, of the primary process[5] nor the existence, in the ego, of differences in the degree to which energies are bound.[6] The second angle from which we have to consider those shades of neutralization is the degree to which certain other characteristics of the drives (e.g., their direction, their aims) are still demonstrable (neutralization with respect to the aims[7]).

Let us now look again, this time from the point of view of cathexes, at the psychology of defense and take as our point of departure a crude schematization of a typical case: preconscious cathexis is withdrawn and the ego defends itself through anticathexis against the reappearance of the instinctual tendency. According to one hypothesis of Freud (1915b), the energy which is used in the formation of countercathexis is the same—or may be the same—as that which has been withdrawn from the drives. Nunberg (1932) cites this process as a particularly good example of the economical nature of psychic organization. In analytic literature, countercathexis is, as a rule, said to consist of desexualized libido. However, most of these formulations belong into a period of analytic theory formation in which aggression had not yet been recognized as a primary and independent drive. Today we would assume that countercathexis may

[5] See also E. Kris (1934).
[6] See now also Kris (1950a) and Rapaport (1950).
[7] This term is no longer used.

equally well consist of neutralized aggressive energy. According to Freud's hypothesis this would be the case whenever the warded-off drive is an aggressive one (another part of the warded-off aggression finds its expression in feelings of guilt [Freud, 1930]). But Freud's hypothesis of the energy of countercathexis being withdrawn from the drives is not necessarily meant to be generally valid; "it is quite possible that it is so," is what he once said in this connection.

Other considerations suggest the possibility that the role of more or less neutralized aggressive energy in countercathexis may be of an even more general nature and greater relevance.[8] I again remind you that Freud stressed the analogy between defense against the instinctual drives and against an external danger. The two processes involved in the schematic example of defense just outlined make such a parallel very impressive indeed: flight and fight can be said to be its main characteristics, withdrawal of cathexis corresponding to flight and countercathexis to fight. This leads to the answer I want to suggest here: that countercathexis widely uses one of those conditions of more or less neutralized aggressive energy, mentioned before, which still retain some characteristics of the original drive (fight, in this case). It seems not unlikely that such forms of energy —it is not necessary to assume that all countercathexes operate with the same degree of neutralization—contribute to countercathexis even if the warded-off drive was not of an aggressive nature.

To assume that the ego uses for defense only and always energy withdrawn from the drives against which it defends itself does not agree too well with what we know today about the high degree of activity and plasticity characteristic of the ego's choice of means to accomplish its ends. Also, it seems of the greatest interest to consider what interdependence there exists between the defensive functions of the ego and other ego functions. There is no doubt, and I mentioned it before, that defense is actually genetically and dynamically under the influence of other processes in the ego and, on the other

---

[8] I want to mention that after having formulated this proposition I found a somewhat similar idea in a paper by M. Brierley (1947).

hand, that defense intervenes in a great variety of different processes in the ego; this I discussed as an essential aspect of developmental psychology. We must assume that this interdependence has also an energic aspect, and this, too, leads to the conclusion that, although countercathexis may draw on energies withdrawn from the warded-off drive—and I shall later discuss one case in question—this is not the only source of energy at its disposal.

At this point I want to remind you of another one of Freud's later hypotheses (1937a), of which I said that their importance for our theoretical thinking has not yet been clearly realized. It points to the possibility that the disposition to conflict may be traced (among other factors) to the intervention of free aggression. Freud, in introducing this thought, gives examples of instinctual rather than of structural conflicts (if we use these terms in the meaning suggested by Alexander, 1933). But he adds that it confronts us with the question "whether this notion should not be extended to apply to other instances of conflict, or, indeed, whether we ought not to review all our knowledge of psychical conflict from this new angle." This disposition to conflict, traceable to aggression, would come into play independently of the nature of the drive against which defense is directed. My hypothesis that countercathexis is fed by neutralized aggressive energy can be based on Freud's ideas if we assume, for the case of conflict between the ego and the drives, that the aggressive energy is (more or less) being bound in the service of the ego's defensive actions. This hypothesis seems more consistent both with what we know about the ego today and with Freud's later thinking than other propositions on countercathexis based on his earlier concept formation.

We may look at the same problem from another angle. In the same paper, Freud describes how, in working on our patients' resistances, we meet what he calls "resistance against the uncovering of resistances" and mentions the well-known fact that in this situation phenomena of negative transference may come to predominate. Is it not possible that, metapsychologically speaking, part of this aggression directed against the analyst is reaggressivized energy of the countercathexes, mobilized as a consequence of our attack on the patient's resistance? This again would well agree with the proposition under discussion.

Before leaving this subject I want to note one more implication, though I am aware of the somewhat speculative character of this inference. Vis-à-vis an external danger an aggressive response is normal, while sexualization may lead to pathology. If the defensive reaction against danger from within is modeled after the one to danger from without, it is possible that the use of aggressive energy —in this case, more or less neutralized—is more regular than the use of desexualized libido. This might also mean that in the case of defense against an instinctual danger, a place for aggression would more easily be found in the defensive reaction of the ego itself (in countercathexis); while the energy of the libidinal strivings, which could not as easily be disposed of this way, would have to be repressed (or warded off in another way). To come back to an earlier point: I would assume that the use, in countercathexis, of energy withdrawn from the drives is more general if they are of an aggressive than if they are of a libidinal nature. I realize, of course, the sketchy character of this statement, and also that I am simplifying what is actually a highly intricate process. However, this hypothesis, though I would not dare to decide whether or not it will prove to be correct, might be helpful (if integrated with others on the subject that have already been accepted in our analytic thinking) toward explaining the etiological predominance of sexual over aggressive factors in neurosis.

A systematic study of ego functions would have to describe them in regard to their aims (for the difference between "aims" of drives and "aims" of the ego, see Chapter 3) and to the means they use in pursuing them; energically, to the closeness to or remoteness from the drives of the energies with which they operate; and also to the degree of structuralization and independence they have achieved.

Here I want to say a few words only about one special group of ego tendencies, as an example of which Freud (1916-17) discusses "egoism." Their importance was, of course, fully realized by Freud, and it would seem desirable to assign them a definite place in psychoanalytic psychology; but their position was never clearly defined on the level of structural psychology, though Freud had tried to account for them on an earlier level of theory formation. At that time, Freud identified the self-preservative tendencies with "ego drives," and the cathexes proceeding from them he called "interests," in contradistinction to the libido of the sexual drives. However, today we no longer speak of "drives of the ego" in the strict sense, since it was realized that all the drives are part of the system id (see also E. Bibring, 1930); this change in theory necessitates a reformulation also of the phenomena Freud had in mind in speaking of "interests." Among the self-preservative psychic tendencies, we think functions of the system ego to be of foremost importance (Freud, 1940; and Chapter 3)—which is not to say, of course, that sexual and aggressive id tendencies, some aspects of the principles of regulation, etc., have no part in self-preservation. The group of tendencies which comprises strivings for what is "useful," egoism, self-assertion, etc., should, it seems reasonable, be attributed to the system ego. Among the factors of motivation, they contribute a layer of their own. The importance of these tendencies has been somewhat neglected in analysis, probably because they play no essential part in the etiology of neurosis and because in our work with patients we have to consider them more from the angle of genetically underlying id tendencies than in their partly independent aspect as functions of the ego. But the relevance of this latter aspect becomes obvious the moment we turn to viewing them from the angle of general psychology, which is what I am doing here, or of social science. Social science no doubt falls short of its aims as long as it bases its interpretation of human behavior exclusively on the model of the interest-directed, we may here say "utilitarian," type of action. On the other hand, many fields of social science cannot successfully be approached by analysis as long as we disregard this layer of motivation.

What position can we attribute to these interests in present analytic theory? May I first suggest that we term these and similar tendencies "ego interests," thus retaining the Freudian name but also implying that we consider that part of what he called "interests" which we have in mind here as belonging to the system ego. They are interests of the ego; their goals are set by the ego, in contradistinction to aims of the id or of the superego. But the special set of tendencies I am referring to is also characterized by the fact that their aims center around one's own person (self). I may add that this is true of their aims only. They obviously also use or serve ego functions that are directed toward the outer world and, among the factors which lead to the change, by man, of external reality, ego interests of this kind play unquestionably a decisive role.

One should beware of overemphasizing terminological questions in this field so little known to us; it might prove practical to include in the concept of ego interests, besides this one, other groups of ego tendencies of an otherwise similar nature, the aims of which do not center around the self; for instance, those which affect the outer world not only indirectly, in the sense just outlined, but whose aims are centered around other persons or around things; or those which are striving toward aims, originating in the superego but taken over by the ego, aims that center around values (ethical values, values of truth, religious values, etc.); and finally, interests of the ego in mental functioning itself (e.g., in intellectual activity) might also be included.

These ego interests are hardly ever unconscious in the technical sense, as are, among the ego functions, in the typical case, the defenses. They are mostly preconscious and may be conscious—but sometimes we meet difficulties in bringing them into consciousness. This often seems to be so because of their closeness to id tendencies underlying them; but I would not dare to decide whether this is always the case. At any rate, we will remember what Freud (1915b) stated about a censorship working not only between the preconscious and unconscious, but also between the conscious and the preconscious mind. The existence of the latter teaches us, according to Freud, that becoming conscious is probably due to hypercathexis, "a further advance in the mental organization." That ego interests are often rooted in id tendencies is obvious (particularly when this is established by analysis). However, this genetic connection is often not reversible, except under special conditions (through analysis, in dreams, in neurosis, etc.). The ego interests follow not the laws of the id but of the ego. They are working with neutralized energy and may, as is often the case, e.g., with "egoism," put this energy against the satisfaction of instinctual drives.

Strivings for wealth, for social prestige, or for what is considered "useful" in another sense, are genetically partly determined by anal, urethral, narcissistic, exhibitionistic, aggressive, etc., id tendencies, and either continue in modified form the directions of these drives or are the results of reactions against them. Obviously, various id tendencies may contribute to the formation of one specific ego interest; and the same id tendency may contribute to the formation of several of them. They are also determined by the superego, by different areas of ego functions, by other ego interests, by a person's relation with reality, by his modes of thinking, or by his synthetic capacities, etc., and the ego is in a certain measure able to achieve a compromise in which the instinctual elements are used for its own aims." The source of the neutralized energy with which the ego interests operate seems not to be confined to the energy of those instinctual strivings out of which or against which they have developed; other neutralized energy may be at their disposal. This is actually implied in thinking of them as sharing the characteristics of the ego as a functionally and energically partly independent system. We may state that many of them (in different degrees) appear to belong to the field of secondary autonomy. As to the comparative

[9] For the categories of problems to the solution of which the ego is consecrated, see Waelder (1930).

dynamic efficacy of the ego interests, what we know about their energic aspects is too small a basis for any definite conclusion.

The self-directed ego interests—egoism, striving for what is considered useful, etc.—can be found in various relations of collaboration with but also antagonism against other ego functions. That the type of action directed by them should not be confounded with "rational action," I have pointed to elsewhere (Chapter 3). They are interacting with object-centered ego tendencies, with that level of self-regulation we call the organizing function, with adjustment to reality and with other functions. We do not know too much about what form of structural hierarchy of ego functions is most likely to be found correlated with mental health in a positive way. But I should like to emphasize one point: the subordination under this group of ego interests of the other ego functions is no criterion of mental health (though it has often been said that the capacity to subordinate other tendencies to what is considered "useful" makes the difference between healthy and neurotic behavior). These ego interests are, after all, only one set of ego functions, and they do not coincide with those, more closely correlated with health, that also integrate the demands of the other psychic systems (synthetic or organizing function).

I have mentioned ego functions opposing each other. Because these contests are clinically not of the same relevance as those between the ego and the id, or the ego and reality, etc., we are not used to thinking of them in terms of conflict. However, we may well describe them as intrasystemic conflicts and thus distinguish them from those other, better-known conflicts that we may designate as intersystemic. The intrasystemic correlations and conflicts in the ego have hardly ever been consistently studied. A case in question is, of course, the relationship between defense and the autonomous functions which I mentioned before. On considering the question of communication or lack of communication between different areas of the ego, I may also quote Freud's statement that the defenses are, in a sense, set apart in the ego. Contrasts in the ego there are many:

the ego has from its start the tendency to oppose the drives, but one of its main functions is also to help them toward gratification; it is a place where insight is gained, but also of rationalization; it promotes objective knowledge of reality, but at the same time, by way of identification and social adjustment, takes over in the course of its development the conventional prejudices of the environment; it pursues its independent aims, but it is also characteristic of it to consider the demands of the other substructures of personality, etc. Of course it is true that ego functions have some general characteristics in common, some of which I mentioned today, and which distinguish them from the id functions. But many misunderstandings and unclarities are traceable to the fact that we have not yet trained ourselves to consider the ego from an intrasystemic point of view. One speaks of "the ego" as being rational, or realistic, or an integrator, while actually these are characteristics only of one or the other of its functions.

The intrasystemic approach becomes essential if we want to clarify such concepts as "dominance of the ego," "ego control," or "ego strength." All these terms are highly ambiguous, unless we add a differential consideration of the ego functions actually involved in the situations we want to describe. It is not possible for me really to go into the much written-about matter of ego strength here (see Glover, 1943; Nunberg, 1939), and a few remarks will have to suffice in this connection. We are used to judging the strength of the ego on the basis of its behavior in typical situations—whether these arise from the side of the id, of the superego, or of outer reality. This would imply that ego strength, like adaptation, can be formulated only in terms of a set of specific relations. We may think of this as a parallel to many physiological problems: in cardiac failure, incapacity of the heart may be due to great and sudden exertion; or to reasons residing in the organ itself; it may also be due to the state of affairs in the blood vessels; and these factors are again interdependent with central regulations and other variables in this complex system. Strength or weakness of the ego—whether habitual or occasional—has been traced to many factors belonging to the id or the superego, and it was pointed out that they are exclusively due to the degree to which the ego is or is not encroached upon by the other systems (Glover). However, I would emphasize here that the autonomous aspect of the ego must also be considered. The discussion of a great variety of elements which one has tried to correlate with the degrees of ego strength—like the strength of the drives, narcissism, tolerance or intolerance against unpleasure, anxiety, guilt feelings, etc.—still leaves us with some confusion. Also, as Nunberg said, the answers are valid only for some, narrowly circumscribed, situations. One typical instance of the difficulties involved, to which Freud drew attention, is the well-known fact that defense, while demonstrating relative strength of the ego vis-à-vis the drives, may, on the other hand, become the very reason of ego weakness. We have to admit—again as in the case of adaptation—that it seems rather generally true that achievement in one direction may cause disturbance in others. In the present context, I just want to emphasize one approach to the problem; I mean the one of carefully studying the interrelations between the different areas of ego functions, like defense, organization, and the area of autonomy. Whether defense leads to exhaustion of the ego's strength is determined not only by the force of the drive in question and by the defenses at the ego's frontiers but also by the supplies the hinterland can put at its disposal. All definitions of ego strength will prove unsatisfactory as long as they take into account only the relation to the other mental systems and leave out of consideration the intrasystemic factors. Any definition must include, as essential elements, the autonomous functions of the ego, their interdependence and structural hierarchy, and especially whether or how far they are able to withstand impairment through the processes of defense. This is unquestionably one of the main elements of what we mean in speaking of ego strength. It is probably not only a question of the amount and distribution of ego energy available, but also has to be correlated with the degree to which the cathexes of these functions are neutralized.

Taking as my main points of departure some of Freud's later and not yet fully integrated findings, I have presented a number of synchronizations and reformulations of and additions to some generally accepted tenets of psychoanalytic theory. May I end by quoting a passage from Freud's writings (1926a, p. 160): "There is no need to be discouraged by these emendations. They are to be welcomed if they add something to our knowledge, and they are no disgrace to us so long as they enrich rather than invalidate our earlier views —by limiting some statement, perhaps, that was too general or by enlarging some idea that was too narrowly formulated."

CHAPTER 8

Technical Implications of
Ego Psychology

(1951)

I N ONE of his last papers, Freud (1937a) wrote that in his opinion the ways in which psychoanalytic technique achieves its
aims are sufficiently elucidated; therefore, one ought rather ask
what obstacles this therapy encounters. However, in the analytic
literature many issues, not only about the practice but also about the
theory of technique, remain controversial. I shall discuss what these
variations mean, and to which differences in the theoretical or practical approach we can trace them.

Progress in the development of analysis is no doubt mostly based
on clinical discoveries; however, now that analysis has come of age,
we realize more clearly also the promoting and interdependent roles
of both technique and theory. Retrospectively, we may say that on
different levels of its development, analytic technique was used in
different ways, not only for the immediate therapeutic aims, but also
in determining the possible scope of observation—of fact finding in
general. Theoretical concepts helped at various stages and in various
ways to facilitate the organization of the data observed (actually also
to seeing the facts), and to advance the exactness and effectiveness of
technique. In the course of its growth, an integration—at times more,
at times less complete—developed among the clinical, technical, and

theoretical elements into a state of reciprocal influence. Faulty theoretical concepts and incomplete insight frequently lead to faulty technique, and there are many examples of adherence to technical mistakes which leads to distortions and misinterpretation of facts.

As to the relation of technique and theory, whenever a lack of integration occurs, both aspects are likely to suffer. A gradual separation of theory and technique, commended by many, would prove inefficient today, as it proved inexpedient in the past. The often used comparison with certain medical specialties is misleading.

A defect in integration of both sides may also be due to one of these aspects outdistancing the other in the course of analytic development. Elsewhere I have tried to demonstrate that the lag is, for the time being, rather on the side of technique than on the side of theory and of psychological insight. The reverse obtained when Freud introduced the systematic analysis of resistances, without at first realizing all its implications for ego psychology. Today we actually know much more than we are able to use technically in a rational way. Genuinely technical discoveries—as was abreaction, and as was analysis of resistances—we do not find in the latest phase of analysis; but the body of systematic psychological and psychopathological knowledge has been considerably increased. However, an equilibrium is likely to be re-established, as has happened and proved fruitful before. For some time, at least one trend in the analyst's interest in technical problems has been following the lead and gradually assimilating the advances in psychoanalytic psychology and psychopathology: ego psychology.

While proceeding along these lines from psychology to technique, we are of course aware of the fact that psychoanalytic technique is more than a mere application of psychological theory. Freud was admittedly and intentionally rather restrained in formulating technical rules; and we are still far from dispensing a collection of technical prescriptions that would cover every given situation. To characterize the present, we may say that we know some general technical principles that help us to avoid some typical mistakes, and in the summarized experience of skilled analysts we have at our disposal a huge potential reservoir of specific technical knowledge, which, in the course of training analysis and supervision, is transmitted to students of analysis. Comparatively few systematic and collective efforts have so far been made to make this potential reservoir available on a larger scale, though, in principle, I do not see any reason why it could not be done. In the meantime, we are trying to develop some rules somewhere in between the generality of acknowledged technical principles and the specificity of clinical experiences, some *principia media.* That is to say, we study variations of our technical principles according to each patient's psychological structure, clinical symptomatology, age level, and so on. Still, considering the interaction of what we may call the aspect of rational planning in our work with its unconscious elements, we cannot but fully subscribe to what Ferenczi emphasized more than twenty years ago: the essential importance of keeping psychoanalytic technique flexible, especially when we are trying to establish what technique may gain from additional scientific insight; also in teaching one must avoid giving the student the impression that actually a complete set of rules exists which just his lack of experience prevents him from knowing. Neither shall we forget that besides the guidance by insight of our technique, every analyst's work with every single one of his patients has also a truly experimental character. There is a continuous sequence of trials and errors, as we check our technical procedures by their immediate consequences and by their therapeutic results.

The technical implications of ego psychology point first and foremost to what a closer insight into defense has taught us about the understanding and handling of resistances; but the ego being what it is, it also means progress in ways of understanding and dealing with the reality aspect of our patients' behavior. Tracing neurotic to real anxiety was one decisive step and obviously an outgrowth of the fact that Freud (1926a) was turning his interest to the clinical implications of ego psychology. Clearly an outcome of this is the way Anna Freud (1936) approaches and deals with conflict with reality, which she constitutes as a field of concern to analysis equal to the conflicts of the ego with the id and with the superego. Thus the way was opened to a better understanding of adaptation and its role in the neurotic as well as in the so-called normal individual. Here, too, there are many practical implications, and we do not feel that we can handle a patient's neurosis without dealing with its interaction with normal functioning. We feel that in order fully to grasp neurosis and its etiology, we have to understand the etiology of health, too. It is true that some degree of realization of all this has always been present in analysis, but the shift of accent is considerable enough to be noteworthy. That in analysis we are dealing with a patient's total personality has become actually true only since this shift in thinking, and in the corresponding technique, was realized. Likewise, the consideration of those interdependencies which we find between conflict and the nonconflictual sphere of the ego points in the same direction. As no concept of ego strength, no concept of mental health, is satisfactory which does not consider nonconflictual functioning as well as the central conflicts (see Chapter 1), this also has a bearing on our technique in so far as it helps to define more precisely the aims of psychoanalytic therapy.

Thinking along the same lines, and if we let our curiosity tempt us to look into the future, we may say that technical progress might depend on a more systematic study of the various functional units within the ego. To the study of the ego's relations with the id or the superego, that is of the intersystemic conflicts and correlations, we shall have to add a more detailed study of the intrasystemic correlations. I spoke of one such unit within the ego: the nonconflictual sphere. But we have to view it constantly in relation to the units of functioning that represent the countercathexes, or the dealings with reality, or the preconscious automatized patterns, or that special functional control and integration that we know under the name of synthetic, or better, organizing function. It would be in line with much research work done today if this intrasystemic approach were to become the subject of more specific investigation. What do we mean when we say that we help the patient's ego; or, strengthen his ego? This certainly cannot be adequately described by referring only to the redistributions of energy between the id and the ego, or between the superego and the ego; shifts from certain spheres of the ego to other functional units within the ego are involved. No definition of ego strength would I consider complete which does not refer to the intrasystemic structures, that is, which does not take into account the relative preponderance of certain ego functions over others; for instance, whether or not the autonomous ego functions[1] are interfered with by the defensive functions, and also the extent to which the energies the various ego functions use are neutralized. No doubt what Freud (1937a) says about resistances in a certain sense being segregated within the ego, or about splitting of the ego in the process of defense (1940b), or what Richard Sterba (1934) says about the splitting of the ego in analysis, are examples of intrasystemic thinking, and I could give quite a few others. What I want to state here is that those insights have so far been gained as byproducts rather than as results of a consistent scrutiny of intrasystemic synergistic and antagonistic relations, and that in many instances in which we speak of "the ego," a differential consideration of various ego functions is indicated.

All this is to show that analysis is gradually and unavoidably, though hesitantly, becoming a general psychology, including normal as well as pathological, nonconflictual as well as conflictual behavior (the two oppositions do not coincide); and that technique is likely to profit further from this development as it has constantly done since this trend was started by Freud.

I have so far not explicitly discussed that aspect of psychoanalysis which we usually designate as the structural point of view. Freud's older conception of the psychic apparatus described it in three strata: the conscious, the preconscious, and the unconscious. The most incisive change which took place in Freud's model of psychic

[1] For a more precise definition of primary and secondary autonomy, see Chapter 7.

personality can be pictured as adding to its description as a series of layers its representation as a (more or less) integrated whole, subdivisible in centers of mental functioning—these substructures being defined by their functions, and their demarcation being based on the fact that empirically he found greater coherence among some functions than among others (Hartmann, Kris and Loewenstein, 1946). This facilitates a multidimensional approach and, so far as psychoanalytic psychology and therapy goes, it has been rather generally accepted as being more useful in giving account of the dynamic and economic properties of mental life. In technique the concept of stratification proved very useful and still is, in so far as making unconscious processes conscious by way of the preconscious is clearly one main and constant factor responsible for our therapeutic results. However, based on the concept of layers and on resistance analysis—maybe because technique at times too violently encroached upon theory—the concept of historical stratification was developed by Wilhelm Reich (1933), and with it a picture of personality that is definitely prestructural, in terms of the development of psychoanalytic psychology. Nunberg (1928) had early warned against this simplification. Fenichel, too, in his book on technique (1941), realized some of its shortcomings and held that certain character disturbances show spontaneous chaotic situations in analysis; and that displacements of the psychic layers may be brought about by the patient's current life, as well as by instinctual temptations or reinforcement of anxiety. I may add that the factors counteracting the establishment of a clear-cut picture of historical stratification seem to be much more numerous. Displacements of historical layers are quite generally an essential part of mental life, as we see it in analysis. Without wishing to discuss that particular theory, it is mentioned in this connection because this approach—not the truest to fact, but obviously containing some truth—had the advantage of linking in the simplest and most radical way the "correct sequence of interpretations" with the patient's life history; but also because, after having outlived its usefulness in this radical form, it may have become more or less of a handicap. It may still be responsible for a certain rigidity in our approach, while we try to utilize more fully in our technique the implications of a structural versus a one-sided "layer" concept.

There is no doubt, however, that a great variety of approaches is gradually converging in this direction. This most clearly appears if one traces the subsequent vicissitudes and implications of the application of Freud's formula, "bringing unconsicous material into consciousness," in the development of psychoanalysis. The formula remained, while its meaning was broadened and deepened by Freud's growing insight into the structure of the neurotic conflict. Its topical significance had already been understood at the time of the *Studies on Hysteria* (1895). But soon Freud found that just to give the patient a translation of the derivatives of his unconscious was not enough. The next step was characterized by a more exact insight into the dynamic and economic problems of resistance, and by laying down accordingly rules for the "what," "when," and "how much" of interpretation; it was defined in its main aspects in Freud's papers on technique (1911-15). He advised the analyst not to select particular elements or problems to work on, but to start with whatever presents itself on the psychic surface, and to use interpretation mainly for the purpose of recognizing the resistance and making it conscious to the patient. Certainly not every analyst works exactly this way even today. Still, these are the fundaments of what we may call the standard analytic technique. Thus, "making the unconscious conscious" is invested with additional significance. The corresponding basic psychological progress is defined in Freud's papers on metapsychology.

Some years later, in the '20s, these principles became the subject of a thorough study, of active discussion, elaboration, and partial modification by other analysts. Soon this discussion came under the impact of the delineation of units of function (ego, id, superego), that is, of the structural aspect. Here, once more a fruitful interdependence of theory and practice became apparent. The unconscious nature of resistance, a fact found through clinical observation under the conditions of the analytic therapy, became a cornerstone in the development of Freud's later formulations of the unconscious aspects of the ego. No less important was the reverse influence of theory on clinical practice with patients. First of all, ego psychology meant, and means, a broadening of our field of view. "Good" theory helps us to discover the facts (for instance, to recognize a resistance as such), and it helps us to see the connections among facts. This part of our psychology also gives a deeper understanding of the forms and mechanisms of defense, and a more exact consideration of the details of the patient's inner experience and behavior; corresponding to this, on the side of technique, is a tendency toward more concrete, more specific interpretation. This approach includes in its scope the infinite variety of individual characteristics, and a degree of differentiation which had not been accessible to the previous, somewhat shadowy knowledge of ego functions. It also sharpened our eyes to the frequent identity of patterns in often widely divergent fields of an individual's behavior as described by Anna Freud.

One problem connected with this development I would like to discuss briefly here: speech and language. Freud found that in the transition from the unconscious to the preconscious state, a cathexis of verbal presentations is added to the thing-cathexis. Later, Nunberg (1937), already thinking along structural lines, described the role of the synthetic function of the ego in this process toward binding and assimilation. One may add that the function of the verbal element in the analytic situation is not limited to verbal cathexis and integration, but also comprises expression. I am referring to the specific role of speech in the analytic situation.[2] This, too, contributes toward fixing the previously unconscious element in the preconscious or conscious mind of the patient. Another structural function of the same process is due to the fact that the fixing of verbal symbols is in the development of the child linked with concept formation and

[2] See now Loewenstein (1956, 1957).

represents one main road toward objectivation; it plays a similar role in the analytic situation. It facilitates the patient's way to a better grasp of physical as well as psychic reality. Besides, the action of speaking has also a specific social meaning inasmuch as it serves communication, and in this respect becomes the object of the analysis of transference. There is also, of course, in speech the aspect of emotional discharge or abreaction. Finally, the influence of the superego on speech and language is familiar to us, especially from psychopathology. This is to say that the different aspects of speech and language, as described by psychologists and philosophers, become coherent and meaningful if viewed from the angle of our structural model, and that in this case actually all the structural implications have today become relevant for our handling of the analytic situation. In trying to clarify the technical aspects of the problems involved, we are actually following the lead of structural psychology.

The necessity for scrutinizing our patients' material as to its derivation from all the psychic systems, without bias in favor of one or the other, is nowadays rather generally accepted as a technical principle. Also we meet many situations in which even the familiar opposition of defense and instinct is losing much of its absolute character. Some of these situations are rather well known, as is the case in which defense is sexualized or—equally often—"aggressivized" (if I may use the expression); or instances in which an instinctual tendency is used for defensive purposes. Most of these cases can be handled according to general rules derived from what we know about the dynamics and economics of interpretation as, for instance: resistance interpretation precedes interpretation of content, etc. In other cases these rules do not prove subtle enough; unexpected and sometimes highly troublesome quantitative or qualitative side effects of interpretations may occur. This, then, is a problem that clearly transcends those technical situations I gave here as illustrations. If such incidental effects occur, our dosage or timing may have been wrong. But it may also be—and this is the more instructive case—that we have missed some structural implications though correctly following quantitative economic principles. It may be that we have considered this quantitative aspect of a resistance only and have not considered precisely enough how the same quantity may involve the various functions of the ego and the superego in a different degree. While concentrating on the analysis of a resistance, we are actually working on many parts of the field at the same time. But we are not always mindful of the possible side effects if we focus too exclusively on the duality "defense—warded-off impulse" only. General rules about the dynamics and economics of interpretation are incomplete as long as we do not consider that, besides the quantitative factors, the resistances represent also the ways in which the various psychic functions, directly or often indirectly, participate in defense—"participation" pointing to intersystemic and intrasystemic correlations, including also their genetic aspects, which here refers to the memory systems. Of course, we do know something about how to handle different forms of resistance differently even when they appear to be equivalent when looked at from the economic angle. I made my point only because I feel that this structural aspect of interpretation is still less completely understood and less explicitly stated than its dynamic and economic aspects. One day we shall probably be able to formulate more systematically the rational element of our technique, that is "planning" the predictable outcome of our interventions, with respect to these structural implications.

This will in part depend on progress in a familiar field of analytic research: a deeper understanding of the choice and of the quantitative aspect of defense mechanisms, of their chronology, typical and individual, but above all else, of their genetic and economic interrelatedness with other functions of the ego. To touch at least on one of the genetic problems involved, we can assume that many defense mechanisms are traceable to primitive defensive actions against the outside world, which in part probably belong to the ego's primary autonomy, and that only later, in situations of psychic conflicts, do they develop into what we specifically call mechanisms of defense. Also, we can say of many of them that after having been established as such, they become in a secondary way invested with other functions (intellectualization, for example). This makes for a complicated overlapping of their role as resistances with various other functions they represent. It is because of this, that if we want to analyze defenses in a rational way, we have to consider their structural, their intersystemic and intrasystemic ramifications, beyond the aspect of resistance they offer to analysis. This is, of course, known in principle, but in a way our knowledge in this respect is not always specific enough. Genetically, some of the pertinent questions of structural psychology can be viewed from the angle of what, borrowing a term from biology, I called "change of function" (Hartmann, 1939a). It is part of what I now call "secondary autonomy."[3] It means relative functional independence, despite genetic continuity, and invites marking off more clearly the functional aspect from the genetic one. This relative independence may be more or less complete. In some cases it is practically irreversible under the conditions of "normal," everyday behavior. But we know from experience that even in many of these instances reversibility can be observed under special conditions, as in dreams, in neuroses and psychoses, and in analysis. It is because of this that the development of secondary autonomy can be made fruitful for the study of those phenomena of overlapping and of ramification which I have just mentioned.

I return to the problem of the incidental effects of interpretation, which frequently transcend our immediate concern with the specific drive-defense setup under consideration, and which are not always predictable. In trying to account in a general way for these and related observations stemming from various clinical sources, we assume that the process set in motion by a stimulus (interpretation being only one instance in question) produces not only, so to speak, "local" reactions. It goes beyond the stimulated "area," changing the balance of mental energies and affecting a variety of aspects of the

[3] In describing similar phenomena, Gordon Allport (1937) has used the term "functional autonomy," approaching the problem from an angle that is closer to psychoanalytic thinking than he seems to assume.

dynamic system. This process activates or sets in a state of preparedness elements functionally and genetically connected with it; its appeal often reaches from one system into the others, and its unconscious side effects may transcend the barriers of countercathexis. It would, however, be rash to assume that these "connections" can always be fully understood in terms of the principles of mere associationism. In contrast to the associationist approach, we imply the presence not only of dynamic but also of structural factors. Also, psychoanalysis, while often using the language of associationism, has from the very first differed from it and does so even more since principles of organization and structure have explicitly become an essential part of our theory.

What I have in mind could be designated briefly as the "principle of multiple appeal." I wish to introduce this approach tentatively, without discussing alternative propositions. A somewhat similar physiological conception has been advanced by brain physiologists, some of whom use the term "resonance effect." I also want to mention that Federn (1938), to some extent, thought along similar lines in trying to prove his point that there is, in the brain, conduction not based on neural pathways—which, however, has no immediate bearing on our problem.

In considering changes in cathexis less as isolated phenomena but rather as occurring in a "field," we are in agreement with a trend in modern science that has proved its fruitfulness in a great variety of domains. I think that as to the phenomena considered here, the introduction of the field concept may facilitate understanding. But I must add that to translate the whole of analytic psychology into field psychology seems hardly feasible without doing it considerable violence—despite the repeated demands voiced by representatives of field theory in psychology.

As in this short paper I have touched on a long list of subjects, I shall summarize. In comparing theoretical and technical development, I believe that the lag today is rather on the side of technique.

In the process of gradual replacement of the older layer concepts by structural concepts, not all the implications have so far been realized. One example is given of how the gradual realization of structural thinking has evolved and helped toward a better understanding and a better utilization of analytic material, in discussing the structural implications of speech and language in analysis. On the technical side, our technique of interpretation has so far been better understood and made more explicit in its dynamic and economic than in its structural aspects. Certain incidental effects of interpretation which, though familiar to all of us, have not yet been taken sufficiently into account by our theory or technique, need closer investigation. In concluding I try to show that it may prove useful to view certain related problems of psychoanalytic psychology from the angle of a "principle of multiple appeal."

CHAPTER 9

The Mutual Influences in the Development of Ego and Id

(1952)

I CANNOT say that I feel too much at ease in introducing this symposium on The Mutual Influences in the Development of Ego and Id. There is in analysis hardly a topic that is more comprehensive. Whatever I could tell you would hardly add up to an integrated picture. The time allotted would not even suffice for a catalogue of the problems involved. But I do hope that this very difficulty, of which you are no doubt as well aware as I am, will prevent you from accusing me of any sins of omission; and that you will extend to me the privilege of a personal approach: the right to accentuate freely and, above all, to select for my presentation only certain aspects of our problem, while discarding many others, though they may be of equal importance for an integrated psychoanalytic theory of development.

I shall submit to you for discussion some possible avenues of approach, trying to place the problem, as it were; make a few suggestions for clarifying, evolving, and integrating some of its aspects; and will start, as is customary, with some historical remarks, which, however, I shall try to limit to a minimum.

The concept of an ego you find already in Freud's physiological psychology of 1895 and in some clinical papers dating from the same period. These first formulations were followed by years of great discoveries: the psychological foundation of analysis in *The Interpretation of Dreams;* the libido theory; the insight into the etiology of neurosis; the *genetic turn*—that is, the discovery of the decisive relevance of early life history; and the development of psychoanalytic technique. During these years the role of the ego is little emphasized and at times even completely submerged under the impact of the theory of instincts. Only in the 20s was ego psychology explicitly defined as a legitimate chapter of analysis. The ego evolves as one system of personality, clearly set apart from the functions of the id and of the superego. This renaissance of the ego concept encompasses Freud's insights into the unconscious and the instinctual drives, the disregard of which had been a deadly limitation of the usefulness of other, preanalytic concepts of the ego. Freud outlined an ego which, in comparison with his earlier formulations, is infinitely richer in importance, dimensions, and specificity of functions. On this later level Freud's ego concept, though elements of early formulations have been integrated, appears as something essentially new, also as to its effects, because of the revolutionizing impact it had on the development of many aspects of psychoanalysis, including the theory of instinctual drives. This development, by the way, always struck me as one rather clear-cut example of a tenet of the philosophy of Hegel, who saw the evolution of concepts in terms of thesis, antithesis, and synthesis.

To approach more closely the ego-id problems under discussion today, we may say that this growing in stature of the ego's role in Freud's thinking can be seen: structurally, in its description as a partly independent unit of personality; dynamically, in Freud's warnings against a simplifying generalization he had noticed in the work of some analysts, which tended to underrate the ego's strength vis-à-vis the id (see also A. Freud, 1936); economically, in the hypothesis of its being fed by a mode of energy different from that of the drives. The independent aspect of the ego is even more conspicuously stressed in one of Freud's later propositions, suggesting the hereditary nature of some of its elements.

In developing his ideas on ego-id relationship, Freud followed the lead of technical and clinical as well as theoretical insights. The interest in these problems extends from technological detail to the most abstract level of theory formation. However, we should not forget that the aspects of the ego we see, viewing it from the angle of resistances, are not necessarily the same as those which are in the foreground in the study of, let us say, psychosis, and neither the one nor the other of these groups of aspects will fully coincide with that part of the ego which becomes visible in the direct observation of children. Thus, partial ego concepts developed which Freud succeeded in integrating in his more general propositions. Different facets of Freud's thinking on ego and id have been worked out by different analysts in different directions. Besides the nature of the data used, theoretical preferences have an obvious influence on an analyst's centering his research on one rather than on another of these partial concepts of the ego. To emphasize only one partial concept of the ego, at the expense of other aspects, may be a question of expediency vis-à-vis specific problems. But we shall remember that the reality ego, the defensive ego, the organizing, the rational, the social ego; the ego that leads a shadowy existence between the great powers, the id and the superego; the ego evolving under the pressure of anxiety situations none of these are "the ego" in the sense of analytic psychology. These are partial concepts to be distinguished from Freud's general ego concept.

Freud knew that the reliability of our statements and particularly of our predictions depends, in analysis, as in other sciences, on how comprehensive and consistent a general theory has been developed. He wanted to get insight "into the entirety of mental functions," as he wrote very early. That is, he aimed, as he repeatedly said, beyond his clinical research at what one could call general psychology, encompassing normal phenomena as well as pathological ones. This has remained one trend in his work through all the years. Its outline in

Freud's work is considerably more comprehensive than what has yet been systematically elaborated in psychoanalysis. He often said that his not yet having dealt with some problem did not imply his negating its relevance.

I mention this here because what we are discussing today is actually one aspect—perhaps the most important one in the present situation of analysis—of such an analytic approach to general psychology. It obviously transcends a narrower concept of analysis that would limit it to the understanding and therapy of neurosis. It aims at normal as well as pathological development. Secondly, dealing with these developmental problems often also transcends what is directly accessible to the psychoanalytic method. I am speaking of the child's growth and development up to the end of the preverbal stage. Still, this trend in analytic research is relevant also for a better understanding of clinical and technical problems, and it will become important particularly in regard to questions of mental prophylaxis.

Guarded extrapolations from what we know about later stages of development to earlier stages are widely used in the genetic hypotheses of psychoanalysis. It is amazing how much analytic reconstruction has taught us even about those primordial stages. Still, a host of questions concerning the relative relevance of our various constructs, the chronology in the development of different functions, and so on, remain controversial. In this situation the most auspicious development is the recent introduction of direct observation of the growing infant and child by analysts or at least analytically trained observers (see A. Freud and others). This can be helpful in checking our genetic hypotheses against observational data; and it can be decisive in giving us positive clues for the formation of hypotheses. We can learn from the correlation of reconstructive data with data of direct child observation how the latter can be used as indicators of structurally central developments, etc. This trend has already given our knowledge of early ego-id development an incomparably greater concreteness, especially as to its reality aspects. Here, then, not only the "negative" aspect of the ego, its role as adversary of the drives, but also many other specific ego functions and their interrelatedness become of necessity a legitimate concern of the analyst. This is a decisive step toward a general analytic theory of motivation.

It has also become apparent, I think, that to speak of the ego in a summarizing way as, let us say, threatened by the id or helpless vis-à-vis the id, as is often done, is no longer a sufficient description of developmental reality even in those early stages. It is not always advisable to conceive of these relations between ego and id as if they were just two opposing camps (Freud, 1926a). The object of research is the great variety of developing ego functions, in their antagonistic but often also synergistic interdependence with the id, and their differential consideration (intrasystemic approach; see Chapter 8).

In speaking of the mutual influences in the development of ego and id, we are used to considering the former, more often, the dependent, the latter, more often, the independent variable. We are impressed by the flexibility, by the learning capacities of at least parts of the ego, and, on the other hand, by the stubborn opposition to change of the instinctual drives. Still, there are those changes in the id that are brought about by the growth or development of the instinctual drives through all their subsequent phases; also, the ego can take a measure of influence by draining the instinctual energies of the id or damming them up; there are those modifications that, via the ego, analysis can induce in the id; there is, although it may not yet be fully understood, the id aspect of the outcome of repression (see also E. Bibring, 1937). Freud (1926a) felt that his originally general assumption that repressed impulses remain unchanged in the id might be in need of revision. This might not be the only possible outcome of repression. Two cases would have to be considered: "mere repression and the true disappearance of an old desire or impulse." Repressed instinctual tendencies may lose their cathexes, which could then be used in different ways. In the case of the breakdown of the oedipus complex, according to Freud, they are sublimated and used in the resulting identifications. In other cases one may think of a kind of displacement of these energies that might help to promote the next step in instinctual development, an important proposition which has been suggested by A. Katan (1937)

The strength of the ego in its relationships with the id lies in finding ways that make discharge possible; or, in other cases, in imposing changes of aims, or of the modes of energy involved; in the capacity to build countercathexes; in its control of perception and motility, and in its use of the danger signal and access to the pleasure-unpleasure principle. One aspect of ego development can be described as following, in several respects, the lead of the drives. We are used to speaking of an oral and anal ego, and so on, and trace specific ego attitudes to specific libidinal characteristics of the correlated phase. This aspect shows the phases of ego development in close connection with the sequence of libidinal phases. However, while rich clinical material and also data of direct observation testify to the importance of this relation, the ways in which ego attitudes are formed by the characteristics of the libidinal phase are not always clear. I think that in some cases the characteristics both of the instinctual tendencies and of the attitudes of the ego may have a common origin in the undifferentiated phase. Of giving, getting, etc., we can assume that they are modeled after instinctual patterns. A partial modeling after instinctual patterns we may also assume in the case of some defense mechanisms, for instance, in identification and projection (Hartmann, 1939a). But to describe ego formation only in terms of its dependence on instinctual development results in an incomplete picture. This is only one of its facets, among several, a point to which I shall return in more detail later. While describing the development of the child in terms of libidinal phases, we are today very much aware of the fact that cross-sections of development cannot be completely described in referring only to libidinal aims—not even if we include the corresponding object relationships in our description. We have to describe them also with respect to the involvement of two other series of factors: the vicissitudes of aggressive drives and the partly independent elements in the ego. It might well be that even the timing and the individual formation of the typical phases could, to some extent, be traced to individual variations of ego development, e.g., to the precocity of certain of its functions, which might become relevant also for pathology (see Chapter 6).

Some aspects of earliest ego-id interrelations could be partly clarified through the study of regressive phenomena in psychosis,[1] and also, for instance, of the phenomena occurring during the process of falling asleep (Isakower, 1938). For the understanding of the same problems, in some instances, and of different ones in others, the approach through the study of the body ego and of object relations has proved essential. The body being the mediator between the inner and outer world, and what we call objects being the emotionally most relevant representatives of the latter, the approach through the body ego and the object relations is also the preferred access to studying how ego-id relations develop in the individual's interaction with the environment. The development of the body ego will be discussed by Hoffer (1952). I shall at this point say a few words about those facets of object relations that seem relevant to our discussion. Freud (1926a) found that as a consequence of the protracted helplessness and dependence of the human child, "the influence of the real external world . . . is intensified and an early differentiation between the ego and the id is promoted. Moreover, the dangers of the external world have a greater importance for it, so that the value of the object which can alone protect it against them . . . is enormously enhanced" (p. 154f.). We may also say that in the human the pleasure principle is frequently an unreliable guide to self-preservation, and that the id, as Freud once said, neglects it. For this reason, the development of a specific organ of learning and

---

[1] I may add that today, as one consequence of progress in analytic child psychology, a clarification also in the opposite direction, from the knowledge about infancy and early childhood to a better understanding of psychosis, seems to be well under way.

adaptation, the ego, has become of vital importance. This we could call a circular process. The ego-id differentiation complicates the relations between pleasure and preservation of the individual. The id, in obvious contrast to the instincts of the animals, neglects the latter. But this very fact probably acts as a stimulus for further ego-id differentiation (Chapter 4). I am emphasizing here the specifically human side of these problems, the distinction between ego-id structures of man and the instincts of lower animals, as a basis for later discussion of ego-id differentiation.

It is in approaching the problem of the child's interaction with his objects, of his indulgences and frustrations, that the study of the "reality factor" and the interest in ever more specific situations in the child's life became particularly meaningful—what Kris (1950b) called the "new consideration for the environment." On the side of theory, one aspect of this trend is clearly based on that part of Freud's reformulations which traces internal danger situations to external ones, and on the subsequent work of A. Freud and others. For the time being it is this trend in analysis, above others, which quite naturally leads to a development that was briefly mentioned before: the integration of the reconstructive data of analysis with data gained from the systematic, not merely occasional, use of direct observation of children, and to an increased concern for a more inclusive view of child development. Some of these studies, as you know, also include an investigation of the most important objects in the child's life (mostly the mother, who is studied together with the child). Thus, for instance, the relevance of the mother's conflicts in the shaping of the child's attitudes and defenses can sometimes be traced (Jackson and Klatskin, 1950).

Such newer studies show in detail the participation of instinctual and ego tendencies in the development of the child's object relations. What we call "satisfactory object relations" has an id aspect, but obviously also an ego aspect. In recent years the impact of incomplete or empty relationships with the mother on ego development has been emphasized repeatedly (Durfee and Wolf, 1933; Ribble,

1943; Spitz, 1945; and others). While these findings are valuable and no doubt valid, the danger of overemphasizing and oversimplifying this side has not always been avoided. The fact that the mother has "rejected" her child in one way or another is frequently, in unilinear causal relation and rather indiscriminately, made responsible for nearly all varieties of later pathological developments and particularly of ego disturbances. That the ego needs, in order properly to function and to develop, a secure relation not only to the drives but also to the objects is obviously true. But ego development and object relationships are correlated in more complex ways than some recent works would let us believe—which we could already expect on theoretical grounds. We do not know much about corrections of very early unsatisfactory situations through later maturational processes.[2] It might also be that on the one hand "poor" early object relations can sometimes be made up for by later ego development, and on the other that so-called "good" object relations may become a developmental handicap—probably, I should think, if and in so far as the child has not succeeded in utilizing them for the strengthening of his ego. Also there is a long way from the object that exists only as long as it is need satisfying to that form of satisfactory object relations that includes object constancy. The work done by A. Freud and her co-workers has an immediate bearing on this subject. This constancy probably presupposes on the side of the ego a certain degree of neutralization of aggressive as well as libidinal energy (a concept we shall discuss later); and on the other hand it might well be that it promotes neutralization.[3] That is, "satisfactory object relation" can only be assessed if we also consider what it means in terms of ego development.

Of all the manifold relationships between ego and id, we are in analysis most familiar with that of conflict, the relationship in which

---

[2] See, however, Lois Murphy (1944); also Beres and Obers (1950); and the important paper by A. Freud and S. Dann (1951).

[3] For this second aspect see also A. Freud (1949) and E. Kris (1950b).

the instinctual drives come to be considered as a danger—in which case the anxiety signal induces defense of the ego. It is the one most immediately relevant for our clinical work and at the same time, because of specific features of our technique, the one best accessible to our method. Thus we owe most of our clinical knowledge on the interaction of ego and id to the study of conflict.

However, we also speak of collaboration of ego and id and in doing so seem to point to a variety of processes: the ego may serve the aims of the id; or the energy of the id is available for the aims of the ego; there may be substitution of ego aims for id aims, or neutralization of instinctual energy. The two last-mentioned processes often go together but may also vary partly independently, as in the case in sexualization.

What the methods used by the ego and its defensive actions are, and what these mechanisms mean in terms of the ego and of the id, has been stated with great precision in the classical contributions of Freud (1926a), Anna Freud (1936), Nunberg (1932), and others. Freud's ideas about countercathexis gave us a metapsychological grasp of the ego aspect. This fundamentally significant subject, conflict and defense, is today among the best known chapters of analytic theory, technique, and clinical practice, though some aspects, as for instance the chronology of defense mechanisms, still pose a number of un-solved problems.

At this point I want to discuss only some aspects, developmentally relevant but more or less at the periphery, of defense itself. It has proved useful to isolate for specific purposes the setup "defensive action—warded-off impulse." But, of course, for the developmental approach—and, for that matter, even sometimes for the clinical or technical aspects—it becomes relevant and indeed necessary also to ask how in a developmental cross-section or in a longitudinal sec-tion, considering the predisposition to or the precursors (and also the aftermaths) of defense, this setup is interrelated to other functions of the ego. This is what I had in mind in speaking of the interrela-tion of the conflictual and nonconflictual spheres of the ego (1939a).

Factors in the nonconflictual sphere codetermine the methods by which instinctual stimuli are dealt with, or, more specifically, the ways of conflict solution, and are in turn influenced by the latter. To study these processes seems particularly relevant in the early stages in which not only the use but the development of the defense mechanisms is in question.

There is a factor of another order that may influence conflict, a factor whose origin also transcends the factors immediately involved in the conflict situation. I am thinking of a proposition formulated by Freud in one of his last papers; it has so far been given little attention. Freud (1937a) suggests that there may exist an individually varying tendency toward conflict which, independent of the conflict situation itself, could be correlated with the presence, or the amount, of free aggression. He suggests that we might ". . . review all of our knowledge of psychical conflicts from this new angle." Earlier I tried to develop Freud's suggestion in a specific direction (see Chapter 7), about which I shall say a few words later.

In the context of today's discussion we may ask what the antecedents of the ego's turning against the id are. This direction of the interest of some analysts is somewhat analogous to the turning toward the preoedipal phases, after the main aspects of the oedipal situation had been explored. In what follows, I shall merely touch on a few points of the earliest phases of this development. In the last part of my paper I shall then turn to a later phase: to an evaluation of the ways in which conflicts with the id have been dealt with and their more remote consequences for the ego.

Earliest stages of ego development can be described from several angles: as a process of differentiation that leads to a more complete demarcation of ego and id and of self and outer reality; as a process that leads from the pleasure to the reality ego; as the development of the reality principle; as the way leading from primary narcissism to object relationships; from the point of view of the sequence of danger situations; as the development of the secondary process, etc. The important thing for a systematic study of the subject, which, as I said, is not intended here, would be to clarify the interrelatedness of all these aspects of ego development.

In the earliest postnatal stage it is difficult to disentangle the nuclei of functions that will later serve the ego from those we attribute to the id. Also, it is often hard to decide what part of it could already be described in terms of mental functioning. Neither is there at that stage any differentiation of the self from the world outside. It is clear that there is no ego in the sense we use the term for later stages; what the state of the id is at that level is unknown. This stage we may term the undifferentiated stage (Hartmann, 1939a; Hartmann, Kris, and Loewenstein, 1946). This conception of the earliest postnatal stage seems to be in agreement with Freud's later thoughts. At least once, in the *Outline* (1940), he speaks of ". . . the id, or rather, the undifferentiated ego-id."

In speaking of ego-id differentiation, Freud introduces hypotheses some of which clearly follow anatomical or physiological models; and he uses not only ontogenetic but also phylogenetic hypotheses. I am not concerned here with studying the interrelation of onto-genetic and phylogenetic propositions, interesting as such an attempt might be. Also, our acceptance of phylogenetic hypotheses depends more on our adherence to this or that school of evolutionism than on our analytic experience and thinking. Be that as it may, in the present context it becomes important clearly to demarcate the two sets of hypotheses.

In ontogenesis, the id-ego differentiation follows the leads of outer and inner perception, of motility, and of the systems of preconscious memory traces, of experience and learning. The replacement of hallu-cination by thinking, of direct motor discharge by action, is an essen-tial element in Freud's theory of ego development. The body in its double position as part of the inner and also of the outer world plays a decisive role in this process—above all, as Freud said, its surface, but also those stimuli that reach the mental apparatus from the inside of the body, and, in a specific way, pain. After Freud, Schilder (1938), Bychowski (1943), Scott (1948), Hoffer (1949, 1950) have helped us to get some glimpses into these many-faceted developments. Hoffer's recent studies of the early connections between oral functions and the use of the hand, and of the role they play in the development of the primitive ego, have clarified one of the earliest and most consequential steps.

I shall discuss one aspect of these differentiating processes in greater detail; not necessarily because it is the one that seems most important, but because its role in ego development has not always been clearly realized. Generally speaking, the apparatus serving perception, motility, and others that underlie ego functions, seem, in the infant, to be activated by instinctual needs. Their use independent of immediate needs, and in a more differentiated relation with external stimuli, is already part of the development of the reality ego. But they are not created by the needs. These apparatus, as well as those that account for the phenomena of memory, are partly inborn; they cannot be traced, in the individual, to the influence of the instincts and of reality, and their maturation follows certain laws which are also part of our inheritance.[4] They will gradually come under the control of the ego; on the other hand, they act on the ego and its subsequent phases of development (Hartmann, 1939a; Chapter 7). They can also be considered as one factor among those to which the ego-id differentiation can be traced. Here, then, is one of the points where phylogenetic hypotheses have to be clearly set apart from ontogenetic ones, if we want to avoid misunderstandings. The differentiation of ego and id, developed by whatever process of evolution through hundreds of thousands of years, is, in the form of a

[4] It is rather generally accepted in biology that part of what we call maturation is developed without the guidance of function as such, and that it may have adaptive significance only in reference to its future function (P. Weiss, 1949). However, the same author adds that there is, of course, no rigid preadaptedness "to fit precisely one particular detailed course of life." For the difference between adaptedness and adaptation see also Hartmann (1939a).

disposition, in part an innate character in man. That is, this differentiation does not start from scratch in every newborn child.

It is tempting to view this aspect of ego development in a way analogous in principle, though not in extent, to that which we have long since accepted in accounting for the libidinal phases. In tracing their significance we are used to considering the anatomical and physiological growth processes underlying them. Freud mentions the importance of the appearance of the teeth, the development of the anal sphincters, etc. I think something similar holds good for the development of the ego—maturational processes in the motor apparatus and the interaction with specific ego functions we may consider one case in point. A detailed knowledge of the stages of development on the side of the ego will be our most valuable guide in extrapolating reconstruction—in deciding what degrees of differentiation and integration of function, what degree of mechanism formation, can be assumed to exist on a given developmental level. Again, here as elsewhere, the fact that I emphasize in this context one facet—in this case, maturation—should not be misconstrued as any underrating of the specific importance of learning processes for the development of the ego.

This consideration of maturational processes also on the side of ego development seems natural enough if we keep in mind that the ego aspect of development is no less "biological" than its id aspect. It seems hard to call nonbiological the functions of adaptation and of synthesis, or integration, or organization (that is, the centralization of functional control), both of which we attribute to the ego. In a late paper (1940) Freud even attributes to the ego, and not to the instinctual drives, the function of self-preservation in man: "The ego has set itself the task of self-preservation, which the id appears to neglect" (p. 111). As to the physiological aspect of the problem, Freud always maintained that in some future time physiological data and concepts would be substituted for the psychological ones, referring to all mental functions and not only to those of the id. I may add that analysts as well as physiologists have, I think correctly, emphasized that it is particularly the study of the ego functions which might facilitate a meeting between the psychoanalytic and the physiological, especially the brain-physiological approach.

In the ego's relationship with the body, we can now describe three aspects: the postulated physiological processes underlying activities of the ego; those somatic apparatus that gradually come under the control of the ego and which in turn influence the timing, intensity, and direction of ego development; and, third, but not necessarily independent of the two others, those special structures that underlie what we call the body ego.

In his last years Freud thought that some aspects of the defense mechanisms may have a hereditary core. At the time he wrote *The Ego and the Id* he did not think that ego functions could be inherited the same way as he assumed that certain characteristics of the instinctual drives were. However, he states in "Analysis Terminable and Interminable" (1937a): "We have no reason to dispute the existence and importance of primary congenital variations in the ego," and "it does not imply a mystical over-valuation of heredity if we think it credible that, even before the ego exists, its subsequent lines of development, tendencies and reactions are already determined" (p. 343f.). I think that in this discussion we should not fail to consider these formulations of Freud's. The role of analysis, vis-à-vis this aspect of development, can be based on what Freud (1924c) once wrote in discussing hereditary versus environmental influences: " . . . it remains of interest to follow out how this innate programme is carried out and in what way accidental noxae exploit his [the individual's] disposition" (p. 174).

Those inborn characteristics of the ego and their maturation would then be a third force that acts upon ego development, besides the impact of reality and of the instinctual drives. We may call autonomous factors the elements on the side of the ego which originated in this hereditary core (primary autonomy). Their development is of course not independent from the development of other elements, but they enter this development as an independent variable (Hartmann, 1939a; Chapter 7).

It may be that very early processes in the autonomous area—cathectic organizations, but also physiological mechanisms that develop in interdependence with them, factors like postponement of discharge and also what Freud calls the protective barrier against stimuli (see also Bergman and Escalona, 1949), and even reflectory defenses against unpleasant stimuli—are genetically speaking precursors of what at a later stage we call defense mechanisms (Chapter 7).

In summarizing this part of my presentation, may I say that certain aspects of the choice and of the chronology of defense mechanisms might become better accessible to our understanding once we possess a closer insight into the development of their precursors. From the point of view of method, I may mention that at least some of them could be approached by direct observation. Little is known so far about the possible role of such factors in what has been called "primary" disturbances of the ego (see, for instance, Hendrick, 1951).

One should also try to describe all ego-id correlations with regard to their energic aspects. I believe, as Freud does, that the ego habitually uses a mode of energy different from that used by the drives. He speaks of desexualized and also of sublimated energy. We also know that if libidinal energy serving the functions of the ego comes too close to the state of instinctual energy (sexualization), this results in a disturbance of function. It does not seem to hazardous to enlarge this idea of Freud's to include neutralization of aggressive energy[5] which may serve functions of the ego and, maybe in a somewhat different state, also of the superego. If the modified aggressive energy used in the ego comes too near to the instinctual mode, this too may interfere with ego function, as is the case with libidinal energy

[5] See Chapter 4. This has also been done by K. Menninger (1938), Jeanne Lampl-de Groot (1947), etc.

(see Chapter 7). The term neutralization, used here and elsewhere, is meant to cover, besides what Freud called sublimation (which he limited to one of the vicissitudes of the libidinal drives), the analogous change in mode of aggressive drives.

If we assume the widest possible concept of neutralization (including sublimation), we may say that, though it may serve defense, it is of a far more general nature than other processes used for defensive purposes. Neutralization in this sense may well be a more or less constant process—if we are ready to assume that all the ego functions are continuously fed by it. But it is this very character that gives it its specific importance for the understanding of ego-id relations, also outside of the sphere of conflict.[6]

It is not unlikely that there exist, viewed from this angle, transitions between instinctual and fully neutralized energy. However, this does not imply that the maximum of neutralization leads in every case to the optimum of functioning. It is possible that aggression used by the superego against the ego is closer to the instinctual condition of energy than the one used by the ego in some of its functions. Probaby correlated with this aspect are the degrees to which the primary process has been replaced by the secondary process.

Neutralization of energy is clearly to be postulated from the time at which the ego evolves as a more or less demarcated substructure of personality. And viewed from another angle, we might expect that the formation of constant object relationships presupposes some degree of neutralization. But it is not unlikely that the use of this form of energy starts much earlier and that already the primordial forms of postponement and inhibition of discharge are fed by energy that is partly neutralized. Some countercathectic energy distributions

[6] Neutralization, even where it is used for defense, stands apart from other defensive techniques of the ego in so far as it is specially defined by its energic aspect (among others), which means here, by the change of one mode of energy into another one. That sublimation is not really a "mechanism" in the usual sense, Fenichel (1945) has clearly seen, and this holds good also for neutralization in general. Also, that its relation to countercathexis is different from the one we find in other forms of defense. However, I cannot follow Fenichel when he simply equates sublimation with successful defense.

probably arise in infancy. Again, these and related phenomena seem easier to understand if one accepts the hypothesis of gradations of neutralization as just outlined.

A further complication is added by the fact that we know a rather wide field of phenomena that we could describe as Janus-faced in the sense that one aspect shows the primary and the other the secondary process. To use Anna Freud's (1936) example, in displacement as a mechanism of defense, a characteristic of the primary process is used for the purposes of the ego. This we also clearly see in dreams. Moreover, processes we describe as vicissitudes of the instinctual drives may at the same time be used by the ego for its own purposes (see also Eidelberg, 1940). In the case of displacement, we may add that in a way it also is a primordial form of learning. It widens the child's experience and is a primitive basis on which the integration and differentiation of experiences may be built. I believe that M. Klein (1930) thought along similar lines in emphasizing the relevance of symbol formation for ego development.

There are many early and important developments which we have learned to consider as two-faced, that is, as to their ego and their id aspects. From the point of view of developmental psychology it becomes relevant to see whether the two aspects are coordinated in the way we would expect, according to our knowledge of parallel development in ego and id; on which side the functional accent—if I may say so—lies at a given stage; whether one of the aspects has outdistanced the other, etc. Cases in which the expected equilibrium between ego and id development is lacking often give us a good opportunity for insight into the psychological structure of the developmental phase in question. Sometimes a disorder in the typical sequence of danger situations may result. We find precipitating or retarding factors both on the side of the id and of the ego; precocious ego development, for instance, may be due to specific instinctual demands (danger situations); to early identifications; to an unusually early development of the body ego; to autonomous elements, etc. Here again I select for discussion only one developmental aspect of object relations. We can view them from the angle of the needs involved, but they also have a cognitive side, a perceptual side, and so on. "Object formation" has a somewhat different meaning in analytic and nonanalytic child psychology. Still, I emphasized long ago that what nonanalytic psychologists have carefully described in their experimental work as the evolving of constant and independent objects in the child's world (as tested, for instance, in the child's handling of toys, etc.), cannot be fully understood without considering the child's object relations in our sense (see also Spitz and Wolf, 1949). One may suggest that the element of identity and constancy in what one calls "objects" in the general sense is partly traceable to the element of constancy gradually developing in what we describe as libidinal or aggressive object cathexis —though, of course, other factors too, partly autonomous ones, are involved. The child learns to recognize "things" probably only in the process of forming more or less constant object relationships. We assume that progress in neutralization is involved in both steps, and that with regard to this factor both steps have a common origin. Further, the development of what one calls "intentionality"—the child's capacity to direct himself toward something, to aim at something, in perception, attention, action, etc., a process that according to Freud probably presupposes hypercathexis—could be viewed as one ego aspect of developing object relations. Actually, intentionality is among the first achievements of the child we would not hesitate to characterize as true ego functions. Others among the especially developmentally interesting, but little explored object-directed ego tendencies should be systematically approached in the same way.

To come back to the energic aspect. What Freud once called "the witch metapsychology" would, by any other name, be what we have to appeal to in questions of general psychoanalytic psychology. Actually today we consider it not so much as something "meta," beyond psychology, but just as the most general level of psychological concepts in analysis. In principle we should be able to describe all the relations we find between ego and id as to the modes of energy they use, but also in terms of cathexis. We are far from fulfilling this demand. Some aspects, after Freud, have been studied, for instance, by Glover and Rapaport. Kris (1950a) recently approached the problem of preconscious mental functions from this angle. The conscious and preconscious phenomena are characterized by the secondary process, one aspect of which is inhibition of discharge, and they are specific of the ego in contradistinction to the id. To describe the preconscious phenomena in metapsychological terms has become even more important since Freud (1940) no longer thought that another characteristic upon which he had previously relied—that is, the addition of word representations to thing representations—is typical of all preconscious mental processes. Evidently, for the questions of ego-id differentiation and interrelation, it is essential to trace how the secondary process originates. Glover (1935), taking his point of departure in the earliest systems of preconscious memory traces, describes the syntheses of such psychic elements associated with drive components of nuclei of ego formations. Out of this stage an organization of memory gradually evolves which has learned to consider elements of reality. Rapaport (1950, 1951) puts particular emphasis on the assumption that involuntary delay of instinctual discharge, due to external circumstances, can later be converted into an ability to delay, that is, into internal control. This hypothesis fits in rather well with what we recognize as one characteristic of ego development: that is, the gradual active use by the ego for its own purposes of primordial forms of dealing with stimuli (see Chapter 7). Internal control is one aspect of the problem of countercathexis, which Freud repeatedly tried to account for, and one fundamental aspect of ego-id differentiation. But the fundamental question, namely, in which way the original transformation of the primary energy distribution into that representing instinct control takes place, is still in need of further clarification. It might be, as I have already mentioned, that those inhibitory apparatus serving postponement of discharge, which are gradually integrated into the ego and which are probably also precursors of later defense mechanisms, play a role in the change of one mode of energy into another one. One may ask what we can say about the nature of the drive energies whose mode is being changed in the process of the formation of countercathexis. Again, it seems hazardous at present to venture a hypothesis with respect to this aspect of the primordial or precursory steps of differentiation. For a later stage, I tried to find an answer in the synthesis of two of Freud's hypotheses: the one, mentioned above, which says that free aggression may be an important factor in the disposition to conflict; and the other, which assumes that the features of defense against instinctual drives are modeled after defense in situations of danger from without. Withdrawal of cathexis would correspond to flight, and countercathexis to fight. On the basis of these two hypotheses we may develop the assumption (Chapter 7) that the ego's countercathexes against the drives are likely to be mostly fed by some shade of neutralized aggression, which nevertheless still retains some characteristics of the original drives (fight).[7] This assumption may well carry us a few steps further also in the understanding of pathological development. I think that the failure to achieve stable defenses, a failure we see in various forms of child pathology and which is also a crucial problem in schizophrenia, is to a large extent due to an impairment of the capacity to neutralize aggressive energy.[8] This hypothesis also implies a double correlation of stable defense with constant object relations, if what I said before is true: that the development of constant object relations on the one hand facilitates, but on the other also depends on, neutralization.

This hypothesis would imply that countercathexis may be a rather general way of utilizing aggression in one of its neutralized forms—a way different from the utilization of aggression in the service of the superego, though maybe not quite independent from it. It might

---

[7] A somewhat similar proposition was formulated by M. Brierley (1947).

[8] For another aspect of impairment of neutralization in the pathology of schizophrenia, see Chapters 7 and 10.

well be that the aggressive superego pressure on the ego also results in the ego's utilizing aggressive energy in its dealings with the id— a kind of turning one aggressive intersystemic relation (superego-ego) into another (ego-id). This may be one energic aspect (the aspect referring to the conditions and distributions of energy) of the role of the superego in repression, and other phenomena familiar to all of us from clinical experience. However, I do not think that this dependence of aggressive ego defense on the function of the superego applies to all of its forms; and it cannot apply, of course, to the early stages of defenses.

I shall devote the last part of my paper to one aspect of ego-id relationships at developmental stages at which the ego has already evolved as a definable psychic system with specific functions. It has acquired, through its prehistory, the capacity to institute and utilize some methods to avoid danger, anxiety, unpleasure. It has developed functions, such as objectivation, anticipation, thought, action, etc.; and it has achieved a more or less reliable synthesis, or integration, or organization, of its own functions and of the whole of psychic personality. The very complexity of the system tends to increase its lability, as Freud has pointed out. However, we find that various functions of the ego may achieve various degrees of virtual independence from conflicts and from regressive tendencies in various individuals. What I have in mind here is the question of their reversibility or irreversibility, the question of their relative stability vis-à-vis inner or outer stress. Obviously many, though not all, attitudes of the ego can be traced to genetic determinants in the id, to the sphere of the instincts—or also to defensive processes. We are used to see that ego interests and other ego tendencies may originate in narcissistic, exhibitionistic, aggressive, etc., drive tendencies. We also see that, for instance, reactive character formation, originating in defense against the drives, may gradually take over a host of other functions in the framework of the ego. That, under certain conditions, the ego's achievements can be reversible, we see in neurosis, psychosis, in the dream, in analysis. Beyond this, we may say that ego functions, if activated, often tend to exert an appeal, sometimes more, sometimes less marked, on their unconscious genetic determinants; also that an attraction from the latter to the former takes place; and there is no doubt that some of this we find also in the normal waking life of what we would call healthy people. But there are relevant differences in the degree to which ego functions maintain their stability, their freedom from those potential regressions to their genetic antecedents. At any rate, in the healthy adult this partial reversibility is not incisive enough to create serious trouble. The degree of secondary autonomy, as I have called this resistivity of ego functions against regression, is a problem equally relevant for our clinical, theoretical, and technical work. It is closely linked up with what we call ego strength and probably is the best way to assess it. The problem of secondary autonomy obviously also overlaps with the problem of mental health and has to be studied in normal development as well as from the angle of pathology.[9]

The relative independence of ego functions from id pressure can be expressed in terms of distance from ego-id conflicts, or distance from the regressive trends exerted by the id determinants. One aspect of the latter can, in terms of the energies involved, also be described as distance from sexualization or aggressivization. As to the developmental aspect of the ego functions' distance from conflict and distance from the drives, it appears relevant that newly acquired ego functions show a high degree of reversibility in the child who uses special devices in his effort to counteract regression (A. Freud, 1951a; Kris, 1951b).

I may add that occasional regressions in the service of the ego (Kris) can be tolerated by the adult ego if its functions are unimpaired. We also know that the healthy ego, for certain purposes, has to be able to abandon itself to the id (as in sleep, or in intercourse). There are also other less well-studied situations in which the ego itself induces a temporary discarding of some of its most highly dif-

[9] I decided, maybe somewhat arbitrarily, to omit from my discussion those aspects of "autonomy" that relate to superego function.

ferentiated functions (Chapter 1). To do this, not only without impairment of normal function but even to its benefit, is an achievement that has to be learned. The child up to a certain age is not capable of using this mechanism, or feels threatened by its attempted use. I think that this is probably one reason why the child fails vis-à-vis the demand of free association (Hartmann, 1939a).

Severe irregularities in the development of autonomy are relevant in pathology, and some of these problems apparently belong to what B. Rank (1949) has called the "fragmented ego." We also have ample clinical evidence of the fact that even in the "normal adult" not all functions of the ego achieve the same degree of stability.[10]

In concluding this paper, may I remind you that in the history of psychoanalysis modifications of concepts or new formulations of hypotheses often followed the opening up of new areas of research, as is the case in other branches of scientific work. At the present time, the integration of reconstructive data with data gathered through direct observation of young children represents one of the more pressing demands on our analytic thinking. One aim of my contribution to this symposium was to facilitate the interrelation of these two sets of data. Some of the concepts and hypotheses I introduced, like the concept of primary autonomy, or of secondary autonomy, will appear unfamiliar to many of you. But I found them to be useful tools, especially in dealing with the type of developmental problems we are mostly concerned with in this symposium. Although they were not used by Freud, I think they are consistently developed along the lines of his developmental theories.

When Anna Freud wrote her book *The Ego and the Mechanisms of Defense,* she refuted, in her introduction, the opinion, still held by many analysts at the time, that stigmatized the theoretical study of the ego as something essentially nonanalytic or even anti-analytic. Since then, these studies have acquired full citizenship in analysis, on an equal level with the study of the id. There is no reason to as-

[10] It seems that certain phenomena described by J. Lampl-de Groot (1947) are relevant in this context.

sume that the desire to conquer "no-man's land" (to use an expression of E. Kris), to extend the reach of the analytic approach to psychological phenomena beyond its present limits, has come to an end. In Freud's ego psychology no less than in other parts of his work we find the kind of truths we would expect to be rather time-resisting. But there is little doubt that he considered his outline of ego psychology, monumental as it appears to us, as a beginning rather than as a systematic presentation—in contrast to, let us say, his psychology of the dream, or of libidinal development; and that he considered this outline in need, but also capable, of reformulation and elaboration.[11]

Concluding Remarks on the Function of
Theory in Psychoanalysis

This symposium was, of course, meant to be a symposium on theory.[12] It deals with developmental and structural propositions. Obviously, it would be impossible to present, on this occasion, the great variety of individual clinical material and of data of direct child observation which underlie our hypotheses. Theory is, in a way, abbreviation; but this is evidently not its only function. Our hypotheses help us to make of the raw material of our data a consistent and meaningful body of knowledge; only the formulation of definite propositions makes our knowledge testable, that is to say, accessible to verification or falsification, and gives us the basis for valid predictions; it

---

[11] I should like to emphasize here the very comprehensive character of the conceptual framework of Freud's ego psychology—though not all of its aspects and implications have so far been actually developed. It is more useful than any other we know to enhance our understanding also of those data of child development which have previously been found and described by other schools of psychologists. There is no reason for us not to avail ourselves of relevant observational data found by others (though their meaning will often be different if seen in our frame of reference), or not to study the methods they use. However, I want to emphasize here that it appears for the most part unnecessary, and often confusing, to borrow, as has sometimes been done, the conceptual framework and the general theories of development from other schools of psychology, or simply to superimpose other conceptual systems on that of Freud.

[12] These concluding remarks are further elaborated in "The Function of Theory in Psychoanalysis" (Hartmann, Kris, and Loewenstein, 1953).

also helps us to ask questions which are meaningful and fruitful, and is a useful tool in directing us toward areas of promising research. All this is well known and accepted elsewhere, and its importance in analysis is in principle not so much different from what it is in other branches of science. It would hardly be worth mentioning here, if it were not for the fact that the function of theory in analysis has not always been too well understood. One occasionally meets a tendency to limit psychoanalysis to a clinical specialty, and also a lack of awareness of how much, especially in analysis, the clinical approach owes to the highly complex structure of hypotheses developed by Freud and others. Some analysts are in the habit of disparaging theory by equating it with "speculation." Or we hear complaints that the limitless and colorful diversity of individual clinical experiences is reduced in the process of hypothesis formation—a view which again disregards the fact that this reduction is one of the most general and most necessary characteristics of every scientific endeavor. There is no analyst who is not fully aware of the fundamental relevance of clinical observation in our field. It is not easy to see why the relevance of theoretical thinking is not equally realized and why sometimes the natural emphasis on clinical data turns into a distrust of theory. The discussion of the role of hypotheses in psychoanalysis would no doubt deserve a special study. At this point I merely want to restate that analysis has been from its beginnings, and is most likely to be also in the future, more comprehensive in its outline, aims, and also means than its clinical aspect. I mentioned before that one trend in Freud's work through all the years aimed at a general psychological theory; to exclude it from psychoanalysis would—*mutatis mutandis*—be somewhat like excluding physiological theory from physical medicine. Also, while we know how much Freud's work owes to his supreme capacity of observation and to his unflinching objectivity vis-à-vis new facts, we should not forget the extent to which the formation of crucial concepts and of "good" hypotheses aided his discoveries as well as their meaningful interrelation. Actually, for a student of the history of analysis, Freud's work is a classical example of the point I am trying to make. It appears, from such study, as a constant mutual promotion of observation and hypothesis formation. We come to understand how much poorer in dimensions and less fruitful his clinical and technical work would have been, had his power of theorizing failed to equal the power of his clinical insight. I do not think that the necessity, not only to enrich our clinical experience but also to develop the body of hypotheses we use in dealing with it, is less obvious today than it was in Freud's time.

CHAPTER 10

Contribution to the Metapsychology of Schizophrenia

(1953)

D ISREGARDING Freud's tentative approach to the problems of psychosis in the nineties, we find in his work two main and characteristically different attempts to understand its specific pathology. I am speaking, of course, of his analysis of the Schreber case (1911b) and of two papers on neuroses and psychoses written thirteen years later (1924a, 1924d). During the interval some essential aspects of the psychology of psychosis had been clarified in his metapsychological papers. The differences between the early and the later work reflect Freud's growing interest in problems of structural psychology and particularly ego psychology. In one of the later papers it is clearly stated that "neurosis is the result of a conflict between the ego and the id, whereas psychosis is the analogous outcome of a similar disturbance in the relations between the ego and the external world" (1924a). The outline that Freud gave us in these papers, and the many hints he gave us in a series of others, have so far not yet been made the basis of a systematic theory of psychosis.

Historically we see in the analytic study of psychosis a mirroring of the trends of psychoanalytic psychology dominant at a given time. The next impulse might come from the advances in analytic child psychology, outstanding in the work of the last two decades. Actually, in saying this, I am not only speaking of the future; this trend has in part already been realized. For quite some time, the study of the regressive phenomena of psychosis has been utilized as one of the main avenues to our understanding of early childhood. While there is certainly no reason to assume that the promises of this approach are exhausted, we see today also a tendency in the opposite direction. What we owe to research in analytic child psychology—through retrospection or direct observation—is more fully utilized for a better understanding of psychosis and the disposition to psychosis. What has become known of the development of early object relationship, ego-id relationship, defenses, and reality testing, constitutes a vast reservoir of data which today we consider essential to any systematic approach also to psychosis. The increasing number of childhood psychoses or related ego disturbances studied in recent years (M. Klein, L. Bender, Kanner, Despert, Geleerd, Mahler, Rank, and others) is an essential part of this knowledge. This approach is the more important as we are aware of the fact that while regressive phenomena give us valuable information on some aspects of early childhood, they often provide us in other respects with a picture that is neither complete nor unambiguous; hence our etiological schemes, based on a study of regression, need to be tested by developmental data.

Freud knew that the instinctual and the ego aspects of the problem of psychosis have never been fully coordinated. If we follow what Freud says in the two later papers to which I referred, the factor that brings about psychosis is a conflict between the ego and a reality that has become intolerable. This seems to be borne out by the clinical findings in psychosis, at least in schizophrenia and in paranoia. However, the question of why some individuals react to a given conflict with reality by fully withdrawing from it, and with regression, could still only be partly answered.[1] Many of those reality factors are of a kind that most individuals would master without any

[1] For an interesting recent hypothesis, see Waelder (1951).

pathological consequences. The ego that reacts pathologically to those situations is very likely already a disturbed ego, but we know little about the specific nature of this vulnerability. In some respects the situation could remind one of that which prevailed in regard to neurosis at the time of the *Studies on Hysteria;* what was then considered as causing neurotic disturbances was later often found to be of an accidental and nonspecific nature, and it was only the later work of Freud that settled the etiological questions for the case of neurosis.

What Freud actually thought was that this conflict with reality, and the ensuing break with reality, could be traced either to features of reality itself or to increased pressure of the instinctual drives—the outcome being the same in both cases "in view of the rival claims made by the id and the external world upon the ego" (Freud, 1940a, p. 114). If in psychosis the ego withdraws from reality, it acts in the service of the id; the instinctual problems cannot be solved without its contact with reality being severed. However, with respect to what I shall say later, I would like to consider here a third factor, in addition to the two of which Freud spoke, which will emphasize more strongly the role of the ego in the process. Increased pressure on the ego by the drives may of course be, and often is, due to a real strengthening of the id forces. But there is the other possibility that, for whatever reasons, the ego's role as a mediator between the drives and reality is impaired: either the defensive countercathexes of the ego, or those ego functions that maintain the contact with reality, may be incompletely developed or weakened. Thus, while a break with reality could ensue in all these situations, "conflict with reality" can, as to its causative impact, be evaluated only by relating outer frustration not merely to the instinctual but also to the ego aspects of the situation.

This last point leads us to what we know about the structure of defense in psychosis, which I shall discuss at this point only as it relates to schizophrenia, and only as to some of its facets. One aspect is the deficiencies of repression and the consequences they have on

the libidinal and aggressive features of schizophrenia. It has sometimes been said—e.g., Nunberg (1920)—that the loss of object
libido destroys the repressions; but how this happens is not altogether
clear. Generally speaking, and keeping in mind the interrelation of
defenses against the outer and the inner worlds, repeatedly emphasized by Freud, one may say here that schizophrenics show a lowered
reactivity to all kinds of stresses (Redlich, 1952). But what is most
obviously lacking is the organized, ego-integrated stability of the
defenses, as compared to what we find in neurotics and in normal
persons. We know, too, that primitive defense mechanisms—turning
against one's own person, reversal into the opposite, projection, and
the most striking of all, the detachment of libido—are more characteristic of schizophrenia than those like repression that demand a
constant maintenance of countercathexes. This lowering of the
ego's defensive potential, first observed in the study of adult schizophrenics, has been confirmed by work with childhood schizophrenics.
Two factors stand out: while there probably is an increased tendency
toward conflict, there is at the same time an incapacity of the ego
to deal with it by the usual methods. What Hendrick (1951) said
about psychosis being "primarily a result of defect of functions
usually considered components of the ego," may be to the point here;
and one may think of a deficiency in those "primary autonomous"
precursors of defense which I discussed in Chapters 7 and 9; or of
some form of what B. Rank calls "ego fragmentation." If it is true
that the ego is a weak link in the psychological setup before the
outbreak of psychosis—maybe long before—we would like to know
more about the genetic side also of the defenses and their precursors.

Disturbed object relations in infancy or childhood have been
widely studied from many angles, not only in order to shed some
light on the fusion of self and world, a central problem in the symptomatology of schizophrenia, but also as to their possible meaning
in its etiology. To quote only a few studies among many, Mahler
(1952) has described two distinct groups of early psychoses: in the
first, the autistic group, the mother seems not to be cathected, while

in the second, the symbiotic group, the early infant-mother relationship is marked, but the representation of the mother is not separated from the self. I also remind you of the cases described by Anna Freud (1951c). She found that surrender to the love object is experienced as a return to primary identification, and these patients fear and defend themselves against this regressive dissolution of personality by a complete rejection of all objects. These cases have not developed schizophrenic psychosis, but they are to the point here because they shed light on another pathological development of early object relationship. In earlier and rarely quoted studies, Hermann (1936) has described that pair of functions: "clinging" to the mother and "going in search" of something away from the mother—aspects of object relationship, I should think, and not partial drives as Hermann supposes they are. But he has perceived some aspects of the pathology of those relations. Another contribution of his (1929) concerns his hypotheses about temperature orientation, and "flowing over," a precursor of projection. These ideas were seized upon by Bak (1939, 1943) in order to explain transitivism and the feeling of being influenced in schizophrenia. Temperature orientation, according to him, would be a causative genetic antecedent of identification and a model of object relation. While its causative role has not been proven, we may well consider it (and "flowing over") regular building blocks of one phase of self-object relations, and frequently later as one of their symbolic representations.

Narcissism and the Disturbance of Specific Ego Functions

The earliest stages of these self-object relations have usually been described as steps leading from primary narcissism to object relation. Essential pathological features of schizophrenic regression could be elucidated from this angle. We know the role of narcissism in causing disturbances of object relation—and also the role of impaired object relation in augmenting narcissism. Since the twenties, when Freud redefined ego functions in terms of his later views, a more differentiated—i.e., the structural—concept of ego-id relations has been more or less generally accepted among analysts, and the developmental description of object relation, on the one hand, and of the ego functions involved, on the other, became more concrete and specific. This broadens the range of our questioning, and also the access to the answers. I described two stages of object relation as the relation to the need-satisfying object and the achievement of object constancy. From another point of view, the emerging of the second from the first stage has also been described by M. Klein (1948) and Hoffer (1952). Anna Freud (1952) sees this progress in quantitative terms; it is, according to her, "determined by a decrease of the drives themselves." My own explanation (Chapter 9) of one aspect of it was that, at the later stage, constant relations with the object, independent of the state of the needs, can be maintained because of a partial change of instinctual to neutralized cathexis of the objects. This hypothesis is basic too for what I shall later develop in regard to the consequences of deneutralization in schizophrenia. It also goes well together with Anna Freud's formulation, if we assume, which I think we may, that neutralization of drive energy will change the balance between the instinctual and the noninstinctual forces and tend to decrease the urgency of the former.

Here I want to say a few words about another aspect of the separation of self and object, which also is a step toward the constancy of the latter. First the infant does not distinguish between the objects and his activities vis-à-vis the objects. In the words of Piaget (1937b), the object is still nothing but a prolongation of the child's activity. Later, in the course of those processes that lead to a distinction of object and self, the child also learns to make a distinction between his activity and the object toward which this activity is directed. The earlier stage may be correlated with magic action and probably represents a transitory step in ego (or, rather, pre-ego) development, interposed between simple discharge and true ego-directed and organized action. The later stage represents one aspect of "objectivation" which is an ego contribution to the development of object relations and an essential element in the institution of the reality principle. Piaget's finding agrees rather well with the findings of analysis, and it means, metapsychologically speaking, that from then on there is a difference between the cathexis of an object-directed ego function and the cathexis of an object representation.[2] I mention these points here because they have a bearing also on our understanding of psychosis, where it is important for us to realize these differences—particularly the second one that has sometimes been blurred in the common use of the term narcissism.

Time does not permit me to discuss intentionality—the capacity to orient oneself toward something, to aim at something, in perception, thought, and action—or attention and anticipation. They belong in the same category as objectivation in so far as they, too, are ego contributions to the building up and structuring of the object and partly also of the inner world. About reality testing I shall say a few words later.

Various forms of disorganization of thought characteristic of schizophrenia can be described in terms of the disturbance of the functions I just mentioned. Here also belongs the impairment (though usually not complete lack) of abstraction, the so-called "concreteness" of schizophrenic thinking, or what has been called its "symbolic" character. An important derangement of the anticipatory function is manifested in schizophrenic anxiety. While anxiety is a frequent and central phenomenon in schizophrenia, it appears that its use as a signal to announce and forestall danger is mostly defective (see also Mahler et al., 1949; K. Eissler, 1953). I also call attention to the impairment of that formation, or organization, of affects which is due to the ego (K. Eissler, 1953).

I shall discuss one of the disturbances in greater detail. One aspect of language plays an essential part in Freud's psychology of schizophrenia. It is the fact that words are subject to the primary process; or that they are treated as if they were things. In the course of the

---

[2] We shall see later an analogous distinction between ego function and self-representation.

schizophrenic process, while the ideas of the objects lose their cathexis, the preconscious verbal presentations connected with the objects become hypercathected.[3] The role of language in schizophrenia has, however, still another feature, which is the reason why I mention it in this connection. Generally speaking, we may attribute three functions to language (see K. Bühler, 1934): it expresses something in the speaker, emotion, for instance; it represents facts or relations of facts, it is what one has called propositional; and it provides signals for communication. The use of signals we also find in certain other animal species. But signals are "operators"—to use an expression of Charles Morris (1938)—while symbolic language (symbol here being used in a more general, not in a more specific analytic connotation) is "designatory." Most important in this context is the deficiency of the second, the propositional or representational function—I am speaking of words meaning something, pointing to something, stating something—that function by which, I would think, language, besides adding verbal to thing representation, is also that function by which the former is made to signify the latter. It is this relation between the word and what it stands for that is so frequently distorted in schizophrenia.[4] This impairment actually transcends language. If what in a normal person would be a symbol (I am now using this as an analytic term) is, in schizophrenia, treated as if it were identical with the object or relation it symbolizes, this is part of the same disturbance. I also want to remind you that the sudden and immediately evident accruing of "new meanings," the investment of banal perceptions with new and often portentous significance, is—though not much studied in analysis—one of the most characteristic symptoms of schizophrenia. It is actually much more characteristic of schizophrenic delusion than the oft-quoted "incorrigible sticking to erroneous opinions," which it shares with other psychopathological states and which is in certain cir-

[3] Freud's later formulation of the contents of the preconscious in his *Outline* (1940a) may indicate a changed approach also to this subject.

[4] I cannot discuss here the distortion in the use of grammar, comparatively frequent with schizophrenics.

cumstances common even in normal individuals. To come back to language: in its ontogeny, expressive sounds and attempts toward communication through them precede the development of its propositional aspect, which develops parallel with the emerging of the ego as a definite system of personality. The undoing of this step in schizophrenia is part of the ego's disintegration. What I had in mind here is to delineate in terms of specific ego function a phenomenon that Freud discovered long ago. If words are treated as if they were things, this is, looked at from this point of view, a loss in the representational function of the ego which normally allows differentiating the signs from what they signify. The keeping apart of the two belongs to that state and distribution of mental energy that we call the secondary process. That is why Freud could describe what happens to words in schizophrenia as their being subjected to the primary process.

Not all the ego functions to which I referred are interfered with in every case of schizophrenia—and this is true also of related childhood disorders (Rank and MacNaughton, 1950); some intellectual functions, for instance, may be preserved. And the ego apparatus—serving memory, perception, and so on—are usually intact; or at least they are certainly not damaged as they are in organic psychoses. It would be highly promising to see in the study of individual cases, or of types of cases, which of the functions I mentioned (and of others related to them that I did not mention) remain intact. Similarly Katan (1953) has recently asked for a closer examination of residual personality. Without an understanding of the residual personality, the pathological features cannot be fully understood. One would expect that the individual preservation of specific ego functions could be related to the degree of secondary autonomy (of resistivity against regression and sexualization or aggressivization) which these functions have reached in the course of childhood development—as we know from the analytic study of children that their tendency to regress is also dependent on the level of ego development (Chapter 9; A. Freud, 1952). But a variety of factors come into play in schizophrenia that make the correlation a more complex one, forcing us to admit that this question has not been sufficiently studied. Moreover, at the present stage of our knowledge, it is difficult to account for the fact that various types of schizophrenic psychoses tend to leave different parts of what in the normal are autonomous ego functions unimpaired.

In emphasizing the ego aspects of schizophrenia[5]—speaking of the deficiencies of defense, of the ego's contributions to object relations, and discussing the impairment of other partly object-directed ego functions—I do not, of course, want to neglect the instinctual factors involved, though I shall discuss only one aspect of them, referring to the economy of aggression. The reasons for my approach are reasons of expediency, dictated by the actual occasion of this presentation (that is, its necessary limitations) but also by the fact that at least some of the instinctual factors in schizophrenia—the detachment of libido, regression, the role of libidinal and aggressive vicissitudes in restitution—have been much more thoroughly studied so far; while the other aspect—the disturbance of the ego, as, e.g., the ego factor in fixation—though recognized in its importance, has never been well understood, or even sufficiently defined. Therefore, in this presentation I shall not go into whatever the nature of the instinctual problems (oedipal and preoedipal, bisexual, aggressive, etc.) may be which the ego tries to escape from in severing its ties with reality. However, I am aware that one of the principal aims of a theory of schizophrenia would be to establish greater continuity between its instinctual and its ego aspects. I shall discuss one such link which, I think, can be found in turning to the economic basis of the phenomena we observe.

Broadening of the Economic Approach

It will be necessary for that purpose to use a broader concept of the economic approach, which is usually understood to refer to the vicissitudes of quantities of mental energy, to include also the con-

---

[5] Freud mentioned the possibility of primary ego disturbances in schizophrenia, without, however, elaborating this idea.

sideration of the different modes or forms of this energy. Here we have to make two distinctions: one between libidinal and aggressive energy, which is commonly accepted, and another one in regard to the place of an energy quantum in the continuum from fully instinctual to fully neutralized energy. The degree to which its instinctual character has been transformed may coincide with the degree to which the primary process has been replaced by the secondary process.

This approach has its origin in Freud's statement (1923a) that ego functions work with a modified form of energy which he traces to the desexualization or sublimation of libido. The reasons why I and others had to widen his statement to account also for desaggressivized aggression are given elsewhere (Hartmann, Kris, Loewenstein, 1949). Sexualization or aggressivization of ego functions leads to their disturbance. Sexualization or aggressivization has, of course, here as elsewhere, one aspect which relates to regression.

I think that the concept of neutralization is relevant also for our understanding of schizophrenia, as it provides us with a vantage point from which several of its features appear to fall into line. One could try to describe the impairment of ego functions I cursorily discussed by reference to narcissistic regression, but such a description is necessarily incomplete. Narcissism is, strictly defined, libidinal cathexis of the self, not of the ego (Chapter 7). Its mode may be either instinctual or neutralized. A description from the angle of narcissism does not account for the distinction between "sexual overestimation" of the self, as we find it, e.g., in megalomania, and other forms of self-cathexis. Nor for the differences between "ego" and "self," or between the cathexis of the self-image (a complex of representations) and of ego functions—a distinction that is relevant in developmental psychology and in the pathology especially of psychoses. These ego functions are not all self-directed, as would be implied if we were to use in their description only a narrow concept of narcissism. What Freud calls typical ego functions, e.g., thought and action, may certainly be self-directed (oriented toward the self), but they may also be object-directed (oriented toward the outer world); in the latter case their cathexis does not mean increased interest in the self.

Freud, in the Schreber case (1911b), has given us a classical description of the pathological process in schizophrenia, the withdrawal of libido from the objects and its subsequent investment in the self. As I said in Chapter 7, the latter is not so much a "reaction" to the former; rather both represent different aspects of the same process. About the narcissistic character of the process there is no doubt. Still, in line with what I said before, one may try to describe the process not only quantitatively but also as to the degree of neutralization of the energies involved. Hypercathexis of the self, or of the ego functions, can hardly, by itself, be expected to account for the failure of the ego functions that we actually find impaired. You remember Freud's critical remarks of Jung, who would not accept his hypothesis that the detachment of the libido from the objects and their withdrawal into the self could cause the loss of reality in psychosis. I think that Freud's correlation of reality loss with libido withdrawal is very likely true. However, to the reasons why it is so I may add: the damaging effect of the withdrawal is due not only to the resulting hypercathexis of self (and ego functions) but also to the fact that in this process they (also the object-directed ego cathexes) are flooded with nonneutralized libido. Self-cathexis is sexualized, which leads to the "sexual overestimation" of the self, and so are at least part of the ego functions, which leads to functional trouble; even more so, because, as I shall discuss later, the schizophrenic ego's capacity for neutralization is damaged. The magic thinking and acting we find in schizophrenia is correlated with this process. The ego functions I described are normally dependent on the use of neutralized energy.

In the example I discussed, ego disintegration, then, is partly a result of object loss and sexualization. On the other hand, the capacity for full object relations and for neutralization, and the resistivity against object loss and deneutralization are in part rooted in ego development. The interconnection of the instinctual and ego aspects of object relation, as of the relation to the outer world in general, is clearly apparent in the development of the child. The ways in which, and the degree to which, objects are built or lost are codetermined by factors we attribute to the ego. Such data are important not only for our understanding of the schizophrenic process; they become particularly relevant as soon as we consider questions of etiology or of predisposition. They also give us a more precise picture of what "fixation" on the side of the ego may mean.

If frustrations, and particularly narcissistic injuries, which in other individuals would be of minor importance, are frequently capable of inducing a detachment of libido and precipitating a schizophrenic process, this is essentially due to the deficiency or to the lack of stabilized power of object relations and certain ego functions. The vulnerability of the schizophrenic ego to frustrations from without indicates that its relation to reality must have been damaged. This has often, and correctly, been described as the "weakness" of the schizophrenic ego (recently by Bychowski, 1952). But it seems relevant to specify the ego functions the impairment of which determines that "weakness." The schizophrenic ego cannot deal with those frustrations in the way they are normally dealt with, because its relations to reality, the object-directed functions I mentioned, and its faculties of defense and neutralization, are impaired. I am speaking of neutralization and not of sublimation, because this impairment also involves the transformations of aggressive energy which I shall discuss later; but the term neutralization is also wider in another respect. It refers not only to occasional energy transformations in certain conflict or danger situations. It comprehends likewise the probably continuous process by which instinctual energy is modified and placed in the service of the ego. Furthermore, in its secondary processes—and dispositions to secondary-process functions—the ego builds up a reservoir of neutralized energy, and energetic interchange takes place among the various aspects of ego activities (Chapter 7).

It has, of course, frequently been observed that in schizophrenia a breakdown of what is usually called sublimation takes place, though certain ego functions commonly resist disintegration. Not much has been made of such observations so far as the theory of schizophrenia is concerned. But I should think—I developed this idea in Chapter 9 —that the lability of neutralization, or its impairment, is a fundamental character of the ego disorder in schizophrenia.

The hypothesis of neutralization and deneutralization of aggressive as well as of libidinal energy also implies that an increase in aggressive strivings in their unmitigated mode would not necessarily be traceable to defusion of libido and aggression. Without undervaluing the importance of instinctual fusion and defusion, we might say that deneutralization is an additional factor to be considered in explaining such an increase in unmodified aggression.[6] By the way, this additional proposition allows a more direct empirical validation, e.g., in child psychology, than do our assumptions on instinct fusion and defusion. That the two factors under discussion—defusion and deneutralization—may be interrelated is possible (Hartmann, Kris, Loewenstein, 1949), but a positive statement in this matter would be premature.

In schizophrenia we commonly find defects in superego structure (Nunberg, 1932), which can partly be attributed to the detachment of libido and to regression. The disintegration of the superego structure often goes together with a great violence that has variously been described as "brutality" and "self-destructiveness," etc. (Zilboorg, 1930; Wexler, 1951; Pious, 1949; Rosenfeld, 1952). At the same time its ideal formation and libidinal aspects may be deranged. The outbursts of unusual violence of the schizophrenic superego may be described as a modification of its energy that brings its already normally aggressive cathexis even closer to the fully instinctual mode. However, a significant feature of the schizophrenic superego is the low level of organization, or integration and differentiation, on which it works; part of which is also its lack of stability or consistency. One

---

[6] Also the power of differentiation between the libidinal and the aggressive impulses (Rosenfeld, 1950) may well be considered from the angle of ego function and the faculty of neutralization.

gets the impression that those layers of it which are closest to the ego, which show the influence of the ego's synthetic and differentiating functions, the impact of all those ego functions that normally account, from a certain age on, for a comparatively stable and workable equilibrium between superego demands and the actual functioning of the ego, have been radically modified. I am, of course, aware that there are many other important facets to the more or less specific superego changes we find, among which the archaization of the predominant identifications seems to be of paramount importance.

Though terminology varies as to this point, I would prefer not to call a superego "strong" that can be erratically oversevere, but rather one that fulfills its functions in a stable and coherent way. One of the striking characteristics of the superego-ego relations in schizophrenia, though it is also not quite specific of schizophrenia, is the disparity of superego severity and the ego's capacity to enforce superego demands. This brings us back to the subject I broached above: the pathology of the defense mechanisms in schizophrenics.

Defense Mechanisms in Schizophrenia (Aggression and Countercathexis)

In Chapters 7 and 9, referring to two ideas of Freud, I stated the reasons which led me to assume that the energy used in countercathexes is probably as a rule one mode of neutralized aggression. Freud compares and partly traces defense against drives to defense in situations of danger from outside and to their main characteristics: fight and flight. Countercathexis used in ego-id conflicts, while being fed by neutralized aggression, would represent a mode of aggression in which at least one feature of the aggressive drive, that is, "fight," is still demonstrable. Yet we know from the study particularly of repression that it normally works with a comparatively high level of neutralization, higher than the one we would ascribe to the functions of the superego. This hypothesis of countercathexis as being based on the neutralization of aggression may prove helpful also for a clarification of certain problems in schizophrenia.

We come to the conclusion that the ego's capacity to defend itself against instinctual drives is—among others—dependent upon its capacity to neutralize aggression. This is true at least of those defense mechanisms, like repression, that presuppose a stable countercathexis. I presume that the schizophrenic's lowered ability to neutralize aggression is one of the main reasons for his failure to achieve workable defenses (Chapter 9); and for the prevalence in schizophrenics of such defense processes in the ego that demand a lesser degree of neutralization.[7] Failure or impairment of neutralization, and of the erection of stable defenses, can be studied in the child. I surmise that these defects—especially in their interrelations with defective object relations, about which I shall say a few words later—can be considered relevant in the predisposition to schizophrenia.

The relations of different forms of neutralized aggression to ego organization are manifold, and it is very likely that these modes of energy play an essential role in the cathexes of a great variety of ego functions. But here we are first of all concerned with defense. Countercathexis appears to be one typical way to utilize aggression (one transformation of aggression) for the aims of the ego. Free aggression can be used in its service if the capacity for neutralization is intact. If it is impaired, the defense mechanisms not only will be damaged and the control of the instincts thus be rendered more difficult; the relative strength of the instincts vis-à-vis the ego will also be increased as a result of the freeing of instinctual aggressive energy that had previously been neutralized in countercathexis.[8] This freed instinctual energy may then be turned against the outside.[9] Also all

---

[7] Again, as so often in biology, the relationship is mutual. The process of libido detachment may, as we saw, lead to deneutralization; but the choice of that dangerous method of defense—it is "pathological in itself," as Freud said—may be codetermined by the ego's incapacity to erect more appropriate defenses.

[8] I do not propose to go any further here into Freud's distinction of "free" and "bound" energy.

[9] I intentionally limit myself to this aspect and shall not discuss here the problem of free aggression traceable to instinctual defusion.

kinds of attempts of defense, on a lower level of integration, as projection and others, may be directed against it. Part of it may be turned against the self, and, under certain circumstances, foster self-destruction. M. Klein (1947) and Rosenfeld (1947) have described, in the schizophrenic, "splitting of the ego" as a result of aggression being turned against the self.

It is the propositions I just developed that I had in mind when I spoke of an attempt to breach at least one of the gaps between the instinctual and the ego aspects of schizophrenia. Nunberg (1920) compares the destructiveness of catatonic patients with defenses; this comparison is even more plausible if we keep in mind what I just said. I also may remind you here of Freud's hypothesis that free aggression increases the proclivity for conflict. If this is so, the deneutralization of countercathectic energy would contribute to an increased proneness to conflict and at the same time to the incapacity to deal with it—which describes rather well what we actually find in schizophrenia. That part of the deneutralized aggression may be interiorized and absorbed by the superego is certainly possible. It would correspond to what we generally know of one of the ways to dispose of free aggression.

What I said may help us to a better understanding also of the superego-ego-id relation in repression, in normal psychology as well as in psychopathology. If defensive countercathexes are fed by a form of aggressive energy, what we know of the role of the superego in repression, or rather repression under the impact of superego demands, can be better described as a dependence of one form of aggressive relation (between ego and id) on another one (between superego and ego) and possibly as a shift of aggressive cathexis combined with an increase in neutralization in the ego. Freud (1932), in discussing the superego's role in repression, speaks also of the case in which the "obedient ego" establishes repression on the order of the superego. What I have in mind could be described by saying that the obedient ego in carrying out the order uses means (modified aggression) similar to those by which the demand has been imposed on it. However, as neutralization is impaired in schizophrenia, the process I just described does not work, which may be an energic aspect of the clinical facts we describe as superego-ego disintegration.

But all this is an obvious oversimplification; e.g., because inner and outer frustrations are interrelated in a very complex way. I remind you of Freud's finding (1930) that outer frustration tends to increase guilt feelings and of his explanation that this is so because frustration gives rise to aggression which is suppressed and "made over" to the superego. There is no doubt about the correctness of Freud's finding. Yet, the increase of guilt feelings as a consequence of frustration (if aggression is not discharged toward the outside) seems to vary rather widely also among normal individuals. I suggest that in cases in which it plays a comparatively minor role this may sometimes be due to the fact that part of the aggression raised by frustration is used in the defensive countercathexis of the ego rather than in the superego. The differences in outcome will depend on the relative strength of the ego vis-à-vis the superego and on its capacity for higher degrees of neutralization.

In ontogeny we see that the defenses against the external as well as internal world develop in close interconnection with object relations and relations to reality in general. Trouble in object relations may interfere with the formation of stable defenses—and vice versa (see also Arlow, 1952). I said before that full object relations (in the analytic sense but also in the more general sense of "object world" used in nonanalytic psychology) presuppose, as one contribution from the ego, some degree of neutralization of libidinal as well as aggressive energy which secures constancy of the objects independent of the need situation. But it has also been emphasized, in particular by Anna Freud (1949) and E. Kris (1950b), that good object relations benefit neutralization. Joining this together with what I said before about the neutralized nature of countercathexis, it appears that there is a common economic aspect to the development of both defense and object relation which may be relevant to their developmental interrelation. Also, this may be a circular process:

constant object relations facilitating stable countercathexis and the latter helping to build up the former. I was speaking above of neutralization of libidinal as well as of aggressive energy. But considering the energic nature of countercathexis, it would be particularly promising to study in children the role played in these processes by the economy of aggression. It is very likely that distorted object relations—though their closer definition escapes us so far—are one predisposing agent in the development of schizophrenia. They have to be considered from the point of view of aggression as well as libido, and also from that of the mutual influences of ego and id—one decisive factor on the side of the ego being the level of neutralization. In schizophrenia this level is lowered—as shown in the defenses, in reality testing and contact with reality, etc. This dedifferentiation of the ego also means that the more differentiated forms of object relations (and, for that matter, objectivation) can no longer be maintained; in their place we find incomplete demarcation or fusion of self and object, and lack of differentiation also between ego and id. We know that in the development of the child self-object and ego-id differentiation run parallel.

A Note on Relations to Inner and Outer Reality

Stable object relation can be a basis for stable relations also to reality in general. On the other hand, we know that also in the nonpsychotic person withdrawal of object cathexis may lead to loosening of the ties with reality. We can view what happens there from the angle of regression. I discussed earlier one specific hypothesis as to the role which, in the case of psychosis, sexualization or aggressivization of ego functions may play in this process. But as I just said, we assume also for the normal person that his attitudes vis-à-vis reality are deeply influenced by the vicissitudes of the unconscious layers of his object relations. In this we usually do not see much of a problem. Nevertheless, I would not say that the metapsychological problem is fully understood.

Speaking of reality testing, I said before that its dedifferentiation, too, may be related to deneutralization. Here I want to add that clinically we see different layers, or aspects, of reality testing; in pathology, not all of these layers are necessarily damaged simultaneously. The basic layer would be the one most often referred to by Freud: the capacity to distinguish perceptions from ideas (presentations); its impairment is also one side of that fusion of inner and outer world we see nowhere clearer than in schizophrenia. Another one appears in what I described in briefly discussing one characteristic of schizophrenic delusions. In the cases I had in mind, perception is unchanged, but the meaning of the perception is radically altered. A further aspect of reality testing, of a more general nature, may be described as the correction, or elimination, of subjective elements in judgments meant to be objective—delusions can be described as a special case of its pathology, which, however, covers a much wider field of phenomena. The basic layers of outer reality testing break down only in psychosis; superficial layers may be interfered with also in neurotic and normal persons. Actually, as mental phenomena are no less "real" than the outer world (though we often refer to the latter only in speaking of "reality"), it might prove useful to broaden the concept of reality testing to include testing of the inner world. Every neurosis adulterates insight into inner reality; and reality testing of the inside is never perfect even in the normal person (with the exception, maybe, of the ideal case of a "fully analyzed" person—if there is such a human being). In schematically contrasting what in a given situation a neurotic and a psychotic would do, Freud (1924d) says: the neurotic represses the instinctual demand, while the psychotic denies outer reality. In this case, we could say that in the neurotic testing of inner reality, and in the psychotic testing of outer reality, is interfered with. However, a higher complexity is introduced by the fact, among others, that the two aspects of reality testing often interact. Repression will frequently affect the picture of outer reality, though never so radically as it is affected in psychosis. On the other hand, while schizophrenics may have a better insight than the normal person into some aspects of inner reality, their picture of it is on the whole distorted and unstable. I cannot pursue this trend of thought here; I just introduced it because I think that the study precisely of the interactions of outer and inner reality testing would help us to describe more clearly some specific features of psychosis. This interaction is, of course, also developmentally relevant. Action can be truly reality syntonic only if it considers not only outer reality but also the inner reality of the actor, and the interactions of both. I think it is a definite step in the child's acceptance of the reality principle (in a wider sense) if he learns not only to manage objects in the outer world, but, in doing so, also to integrate expectancies as to outer with expectancies as to inner consequences.

Clinically, we know of a great variety of relations between defense (working with one form of neutralized aggression) and the other ego functions I spoke of (which are fed by energy of the highest degree of neutralization of both libidinal and aggressive drives). The synthetic and differentiating functions which belong in the latter group are definitely correlated with the control of instinctual drives. On the other hand, the defensive functions influence in various ways those ego tendencies that keep up the contacts with reality, and so on. The pathology of these interactions of ego functions would be of particular interest in a systematic study of psychosis. While as a rule stability of defenses certainly enhances the stability of contact with reality, we see in schizophrenia that also the opposite can happen. This is so because of what I discussed before: contact with reality is also based on object cathexis. Therefore, defense against (withdrawal from) object relations may result in a loosening of the ego's attachment to reality. In these cases the ego is, as it were, confronted with the choice between the maintenance of defense and the clinging to reality.[10] Economically, what we actually see in schizophrenia is, as I said before, that some of these functions may be kept on a high degree of

[10] This point is discussed in greater detail by M. Katan (1953).

neutralization, while others have been aggressivized or sexualized; I tried to explain one aspect of these differences—but I certainly do not think that any systematic presentation could even be attempted today. One gets the impression that there is not only a partial impairment of neutralization, but that also the "operation of displacement," the distribution of neutralized energy, its free shift to the points where it is needed, are interfered with (see also p. 233).

Predisposition to Schizophrenia

Nowhere else in pathology is it so important to trace the development of mental processes back far beyond the stage of fully developed function as it is in the search for the predispositions to schizophrenia. As to its instinctual side, this predisposition has been situated in the oral-aggressive stage (M. Klein, 1948). But the problem has actually been investigated also as to different aspects of the unfolding of object relations. However, for a fuller understanding of etiology and of fixation we need a far more specific knowledge of the evolution also of certain other ego functions, some of which I discussed today. Why hypotheses on narcissism are in one sense too broad and in another too narrow to account fully for the subject, I have said before. In the context of this paper, insight into the development of neutralization and countercathexis appears to be essential.

The question of how far my suggestion in regard to the mode of energy found in countercathexis may be true also of the first countercathectic structures which we would expect to be present very early in life cannot be answered so far. In Chapter 9 I ventured the hypothesis that those primitive inhibitory apparatus which are parts of the primary autonomous equipment of the ego may contribute to the development of these very early countercathexes. Brierley (1952) has recently again called to our attention the role identifications may play in the setup of these countercathectic organizations. According to Rapaport (1950), "It is a rather common occurrence for energy distributions which usually strive for discharge, when they are prevented from doing so, to structuralize to prevent or regulate their own discharge." The concept of secondary energy distributions actually covers one aspect of what we call neutralization. These countercathectic energy distributions are essential, e.g., for the acceptance of outer reality; without them not even the separation of outer and inner world could come about. They are one aspect also of synthesis and differentiation, and, of course, of defense. What I want to emphasize here is that these countercathectic structures, factors like postponement of discharge, but also what Freud called the "protective barrier against stimuli," are probably among the genetic precursors of later defense mechanisms (Chapters 6 and 7). Bergman and Escalona (1949) used the concept of a "thin" protective barrier against stimuli in accounting for the unusual sensitivities of children, most of whom they described as schizophrenic. Sensitivity against stimulation from outside actually plays a large role at least in one phase of schizophrenia (Glover, 1949). Bergman and Escalona (1949) assume that a thin protective barrier may lead to precocious ego development (Chapter 6). Actually, these early developed ego functions may prove highly vulnerable. Sometimes, they subsequently seem to achieve a comparatively high degree of secondary autonomy, but often their resistivity is impaired. It is not impossible that the difference between precocious functions of the one and the other type may reveal itself to direct observation.

Summarizing my own impressions, I am inclined to consider as valid the hypothesis according to which deficiencies in primary autonomous factors in the ego contribute to the vulnerability of defense and of neutralization (and of other ego functions), and thus represent one etiological factor in schizophrenia. I want to state again that these agents in the course of development act in continuous interdependence with others. I of course do not deny, but, on the contrary, would like to emphasize, the causative role also of different factors, the best studied of which are certain aspects of object relations. But it is not impossible—as I said before—that anomalies of primary autonomy also represent part of the hereditary core of schizophrenia (there may be others, as bisexuality). However, the hereditary core is only one of the factors determining schizophrenia. While there can hardly be any doubt about its existence, the probability of its manifestation is still under discussion. If we accept Freud's statement (1937a) that defenses (and other ego functions) may normally have a hereditary core, we will not be too surprised to find that this is true also of the anomalies or vulnerabilities of defense (and other ego functions). This does not, of course, decide the question whether, as a rule, hereditary or environmental factors are prevalent in the etiology of schizophrenia. I shall not describe here the role of early traumatic and other environmental influences, nor their interaction with maturational factors. Moreover, it is not unlikely that pathognomonic features which in certain cases seem to be traceable to early weakness or distortion of ego functions may come about in others as a consequence of later organic impairment.[11]

Summary

I have made an attempt to account for some aspects of schizophrenia in terms of the impairment not so much of "the ego" as of specific ego functions. I tried to integrate or, more modestly, to account for certain well-known data about schizophrenic defense, object relations, language, reality testing, and so on. This was done from one point of view, but did not exclude different ways of approaching the problem. While I abstracted, for the purpose of this presentation, one aspect, I repeat here what I said before, that the meaning of this aspect is fully realized only when viewed in its interrelations with others. That many aspects of schizophrenia cannot

[11] An attempt to correlate our findings with those of physiology might well appear premature, though there is no doubt that Freud considered such correlations as the final aim of psychoanalysis. But I just want to mention here that some recent work on the pathophysiology of schizophrenia, particularly of the adrenal system, if it can be confirmed, appears to be relatable to what we think in psychoanalysis about the schizophrenic's defenses. Of course, we would have to differentiate the concept of "stress" that has proved useful in physiology in order to make correlations with analytic data and hypotheses more meaningful. That is, we would have to work with the elaborate framework of "danger" and "conflict" situations which we use in analysis.

be really understood unless we approach them in terms of meta-psychology has been clearly stated by Glover (1949). The meta-psychological hypotheses I used allowed me at least partly to bridge the gap between the instinctual and the ego aspects of schizophrenic psychosis, and to establish some connections between them. They gave me some insights into the economy particularly of aggression and into its role in the normal as well as in the schizophrenic individual. And they led me to some conjectures about the problem that is for many of us in the foreground of interest: the predisposition to schizophrenia. Some of the clinical phenomena that can be explained in the framework of these hypotheses will also be discussed at this symposium by Bak (1954). In a paper like this one, with its operational, or heuristic, one-sidedness, we are of necessity confronted with a large number of question marks surrounding an island of tentative propositions; but I think I am safe in saying that the hypotheses I suggested are at least not in contradiction with empirical data, or with the main body of tested psychoanalytic theory.

CHAPTER 11

Problems of Infantile Neurosis

(1954)

BOTH Anna Freud and Greenacre have contributed toward the understanding of the earliest, prestructural phases of development. Anna Freud (1954a) spoke of frustrations of very specific needs, needs for eating, sleeping, breathing, body contact, elimination, and the interaction of these needs at a period before the drives find a more definite and characteristic expression. Greenacre (1954) too referred to phenomena occurring at that period of development. Both authors claim for these factors no really specific etiological significance, but consider them as creating some degree of predisposition for later disease. Such studies show our growing awareness of the complexity of these predispositions to pathological development, and the search for an understanding of these predispositions in their interaction with those that had been known to us before.

It is not, however, apparent how far the factors described determine in their own right some kind of phase-specific vulnerability for neurotic development; or how far they act by contributing to the phase-specific conflicts of later stages, let's say to the oedipal conflict in the phallic phase. Obviously, all these factors mentioned influence

This paper was part of a panel discussion. Dr. Greenacre and Miss Freud had preceded me. Unless otherwise indicated, my remarks refer to their contributions to this panel.

the form and intensity of object relationships, and the development of the ego. But there are missing links between these very early happenings and what we know now about the etiological significance of later phases. There is still a gap, and what is being done here and elsewhere, is actually to lead up to a kind of inventory of contributing factors, and of their interrelationships, beyond Freud's classical formulations concerning the etiology of neurosis.

I have to mention here, because it has not been mentioned so far, that many of these factors are actually part of the child's equipment. For instance, the core of the differentiation between the ego and the id, and of individual variations of this differentiation, is among the factors that are part of man's equipment. This is relevant, because, as you remember, Freud considered the differentiation of ego and id to be a basic prerequisite for the development of neurosis. All these questions, however, are very much in flux right now, and it becomes difficult to evaluate the problems infantile neurosis poses in regard to its origin, its structure, its significance for later development.

You will have noticed that in both Greenacre's and Anna Freud's paper, relatively little has been said about infantile neurosis proper, which is of course significant for the state of affairs today. I would say that most of what Freud said about infantile neurosis long ago remains true today. But it is also obvious that in the course of the development of analysis reformulations are inevitable.

As to our topic of infantile neurosis, at present we have more questions than answers. Still, it is pleasant to think that most of the discomfort many of us feel in approaching this problem today is due to the fact that we know actually much more; that is, we know much more about developmental psychology in general, which makes us more ambitious in specifying our hypotheses. We know more about normal development, and we all agree that an understanding of neurotic development is not possible if it is not based on a very detailed analysis and on precise knowledge of what normal development is. Consequently we have to deal with a greater number of hypotheses on this subject today.

I may mention here, for instance, what Anna Freud said about those primitive needs, which she traced in their interdependence, some of them acting in a synergistic way, others in an antagonistic way. This body of hypotheses about the earliest phases has the great advantage that it can be validated, that it can be tested (though only on the basis of both direct child observation and retrospective analysis of adults), while quite a few earlier hypotheses on the subject were actually scarcely accessible to any validation or invalidation. But, as for the present, the concepts of developmental phase, conflict, trauma have become much more complex for us, and, I think, they will become ever more complex before we again reach that beautiful, peaceful state of affairs when both simple and general formulations become possible.

I may mention another difficulty in this context. It is actually not so easy to say what we call an infantile neurosis. You remember that when Freud first approached this problem, he found that what he actually considered a neurosis was frequently considered naughtiness or bad upbringing by the parents and by the teachers. Today we are confronted with the reverse situation; i.e., in rather broad circles, every naughtiness, actually every behavior of the child that does not conform to the textbook model, every developmental step that is not according to plan, is considered as "neurotic." What does this mean? It means that the broad range of normal variations of behavior is not recognized, and that the specific features of what analysts call a neurosis get lost sight of. Apart from this, however, many of the very early neuroses are really different from what we are used to calling neurosis in the adult. Many problems in children which we call neurotic are actually limited to a single functional disturbance; and the way from conflict to symptom is often shorter than in adult neurosis.

I may also mention that another aspect of the problem of childhood neurosis has not been systematically studied, i.e., its developmental significance, the simple clinical question of what the actual correlations between childhood neurosis and form and intensity of

adult neurosis are. In some well-analyzed cases, we know the sequence of early childhood neurosis, latency neurosis, and adult neurosis—for instance, in the best analyzed of all, in the Wolf Man. But
even today, it would not be easy to make even a moderately general
statement about many of the problems involved. However, this question can be approached, for instance, by using the material of one
of our analytic clinics. As a matter of fact, it is among the topics
suggested for the research program of the New York Treatment
Center.

Though our literature contains some beautiful analyses of childhood neuroses, the analytic interest of many has, I should think quite
consistently, searched for answers in turning from the purely clinical
aspects to the underlying developmental processes, that is, to the
more or less general laws governing the development of libido,
aggression, the ego, object relations; and to what we can say, in a
general way, of the strong points and weak points of these developments. Of course, on this level of research, no longer merely clinical
but also developmental, it remains true that the fixations and conflicts that we find in infantile neurosis are frequently also found at
the basis of the neurosis of adults. The latter is often modeled after
the former, but this is not always the case. No doubt, certain con-
stellations in drive and ego development, whose interactions we have
come to understand to some degree, are pathogenic. However, the
mere fact that these conflicts and fixations of the child resulted also
in the formation of a neurosis during childhood is not of necessity
an additional pathogenic factor for later life.

I may remind you here, to clarify this point, of a similar finding
made in a different field by Helene Deutsch (1937), who showed
that in certain situations the fact that a depression develops is less
damaging than the not coming about of a depression. We have to
ask ourselves whether phase-adequate neurotic reactions of the child
should not often be considered with this view in mind. We could
formulate this in a more general way by saying: what appears as
"pathological" in a cross-section of development may, viewed in the

longitudinal dimension of development, represent the best possible solution of a given childhood conflict.

What Anna Freud said long ago (1945) is, of course, true, namely that the apparently strong ego of a neurotic child is actually weak, and also that infantile neurosis may mean "calcification." This danger is inherent in rigid fixations on certain instinctual aims, or on certain defenses, or also on those patterns Greenacre spoke about. The consequence then is that parts of the growing personality are, at least temporarily, excluded from further development. But there are several points to be considered here. First of all, there are also very recalcitrant and durable fixations that do not lead to neurosis or psychosis and still interfere with some aspects of later development. I remind you, for instance, of those "distortions" of the ego (Freud, 1937a) with whose help the development of a neurosis may be avoided. Such phenomena, though still little considered in analysis, are probably very frequent. Also the fixations on early specific frustrations, described by Anna Freud, do not necessarily lead to neurosis; though they may determine symptom formation if a neurosis develops. Early traumatization may have similar effects, as Greenacre mentioned. Grinker (1954) thinks that many psychosomatic disorders are traceable to such factors. The decisive question is, of course, whether these various developmental vicissitudes are reversible, capable of compensation, or irreversible.

Thus, there are in childhood a variety of factors that may, in a sense, be called "pathogenic," but do not by themselves lead to neurosis or psychosis. On the other hand, there are also neurotic phenomena in childhood that are amenable to correction, to modification in the course of growth and development, which I have to mention here in order not to make the picture too one-sided. The theoretical basis on which we can build here is a thought Freud expressed in some of his later papers (e.g., 1926a), namely, that the repressed instinctual demand is not necessarily rigidly preserved in the id. That is, it may be elaborated by the ego, or used by the ego, as is commonly the case in the more normal passing of the oedipus complex when repressed instinctual drives are sublimated and used in the resulting identifications. A paper by Anny Katan (1937) develops this proposition of Freud's. This gives us an explanation for the fact that the calcification we often find after childhood neuroses may be only a transient phenomenon; and this will make us less inclined to dispute, on theoretical grounds, the possibility of a spontaneous cure of these neuroses. It will appear even more plausible if we keep in mind the modifying power of maturation, also mentioned by Anna Freud, on the side of the id, but also of the ego, through which some anxiety conditions may lose their importance.

There is no yardstick for the pathogenic potential of infantile neurosis except for the long-run developmental consideration. We have to bear in mind that every new phase of maturation creates new potential conflict situations and new ways of dealing with these conflicts; but, on principle, it also carries with it, to a certain degree, the possibility of modifying the impact of earlier conflict solutions. The new aspect of the subsequent phases is the changed dominance of certain instinctual and certain ego functions; this includes also phase-specific capacities to deal with conflict situations and, in some degree, to revise old conflict solutions. The main thing in approaching these problems—and this touches on what both Greenacre and Anna Freud said—is that the genetic, the historical, aspect of later conflicts must be clearly distinguished from their phase-specific possibilities (see also Chapter 6).

As to another point: if we try to determine a developmental potential, we should not forget that many of the concepts we use here (e.g., trauma, ego strength, etc.) imply relationships. The facts to which they refer cannot be evaluated without knowledge of the context in which they appear. This is obvious in a concept like trauma and relevant to what Greenacre said. Because of similar reasons we became accustomed to describing many developmental phenomena in terms of their "id aspects" and their "ego aspects"— this category of relations, between ego and id, being fundamental for our understanding of so many others.

The assessment of a developmental potential also includes, as an important factor, the study of the pleasure potentialities in the three psychic systems, and their changes on the different levels of growth and development. I remind you here of what Greenacre said about two biological rhythms (pleasurably soothing and orgastic); but also the rhythmical aspects of ego activities should, I think, be studied in this context. Various forms of rhythmical activity can be connected with various conditions for pleasure gain, and the question always is: which forms of pleasure gain are prevalent on a given developmental level?

Another point refers to what we just heard from Anna Freud (1954b). It is certainly true that the persistence of earlier phenomena in later phases is often, beyond certain limits, suspicious or ominous. I may add that precocious development of certain functions probably can also lead to pathological development.

I want to make just one more point about the capacity of modifying, reversing, or compensating for developments which, if unchecked, may lead to pathology. An essential aspect of this is the capacity of the child to neutralize instinctual energy, libidinal and aggressive. This faculty for neutralization may be different in regard to libido and to aggression, as is, e.g., clearly traceable in a case analyzed by Berta Bornstein.[1] And this faculty for substituting neutralized for instinctual energy must be viewed in connection with the substitution of ego aims for instinctual aims—the two processes varying partly independently, as seen in the cases of sexualization or aggressivization of ego functions. This is particularly relevant for the understanding of fixations and their consequences—which show a continuum from the rigid fixation on an instinctual demand to those, on the other end of the line, that finally survive predominantly as an individual form, or direction, or intensity of an ego function.

All this goes to show that the impact of development on infantile neurosis cannot be judged without using, in each individual case, all

[1] Personal communication.

the tools that child psychology has developed as well as a knowledge of the relative relevance of these many factors mentioned, and of many others not mentioned here. The question of the extent to which infantile neurosis will determine later neurosis, or psychosis, or character development, or positive achievement is basically an empirical question. But developmental theory can give us models, it can tell us what factors have to be considered in such a study, and what their most likely interaction is. Thus, theory can direct clinical studies on childhood neurosis, but it could not possibly replace them. And that is why we hope that in the following discussion, we will hear many clinical examples to enrich and also to test our developmental hypotheses.

CHAPTER 12

Notes on the Theory of Sublimation

(1955)

I T HAS frequently happened, in psychoanalysis as in other fields, that concepts first devised to account for some more or less occasional observations were later used to refer to phenomena of a far more general nature than had been anticipated. In such cases, these concepts often preserve for a time the imprint of the specific situation they were originally meant to cover, but gradually detach themselves from the particular discoveries which had given rise to their formation. They get more or less integrated into the total field of experience and thought, which process often requires redefinition. To demonstrate this in detail would certainly be a worth-while subject for the historian of psychoanalysis. Suffice it here to remind you of Freud's concept of defense of the nineties, as compared to a later phase in which defense had acquired a structural definition and was recognized as one aspect of general psychology equally relevant for the development of the normal and the later pathological individual. Or think how the conceptualization of aggression has changed, until finally aggression was realized to be, and defined as, one of the basic instinctual drives. As a third example, I may mention narcissism. Here, too, several reformulations occurred; the fact that Freud has not quite consistently synchronized the concept of "narcissism" with the level of his later insights and theories has, in this case, led to quite some uncertainties and contradictions in psychoanalytic thinking and literature.

The concept of sublimation shows a somewhat similar development. When first used by Freud, "sublimation" referred to certain cultural or otherwise highly valued achievements and to their derivation from instinctual sources, which meant at the time sexual sources. These phenomena were also studied as ways to avoid conflict while still achieving discharge, to escape the necessity of repression; their relations to the reaction formations of the latency period, their role in artistic creation was recognized. Partly realized was also their relation to symptom formation on the one hand and symbolization on the other hand. All this was described by Freud and other analysts before ego psychology had come to be acknowledged as a chapter of psychoanalysis in its own rights. Later studies on sublimation tend to emphasize its relations to the build-up of the ego in general and to specific ego functions. As in the case of narcissism, we find in Freud's later work new ideas on the subject which, however, he has not quite explicitly developed or used for a redefinition of "sublimation" in terms of his more recent work.

Despite the broad and general use made by analysts of the concept of sublimation and despite many attempts to free it from ambiguities, there is no doubt that a certain amount of discontent with some of its facets is rather common among us. Different aspects of sublimation, as usually defined, have been criticized by Sterba (1930), Bernfeld (1931), Glover (1931), Levey (1939), among others. Brierley (1947) speaks of sublimation as an "omnibus term" which comprises a great number of actually different activities. Jones (1941), limiting his indictment to earlier usage only, refers to "the days when analysts were prone to cite the blessed word 'sublimation' as the deus ex machina in all social and idealistic impulses."

The most common definition refers to sublimation as a deflection of the sexual drives from instinctual aims to aims which are socially or culturally more acceptable or valued. There may also be a change of objects. In this definition, sublimation is actually a special case of displacement, special in the sense that it includes only those displacements that lead to the substitution of worthy aims. The advantage of this approach was that it clearly stated that the highest achievements of man—art, science, religion—may have and often do have their origin in libidinal tendencies. But some authors, e.g., Bernfeld (1931) and Sterba (1930), have objected to this definition, pointing out quite correctly that it is always questionable to include value judgments in the definition of a mental process— which, of course, does not mean that the function of valuation cannot be made the object of empirical studies. At any rate, on the basis of such a definition every inquiry into the relations between sublimation and the creation of values rests more or less on a *petitio principii*.

It was, therefore, a reasonable suggestion to eliminate the element of value judgment and to speak of ego-syntonic aims (Bernfeld). This important emendation still left many questions unanswered. We are used to saying that in sublimation ego aims are substituted for instinctual aims, which may be accompanied by a change of objects. But is it really true that it depends only on the aims (and objects) whether or not we can speak of sublimated activities? Here we meet the problem of the relations between sublimation and sexualization. Some definitions of sublimation leave open the question what the differences between the two processes are; or rather, they forget to make this distinction. Clinically, we know that sexualization of ego functions, beyond a certain limit, interferes with proper functioning, while in a large field of human activities successful functioning depends on sublimation.

In the case of sexualization, we often say that an ego function has, mostly unconsciously, been invested with a "sexual meaning"; I remind you also of certain forms of inhibition which may ensue (Freud, 1926a). However, this concept of "meaning" is in need of clarification. Obviously, in the case of sublimation, too, we may find unconscious genetic determinants of a sexual character. One could try to relate the differences between sublimation and sexualization to the preponderance of the secondary or the primary process; to the degree to which the functions in question are, or are not, reality-syntonic; to whether suppression of the function can lead to anxiety; to how likely it is that the ego activity changes into direct instinctual gratification, and so on. All these are no doubt relevant aspects of that distinction and some of them I will take up later. At any rate, it seems that a clear presentation of this problem calls for the introduction of metapsychological concepts. And for the purpose of this discussion we will retain the fact that basing the concept of sublimation on the aims of behavior only will of necessity fall short of a satisfactory definition. We will also realize that one shortcoming of such a definition that makes no distinction between sublimation and sexualization is caused by its neglect of the considerable differences we find in the stability of ego functions, even of those whose instinctual core is very much alike; differences in resistivity against regression and sexualization—that is, its neglect of what I am used to calling degrees of secondary autonomy of the ego. Postponing the discussion of the energic aspects, the aspects of the modes of energy involved, we may say that the stability of sexualized ego functions and their integration are usually less secure and that they more easily follow the pull of regressive tendencies.

Developmentally speaking, one main trend can be characterized as away from instinctualization of ego functions toward greater (secondary) autonomy, that is, better protection against instinctualization and regression. The degrees of autonomy vary, of course, from individual to individual, according to the developmental stage, and to different functions of the ego.[1] If we take an over-all picture of an individual ego, the degree of autonomy is correlated with what we call ego strength, though it is not its only source.[2]

[1] For an interesting discussion of the stability of ego functions in the psychoanalytic process, see Jokl (1950).

[2] In discussions of this kind, the early value-tinged concept of sublimation proves to be still very much alive in the minds of many of us. At the end of this paper I

The dependence of ego function on needs is marked in the infant. During the whole of childhood, newly acquired ego activities show a considerable lack of stability, or a tendency to get temporarily reinvolved in the conflicts and instinctual demands that contributed to their development. The child develops special methods to counteract such regressive tendencies (Anna Freud and Dann, 1951; Kris, 1951b).

We probably all agree on the developmental relevance of early libidinal cathexis of ego activities. But in this case I should not yet speak of sublimation—which has been done, though, by some analysts—because of the reasons just mentioned and because of others not mentioned so far. However, I think that there is a variety of ways in which these early libidinal cathexes of ego activities may influence later sublimations. Melanie Klein (1923a) equates the capacity to cathect ego activities with libido with the capacity to sublimate. She also thinks that libidinal fixations on speech and pleasure in movement constitute the preconditions for the capacity for sublimation.

The spreading of cathexis on objects, functions, and aims somehow or other related to the original ones is in fact part of the primary process. Thus the ego, and already the precursors of the fully developed ego, becomes invested with drive energy. This is a significant factor which partly accounts for the relative emphasis on certain ego functions in the growing child and also for the timing of their development.[3] But such characters of the primary process, e.g., displacement, come soon to be partly integrated by the ego and to be used for its own purposes, e.g., defense (Anna Freud, 1936). Displacement is, in a way, also a form of primordial learning, inasmuch

---

shall briefly outline the problems at which the theory of sublimation originally aimed and discuss their place in the present theory in terms of Freud's later ideas. At this point, however, it may be good to remind ourselves that the concept of secondary autonomy refers to the stability of ego functions only, in the sense just outlined, and not in any way to the "value" of the activities in question or of their results.

[3] I do not propose to discuss here the factor of primary autonomy of the ego. Later I shall say a few words about the not unlikely hypothesis that the ego draws, in its development, also on other than instinctual sources of energy.

as it widens the child's grasp of his outer and inner world (Chapter 9). As to symbolization, its importance for the development of the ego and particularly of sublimation has repeatedly been stressed by Melanie Klein (e.g., 1930). Hand in hand with the full integration of the precursors into the gradually developing ego go certain changes in the mode of cathexis we shall have to describe. From that stage on, while one aspect of these functions can still be described as "vicissitudes of an instinct"—you remember that Freud (1915a) describes sublimation in this way, among others—it becomes necessary to add a description of their role in the setup of the ego.

I think it should greatly facilitate our understanding of these developments if we here introduce some distinctions. Speaking of sublimation: quite apart from the specific process of sublimation,[4] which I will discuss later, there is a difference between the (sublimated) cathexis of an ego function, on the one hand, and the (sublimated) cathexis of the aims toward which this function is directed, and of the objects through which the aims are achieved, on the other hand. The cathexis of objects of thought or action is not identical with the cathexis of the functions of thought or action. Clinically, we know that aims which presuppose a high degree of sublimation may be retained, though the functions are regressively instinctualized (as in sexualization). This difference holds good also in another respect: we have to distinguish the pleasurable character of an activity from the pleasurable character of its aims. It also seems advisable, which I may note here parenthetically, to differentiate between ego function and the representation of the self, the neglect of which has considerably handicapped our understanding of a variety of phenomena that are frequently lumped together under the heading of "narcissism" (Chapters 7 and 10). There is, of course, interaction between the two aspects I mentioned. What I want to

---

[4] The word "process" has, in analysis, been used to cover different meanings. One, I think, fruitful attempt to give it a definite place in our field has been made by Brierley (1944).

note here is that some concepts of sublimation referring only to the aims and not to the functions, which are equally important for our understanding of the ego, are less suitable for the advancement of ego psychology.

Even today, we know much more about the origin of specific contents of sublimations, of specific goals, or of interests in a given material or subject, etc., than of the role of sublimation in the build-up of ego functions (though here, too, important work has been done[5]), and the genesis of the process of sublimation is far from being clearly understood. To trace the specific contents of sublimation to their sources was actually the central issue of research on sublimation for a long time. We can establish genetic connections of this kind in much of our clinical material. That the child's conflicts, his instinctual behavior and fantasies, and his anxiety reactions at least codetermine the contents of later sublimation was, of course, an important discovery. If one would say—and it has been said—that sublimation is the repetition of an infantile situation, this is certainly in a way true as far as the contents are concerned, though it does not fully clarify what the particular features of sublimation are. The knowledge of an artist's conflicts and unconscious fantasies often does not sufficiently explain why their working out takes the form of art (see also Kris, 1952). The thesis which considers sublimation a victory of the id (over the superego; Róheim, 1943) is certainly due to a failure to distinguish between the function of sublimation and its genetic aspect. This hypothesis neglects the fact that forces originating in the id may be used by the ego and even turned against the id. It is again an instance—I touched at the problem before, in speaking of secondary autonomy—of a kind of genetic fallacy: the actual function is equated with its history, or rather reduced to its genetic precursors, as if genetic continuity were inconsistent with change of function.[6]

[5] See Anna Freud (1936) on intellectualization, and more recently, for instance, Rosen (1953).

[6] I think that the distinction between function and genesis, and the recognition of the principle of change of function, are inherent in what, in analysis, we call the

Fortunately, detailed genetic studies usually do more than empha-size the persistence of past conflicts and fantasies in the contents of present sublimations. They often show us the functions that sub-limation had in *statu nascendi* and how it is used in the development of the ego, in its relations to id, superego, and reality. They can give us answers to the question: which are the actual situations that either promote sublimation or interfere with it? In this respect, child observation which has given us certain clues might become even more helpful in tracing the impact of objects, object relations, identi-fications, etc., on concrete sublimatory achievements as well as on the different question of the individual capacity for sublimation.[7] It is probably true that, as Freud states, this capacity is partly inborn —which will appear to us even more plausible today, since we have come to realize that ego functions no less than instinctual tendencies may have a hereditary core; but Freud never doubted that external influences, too, have a part in it. Also we would be glad to hear more, in this discussion, from the child analysts and analytic child psy-chologists, about the typical or individual timing of sublimations. The "beginnings of sublimation" are variously described to coin-cide with the latency period, with the beginning of the oedipal phase, but also with much earlier stages of development. Of course, the answer to this question will be different according to whether the original, narrower concept of sublimation is used, or a much broader one, to which I now turn.

In *The Ego and the Id* (1923a) Freud equates desexualization and sublimation; and thought processes are quite generally sub-

---

structural point of view. Of nonanalytic psychologists, Bühler (1929) and Allport (1937) have clearly stated the problem, and the latter has systematically developed this aspect of psychology. Both, though, failed to realize its actual role in the frame-work of psychoanalytic theory, and they consider it contrary to basic tenets of analysis. Most analysts, however, would, I suppose, agree that it is one of the significant features of psychoanalytic psychology that Freud has succeeded in integrating the genetic approach with a structural viewpoint. See also Hartmann (1939a) and Chapter 7.

[7] After having written this paper, I read the one by Ernst Kris (1955) on "Neu-tralization and Sublimation: Observations on Young Children." His child observations actually fulfill, in a highly suggestive way, what I had in mind here.

sumed under sublimation. Somewhat later (1926a) he stated—again quite generally—that the ego works with desexualized energy. As I said in the beginning, Freud did not systematically synchronize the concept of sublimation with the new level of his psychological thinking; but his later statements imply fundamental changes which ought to be spelled out and challenge further development. Here the stage is reached at which sublimation, as other psychoanalytic concepts before, refers to a psychological process, this process being a change in the mode of energy, away from an instinctual and toward a noninstinctual mode. This formulation eliminates the doubts concerning earlier concepts of sublimation that did not account for the clinically essential differences between sublimation and sexualization. Moreover, we see the relations between displacement and sublimation in a new light; not only the aims are (usually) changed in sublimation, but also the mode of the cathexis is. It is even likely that the same aim of the ego may be pursued at times with less, at times with more, sublimated energy; this can be studied in the play of children and in other developmentally relevant ego activities.

The process of sublimation can be linked with several mechanisms, of which displacement is only one. I just mention identification, whose importance in this respect has often been emphasized by Freud and many others. Even more important, the correlation between change of mode of energies, on the one hand, and change of aims or objects, on the other hand, has again become a topic of empirical research, being no longer prejudged, as it was, by too narrow a definition. On this basis, the role of sublimation in the formation of objects, particularly constant objects, can be hypothesized (Chapter 9). Freud approached this subject in speaking of the "tender" or "aim-deflected" strivings toward an object and thought that "if we want," we could consider them as a "beginning" of sublimatory processes. I suppose we could assign them their place as one of the many shades of neutralization in the continuum from fully instinctual to fully neutralized energy, a subject we shall have to deal with later.

That all ego functions are fed by desexualized or sublimated energy (later we will say: by neutralized energy), is indeed only the last touch Freud gave his gradually evolving ideas on the ego, which step by step emphasized its importance in the mental economy. It is with this turn in his theory formation that the problems which sublimation poses become essential for our metapsychological understanding of the ego. If we agree with Freud's later proposition, we will tend to see in sublimation not a more or less occasional happening but rather a continuous process, which, of course, does not exclude temporary increases or decreases in sublimatory activities. This hypothesis will, of course, also be one more reason for us, and a decisive one, no longer to limit the study of sublimation to culturally or socially valuable achievements only. The earlier definition assumes an essential difference between some striking sublimatory achievements and other, less obvious ones, though the fundamental psychological process we want to define is probably the same in both cases; and, continuing this trend of thought, we cannot attribute, as was done in the past, the "capacity for sublimation" to "the few" only. Obviously, while Freud's later definition emphasizes an essential relation between creativity and the ego, this does not do away with the many psychological problems creativity poses. The striking expression of sublimation we call "creativity" may differ quantitatively, but certainly also in a subtler way, from other ego achievements.

Taking as his point of departure the same passages in Freud's later work I just mentioned, Glover (1931), in a penetrating study of the subject, comes to the conclusion that "some qualitative change in energy may prove to be the only metapsychologically valid criterion of sublimation." The advantages of the concept are manifold, particularly in the study of specific ego functions, and some of these advantages have been mentioned. Glover suggests a definition which includes displacement together with the change in the mode of cathexis. About the role of displacement, I said a few words before. But the question of what the relations between various mechanisms, such as displacement, identification and others, and the energy transformation actually are, is in many respects in need of further study. At any rate, it seems essential that the nature and relevance of this basic process of energy transformation be clearly conceptualized and that we comprehend its role in the build-up and the functions of the ego.

Something similar to this, i.e., a conceptualization aiming at the basic processes, has been attempted in regard to other concepts of psychoanalysis and has considerably helped to clarify our thinking on developmental psychology, on clinical problems, and so on. Thus we are used today to defining "defense" in general terms, topographically, dynamically, economically, and structurally. In speaking of a particular defense mechanism, we will add a statement about its specific characteristics and functions. We would rather not include into its definition anything beyond this, as, for instance, the possible long-range consequences of defense as regards neurosis, health, perversion. Many of us would agree today that in speaking of "successful defense," we refer to the fact that the function of the defense mechanism has been performed, its aim has been reached—and not to the possible long-range outcome of health or disease.[8] The latter type of definition would threaten every study of the relations of defense to health and disease with the danger of begging the question.

If we want to achieve the same level of psychological definition in the case of sublimation, we will here, too, have to eliminate all references to "normalcy" or "abnormality," which are frequently included. Thus we cannot accept the frequently used distinction between "true" and "not true" sublimation, if it is drawn with this implication in mind. This certainly does not mean that no correlation of capacity for sublimation, or degree of sublimation of specific ego functions, with states of health or disease exists, or that it is

[8] I know that Fenichel (1945) defines this differently.

irrelevant. The opposite is true (which, of course, does not imply that in the concatenation of factors that lead to disease, no functions enter which are fed by sublimated [neutralized] energy; see later). At any rate, it is preferable not to prejudge the question. Thinking again of the analogous situation of defense, you will remember how many misunderstandings were created when on the basis of the correct insight into the role of defense in neurosis, it was deduced, which is not correct, that every defense leads necessarily to pathology.

I will treat the next question rather briefly, though it is essential for our orientation in this field. I have discussed this aspect of our subject in a series of papers published partly together with Kris and Loewenstein, in the last few years. We have accepted Freud's idea that sublimation of libido is a process by which the ego is provided with energy appropriate to its special needs; that is, the energies the ego uses for its specific functions are as a rule not instinctual, they are desexualized. But is there a parallel to this with aggressive energy? I assume, in agreement with Melanie Klein, Kris, Loewenstein, Menninger, Lampl-de Groot, Hart, and others, that the mode of the aggressive energies too can be changed, in a way comparable to desexualization. It also appears that this desaggressivized energy is no less important for·the formation and the function of the ego than is desexualized libido. This, then, implies that self-destruction is not the only alternative to aggression being turned outward; neutralization is another alternative (Menninger, 1942;[9] Chapter 4; Hartmann, Kris, Loewenstein, 1949). If desexualization is really correlated with defusion of instincts (Freud, 1923a), the possible dangers inherent in such defusion could still be counteracted, as long as the capacity to neutralize aggression is unimpaired. If we further assume that self-preservation is, in man, to a considerable degree a function of the ego (Freud, 1940a), we will come to the conclusion that it is actually dependent on neutralization.

[9] Menninger (1942) even considers aggression more important in "sublimation" than libido. See also Brierley (1932).

We call neutralization the change of both libidinal and aggressive energy away from the instinctual and toward a noninstinctual mode.[10] The process of neutralization is essential in what we usually call sublimation, and it is mostly this aspect I am dealing with in this paper. But what is the relation of the two terms? There are several terminological possibilities. We may continue to speak of sublimation only in the case where neutralization of libido is involved, because this is the way it was meant by Freud and is still dominant in analytic literature. One may also use the word sublimation for the desinstinctualization of both aggression and libido, making it a synonym of neutralization (Menninger, 1942). An alternative suggestion (Kris, 1952) would reserve the term for the change of aims, often associated with neutralization. Again, the term is sometimes used for the nondefensive, in contradistinction to the defensive, ego functions, and for their aims and cathexis. This question of nomenclature cannot be too important in itself and, for the purpose of my presentation, a decision between these alternatives does not seem necessary. What I want to remind you of here is just that much of what I said before about "sublimation" refers to the process now defined as "neutralization." In what follows you will see from the context where I speak of this process and where I

[10] This term has occasionally been interpreted as referring to instinctual energy somewhere in between libido and aggression. But this is at variance with the term as we use it here. Also, "neutralization" does not mean instinct fusion—though the two processes may be interrelated (Hartmann, Kris, Loewenstein, 1949). In Freud's work one occasionally finds the word *neutralisieren* (to neutralize); e.g., "as a result of the combination of unicellular organisms into multicellular forms of life, the death instinct of the single cell can successfully be neutralized" (1923, p. 41); or "libido . . . serves to neutralize the destructive impulses which are simultaneously present" (1940, p. 22). However, this word is not defined by Freud as a technical term, but rather is used as interchangeable with a number of other words. At any rate, it is clear that its use does not coincide with "neutralization" as defined above. In another context Freud speaks of *"indifferente Energie,"* which is assumed to be "desexualized libido" and "sublimated energy." *"Indifferente Energie"* is rendered by the translator of the *Standard Edition* as "neutral energy." Still what Freud describes in that passage is in some respects but not fully identical with either "neutralized energy" or "primary ego energy," in the sense in which these concepts are used here. The latter concepts are closer to what is a later and clearly different hypothesis advanced by Freud (1926) (it has been widely neglected in analytic literature): the general assumption that the ego works with desexualized energy.

refer to other aspects often associated with the concept of sublimation.

Beyond emphasizing the central position of the process of neutralization in general in the build-up of the ego, and in its differentiation from the id, a certain number of more specific hypotheses are necessary to organize and clarify our thinking on the great variety of phenomena we have in mind in speaking of ego functions. In what follows, I shall, then, attempt to develop some such propositions based upon Freud's statements quoted above, on the desinstinctualized character of the mode of energy used by the ego. It is, of course, in elaborating the implications of these propositions, and their applications with respect to specific problems, that their usefulness will have to be tested.

The question is often discussed in analytic literature whether moral masochism, or play, or any number of phenomena "are" or "are not" sublimations. But this is not just an either-or question. I think, it comes closer to observable facts if we speak, as I suggested, not just of two modes of energy of each drive: instinctual or neutralized. Both clinical experience and theory point to the probability that there exists a continuum of gradations of energy, from the fully instinctual to the fully neutralized mode (Chapter 7; Kris, 1950a; Rapaport, 1950).

If we accept this proposition, the next problem would then be what degrees of neutralization are commonly used for certain ego activities. Individual differences, differences as to situation and developmental level, must of course be considered. But some generalizations may be hypothesized. To draw my example from aggression: there is the unmitigated form of free aggression; the aggression the superego uses in its relations to the ego is already partly modified; even further removed from instinctual energy is the one the ego, according to a hypothesis I developed in Chapter 7, employs in countercathexis—but it is still aggression and also retains that element of aggression, "fight"; we find the highest degree of neutralization of aggression in nondefensive ego activities. It is not unlikely that differences between instinctual and neutralized energy go mostly parallel with the differences between primary and secondary processes. This would mean that in this respect, too, transitory phases have to be considered.

That changes in the degrees of neutralization do not without exception coincide with a change of the aims, I have mentioned before in discussing sexualization (see also Chapter 9). To trace systematically the ontogenesis of ego functions from the angle of change of aims and change in the mode of energy is obviously a subject too broad to be broached here. May I repeat what I said before: that, aside from primary autonomous ego functions, and before the ego has been established as an organization, primordial aims and functions come under the influence of libidinal and aggressive cathexes. In the course of development, their cathexes will be neutralized, and they will gain a certain degree of autonomy vis-à-vis the instinctual drives, which happens in constant interdependence with processes of maturation. Secondary autonomy is certainly dependent on neutralization. But it would be erroneous to assume that every—maybe transitory—cathexis of a function with neutralized energy constitutes autonomy in the sense I use the term (that is, stability of an ego function, or, more precisely, its resistivity to regression and instinctualization).

Once the ego has accumulated a reservoir of neutralized energy of its own, it will—in interaction with the outer and inner world—develop aims[11] and functions whose cathexis can be derived from this reservoir, which means that they have not always to depend on *ad hoc* neutralizations. Stating this more completely and with reference to the relationships of the ego and the id (here I do not want to broaden this statement to include the interactions with the superego), we may say: the ego accepts some instinctual tendencies and helps them toward gratification, without change of aims or of the mode of energy involved. In other cases, it will substitute ego aims for aims of the

[11] That the ego sets itself aims was emphasized by R. Waelder long ago (1930).

id. This can be done in a variety of ways. The ego aims may lie in the direction of id tendencies; they may be opposed to them (counter-cathexis); the third group are those nondefensive aims the ego, as I just said, sets itself in the course of development. Ego aims will normally be fed by neutralized energy and achieve a certain amount of secondary autonomy. But ego aims may, under certain conditions, also be cathected with instinctual energy—the case we call sexualization and aggressivization. In the first case, in which these aims use neutralized energy, the energy is either drawn from *ad hoc* acts of neutralization, or provided by the reservoir of neutralized energy at the ego's disposal.

We see that the ego gradually gains a comparative independence from immediate outside or inside pressure, a fact that one is used to considering (though usually not in this terminology) as a general trend in human development. Thus we may say that while displacements partly determine the directions neutralization takes, it is also true that neutralization can lead to displacements, because, as a rule, different degrees of neutralization are not equally well suited for all aims and functions of the ego (I remind you of what I said about degrees of neutralization of aggression, in their relation to different functions; see also Kris, 1952).

There are considerable variations in this respect also from one individual to the other. And in the same individual the level of neutralization, as to one specific function, is not constant.[12] It seems, furthermore, that neutralization of libidinal and of aggressive energy varies independently—or rather partly independently. Berta Bornstein (1955) has discussed this point.[13]

Sublimation (which here means neutralization) of instinctual energy is mediated by the ego (Freud, 1923a).[14] Freud has particu-

[12] Kris (1952) introduced the concept of "energy flux," defined as "the transitory changes in energy distribution and redistribution such as the temporary and shifting reinforcement, of sexual, aggressive or neutral energy as it may occur in the course of any type of activity."

[13] Her material has not yet been published.

[14] And, in view of what I shall discuss later, I may add: already by the precursors of the ego, before the ego as a definite system has been established.

larly emphasized the role identification plays in this process (it is a well-known fact that disturbance of identification often leads to disturbance of sublimation), but it is unlikely that neutralization can be achieved in this way only. Whether, generally, in neutralization object libido must first be transformed into narcissistic libido—a problem related to the one I just mentioned—is a question not easy to decide. Because of certain variations in terminology, I could not even say positively that this was always Freud's opinion. You know that Freud, and others, have often equated "narcissism" with the libidinal cathexis of the ego. In this sense, the statement that neutralization proceeds through a narcissistic phase could be tantamount to the one mentioned before: that neutralization is mediated by the ego. But narcissism was also meant to refer to the libidinal cathexis of the self (not the ego), as opposed to object cathexis, and this definition of narcissism seems to me in many respects preferable to the one mentioned before. If we accept it, we may then speak of self-representation (in the case of libidinal cathexis: narcissism) in opposition to object representation; but self-representation in this sense is not identical with the cathexis of ego functions. It becomes clinically and theoretically important to make a difference between the cathexis of the self-image, on the one hand, and of ego functions, as thought or action, which may be object-directed as well as self-directed, on the other hand (see Chapters 7 and 10). Applied to our subject, this leaves the hypothesis that neutralization proceeds through the ego (or its precursors) unchanged. But if we make that distinction, we will be inclined to say that while a change to narcissistic cathexis will certainly often be one step in neutralization, as, for instance, in identification, this step is not a necessary prerequisite of neutralization in general.

It is well known that in sublimation (neutralization) the ego allows a certain amount of discharge of the original tendencies, provided that their mode (and, often, their aims) have been modified. Pleasure gain by sublimation has often been emphasized by Freud and others. The amount of energy that can be discharged this way varies in the estimate of different analysts. The fact itself that sublimation provides us with an outlet, in a different mode, of instinctual impulses has been made the basis for its distinction from reaction formation (Sterba, 1930; Glover, 1931; Fenichel, 1945). Reaction formations originate in defensive measures of the ego. They will also later be used in their countercathectic aspects, but we should not forget that, e.g., reactive character traits will, in the course of development, be invested also with other, nondefensive functions in the framework of the ego (quite apart from the fact, noticed by Freud long ago, that they may also feed on instinctual tendencies opposed to the ones they were built to ward off). This confronts us with a rather complex issue. Glover subsumes reaction formation under displacement, defining it as a displacement into the opposite. The next step would try to account for it in energic terms. It sometimes appears from analytic writings that sublimation is used as a word for the nondefensive achievements of the ego (see, however, later), which points to the dynamically speaking correct opposition of defensive and nondefensive ego functions. With respect to the modes of energy used, according to Freud's later formulations which I take as a point of departure here, reaction formations too (and for that matter, all countercathexes) work not with instinctual but with some shade of neutralized energy. Still it may be that countercathexes can be characterized as also energically differing from other ego functions, which may, at least partly, explain why, according to Freud, they are "set apart" in the ego. As I mentioned before, it is likely that defense against the drives (countercathexis) retains an element (fight) that allows of their description as being mostly fed by one mode of aggressive energy, and that this mode is not full neutralization. In this sense, countercathexis in repression appears to be a good example to be contrasted, also as to the energy it uses, with the nondefensive ego functions. Reaction formation (e.g., in character traits) is a less good example, because, as I said, here the countercathectic function is often overlaid with other functions of the ego. It is not unlikely, though it may appear paradoxical from a certain point of view (see below), that the nondefensive ego activities have a higher discharge value than the countercathexes. The typical reactive character formations would have an intermediary place—representing on the one hand a defense, on the other hand non-defensive functions.[15] Furthermore, the shift of energy from one ego function to another one seems easier achieved among the nondefensive functions. But this is not to say that defenses cannot also to some extent draw on the reservoir of various shades of neutralized energy that the system ego has at its disposal. The comparative rigidity of the cathexis of some ego functions, as against the comparative ease with which the cathexis of others is changed, is a scarcely explored chapter of psychoanalysis.[16] We have learned from Freud the differences in mobility between primary and secondary processes, and also that, as a rule, secondary processes are characteristic of the ego functions.[17] However, we see that there are differences in mobility also between various ego functions. We could try to correlate these differences with degrees of neutralization, and this might actually be part of the truth—but maybe not the whole truth. Some of the most challenging problems of psychoanalysis might become approachable if one were to resume Breuer's and Freud's work on bound and mobile cathexis extending it to the varieties of ego cathexes.[18] Here I merely remind you that the system ego, besides the more localized investments of specific ego functions, disposes of reserves of neutralized energy that can be shifted to points where it is needed. It is probable that in certain psychoses these operations are interfered with, maybe concomitantly with impairment of neutralization (see Chapter 10).

I spoke of various degrees of discharge being correlated with various ego functions. But there is also another case relevant for our understanding of the discharge aspect of neutralization. In many

[15] Freud occasionally describes reaction formation as a case of sublimation.

[16] See, however, Chapters 7 and 10; Kris (1951b, 1952), Rapaport (1951).

[17] For the cases in which ego functions depend on the use of the primary process, see Kris (1934).

[18] See now the thorough discussion of these and related questions by Holt (1962).

situations that call for action, it is probable that the ego appeals to the id for energic support (this is, of course, an anthropomorphic description; but you understand what I mean). It is further likely that the appeal is mostly made to those forces in the id which, genetically speaking, represent the precursors of the ego activity in question (see Chapter 9). Ego and id activities, though often antagonistic, would here be synergic, as they frequently are (Freud, 1926a). In these cases there will be an increase in the amount of instinctual energy of the id discharged through the ego, in a more or less neutralized mode. It would be an example of one of those "switching" operations of the ego, of which there are many.

This way of admitting the forces of the id will not interfere with autonomy, as long as the ego's capacities for control and neutralization are unimpaired. The ego's faculty to accept this help without functional disturbance varies from one individual to the other, and also as to specific functions. The process, though in itself normal, has one aspect that can be described as regressive, and I want at this point to remind you again of Kris's work on "controlled regression" (since 1934).

So far, in opposing defensive and nondefensive ego functions, I have only scantily referred to the fact that there is a defensive aspect to neutralization (or sublimation) too. Sublimation has often been described as a defense mechanism, and it is true that it represents one of the most efficient means to deal with "danger" threatening from the drives. Thus it can be used as defense, though it is not always and often not only defense, as it takes care, economically speaking, of the nondefensive functions of the ego too. I may add that even where it serves defense, sublimation is hardly a "mechanism" in the usual sense (Fenichel, 1945; and Chapter 9). If we compare it with other defensive measures, there is also this difference that the change of instinctual to neutralized energy forms at least one element of its definition, thus setting sublimation apart from other defense methods, the concept of none of which refers to a change in the mode of energy. We may say that the process of neutralization in itself, and in general, can serve defensive purposes, far beyond the more special case in which certain shades of neutralized aggression are used in countercathexis.

As I mentioned before, it can also be closely linked with some real defense "mechanisms," as identification or displacement. More complex is its relation to repression. It has often been said that early repressions may interfere with neutralization (Freud; Melanie Klein, 1932; and others); but also that successful repression may be a prerequisite for neutralization (Nunberg, 1932). Jones (1941) states that there is "an optimum point, where there is neither too much nor too little repression, in relation to which the maximum amount of sublimation occurs." That repressions can handicap neutralization is an uncontested clinical fact. Still, this is certainly not the necessary outcome of every repression. Also, while Freud originally thought that repression makes the energy of the repressed drives definitely unavailable for other purposes, he later (1924c, 1926a) considered an alternative to this outcome, namely, that it may be taken over by the ego and used, e.g., in identifications. Just in passing I may mention that if we use the broader definition of neutralization, there is actually a double correlation with repression; while repression often interferes with neutralization, impairment of the latter can, on the other hand, prevent the formation of stable repression, as, I think, is the case in schizophrenia (see Chapters 9 and 10).

From what I said, it already clearly appears that neutralization (the change of the purely instinctual strivings into a mode of energy more appropriate to the functions of the ego, together with the delay of immediate instinctual discharge, the control by the ego) plays a decisive part in the mastery of reality. The formation of constant and independent objects, the institution of the reality principle, with all its aspects, thinking, action, intentionality, all depend on neutralization. According to Hart (1948), it is a compromise between instinct and reality (see also Hendrick, 1943). As I said before, if we accept Freud's statement that self-preservation, in man, is mostly taken care of by the ego, we come to understand neutralization also as a powerful help to this central biological aspect of man, not as its opponent as it has occasionally been described. Besides reality testing and the mechanisms of adaptation, the integrating (or synthetic, or organizing) functions share in the maintenance of self-preservation; and they too are not purely instinctual in character but mostly belong to those that work with neutralized energy, though they may be in part genetically traceable to the instincts (Freud, 1923a; Nunberg, 1932), as are other neutralizations.

I have discussed the neutralization of libidinal and aggressive drives, pointing to what these two forms of neutralization have in common, but also to some of their differences, e.g., in relation to specific functions of the ego; I also mentioned that neutralizations of libido and aggression do not of necessity run parallel to one another. Here I want to add a few words to what was also hinted at before: the possibility that there exist other, noninstinctual sources of neutralized energy. Most of the energy active in the psychic apparatus originates, according to Freud, in the drives. But a later hypothesis of his which may be relevant for this question assumes that there exists a hereditary core not only of instinctual but also of ego functions. I have developed some implications of this idea in my work on the primary autonomy of the ego (1939a; and Chapters 7 and 9), which prepares the ground for the possibility just presented: namely that part of the mental energy—how much or how little we can hardly estimate—is not primarily drive energy but belongs from the very first to the ego, or to the inborn precursors of what will later be specific ego functions, and maybe also to those apparatus that come gradually under the influence of the ego and in turn influence its development. It is true that such a hypothesis, though appealing on many grounds, cannot today be proved. But this is equally true of the hypothesis that really all mental energy stems from the drives. Both assumptions lead ultimately back to physiology (Chapter 7).

Not only the longest known, but also still the best studied sources of neutralized energy are the sexual drives. May I insert here some remarks on a problem, widely discussed in analytic literature: the question of what kinds of sexual energy lend themselves best to sublimation. The question has been answered in various ways. In one passage, Freud (1916-17, p. 302) states that sublimation "consists in the abandonment, on the part of the sexual impulse, of an aim previously found either in the gratification of a component-impulse or in the gratification incidental to reproduction, and the adoption of a new aim." Freud (1908b) also considers the occurrence of sublimation as a consequence of sexual abstinence (for the case of the scientist). Here he implies the sublimation of genital libido, and, in the first quotation, he states that both pregenital and genital libido may be sublimated. In another passage (1908) he assumes that the greatest part of sublimation has its origin in pregenital strivings. Fenichel (1945) and even more definitely Deri (1939) think it unlikely that genital libido can be neutralized, and Flescher (1951) seems to share this opinion; while others, like Sterba (1942), allow at least of the occurrence of some degree of genital sublimation. Both Fenichel's and Deri's thesis is deduced from theoretical premises which I cannot go into at this point. Personally, I cannot fully agree with those premises or, for this reason, with their arguments for discarding genital sublimation. That normally a considerable part of pregenital impulses is sublimated, is very likely true. But I do not see any definite reason to deny the occurrence also of neutralization of genital libido. Alpert (1949) emphasizes the apparent contradiction that even when the genital level has been reached, only pregenital strivings should be sublimated. There is some uncertainty also concerning the question whether only object libido can be sublimated. Glover (1931) points to the fact that at least part of the pregenital tendencies, from which so much of the sublimation is derived, are not object-directed. These and related questions do not necessarily enter the definition of sublimation. But these and other differential considerations may become relevant if we study the developmental aspects of neutralization, or the relations between certain of its forms (as to gradation, origin, and so on) on the one hand, and specific contents, or functions that it serves, on the other hand. I first realized the relevance of this latter category of problems in studying the energic aspect of countercathexis, about which I said a few words earlier in this paper.

As mentioned before, it is difficult to ascertain when neutralization starts in the child. It has often been traced to early frustrations and renunciations. Hart (1948) has particularly emphasized that renunciation which comes from love is more likely to promote neutralization than the one which comes from fear. The child's siding with reality demands (Anna Freud, 1954a) and the early identifications are no doubt an important step in the use and spreading of neutralization.[19] At any rate, we have to assume that neutralization starts very early, if we follow the lead of Freud's later definition which seems to me the most logical one. It must start even before the ego as a definite system is established and before constant objects are constituted—because it is likely that these achievements already presuppose some degree of neutralization.[20] This also implies that neutralization cannot be assumed to be initiated by the superego, though its secondary relations to the superego are clinically and developmentally of paramount importance. That certain types of superego formation may interfere with neutralization is amply documented clinically. Alexander (1923) stressed the point that every tendency of self-injury may handicap it. On the other hand, the aspect of the superego that Freud calls the ego ideal is most influential in determining the direction of neutralization on certain aims or functions—which does not mean, as Freud reminds us, that the capacity for sublimation is in any way proportional to the sublimity of the demands.

This is obviously one of the problems that stood at the beginning of psychoanalytic research on sublimation: the question of the mean-

[19] For the formation of early countercathectic energy distribution in their relation to neutralization see Rapaport (1950, 1951) and Chapters 9 and 10.

[20] Aspects of sublimation such as the elaborate stratification described by Bergler (1945) obviously belong to a much later age.

ing and the origin of those sublimations which are syntonic with the demands of the ego ideal. Today we would say that this is not "the problem" of sublimation or neutralization, but it is certainly one aspect of it. It was necessary to broaden the concept—maybe so much that some of you feel uneasy with it—in order to make it maximally fruitful for our understanding of ego functioning (some of the pertinent problems I have presented here) and for a comprehensive view on ego-id relations. On the basis of these insights, the old sub-limation problem, sublimation in art, religion, etc., has, then, to be attacked anew. If our reasoning is correct, we should expect to find that the later formulations prove more elucidating, even in regard to those "cultural achievements," than the original concept was meant to cover. So far differential research along these lines has not been done in all the fields relevant to that subject. But it has been done for one of them: art and the artist. I think that a work like that of Kris, *Psychoanalytic Explorations in Art* (1952), which uses the later and more complete conceptual framework, does bear out this expectation.

To summarize: while conceptualization of "sublimation" has changed, the most important single factor among several that at one time or another entered its definition is the process of desinstinctual-ization (neutralization). In adopting a broad concept of neutraliza-tion I follow Freud's later formulations on desexualization. It opens the way to many problems essential for the metapsychology of the ego and of ego-id relationships. Because of obvious reasons, the earlier concepts have not become, and could not become, equally meaningful in this respect.

In studies of "sublimation," situations that give rise to neutraliza-tion, or the genetic determinants of its contents, or the mechanisms that are often connected with it, etc., are sometimes not clearly set apart from the process itself, a neglect which has often led to am-biguities. In this paper I have suggested that we consider, besides the general character of the process, the twofold (or probably trifold) origin of neutralized energy in the two drives (probably also in the ego);[21] the capacity to neutralize which varies individually, according to the developmental level, to the situation, etc.; the incentives to neutralization, under the pressure of the id, under the direction of the ego (and later of the superego); the ontogenesis of neutralization; the neutralized cathexis of aims of the ego, as opposed to that of ego functions; the role of neutralization in defensive as well as nondefensive ego functions and the difference of cathexis of these two sets of functions; the gradations or shades of neutralization, in particular with respect to the various functions they serve; the partly different use of neutralized libido and neutralized aggression; the correlation of neutralization with secondary ego autonomy.

I know that this introduction to our discussion is incomplete in many respects, and I am fully aware of the tentative character of some of the hypotheses I introduced. The accent was on the importance of Freud's later concept of desinstinctualization for the psychology of the ego, and, on the other hand, on how our understanding of some aspects of sublimation (neutralization) can benefit by the introduction of ego-psychological propositions. I also tried to give some indications where potential ambiguities lie, and where, on the other hand, fruitful possibilities of future investigation may be found.

---

[21] A terminological note is to the point here. Strictly speaking, energy that from the start belongs to the ego can, of course, not be termed "desinstinctualized" or "neutralized." It could be called "noninstinctual" and probably is best called "primary ego energy."

CHAPTER 13

Notes on the Reality Principle

(1956)

I F WE are to study the processes and the problems which the concept "reality principle" is meant to cover, there is still no better point of departure than Freud's paper on the "Two Principles of Mental Functioning," first published in 1911. This work is important and interesting in another respect also. It deals specifically with a number of ego functions, such as consciousness, thinking, attention, judgment, action—and does so *avant la lettre,* if I may say so, before ego psychology had become an integrated part of psychoanalysis; that is to say, his studies of ego functions had not yet appeared in the framework of the set of propositions which we call ego psychology today. At the time Freud used the terms pleasure ego and reality ego, and what was later to become the distinction of ego and id was still represented as an opposition of ego drives and sexual drives. One of the many essential contributions of the paper was the observation that while the ego drives are ready to yield to the influence of the reality principle, the sexual drives remain much longer under the dominance of the pleasure principle, a fact that is significant for mental development in general and for neurosis in particular.

The idea that pleasure and unpleasure are dominant forces in motivating human behavior had, of course, not escaped the attention of earlier thinkers; it goes far back in the history of philosophy and has been strongly emphasized especially by a school of British philosophers. Bentham, to quote at least one of them, said that nature has put man under the control of two sovereign masters, pain and pleasure. We find also in the pre-Freudian literature references to a development toward a more adaptive state of affairs. Freud has never claimed property rights in this respect; on the contrary, in discussing the pleasure principle, he said that "Priority and originality are not among the aims that psycho-analytic work sets itself" (1920). Originality was not the aim of his work, although it was, in the case of Freud, invariably its outcome. It was with Freud's pleasure and reality principles in a way as with his concepts of the unconscious mental processes. While the terms had been used before, the decisive achievements of finding a method to study these processes, of filling the terms with specific psychological meaning, and of assigning them their place in a coherent structure are Freud's.

If the infant finds himself in a situation of need, and if attempts toward hallucinatory gratification have proved disappointing, he will turn toward reality; and the repetition of such situations will gradually teach him better to know reality and to strive for those real changes that make gratification possible. This is what Freud says in the "Two Principles." It gives us a solid basis and point of departure for the following considerations. In the case described, the first step, the turning toward reality in search of gratification, simply follows the pleasure principle. We attribute to functions of the ego both the cognition and the purposive change of reality involved in the process. But the reality principle, according to Freud, means also that uncertain pleasure is renounced, with the purpose of ascertaining, in a new way, that an assured pleasure will come later. This clearly presupposes two other ego functions of the greatest importance—postponement and anticipation. Thus the question arises (Hartmann, 1939a): how far does the development of ego functions enter as an independent variable into the processes described by Freud? It is true, we are wont to say that the "demands of reality" are responsible for them. But this is, of course, a metaphorical way of putting the case;

it is correct only if we presuppose the existence of something in the individual that speaks out for reality—a tendency toward self-preservation which, in the mental life of man, we attribute mostly to the ego and to its precursors. The question whether the ego plays a primary role in the institution of the reality principle will be answered differently, according to whether we view the ego as an agent active from the beginning, though only in a limited way (as Freud did in later writings), or as something traceable only to the impact of the interaction of reality and drives (as he did earlier). Freud's formulations of the reality principle vary. In quite a few passages he simply states that the institution of the reality principle is due to the influence of the external world on the individual. And often he describes the reality principle just as one form of regulating mental processes and achieving mastery of part of them. In these definitions it is not traced to the activity of specific mental functions or groups of functions. But I can also quote some passages in which he explicitly describes the influence of the ego on its emergence. In *Beyond the Pleasure Principle* (1920) we read that the substitution of the pleasure principle by the reality principle is due to the "self-preserving instincts of the ego"; in *The Question of Lay Analysis* (1926b) he says that the ego replaces the pleasure principle, which before then had been the only dominating force, by the reality principle. In the *New Introductory Lectures* (1932) we find a similar statement. These latter descriptions seem to me to be more in line with what we know about the facts, and more in line also with Freud's later formulations concerning the role of the ego.

There is another aspect to this same question, one closely related, though, to that just discussed. Freud distinguishes three principles of regulation which he calls pleasure principle, Nirvana principle, and reality principle, respectively. They are described as tendencies which in a general way aim at regulating the excitations in the mental apparatus, in modifying them as to quantity, quality, or rhythm. The first two, the pleasure and the Nirvana principles, easily fit this definition; their regulating activities are concerned with the whole mental apparatus. Here again, the reality principle stands apart. It originates in one mental system only; also, its power over the mental apparatus extends no further than the power of this system. The reality principle seems to represent the modifications imposed by the ego on the functions of the two other principles and is therefore not quite on the same plane as the others (see Chapter 4). It is, indeed, an ego principle; that is, the concept of the tendencies we ascribe to the reality principle is identical with that of a group of ego functions (though not of the ego as a whole). It seems advantageous to keep this in mind when we speak of the reality principle.

In our literature two meanings are currently attached to the term reality principle. Used in one sense, it indicates a tendency to take into account in an adaptive way, in perception, thinking, and action, whatever we consider the "real" features of an object or a situation. But in another, maybe we could say, narrower sense, we refer primarily to the case in which it represents a tendency to wrest our activities from the immediate need for discharge inherent in the pleasure principle. It is in this sense that we speak of the reality principle as the natural opponent, or at least modifier, of the pleasure principle. This poses a problem. One cannot state in a general way that reality-syntonic behavior curtails pleasure. This would be a quite illegitimate generalization, and not only because—as Freud repeatedly emphasized and I have just quoted—behavior under the guidance of the reality principle is aimed at gaining, in a new way, assured pleasure at a later stage, while giving up momentary pleasure. In this case, its timing determines whether or not discharge is reality syntonic. But beyond this consideration of expected or assured gains, there is also the fact that the activities of the functions that constitute the reality principle can be pleasurable in themselves. I remind you at this point of the pleasurable potentialities of sublimated activities. Organized thought or action, in which postponement is of the essence, can become a source of pleasure. While this, at first sight, seems to complicate things, there is no way denying it; indeed, it becomes perfectly clear if we think of the reality principle in terms of ego functions. If I have emphasized here the double meaning of the term reality principle, it was in order to forestall possible misunderstandings; failure to note the double meaning has occasionally led to a misrepresentation of Freud's thinking on the subject. In opposing reality principle and pleasure principle, he certainly did not mean to negate the pleasures we derive from the world outside; and he repeatedly commented on the advantages the ego provides for instinctual gratifications, aside from its different role as an opponent of the drives.

Freud emphasized, as I reminded you before, the importance of situations of frustration in the development of the reality principle.[1] The assumption that in the hypothetical case of continuous and full gratification the objectivating and anticipating functions would be badly impaired is, indeed, quite convincing. But we should also consider here the thought first expressed, I think, by Anna Freud (1936), that the postponement or control of discharge is one of the essential features of the human ego from its beginnings; it is probably an essential feature already of its forerunners, before the ego as a system of personality has been fully established. We should also

---

[1] Recently, two interesting papers, replete with thoughts pertinent to this point, were published by Loewald (1951) and by Székely (1951). It is emphasized that Freud's concept of reality is bound up with the figure of the father, and that in Freud's mind the castration threat is the clearest representation of the demands of reality. On the other hand, the concept of reality is also connected with the role of the mother. It is not possible to discuss here in detail the contributions of these authors. I just want to note the obvious truth that the child's attitudes toward reality and conceptions of reality pass through several stages of relations to the objects which leave their imprints on them. I fully agree with the authors that those stages of the child's attitudes toward reality which they put in the center of their presentation are important, though I do not propose to include these aspects in this paper. Both mother and father play a dominant role in the vicissitudes of the child's relations to reality. But I think that the concepts both of reality and of the reality principle as presented by Freud are of a far more general nature. The child's concepts of reality can be followed through the vicissitudes of object relations and conflicts. But "the reality concept of psychoanalysis" cannot be defined by these. Nor would such an attempt at defining our concepts be of any advantage in dealing with other psychological processes of a general nature. In this context it may be instructive to remember how Freud rejected what he called the "sexualization" of the concept of repression, the attempt (suggested to him by Wilhelm Fliess and Adler) to limit this concept to the opposition of two specific groups of instinctual tendencies, masculine and feminine (Freud, 1919).

consider what is, I think, a necessary assumption (see Chapter 9), that the child is born with a certain degree of preadaptiveness; that is to say, the apparatus of perception, memory, motility, etc., which help us to deal with reality are, in a primitive form, already present at birth; later they will mature and develop in constant interaction, of course, with experience; the very system to which we attribute these functions, the ego, is also our organ of learning. What I have said is to the point here, because it means that some preparedness for dealing with reality precedes those experiences Freud referred to in the passage quoted.

Another point, related to the foregoing, though not identical with it, is the question of the occurrence of the first "positive" attitudes of the infant to the world outside. It is a complex problem, to which both Spitz and Erikson have given considerable thought. In a remarkable paper by Charlotte Bühler (1954), which in part follows analytic reasoning, great emphasis is put on "primary positive responses" to reality alongside the primary negative ones—and this both on observational and theoretical grounds. There is no reason to deny these findings; moreover, the assumption that later on, when the differentiation of self and object has taken place, the positive object relations also draw on these primordial experiences is plausible enough. However, while the child does not have to learn everything the hard way, for many important functions this situation proves unavoidable. And there is certainly nothing to invalidate any of Freud's statements on the impact of situations of deprivation on the evolution of the reality principle. While Freud has not discussed all the implications of his theory, we find here and there in his work contributions to some facets of the problem, e.g., in his paper on "Instincts and Their Vicissitudes" (1915a).

Sooner or later, though not every step has been clarified thus far, the child unlearns and outgrows the distortions inherent in the purified pleasure position described in that essay. The impact of all stages of child development—the typical conflicts, the sequence of danger situations, and the ways they are dealt with—can be traced in this process. The problem has been most extensively studied in relation to the development of object relations. Perception, objectivation, anticipation, intentionality, neutralization of energy—all participate on the side of the ego in this process. One may well ask why this whole development of the reality principle (or the corresponding ego functions) shows such a high degree of complexity in man, a complexity to which there is hardly a parallel elsewhere, except, perhaps, for some other higher mammals. No doubt, one reason is that in the human the pleasure principle is a less reliable guide to self-preservation. Also, self-preservation is mainly taken care of by the slowly developing ego with its considerable learning capacity. But pleasure conditions for the ego on the one hand and the id on the other differ significantly, while the instincts of the animals represent at the same time what we would call in man ego functions and functions of the drives. Also, probably as a result of the differentiation of the human mind into systems of functioning, the id is here much farther removed from reality than are the instincts of animals (Hartmann, 1939a).

But let us return to the meaning of the relationships of the reality and pleasure principles in individual development. It is here, in the study of ontogenesis, that the mainsprings of psychoanalytic knowledge lie, and most of what we say analytically about the differences of man and lower animals, or about the special characteristics of the human mind and related questions, is ultimately traceable to what we know about ontogenesis. The reality principle includes postponement of gratification and a temporary toleration of unpleasure. Another source of unpleasurable experiences, and an essential one, "is to be found in the conflicts and divisions that take place in the mental apparatus" (Freud, 1920) in the course of development. That is, what would have been a pleasurable experience under other conditions—namely, without the differentiation into ego, id, superego—may now be felt as unpleasure. This is a process clearly distinguishable from the one I discussed earlier. In the case of postponement of satisfaction and temporary tolerance of unpleasure, the pleasant or unpleasant nature of the elements involved is a "given thing." But the second case we could state only in a general way by saying that the conditions themselves on which the pleasurable or unpleasurable characters of a situation rest have been changed. There is no other way of accounting for this than, again, to attribute it to the development of the ego (to which, however, we must add here the development of the superego). These developmental changes in the pleasure conditions, consecutive to ego (and superego) development might, in so far as maturation participates in them, be compared to the changes of pleasure conditions induced by the sequence of libidinal phases. In the statement which I just quoted from Freud, he finds an explanation of the reasons why structure differentiation can induce a state of affairs in which earlier sources of pleasure, in the course of development, lose their pleasure qualities. If we look at it from a point at which structuralization has actually taken place, we have the right to draw from this finding two conclusions. The reality principle, in the narrower sense, imposes restrictions on the pleasure principle, if only to secure a future pleasure gain. But the aspect of structure formation under scrutiny now has changed also the conditions for pleasure gain; it has not only limited them but also newly defined what is and what is not pleasurable (or less unpleasurable). This is the more remarkable as we are impressed by the tenacity with which man so often clings to the sources of experienced pleasure. But there is no denying that a reassessment of pleasure values does take place, a differentiation according to their various sources, which one may well describe as a modification of the pleasure principle, or perhaps as a partial domestication of the pleasure principle—different from the reality principle in the stricter sense. Not only the reality-tuned functions of the ego but also its organizing function play a role in it. Obviously, this change in pleasure-unpleasure conditions grows parallel with other developmental changes.[2] One may

2 The hypothesis that certain activities or organs owe their exceptional pleasure potentialities to the important biological functions they serve is familiar in analysis from phylogenetic propositions (Ferenczi, 1924); see also Hartmann (1939a).

say that this aspect of the pleasure principle develops a bias in favor of the ego and superego or, better, it comes partly under their control. However, what I have said certainly does not apply to the id, where we find only instinctual tendencies seeking discharge, but it does appear to be valid for the interactions of the systems. If you remember what, for the case of repression, Freud says about the ego setting the power of the pleasure principle in motion (1932) or his statement that the essential point in turning "a possibility of pleasure into a source of unpleasure" is that "pleasure and unpleasure, being conscious feelings, are attached to the ego" (1920, p. 11), then it seems to me that you will not be very far from the interpretation I have just given you. This is an interesting development indeed, particularly if we consider the discharge value of the primary as against that of the secondary processes. It may seem difficult to account for this in metapsychological terms. It would be especially hard on the basis of Freud's earlier theory which established a direct coordination of the feelings of the pleasure-unpleasure series with the lowering or heightening of the stimulus tension in the mind. Later he said that this view could not be correct. He thought rather that pleasure and unpleasure could be referred to peculiarities like "something rhythmic, the periodical duration of the changes, the risings and fallings of the volume of stimuli" (1924b). This problem is one of the most obscure among those psychoanalysis has to deal with. But I think it is not inconceivable that changes in the relations of the factors Freud mentions here with pleasure and unpleasure go on parallel with mental development. At any rate, whether we chose to interpret it metapsychologically in this or in a different way, we can say that the pleasure principle itself has a history too, besides the limitations imposed on its manifestations by the reality principle in the narrower sense of the term. To avoid a possible misunderstanding I may repeat: it is, of course, not the essential characteristics of the pleasure-unpleasure principle by which we define it (that is, the striving for pleasure and avoiding of unpleasure) that change in the course of development; what does change are the conditions of pleasure and unpleasure.

The second reflection relevant at this point brings us back to another aspect of the reality principle. I said earlier that in man the pleasure principle is not a very reliable guide to self-preservation. There are, though, exceptions to this rule; the avoidance of pain (*Schmerz*), e.g., retains its biological significance. As a very important exception we might also consider what I am discussing just now. In those situations in which pleasure in one system (id) would induce unpleasure in another one (ego), the child learns to use the danger signal (a dose of unpleasure) to mobilize the pleasure principle and in this way to protect himself (Freud, 1926a). He will not only use this mechanism against danger from within but also against danger from without. The process is directly guided by the pleasure principle; it is really the pleasure principle that gives this move its power. What interests us in this connection is that through a special device an aspect of the pleasure principle itself (avoidance of unpleasure) is made to serve one of the most essential functions we make use of in our dealings with reality. It is a definite step in development to be distinguished from what I called the reality principle in its narrower sense (the so-called modification of the pleasure principle, meaning postponement of discharge, temporary tolerance of unpleasure)—and I may refer you here to what I said, partly with this case in mind, about the necessity to keep apart the two concepts of the reality principle. Genetically, of course, the use of the pleasure principle I am discussing now is also dependent on the development of the ego, as is the reality principle in the narrower sense.

Over and over again we see how our understanding of these problems depends on our insight into the evolution of the ego, but also that this insight has not yet made sufficient progress to allow us more than highly hypothetical answers to a number of questions. Summarizing this first part of my paper, I may say: we assume that at birth (and actually before) there exist certain dispositions for future ego functions whose growth will later influence the pleasure and reality principles in a variety of ways. Freud assumes that the tendency to pleasure gain is there from the beginning and that at an early stage it predominates over the tendency to avoid unpleasure. Both together, however, cannot fully account for the institution of the reality principle, in the sense of postponement of discharge and toleration of unpleasure; we have to assume that the development of ego functions enters the process as an independent variable. At this point, objectivation and anticipation begin to play a decisive role. What one could call the pleasure-unpleasure balance (that is, the sum total of pleasurable and unpleasurable elements in a situation, an activity, and so on) will now include, beyond the consideration of the present, also the consideration of the future.[3] The question of whether the accent is on pleasure gain or on avoidance of unpleasure remains relevant for the "acceptance of the reality principle" as a factor variable not only developmentally but also individually. According to this, quantitatively identical pleasure-unpleasure balances may produce different reactions. The foresight I spoke about includes judgments on the relations of cause and effect, both as to what happens in outer reality and in the child's mind. Structure later induces, as a new element, a change in the pleasure conditions, as described above. At this point the direct use by the ego of the pleasure principle for the mastery of outer and inner reality becomes important in a specific way. And, as a further step, in the case of the danger signal, an unpleasant feeling is intentionally reproduced by the ego for that very purpose.

This summary is, of course, strikingly sketchy. It does not even exhaust the knowledge of which we feel reasonably sure. May I at least add that the pleasure-unpleasure balance is decisively changed as a consequence of the fact that the child renouncing an instinctual desire expects, and often gets, a recompense in the form of love or

---

[3] Once a certain level of differentiation and integration has been reached, it becomes inadequate in an increasing number of cases to describe an experience (actual or expected) as simply "pleasant" or "unpleasant." What we are confronted with is rather a series of pleasant elements, weighed against a series of unpleasant elements. It is to account for this fact and to warn of oversimplification that I use the term "pleasure-unpleasure balance."

approval by the parents. There is also the pleasure the child derives from participating in the world of the grownups. Here we have, then, a substitution of one form of gratification (through the object) for another one. We also know that once the superego has been established, the child will often feel pride in foregoing a pleasure (Freud, 1940a). This is certainly a strong motivation for accepting certain demands made by the reality principle. As I have said, I think that the gradual development of the pleasure potentialities provided by the ego works in the same direction—not only in so far as it provides us with ways in which to achieve instinctual satisfaction, but equally because of the pleasurable feelings so often connected with sublimation. Of course, the pleasure principle does not stop at the door of the ego; it is simply that the psychology of discharge has been much better studied as to the instinctual drives than as to the secondary processes.

The reality principle includes both knowledge of reality and acting in regard to it. Biologically speaking, it is part of what we usually term adaptation. As you know, Freud called the two ways by which a more suitable relation to reality can be achieved alloplastic and autoplastic behavior respectively, according to whether the individual effects a change in the outside world or in himself. Incidentally, I may add what we could consider a third case (Hartmann, 1939a) in which the individual does not effect changes of himself or of the world outside; instead the relationship between him and the outside world is changed: I am thinking of the search for and finding of a more appropriate environment. This process, too, plays a considerable role in the development of the species and also of the individual, very clearly in the case of man.

But in this context I want to make only one point, referring to the relations of the knowledge and action aspects of the reality principle. First of all, in a general way, maximal utilization of one partial function of those that serve adaptation is not always compatible with the optimal functioning of the whole system (see Chapter 1). More-over, if we state, let's say, that a certain thought is reality syntonic in a given situation, this may refer to either one of two meanings. It may mean that the thought is true in the sense that it corresponds to reality. On the other hand, it may also mean that its use, in a given reality situation, leads to a successful mastery of this situation. That in a large sector of human behavior there is no simple correlation between the degree of objective insight and the degree of adaptive-ness of the corresponding action is not in need of being proved. Objective knowledge of and practical orientation in reality do not necessarily coincide. We all know that action in line with "common sense," which is practically oriented, can be more efficient. But it is hard to state in general terms where it will be efficient and where, on the other hand, the kind of thinking we call scientific is called for. The French, very aptly, distinguish *savoir-faire, savoir-vivre,* and *savoir tout court.* If we sometimes tend to forget these differences, it is probably because in our analytic work the relation between truth-finding and an effective therapeutic change is a particularly close one. This therapeutic value of insight in analysis we can take for granted and I do not propose to discuss it here. It is rather in a broader psychological framework that the distinction I have in mind becomes significant.

Developmentally speaking, a degree of avoidance of outer reality, of restrictions of insight, or of denials can often be harmless in the child and even, in certain situations, useful, which, as Anna Freud (1936) has explained, in the adult would lead to far more serious consequences. As to inner reality, there is no doubt that withdrawal from insight, the restriction of inner reality testing, in the wake of the typical repressions, occurs also in normal development. It appears that later, though less incisive, techniques of compromise in the grownup, which neglect some aspects of reality but nevertheless remain adaptive, are partly built on the early models. Of course, we are very familiar with the cases in which such compromises miscarry; but in this context, dealing with general psychology rather than with pathology, my point is just the opposite: that they often do not. Minor refusals to acknowledge part of reality without a consequent impairment of reality-syntonic action are pretty much ubiquitous. They may even serve a more reality-syntonic behavior, in the second sense, a subject to which I will turn. These phenomena may be situational and are often more or less mobile. They may also become parts of automatized patterns. These are, in a way, defensive maneuvers, but hardly always defense mechanisms, in the stricter sense in which we use the word as an analytic term. I think we should say that, in these phenomena, what is not conscious avoidance is very often, though by no means always, preconscious rather than unconscious; it is kept from consciousness by that censorship which, according to Freud, works between the conscious and the preconscious mind.

I return once more to problems of development. We take man's unique learning capacity for granted, but we are impressed again by the complex steps, the detours, one might say, the devious means necessary to achieve "acceptance of reality." It has been said that in man "there is a long way from pleasure-principle to self-preservation" (Freud), and this may be one reason why so much of adaptive behavior has to be wrung from the pleasure principle. We may now add that this is not the only cause of those complexities. We have to face the fact that what is adaptive in one respect may interfere with adaptation in another. I just touched upon the question in speaking of the relations between objective knowledge of and action vis-à-vis reality. An equilibrium between the various adaptive trends will finally, more or less successfully, be established by experience and by the integrative, or synthetic, or organizing function of the ego, which works on several levels and correlates aspects of mental functioning with each other and with outer reality. However, what I want to emphasize next is that there exist similar discrepancies even in regard to the forms of "knowledge of reality" itself; also that from the beginning the very ways in which the child acquires knowledge of reality are fraught with instigations to distort it.

The main early sources of learning about reality are in the child's relations to his own body and to the objects. Identification and object relations will for a decisive period of time dominate this process and will, even later, never become quite irrelevant to it.[4] Both the development of ego functions and the constitution of constant objects represent a moving away from what Freud calls primary narcissism, and are closely interrelated. They probably already presuppose the use of a mode of energy different from the instinctual one. In contact and communication with the object, the child learns to demarcate his "self" and to realize the first vestiges of objectivity. The transition from "egocentric" thinking to recognizing the relativity of qualities depends on insight into the relativity of the "me" (Piaget, 1937a; Rapaport, 1951). Much careful and interesting work on the subject has been done recently, inside and outside of analysis.

The protracted helplessness of the human child causes a situation in which "the value of the object . . . is enormously enhanced" (Freud, 1926a). One may well say that in man the human objects are by far the most important sector of reality. The dependence upon the object, as is well known, becomes an essential factor in the human child's learning about reality. It is responsible also for typical or individual distortions of the picture of reality which the child develops. Thus the same factor acts in both directions (on either side, of course, it is combined with others). Its "not-objective" imprints will differ in different sectors of the child's thinking. We may expect them to be comparatively insignificant in the area of perception, though even here the higher processes by which sensory data are integrated are accessible to subjective modification. They are certainly clear in concept formation, in habits of thought and of emotion. Language, one of the most characteristic achievements of man, and one the child largely owes to the objects, might be one of the most general examples because it opens a decisive avenue to objective knowledge, but at the same time preserves forms of thinking that are often

[4] See also de Saussure (1950), and Axelrad and Maury (1951).

neither realistic nor logical. One aspect of this, the taking over of "stereotypes" by the child, has been discussed by Sullivan (1953). It is, of course, not possible to present in this paper the manifold practical problems raised by this double-faceted impact of socialization on the child's learning about reality.

A "realistic" object can be of great assistance to the child in discriminating fantasy and reality; it will help him to meet real dangers on their own grounds, as Anna Freud has said recently. When Freud speaks about reality testing he usually means the capacity to distinguish between ideas and perceptions. In a broader sense, reality testing also refers to the ability to discern subjective and objective elements in our judgments on reality. The former we expect to function rather reliably in normal adult persons; the learning of the latter is an unending process. It is here that the criteria are, in most people, rather poorly defined and the temptations to tamper with objective judgment are considerable. There are, of course, many well-known reasons for this, but I propose to limit myself to the one point under discussion only. I mentioned the well-known fact that pleasure premia are in store for the child who conforms to the demands of reality and of socialization; but they are equally available if this conforming means the acceptance by the child of erroneous and biased views which the parents hold of reality.

What I said concerning the essentially helpful, but also prejudicial, impact of the objects on learning about the outside world is true also in regard to the child's inner world, and self-deceptions are the inevitable result. The ways in which the data of inner reality are organized or integrated, the image of his own self and its evaluation, are codetermined by these powers in their role of models or of prohibiting agents. This does not start with, but finds its clearest expression in, the formation of the superego, which of course includes, among other and partly opposite results, also some degree of narrowing or distortion of the child's knowledge of inner reality. We should not omit that the superego may occasionally influence even the testing of outer reality (Freud, 1936). On the other hand, the superego may add to the motivation for objectivity, at least in so far as the characters of objectivity, intellectual honesty, truthfulness, etc., are included in its demands. Actually, these are rather widely emphasized, even in otherwise divergent value systems (see Hartmann, 1960a; Hartmann and Loewenstein, 1962).

There is, then, interference with objective cognizance of the world not only through the action of instinctual needs; it may be handicapped also by ego (and superego) functions, even by functions which in other circumstances can lead to adjustment. And, more specifically, there is the case I am discussing here, namely, the taking over by the individual of the picture of reality accepted and taught by the love objects, but also, in a broader sense, of the picture commonly accepted in the culture to which he belongs. The child learns his approach to reality in constant relation to the adult's approach to it. It adjusts to a world which is not only to a considerable extent man-made, but also man-thought. As a consequence, two different criteria of reality develop, and in the world of every individual both play a role.

Without entering into the philosopher's discussions of what constitutes reality, a few words about how we use the term in analysis may be to the point here. The criteria chiefly used by Freud are those of science, or more correctly, those that find their clearest expression in science. Science strives for validation of its statements concerning reality, it accepts as "objective" what is verifiable by certain methods. Intersubjectivity plays a role in scientific validation. But "conventional" or "socialized knowledge" of reality means, in contradistinction to scientific knowledge, often not so much what allows intersubjective validation, but rather what is intersubjectively accepted, to a considerable extent without validation, or attempt at validation. For the child, this means accepted by the objects closest to him.[5]

---

[5] In enlarging upon Piaget's concept of "realism" in the child, we could speak of "social realism": opinions of the objects are taken for objective. For the same problem (and also for the difference of "reality testing" and "sense of reality") see Weiss (1950).

What the mother, according to objective standards, is "neurotically" afraid of can (but in this second sense only) mean "real" danger for the child. Incidentally, there is in this socializing of reality knowledge also a tradition-forming element, besides the one recognized in the superego.[6]

In our clinical evaluation of "realistic" behavior we commonly use both concepts of knowledge; in theoretical discussions we mostly refer to the concept of "objective knowledge." How the relations between the two concepts of reality knowledge or, maybe we should say, how the criteria of "truth"[7] about reality evolve, I cannot discuss here in detail. In his stages of rebelliousness the growing individual also rebels against the commonly accepted view of reality. His tendency toward objective knowledge may also muster the help of instinctual drives. However, after having become autonomous, it may reach a considerable amount of stability. In certain situations the resistance against group contamination can be considered an indication of ego strength (Redl and Wineman, 1951).[8] Actually, many factors would have to be considered if we were to study the various types of independent as contrasted with the various types of conforming behavior. My main point here is only that the preponderance of one adaptive ego function may mean the weakness of another one, equally adaptive in itself. The scientific conception of knowledge of reality will never entirely eliminate the other conception except in the case of the scientist, and, even here, only as long as he does scientific work. It is not to be forgotten that much of our "knowledge" of reality is of the socially accepted kind, with most of our actions based on it.

---

[6] I would like to mention in this connection also another aspect that often leads to distortions of objective thinking. The child is constantly confronted with value judgments which cannot be validated objectively but which are presented to him as statements of fact. "This is good" and "that is bad" are often presented to him in the same way as "this is red" and "that is green." Such presentations also become part of "socialized reality," which may well be one of the reasons why many adults (some great philosophers among them) cannot accept the logical difference between a moral imperative and a factual statement.

[7] Gide speaks about *vérités de constatation* and *vérités de convention*.

[8] I need hardly remind you that, on the other hand, the inability to conform is very often of a pathological nature.

"Objective" knowledge does not, of course, have to contradict the accepted picture of reality; but it often does. Perhaps the best example of this second case is psychoanalysis, which put objective knowledge into a field where only socially accepted knowledge had existed, and thus interfered with conventional thought in a particularly sensitive area. What Einstein (1950) said about the desirable freedom of thought "from the restrictions of authoritarian and other social prejudices as well as from unphilosophical routinizing and habit in general," is to the point here and closely corresponds to Freud's thinking. It is clear that not every judgment of or dealing with our fellow men calls for the same level of objective thinking. What one usually calls *Menschenkenntnis* belongs to a greater part to the level of common sense. However, it is one of the most characteristic features of psychoanalytic work that it transcends the conventional level of our thinking on man, not only occasionally, but essentially. In this field, the usefulness of an approach on the common-sense level seems rather limited. It is, I believe, empirically true that adherents of a great variety of philosophies, of political and religious denominations, may be competent psychoanalysts; and it would be quite unrealistic to expect that the analyst cannot share some of the prejudices of his culture, his nation, his social class, or his age group. But it is probable that too strong a bent toward general conformism, or conformism beyond a certain threshold, can create a disposition unfavorable to his professional work. At any rate, he can, strictly speaking, be an analyst only in so far as he is able, in the thinking and acting which constitute his work, to detach himself from the socialized knowledge of man and to move on the level of what Freud calls reality.

There are, then, two pictures of reality opposed to the concept of "objective" reality, which Freud mostly used: the one, as we know, corresponds to what we usually, in a simplifying way, call magical thinking; the other, to a view in which not validation but intersubjective acceptance is used as a criterion of reality. Though the two undoubtedly overlap to some degree, nevertheless their structural and economical differences are very significant. I think the distinction proves useful also for the understanding of certain aspects of pathology. To give you a simple example: if somebody tells you the prophet Elias has ascended into Heaven, this will not lead you to any doubts as to his mental health, though you may not share his opinion. If he says the same of his neighbor, you can make the diagnosis of a psychosis. This means that of the two reality concepts which are opposed to the concept of objective reality, one may be pathognomonic while the other is not. It has often been said that the incorrigibility of an idea which is not substantiated by objective criteria marks it as a delusion. But this idealizes the critical faculty of man. Everybody has his share of erroneous and incorrigible ideas. It would seem that for an understanding of why we consider an idea pathological, the distinction between "conventional" or just socially accepted "knowledge" and objective knowledge can be helpful.

I spoke of various functions serving the reality principle, such as cognition and action—both obviously adaptive but also occasionally in contradiction with each other. I added that even for knowledge itself at least two different concepts are developmentally significant. These complexities of the reality principle are more easily understood if we think of them in terms of a variety of partly independent ego functions, of their synergisms and antagonisms, and of various states of intrasystemic equilibria. This necessity for considering the specific functions which determine our relations to reality in addition to the more global concept of the reality principle becomes clearest, of course, where these functions are at least partly opposed to each other. Thus, to make my point I had to emphasize this aspect; I do not overlook or underrate the more familiar situations in which they work together in the service of adaptation.

Taking as my point of departure the discussion of objective versus conventional knowledge, I suggest that we take one more step toward clarifying our thinking on reality, a step which will again land us in a kind of dichotomy; this dichotomy, too, can in principle but not always in practice be accounted for in psychological terms. The problem I have in mind has not been much discussed in analysis,[9] but I thing it belongs in the context of my presentation.

Scientific thinking, the purest form of objective thinking, gives us a knowledge of reality which is formally but often also materially different from everyday knowledge. I discussed the case of conventional knowledge, but there is still another aspect to this difference. As an attitude, objective thinking presupposes a certain degree of detachment from immediate experience. Freud describes thinking in general as a trial activity with small amounts of cathexis. That is, trial is interiorized. Thinking is a detour activity which requires first some detachment from the outer world, in order better to understand, predict, and master it. This detour is necessary for the efficiency of objectivation. Objective thinking is the more essential in man, because his drives are much further removed from adaptive aims than are the instincts of lower animals. I spoke of detachment from immediate experience. This world of immediate experience, which is what we commonly mean in speaking of "the world we live in," is not easy to define. Not speaking scientifically, most people would call it the "real" world.

This poses a number of interesting problems. However, what interests us here is only one aspect, namely, the relation of this world to what I said before about "reality." On the one hand, it is obviously not what we call an "autistic" world. On the other hand, the world of exact science certainly does not simply coincide with that "world" we are considering now. For one thing, the latter contains the element of quality, of color, sound, touch, and taste, while the world of strict science does not. The biological meaning of quality has been accounted for in various ways. Freud seems to have been interested in the problem (and, in connection with it, in the function of consciousness) in his early work. He wrote about it in the "Project" (1895) and in *The Interpretation of Dreams* (1900), where he said that qualities direct cathexis, that they act as regulators. Of

[9] See, however, Winnicott (1953).

course, quality is only one of the differences between the scientific concept of the world and its everyday meaning. Specific factors of coherence and organization have entered our everyday perceptual picture of reality, and this is true also of our thinking about reality. That is, data are assimilated in a way which gives us knowledge of the outside but which also tries to give them a meaningful place with respect to our mental functioning. This is based on the structure of our mental apparatus (it certainly has a physiological aspect too), on conscious, preconscious, and unconscious previous experience, and on present mental activity also. If we speak of assimilating a part of reality, or of making it our own, this does not refer only to the knowledge of objective data; it also refers to their cathexis and integration. There may be a difference in cathexis of objective data and those that are also in a more personal sense part of "our world." At any rate, the economic and dynamic status of knowledge is changed by this process of assimilation which introduces it into the interplay of our psychic tendencies. This world we are discussing now, different from the world of science, is clearly an important aspect of our relations with reality and it is, particularly as a developmental problem, a very much worth-while subject also of scientific study. The absence of, or rather restrictions on, the capacity to build this world we know as pathological phenomèna. It is seen most frequently in schizophrenics that reality becomes meaningless, reduced to "pure environment," that they are deprived of the processes which normally give it a place in one's personal world. In this case, we speak of a withdrawal of cathexis from reality (or rather from the presentations of reality), which is correct though probably incomplete. Beyond this, it is likely that in the schizophrenic there is an impairment of specific ego functions which normally account for our world being meaningful also in a personal way. Also, in so far as the world is personally meaningful for him, the meanings have often changed as compared to his earlier, normal stage.

What is commonly called "reality" outside of science is formed, then, also by the nature of our mental apparatus in general and by our history. A constant process of taking in—assimilation—and putting out is going on in our minds. This brings us face to face with a familiar problem, rather well understood psychologically in some aspects—although other aspects raise questions which concern physiology, and a third group constitute one of the central issues of epistemology. In a thoughtful paper on the "Sense of Reality," Zilboorg (1941) states the question: what is "external" and what is "externalized"? He also remarks that "the ego's actual manipulation of reality has hardly been taken into consideration," which was more true at the time of writing than it is today, though even now this aspect of our studies is still in its beginnings. We know projection as a pathogenic mechanism, but it is, of course, also part of normal functioning. In the grownup, a workable equilibrium is normally established between what we here call "our world" and the objective knowledge of reality. It is workable if the ego is strong enough not to be impinged upon in its essential functions by the id, and strong enough also not to exhaust itself in its struggles against the drives—that is, if those of its functions which serve reality and synthesis have reached a certain degree of autonomy. Reality testing can then function not only in the narrower sense—the distinction between perception and idea, which is normally established rather early in life—but also in the broader sense I mentioned before. However, it does not, of course, always reach out into strictly "objective" knowledge but mostly balances one element of the "world of immediate experience," in the somewhat hazy sense I use the word here, against others.

Thus we have actually two organized systems of orientation, the world of science and the world of a more immediate experience. The principles inherent in these organized systems differ; both are "selective," though in a different way. There is also, as I have just said, overlapping. The cues to our actions are widely found in the world of immediate experience. There is no doubt that the evolving of this world, though it falls short of exactly reproducing or corresponding to "objective reality," is helpful toward developing our relations to it. By assimilating it, we learn to handle it. The transformation, or molding, of data into this more or less coherent world fulfills, then, a necessary function. Here again, we see a compromise formation between two ways of dealing with reality, each one of which is in itself adaptive. The coherence of this "world" is dependent, among other factors, on the ego's capacities for integration, which in dealing with outer reality at the same time consider the state of the mental systems. This is a contribution of the synthetic function to our approach to outer and inner reality. Nunberg (1930) relates the development of causal thinking to the synthetic function. I may add that causal thinking is only one, though an essential, aspect of the processes I have in mind here.

Part of what I have said can also be presented in different language by stating that the relation between stimuli from without and our response to them is commonly a rather complex process. The stimulus can, of course, be complex in itself, but there is also the fact that the same individual does not always react in the same way to the same stimulus. There is usually no one-to-one reaction. The basis of the reaction includes the structure of the mental apparatus, intersystemic as well as intrasystemic relations, and is formed by earlier experience. The nature of this integrated response determines also whether a situation is "meaningful" for us or not. In this sense, Freud (1926a) speaks, e.g., of the fact that "the external (real) danger must also have managed to become internalized if it is to be significant for the ego. It must have been recognized as related to some situation of helplessness that has been experienced" (p. 168). Dealing with similar problems, though from a different point of view, and exemplifying them by the problem of pain, Buytendijk (1955) said recently in an interesting paper, which is representative of a definite trend in contemporary thinking, that "one's world . . . is no system of objective correlations, but a system of meanings and thus of values." He regrets that the possibility that something acts through its meaning is an annoyance to the scientifically oriented physician. I do not think the possibility is annoying to the scientifically oriented psychoanalyst, though the analyst will tend to look at it from a different angle. First, while we realize that both values and meanings enter "one's world," we would keep "value" and "meaning" conceptually apart. And, beyond this, meanings, in our sense, that is, regarded in the framework of our thinking, are considered as psychological facts; they refer to mental tendencies involved in a situation; they refer to the sign or the symbol characters with which we invest our experiences. That an attitude to reality is "subjective" does not mean, to us, that the psychological factors accounting for this "subjectivity" cannot be studied objectively. This reorientation in regard to the problems of "subjectivity" and "objectivity" is actually an essential feature of psychoanalysis, which has subjected that "world" I spoke of in relevant aspects to objectifying thinking. In the process of analysis itself, the patient's relations to inner and outer reality are restructured, distortions are undone, and a more "objective" picture is substituted for them. Particularly with respect to childhood material, the resulting picture is far more "objective" and also coherent than the one the child could form at the time the experience took place. In regard to this, analysis means increased knowledge of reality, outer and inner, in the strict, objective sense. Also, psychoanalysis tends to eliminate "quality" from its basic concepts (Hartmann, 1927). But in the course of analysis, these objective insights are also integrated, though the degree to which this is done varies with each individual, into the patient's "world," in the sense I use this term here.

In the foregoing, I have repeatedly referred to inner as against outer reality. I have now to make clear that inner reality is not quite the same thing which Freud had in mind in speaking of "psychic reality," a concept he used in his explanation that fantasy activities can have the same motivating power as realistic behavior, and that in parts of our mental apparatus reality testing does not exist. In speaking here of "inner reality," I am referring to the fact that in a sense all mental functions, tendencies, contents are "real"; fantasy activity also is real, though not realistic. That is, to recognize that a fantasy is, as a mental act, real does not mean that its contents reproduce reality.[10]

Problems of acceptance, of distortion, of denial occur in relation to inner as well as outer reality. How the attitude toward the one affects the attitude toward the other is a fascinating object of study. Developmentally, the problem has been extensively investigated by M. Klein (1932), who emphasizes that the relation to inner reality has already become important at the time when the reality principle is instituted; by Winnicott (1953), who refers to an intermediate area of experience, in which both inner and outer reality participate; and recently by Frumkes (1953), among others. To speak only of one later developmental phase, it is certain that after a given age the child learns, in his successful dealings with external reality, to include in his plans of action the consideration also of his own mental processes (see Chapter 3). He learns to anticipate the interaction of inner with outer reality. This has been well described in regard to one aspect of action by Parsons and Shils (1951); "In accordance with a value standard and/or an expectation, the actor through effort manipulates his own resources, including his own body, voice, etc., in order to facilitate the direct or indirect approximation to a certain cathected goal—object or state." What has been called "attitudes on a realistic basis" includes certainly also some knowledge and consideration of one's own person. About the distorted pictures of inner reality, about typical and individual self-deception, we have learned more from analytic work than from any other source. To account for it, it seems reasonable to speak of a testing of the within, in addition to the testing of the without—that is, to distinguish inner-reality testing from outer-reality testing. Impediments of inner-reality testing are so common that, as to certain functions and contents of the mind, we do not expect much objectivity even in a normal person, except in the course of the psychoanalytic process. These impediments will, of course, sometimes also alter the picture of outer reality, as a con-

[10] See also Dorsey (1943).

sequence of repression, for instance. But in the neurotic, interference with the testing of inner reality is in the foreground. The basic properties of outer-reality testing, we know, break down in psychoses only.

In summary, my paper dealt with problems of general psychology, not specifically with the theory of neurosis. This is in line with Freud's approach in the paper I took as my point of departure. You may well feel that I have introduced a bewildering number of differentiations and complexities into a basically simple question. I shall be glad if at least some of you agree that these complexities are not arbitrarily introduced but are features of the problems under consideration today. Once one gets used to the manifold aspects of "reality" and "reality principle," this variety no longer appears bewildering. It seems to correspond rather neatly to the variety of those ego functions and their interactions which led Freud long ago to speak of the ego as a "representative" of reality. I also think that their differential consideration proves helpful in practice in evaluating the different modes of reality-syntonic behavior.

CHAPTER 14

The Development of the Ego Concept in Freud's Work

(1956)

THE choice of my topic for today may need some explanation. For the analyst in his daily work, Freud's thought continues to be very much alive; indeed, an essential element. In this sense, Freud has not yet become a "historical figure" for us, and an intellectual effort is required to change the perspective to view him from the vantage point of a historian. But the effort is necessary, for the presentation without historical discrimination of his discoveries as well as his thought tends to create uncertainties and promote confusion. Furthermore, we can hardly do justice to Freud's thought without an intimate knowledge of the remarkable growing power inherent in it, and of the ways in which this development came about.

We find in Freud's work, even after the foundations of psychoanalysis had been laid, many rather radical new departures and many reformulations, continuing through his last papers. There are a number of chapters of psychology whose importance he freely admitted, but which, as he often said, he had not yet come round to. It is this quality of not being finished, of not having said the last word, that Freud had in mind, when, confronted with misunderstandings of his teachings, he found it necessary to draw a demarcation line between psychoanalysis as an empirical science and the philosophical systems. He was not, of course, implying that analysis is less bound to the principles of systematization than other sciences of nature. Freud's hypotheses are interrelated in a systematic way: there is a hierarchy of hypotheses in their relevance; their closeness to observation, their degree of verification. It is nonetheless true that there exists no comprehensive presentation of analysis from this angle. Here again recourse to the historical approach seems imperative—for the present, as a substitute for such a system, also as a help toward achieving a system in the future, by showing the actual problems in their right proportions and in the right perspective.

As we all know, Freud was not much given to stating systematically, by way of a cross-section, where and when new thinking had supplanted earlier concepts. Although he did so occasionally, in many cases his changes of thinking are not made explicit, but must be deduced from the changes he makes in the use of his concepts. It also happens that ideas long abandoned are revived again and filled with new life, often after a considerable period of time. This state of affairs might well have facilitated the development of a phenomenon not rare in the history of analysis: the fixation of some analysts on a single phase of Freud's thinking—everything before being considered merely preliminary to this phase and everything later as just its aftermath. Obviously, in any single case many other factors determine such preferences and limitations. To some extent at least these arbitrary judgments can be counteracted by a closer study of history. To the study of biology, social science, literature— which Freud felt we ought to include in the curriculum of the student of analysis—we should add a detailed study of the history of his own field.

None of Freud's own historical writings is aimed at a really comprehensive or detailed presentation of all the adventures of discovery and adventures of inventive thought that went into the making of psychoanalysis. Fortunately, we have in some of his not primarily historical papers a number of summarizing excursions into certain historical aspects of analysis, as, for instance, the development of the theory of instincts—a history to which other analysts have added several significant contributions (e.g., Jones, 1936; Bibring, 1936). More recently, we have witnessed a renaissance of historical awareness in analysis. There is, of course, Jones's imposing work (1953-57), infinitely rich in relevant material and in penetrating thought; there is Kris's brilliant introduction to Freud's letters to Fliess (1950c); there are the invaluable introductions and notes by Strachey in the *Standard Edition,* the detailed investigations of Bernfeld (1944-1953) and a few others. To all of these I am grateful, particularly with respect to this paper.

One could not say, though, that historical studies on specific aspects of analysis abound, even today. But such studies seem to be more needed at the present state of affairs in our field than are summarizing accounts of the main lines of its development, of which there exist quite a few. As to ego psychology, despite the fact that the concept of an ego has been present in analysis since its beginnings, it became a chapter of analysis in its own right comparatively late. Its importance with respect to general psychology, beyond the reach of problems it was originally meant to cover, was realized even later. Thus for a long time less has been said about the history of ego psychology, by Freud and by others, than about the history of other chapters of our field. There exist, however, a few prolegomena on this topic, as, for instance, an article by Kris (1951a) which deals specifically with our subject, and this paper, too, was helpful to me, as were quite a few scattered but revealing points in some others.

The choice of this topic seems appropriate also because the historical study of the ego concept leads directly to some later reformulations of Freud—new departures, suggestions, hints, or whatever you like to call them—which he could not work out in a more systematic way and which have been unduly neglected by many of us. Though their importance is considerable, they have not yet gained the place in research and in teaching which they actually deserve. Some of these reformulations have a bearing not only on ego psychology itself, but seem to reveal (or imply) a changed approach also to other fields. Freud's last contributions seem to me to have a special interest, as they may well give us some indications as to the direction in which his thought might have developed.

Today, however, I do not set out to speak about the future of analytic ego psychology, but about its past; I have decided to limit my observations to Freud and, occasionally, to some of his immediate precursors, whose concepts of the ego obviously influenced his own. I do not propose to speak about work on ego psychology contemporaneous with or subsequent to his. Even so, I am sure you will not expect anything like a comprehensive study of this rather complex and, even today, in many respects baffling subject. I cannot do better than select, and follow, a few strands only among the many that went into its formation—though I know that every such selection is open to questioning. I will not discuss the development of Freud's ideas on the superego—which makes my selection already a somewhat artificial one, though one easily understandable as imposed by the natural limitations of a lecture. Also I shall place the accent on concept and hypothesis instead of data, and here I will not plead limitation of time only; I feel that this approach is, in the case of Freud, unusually rewarding. And, speaking to this audience, I feel assured that the observations these concepts are meant to account for are familiar to all of you. Furthermore, a certain conceptual vagueness which has crept into many discussions tends to become a serious handicap to an understanding among analysts and also to an understanding of psychoanalysis in general. In emphasizing the conceptual aspect I also think of the fact that while in earlier days the detractors of psychoanalysis used to reject it *en bloc,* more recently a tendency has developed to accept the discoveries, or, let us better say, some of them, and to concentrate criticism on the Freudian concepts and hypotheses.

As to the prehistory of psychoanalysis, you probably all know the book by Dorer (1932), if not in the original, then from the extensive use made of it and the many quotations from it in the first volume of Jones's biography of Freud. Not being an analyst, Dorer misses many of the more subtle implications of Freud's ideas, and is often not able to discern clearly the use Freud made of ideas and concepts carried over from his teachers. Her statement that Freud's psychology was in the main derived from earlier sources is quite obviously wrong, and Jones's objection to it is indisputable. What happened to that historian of preanalysis has happened to other historians before: looking at even the greatest work from the angle of "precursors" only, one cannot help finding similar ideas in the history of human thought. If we look at it from the other side, tracing how the ideas were used or modified, how they were integrated with experience and with each other, we may come to look at the same work as one of the most original creations of the human mind, as is the case with analysis. This is true of all its chapters, and very clear in ego psychology—which does not, of course, obviate our interest in the building stones Freud selected for his work.

Having disposed of Dorer's misunderstanding of what originality actually means, we can acknowledge that her book is richly documented and in a way quite valuable; we shall turn back later to one of her points. There are, then, two questions, both relevant to history. What was the set of concepts with which Freud approached his work in its beginnings? When and why were they discarded or modified; what has taken their place; what part has experience, and what part thinking to play in the evolution of his later concept of the ego, highly original and quite his own in the sense just outlined?

Freud's earliest conception of the ego defines it as an organization with constant cathexis. In the language of physiology, it is a group of neurones, and, where it is psychologically characterized, a group of ideas. We find as early as the "Project" of 1895 the three approaches to psychology which he was later to call the topographical, the dynamic, and the economic. The imaginativeness and, at the same time, strictness of the hypotheses presented in this work is extraordinary indeed. It has been discussed by others in greater detail, and I shall refer to it only in so far as it reveals something of Freud's ideas on the ego at that time. As one would expect, they find a more precise formulation here, and are less limited in scope, than in the simultaneous clinical writings. The functions which form the body of the ego concept are set apart from other mental processes. The distinction between primary and secondary processes is clearly outlined. One of the functions, defense, became dominant at that time in his clinical research. Other functions studied in this outline—to all of which Freud's interest returned at various stages of his thinking—include reality testing, perception, memory, thinking, attention, and judgment, among others.

The idea of an ego characterized by its functions and its relations to the external world and to other mental processes is presented here with the greatest definiteness and has proved to be of lasting value. But, of course, most of the data that were later to fill it with concrete meaning had not yet been discovered; and particularly of the great inner antagonists of the ego, the drives, Freud had in those years only a rather limited knowledge.

A few words about the ancestry of this early ego concept are appropriate here. We know that Freud became familiar with the psychology of Herbart in the gymnasium, though, as Jones says, we have no proof that Freud studied his original writings. At any rate he knew that, according to this author, ideas are the true subject of psychology. He was acquainted with Herbart's propositions of a quasi-dynamic nature, with the mechanics of association, with one concept of unconscious thinking; perhaps he adopted the term "repression" from Herbart. However, while Freud certainly wrote, in the beginning, in the psychological language of Herbart, it does not appear that his psychology had great stimulating power for Freud, who gave the concepts new meanings or discarded them altogether; even more important, it does not seem that Herbart's concepts were helpful in a specific way for the solution of any of the concrete problems with which Freud was confronted—an essential difference, whenever we try to evaluate "influences." With Fechner, it was a different case. Some of his propositions did help Freud in a more specific way, though not particularly with respect to the field with which we are concerned today. The concept of truly dynamic unconscious processes has a quite different ancestry; it is, in German philosophy, found in the works of Schopenhauer and Nietzsche, and in certain romantic philosophers before them. But about this ancestry comparatively little is known, or rather little is known about the degree to which, and the ways in which, this thinking might have left an imprint on Freud's work. However, I want to remind you that Freud said of Nietzsche in 1907 "that he had a more penetrating knowledge of himself than any other man who ever lived or was ever likely to live" (Jones, 1953-57, 2:344). At any rate, it is noticeable that while the traces of Herbart's psychology were soon overcome, the correspondence with Nietzsche's thought—whether or not "influence" played a role in it—is striking even in some of Freud's later theories.

Much broader and more specific—in the sense in which I have just used the word—than Herbart's, was, I think, the impact of Meynert on Freud's concept of the ego. This is natural enough. He was, for Freud, "the great Meynert in whose footsteps I had trodden with such deep veneration," and the man of whom Freud had repeatedly said that he came, of all those he personally knew, closest to genius. That Freud knew Meynert's every written work, and also his lectures, seems obvious.

When I read not just quotations from Meynert but some of his works in the original, I was impressed by some definite correspondences with Freud's ideas. You will allow me to give you a few examples. Meynert (1884) distinguishes a primary and a secondary ego (this is quoted by Freud in *The Interpretation of Dreams,* and also by Dorer and by Jones). The primary ego represents that part of mental life which is genetically early and unconscious. Superimposed is the secondary ego. The core of the ego is given by the demarcation of the child's body from the environment. Also, the ego has the function of a controlling agent. Closely related persons may be included in it, and in the course of development what we would call a person's ideals will become part of it. Another point worth mentioning is that perception is here described not as a passive but an active process.

All this, I suppose, will sound rather familiar to you, though the conceptual framework in which it is presented in Meynert's writings is, of course, different from the one of psychoanalysis. But the analogies between the primary and secondary ego, and ego, superego, and id, in Freud's sense, are obvious. Nor do I have to point out the parallels with Freud's concepts of the body ego and of identification. The idea of the active character of perception was developed by Freud in a very interesting way later; and by the way, quite recently a great number of experimental investigations have come to the same conclusion. Here, then, according to the distinction I just introduced, we have not only the use, by Freud, of a given terminology, but the continuity of this approach was a guide for him also in specific problem solving. The powerful influence of Meynert was emphasized by Dorer, though her presentation suffers from the bias I mentioned before, and Kris shares this view, at least to some extent. For a different opinion, I refer you to Jones, who treats, in what is certainly the most penetrating study of those "formative years," Meynert's influence as one among others of similar importance.

Although Meynert's ideas were widely known at the time, they were integrated with clinical experience, freely modified, and assigned their place relative to others in an incomparably broader frame of reference only by Freud. There is but one exception, and that for the first steps only in this momentous transformation and elaboration: that is, Josef Breuer. Freud always admiringly acknowledged Breuer's theoretical contributions to the *Studies on Hysteria* (1895). Unfortunately for the historian, the respective shares of Freud and Breuer in this essay are not clearly traceable even today.

The first layer of Freud's conception of the ego looks, I know, rather forbiddingly "theoretical," or maybe "speculative," to some and too far removed from clinical usage. This is not quite so; in the "Project" Freud already allowed an important place to his studies of the dream and of neurosis. Later, after he had made the decisive step of abandoning an approach through anatomy and physiology and of dealing with psychological problems in terms of psychology, the continuity with some of his earliest concepts is still noticeable in at least some aspects of his reorientation. It is clear that his earlier theoretical work, together with his clinical work of the same time, reveals the two-way approach that was to remain highly characteristic of his work throughout his life. Freud has been variously described as a great discoverer, thinker, liberator—and he was certainly all these and something more. In the context of studies like this one, the important thing is to know exactly when, in his work, he was the one and when he was the other. Summarizing presentations of psychoanalysis often do not clearly distinguish between the roles which observation and hypothesis formation respectively played in Freud's work. Among the truly great thinkers Freud was one of the very few who was also a great clinician. One may also reverse the statement and say that among the great clinicians he was one of the not too many who were equally great as thinkers. Thus there is hardly a better example in the history of science than Freud's work, if one wants to study the interaction between clinical observation and theory. Of course, the role of fact finding for the formation of theories has long since been established, but today there is also a more general awareness of the role of "good" concept formation and "good" theory, not only for integrating facts, but also for discovering them. This was always, of course, known to a few. Darwin said that without speculation (which, I suppose, means theorizing) there is no good and original observation. For Einstein, theories were a free creation of the imagination, limited by two principles: there must be confirmation by experience, and the fundamental laws should be as few in number as possible and be logically compatible. In Freud, the capacity for fruitful theorizing was on a level with his clinical genius. Of course, I do not want to imply that his concepts have always the precision of those used in exact science. But I do want to assert that they are by far the most fertile at our disposal in the field of psychology. In his constant concern with both aspects of analysis, it often happened that hypotheses anticipated observation. This is to the point here, because a characteristic of his early thinking was that in some respects it anticipated his clinical work. Some early ideas re-emerged many years after he had first formulated them, becoming clinically essential only at this later level. The reverse case, postponement of conceptualization, will occupy us later.

While various functions of the ego are described, more or less occasionally, in the early clinical papers, it is the function of defense that becomes very definitely the focus of interest. Here already, instead of the pure empiricism of older medicine, attention is directed toward the mechanism of nosogenesis. During their collaboration, it was Breuer who developed the idea of a hypnoid hysteria, while Freud, perhaps from the first but certainly soon afterwards, saw defense as the decisive agent. Inasmuch as they shared their clinical experience—incidentally, similar observations were made by Janet at about the same time—one would like to know how to explain the differences in their conclusions. Freud said later (1914c) in comparing his interpretation with Breuer's: "I had taken the matter less academically; everywhere I seemed to discern motives and tendencies analogous to those of everyday life." He also spoke of a number of simple psychological formulas, that is hypotheses, with which he approached the field. This may then be one of the cases in which the formation of fruitful hypotheses is decisive to the scientific momentum of a discovery. Freud's dynamic thinking, his concept of a defensive ego, opened the way to the reality of psychic conflict, and we can say in retrospect that this emphasis on conflict, on defense, and on the dynamic unconscious, was to become the cornerstone of analysis in its clinical and technical as well as theoretical aspects. We owe entirely to Freud the possibility of studying conflict in a systematic and objective way and of tracing its role in normal and abnormal development. Conflict, of course, had always attracted the interest of writers, of philosophers, and of religious thinkers. But no psychologist before Freud had had either the method or the courage to make it an object of scientific investigation.

The ego, we remember, was at that time still an organized group of "ideas." Certain ideas could be admitted while others were excluded. Although other possibilities were also considered, the assumption prevailed that this exclusion implied exclusion from consciousness, and thus a decisive step was taken toward linking the dynamic with the topographical viewpoint. Still, it is noteworthy that Freud had already found in 1896 that the defenses themselves are, or can be, unconscious. It was only much later that this insight became relevant for a reformulation of his ego psychology.

Even after the ego's propensity to defense had been recognized, the dynamic factors involved on both sides of a conflict were for some time not explicitly defined. But to the mechanics of association was added the directing influence of psychic tendencies, and in the interplay of associations the role of purposive ideas was appreciated. This appeared, tentatively, in the "Project" and found its clearest exposition in *The Interpretation of Dreams.* The pure association theory of earlier days was soon modified by Freud and adapted to the demands of his rapidly evolving experience and thinking. For some time there was an overlapping of the old and the new. Then concepts like "purposive idea" and "psychic tendency" became dominant. Also, a realization of the determining force of what Freud called, in a general way, "wishes" was an early mark of his theories; occasionally, he spoke of wish fulfillment on the side of the repressing as well as the repressed forces, and in these cases the word seems synonymous with psychic tendency, or intention. Freud sometimes spoke of the intention of the ego to forget, or to repress—a deviation from associationism which reminds one of the fact that another critic of that theory, Franz Brentano, was among Freud's teachers in Vienna. In the history of psychology his name is linked to the concept of intentionality. I may add that about the time *The Interpretation of Dreams* was written, a new trend started in experimental psychology, too, with the central concept of determining tendencies.

The latter departure Freud might not even have known, but this type of historical parallel to analytic concepts retains its interest, if only to show how differently similar ideas, originating at the same time, are worked out by different thinkers. The two parallels to Freud's thinking here mentioned never reached a stage, and entirely lacked the method, in which and by which the central dynamic factors could be approached.

Before leaving our discussion of Freud's early ego concept, I want to add, because it will become relevant for later developments, that what I have discussed here has been only the dominant and the best defined part of the picture. The term "ego" was used at the time in science, and is used also today both outside analysis and even inside, in a variety of meanings beyond the one Freud defined. The expression often points to the subject of experience in contradistinction to its objects. It is also used to indicate one's own person as against other persons. For some it is synonymous with what Freud calls the psychic apparatus. Others call "ego" the awareness (or the "feeling") of one's own self. Freud did not use the word in its last-mentioned, that is, in its phenomenological meaning; for him, the subjective experience of one's self was a function of the ego, but not the ego. Nor did he accept the meaning I listed first, familiar in epistemology. Perception and thinking, according to Freud, depend on the ego, but the activities of the ego can also be objects of perception and thought. But as to some other meanings of the term, it is obvious that at one time or another they played a role in Freud's thinking. The ambiguous use of the term, especially its use to designate not only what we now call the ego as "system" but at the same time also the self, and one's own person in contradistinction to other persons, influenced Freud's theories only later, so we shall discuss it at a later point.

In the period immediately following the conceptualization outlined above, some important additions were made without changing the basic characteristics of the ego concept. Freud's first classical work, *The Interpretation of Dreams* (1900)—in which he formulated general psychological laws for the first time comprehensively and in the language of psychology—describes the contributions of the ego to the dream (though not in the first edition; see Strachey's notes): "The wish to sleep which the conscious ego is concentrated upon, and which, together with the dream-censorship and the 'secondary revision', . . . constitute[s] the ego's share in dreaming." Censorship of the ego is a term used earlier in Freud's clinical papers. The secondary revision, in so far as it represents a tendency to unify and to contribute to intelligibility, reminds one of Freud's later concept of a synthetic function of the ego. Elsewhere, the dominating influence of the ego upon mental impulses was emphasized and explained by its "relation to consciousness and to voluntary movement." These were essential contributions indeed to the psychology of the ego. But soon afterwards a period of latency, as it were, set in, so far as the development of ego psychology was concerned.

What were the reasons for Freud's temporarily receding interest in the ego? Several come to mind, but their respective influences on the trend of his work at the time are not easy to judge, and a certain amount of interpretation becomes unavoidable. Though he was more outspoken in his writings about some aspects of his mental life than any man before or after him, Freud was in general not too much given to thinking about his thinking in developing his ideas. Nor does he seem to have communicated extensively about it. The important exceptions we know of are in the letters to Fliess and in some of the letters to other friends, published in Jones's biography. As to this point, students of the thinking of other great men, for instance, Nietzsche, have it remarkably easier. With Nietzsche—the only man of the nineteenth century comparable to Freud in the depth of his psychological insights—the self-interpretation of his thinking, descriptions of how his intuitions came about, and explicit or implicit dialogues with himself abound. This kind of interpretation is not completely absent from Freud's work (I shall quote one example later) though, in studying the evolution of his thought, one often wishes there was more of it. We know from some instances, and assume it from others, that his thoughts went through a slow maturative process, from the moment they occurred to him for the first time until he gave them their precise and explicit place in his work. In some instances the reasons for such postponements seem easy to grasp, while in others they pose interesting problems. It is true also of certain of his clinical observations that their clear-cut conceptualization and integration occurred only in much later phases of his work. The best examples here are aggression and the unconscious nature of defenses. In the former case, Freud himself later (1930) wondered why he had overlooked the ubiquity of nonerotic aggression.

The most obvious reason for his temporary postponement of ego psychology was no doubt his momentous discoveries of those years in other fields of analysis. The great superiority of his later ego psychology lies to a considerable extent in the very fact that his work on the unconscious mind and on the drives, and his insights into human development, had preceded it. About essential properties of the ego we may say that any attempt to force an understanding of them in a way which neglects those other aspects of the mind is doomed to failure. From this angle, the retardation of Freud's interest in the ego appears as a rather fortunate event. Nobody could, I suppose, say with assurance how far this order of succession in turning his interest to different fields, was consciously intended; part of it was probably due to the impact of clinical and technical problems; certainly his reliance on the proven guidance by his preconscious thinking played a part in it. Perhaps what he wrote to Jung about the way he worked, in a letter published by Jones (1953-57, 2:449), is to the point here: It is "to be on the look out in whatever direction you feel drawn and not take the obvious straightforward path. I think that is the best way too, since one is astonished later to find how directly those circuitous routes led to the right goal."

An accessory reason at that time for Freud's changed attitude toward the study of the ego was probably that since this concept had originated only partly in analytic experience, he found it difficult to assign it, or certain of its aspects, the right place in relation to some of his discoveries in other fields of mental activity which he owed totally to the psychoanalytic method. And then it was his avowed endeavor, at least for some time, to study precisely what the others had neglected. Furthermore, there is no doubt that Freud disliked what the philosophers had said about the ego and was suspicious of its possible metaphysical implications. The term was burdened with the metaphysical meanings the philosophical system builders of the early nineteenth century had given to it, and these systems, we know, represented just the kind of philosophical thinking Freud found uncongenial. Nietzsche, who shared this antipathy, had written not much earlier that the superstitious belief in the "soul" had not yet ceased to make mischief in the form of a superstitious belief in the subject and in the ego. In early papers Freud often put the word "ego" in quotation marks (as, by the way, Meynert also did occasionally) which gave it the look of a foreign body. It was probably also to counteract metaphysical implications that Freud described the ego as part of a mental "apparatus"—a term that clearly reveals its origin in the "physicalist" thinking whose influence on Freud Bernfeld has clearly stated. You know that in later years, though still critical of philosophers and, inversely, disliked by most of them, Freud developed ideas which according to common usage one would call philosophical. But we do not find such ideas in his ego psychology; they are rather concerned with a speculative extension of his theory of instinctual drives. It would certainly be worth while discussing what kind of "philosophical" thinking Freud considered fruitful, or considered legitimate, and where the limits of its legitimacy lay for him; but this is beyond the scope of this paper. Suffice it to mention here that he would certainly have rejected various recent attempts to distill from analysis some kind of "philosophy of life," and to base the evaluation of the empirical findings of analysis on the evaluation of such allegedly implied "philosophies."

It took more than twenty years after Freud's early formulations, before ego psychology could definitely be established as a chapter of psychoanalysis and before the interest of the analyst became equally distributed between the id, the ego, and the superego. As is the case with the theory of drives, we can thus describe three consecutive phases in the development of Freud's concepts. Neither here nor in instinct theory, though, are these phases sharply demarcated; there is continuity as to many aspects, and there is to a certain extent over-lapping even of the central themes of the consecutive phases.

At the turning point from the first to the second phase Freud did not explicitly revoke what he had previously stated about the aspects of the ego closest to the later "system" ego, but the change in accent is obvious. Under the impact of the unparalleled series of discoveries on the unconscious mind, on sexuality and its ontogenesis, and of others, all mainly in the realm of what was later to be called the id, ego psychology came gradually to be looked on by analysts as a field somehow outside real analysis and became quite unpopular (as Anna Freud was to say later, in a book which with some of Freud's marked the end of this trend [1936]). But even in the intervening second stage, when the direct approach to the ego was in the background, changes in the conception of the ego took place as a kind of secondary effect of the developing clinical and theoretical and technical principles.

Once Freud has disclosed the dominance among the motivating factors of the instinctual drives, and especially sexuality, the question of dynamics—that is of the forces active in the mental apparatus—could be defined in a more specific way than had been possible in his earlier work. However, the nature of the forces opposing the drives in the typical situations of inner conflict, that is of the ego, was for some time rather indeterminate. But even though mental phenomena were primarily looked at from the angle of their instinctual implications, the actual contributions to the understanding of the ego were considerable. The genetic viewpoint, which was first introduced in those years in regard to the drives and was soon to become all-pervasive in analysis, also helped toward an understanding of the developmental aspects of certain character structures now being viewed as "transformations of instincts." The introduction of "reaction formation" and "sublimation" went a long way toward clarifying the role of the ego, although it was only twenty years later that "sublimation" was linked in a much broader sense with ego function in general. The word "sublimation"[1] occurs in Freud's letters to Fliess (see also Strachey, 1953). Then, in 1905, after a period of latent maturation, the concept emerges fully grown, well defined as the center of a theory.

In most of the great case histories of those years little is said about the ego. But in one of them, the Rat Man (1909), we find an unsurpassed clinical description of a number of defensive techniques (regression, isolation, undoing, displacement) which, though not explicitly defined as to their position in the ego at the time, represent an essential basis for Freud's later theory of the defense mechanisms of the ego.

The most penetrating analysis of a psychotic patient in existence, the Schreber case (1911b), contains, in line with Freud's style of case history writing, a great wealth of theoretical thinking beyond its clinical contributions. It gives us, among other things, an extremely interesting insight into the interactions of libido and ego, the discussion of which would transcend the more limited aims of this paper. I do, however, want to point to one passage which shows that overlapping of two sets of theories I mentioned before: in this case, the anticipation by Freud of the concept of a more independent ego, which later became the one adopted by him, although at the time he wrote the Schreber case a different set of propositions was in the foreground. At one point in this paper he noted, in addition to the possible effect of libido disturbances on ego cathexes, the secondary or induced disturbance of libidinal processes as a result of abnormal modifications of the ego. Such formulations were excep-

---

[1] The origin of this term in Freud's work is unknown. Nietzsche used it, but whether it came to Freud this way, directly or through an intermediary, has not been ascertained. It is, of course, equally possible that Freud, a great creator of suitable terms in his own right, devised it himself.

tions at the time, but exceptions like this one deserve our interest because they sometimes announce later developments.

Like an anticipation of an ego psychology that was still to come is the important part of the "Two Principles" (1911a), which clearly traces the development of specific ego functions. It represented a major step forward, beyond what Freud had long known about the specific relations of ego and reality. However, from the point of view of explicit conceptualization, with which we are primarily concerned here, the paper mostly deals not with the development of "the ego" but with the ego drives and the impact of the reality principle on them (in contradistinction to its influence on the sexual drives). Only later did it become evident that this problem of the relations between dynamics, function, and structure had to be solved in a systematic way.

In the second decade of this century the role of the ego as an agent in its own right, in contradistinction to the drives, was at its lowest point. The ego was seen not only as a satellite of the instinctual drives but, at times, as close to an eclipse. I do not propose to review at this point the development of Freud's theory of the ego drives and his introduction of the concept of ego libido (or narcissistic libido). This theory is outlined in his paper "On Narcissism" (1914a) and in his additions to the *Three Contributions,* dating from about the same time; what are in part restatements and in part variations on these themes are to be found in other places. Again, there is an element of continuity with the past in so far as other forms of mental energy besides the libidinal ones are, in principle, recognized, though it is not explicitly stated whether or not the former are instinctual too. But the essence of Freud's reformulation lay in the introduction of his concept of a libidinal cathexis of the ego and in his statement that we have no means of immediately distinguishing it from the other energies active in the ego. Also, he found that ego libido is conveniently accessible only where it is used for the cathexis of objects. At any rate, those "other energies" remained in the background, at least for the time being. This instinctualization of the ego was a radical departure from the earlier ego concepts whose hallmark had been distinction from and opposition to the drives in general. Neurosis is now described as the result of a conflict between two agents which are both instinctual in character. Repression is defined as directed against libidinal object cathexis. But we sometimes get the impression that even at that time Freud was not quite satisfied with these formulations.

At any rate, not long afterward, Freud made an attempt to differentiate those "other energies active in the ego" from the libidinal ones, at least as to some ego tendencies (in the "Metapsychological Supplement to the Theory of Dreams," 1917a, and in the *Introductory Lectures,* 1916-17). He asked: what are the conceptual differences between egoism and narcissism? Egoism, he answered, is the individual's aiming at advantage, while if one says "narcissism," one thinks also of the libidinal gratifications which are implied. Narcissism is thus the libidinal complement to egoism. He added that one can go a considerable way in tracing the two separately as motivational forces. With these statements Freud opened a wide field of potential research, but unfortunately he did not conceptualize it in his later, more systematic, exposition of ego psychology. This, then, led to the near-complete neglect in psychoanalysis of that important chapter of psychology, though there is no reason to believe that he questioned the motivational power of self-interest.

I mentioned that in the period we are dealing with the interest in that concept of the ego which, in anticipation of things to come, we may refer to as the beginning of the system concept receded and was overshadowed by the interest in the ego's instinctual and particularly libidinal aspects. But I want to repeat that one part of ego psychology that decidedly gained from this phase was the developmental aspect, so far as the development of the ego functions follows the lead of the consecutive libidinal phases.

I must now speak of a modification of Freud's ego concept which seems to derive from the changed approach to ego psychology during that period. I mentioned that Freud, as did others, sometimes used the term ego in more than one sense, and not always in the sense in which it was best defined. Occasionally before, and more often in the phase I am discussing now, the term ego became interchangeable with "one's own person" or with "the self." In most instances it is clear whether Freud referred to the latter (sometimes also to the image of one's self) or to the former; in some it is debatable. However, this usage rather tends to obscure the fact that in the study of the problems I have in mind here (particularly narcissism) two quite different sets of propositions were involved, the one referring to the functions and cathexes of the ego as a system (in contradistinction to the cathexes of different parts of the personality), the other to the opposition of the cathexis of one's own person to that of other persons (objects). The distinction of the concern for one's own person as against that for the objects, on which the distinction of ego drives and object drives had been based, is clearly not the same as that between the ego on the one hand and the other systems of the personality on the other hand. Also, it is clear that ego tendencies are very frequently object directed—to mention another difficulty of the earlier theory. At any rate, the term narcissism was at that time used to cover the libidinal cathexis both of the ego and of one's own person. In this usage originated also the frequently found formulation that at the beginning of life all libido is in the ego, part of which is sent out later to cathect the objects. In this case it seems perfectly clear that what Freud thought of was the cathexis of one's own person preceding that of the objects—if for no other reason than that, at least at the time, he did not think that anything comparable to an ego was present at birth. Later, when the system concept of the ego became dominant, Freud corrected his statement that the ego was the original reservoir of libido (1923a)—very characteristically, I should think, in a footnote, as if to indicate that what he said was obvious and did not need any further discussion. It is, however, not explicitly stated that this correction also implied a detachment from the often used formulation that narcissism is to be defined as the libidinal cathexis of the ego (as system). This, of course, could certainly not mean that there is no libidinal cathexis of the ego. Rather it would mean that, for the definition of narcissism, the distinction of the libidinal cathexis of one's own person, as opposed to that of the objects, is the essential element.

In a later work (1926a) in which Freud found it necessary to reformulate some of his earlier ideas, he spoke of the desirability of making such emendations and mentioned two forms: "make a generality more specific" and "broaden a conception which was too narrow." As to the ego concept of the phase now under discussion, it represents the interesting case in which the observations (on narcissism) are indubitably well founded and have proved of signal importance for the development of psychoanalysis. The theory of the libido applied to account for them is one of the greatest devised by Freud, and its fruitfulness is above doubt; still, at one point it oversteps the limits of maximum usefulness. A somewhat similar case was the attempt to explain anxiety in terms of the libido theory. In this case Freud made the "emendations." It was different in a third case (1919): he refused from the start to accept what he called the "sexualization of the process of repression" implied in certain hypotheses of Fliess and Adler.

When Freud established ego psychology as a legitimate chapter of psychoanalysis, the ego concept he evolved had, then, a long and eventful history. The reasons which prompted this decisive step in the twenties were of various kinds. There was his technical experience, which led him to an increasing emphasis on resistance and on the relations of resistance with defense; there was certainly also the fact, early noticed but so far not fully accounted for, that defenses were mostly unconscious. Another determining factor was his clinical experience with psychoses and with other, though not psychotic, impairments of the ego; another was the great wealth of phenomena that became accessible through his discovery of the conflicts between ego and superego; there was the insight into the role of unconscious guilt feelings; the difficulties he encountered in using his earlier theory of anxiety; also the importance of the child's conflicts with reality, sometimes paralleling, or being consecutive to, but sometimes also preceding, the conflicts between ego and id; and a number of other factors I will not mention here. As to theoretical reasons, I suppose one decisive reason must have been his understanding that in order to approach more nearly a systematic presentation of mental phenomena—and the trend toward a general psychology has been inherent in psychoanalysis from its inception—the genetic viewpoint has to be supplemented by a structural approach, though Freud never quite explicitly stated this in a general way. At any rate, his successful integration of the genetic with the structural viewpoint has no parallel in psychology outside psychoanalysis, and represents one of the most distinctive marks of his later theories. Freud's demarcation of mental structures was, of course—and here again we discern a most fertile interaction of clinic and theory—closely geared to the typical conflict situations of man. It helped, too, toward a better understanding of some important aspects of the vicissitudes of instincts. Here, the role of the superego in the economy of aggression is perhaps the most clear-cut example, but we will not forget that the ego is also, passively and actively, involved in the economy of the instinctual drives, and about one aspect of this a few words will be said later. Of course, among the theoretical reasons which induced this development, we cannot forget that many topographical, dynamic, and economic problems that Freud had intermittently made the center of his interests, in *The Interpretation of Dreams* and in the metapsychological papers of his middle period, found a not always simpler but often more satisfactory solution on this new level of metapsychology.

The structural hypotheses intended to account for and to organize his psychological experience, and at the same time to determine the direction of future research, are in many ways more operational, more workable, and also, if we may say so, more elegant than Freud's earlier attempts to cover the same, or partly the same, subjects. As was his wont, not all implications of this new level of his thinking were worked out in a systematic way, nor did he indicate in every case where his new thinking implied a departure from views previously held. The continuity of new formulations with earlier ideas was occasionally emphasized by Freud. Consequently, with some the impression took shape that what had been added was actually a new language, a new conceptualization which could be used interchangeably with the older one; this, however, I do not believe to be the whole truth. Of course, it would be correct to say that many new elements of these theories were anticipated by more or less casual remarks in his earlier work, and it is true also in this case that older and more or less discarded concepts re-emerged after a long latency. Without wanting to labor the point of earlier models, I mention here that in the later concept as in the earliest, the organization of the ego is strongly emphasized, more strongly than in the intermediate phase. The ego is defined as a system of functions—we could add: again defined this way. Now as in the early beginnings, the relative independence of the ego, the fact that human behavior cannot be predicted on the basis of the instinctual data only, is more definitely stated. But while the affinities with Freud's first layer of theory formation are indisputable, it is also obviously true that in every respect new meanings have accrued to them, that the new formulations are incomparably more comprehensive, more systematic, more specific, and more fruitful, being based on a whole new world of experience and thinking. The center of emphasis was changed in a sufficient number of essential aspects to permit us to speak of new theories. Psychoanalysis, in those decisive years, had changed its face and its potentialities.

In the structural phase of his theories, Freud emphasized more definitely than in the preceding decades the biological function of the ego. It is highly characteristic of Freud's approach that in tracing the development of the ego he often tried at the same time to account for its phylogenesis. But another point was to become more important: while the drives had often been referred to before as "the biological aspect" of personality, now the powerful triad of functions: adaptation, control, and integration (synthetic function), attributed to the ego, underscored its significance as a biological agent. Again, some statements, for example on the synthetic function, are encountered in previous writings; but it is only at this later point that they have become invested with that dignity which systematization confers on a concept. To stress the biological role of the ego is not superfluous even today, as the so-called "culturalist" theories —*intra muros et extra*—tend, I feel, to underrate this aspect. I may mention here that it became even more accentuated in some of Freud's latest papers. It was said by physiologists, and by psychoanalysts, that especially the conceptualization of the ego as, we may say, an organ of "centralized functional control" brought it closer to the thinking of brain physiology. The integrative function of the ego also added a new aspect to earlier ideas of Freud on the problem of equilibrium in the mental apparatus. The recognition of the synthetic function (not exclusive of, but in addition to, other regulations) made the ego, which had always been considered an organization, now also an organizer of the three systems of personality. This has rightly been compared with Cannon's concept of homeostasis, or described as one level of it. Here a harmonizing factor is added to Freud's predilection, justly emphasized by Jones, for basing theories on two opposing forces. There is no longer only "compromise" as result of opposing forces, but intended harmonization by the ego. And, on the speculative level, we find an analogous tendency in the binding power of Eros.

The equilibrium in Freud's grasp of reality—a prerequisite of this great sign of courage, objectivity—did not allow his biological approach to the ego to be paid for by a neglect of its social or cultural aspects. We may say that he liked to study cultural phenomena in their biological context or significance, and biological phenomena in relation to the sociocultural environment. What is certainly to be called a biological factor, "the protracted helplessness and dependence of the young of the human species," promotes the influence of the environmental factors, alongside the early differentiation of the ego from the id, and this also refers to man's capacity for learning.

Also "the value of the object . . . is enormously enhanced" (1926a). This conception of ego development is at the origin of much of what Ernst Kris (1950b) has called "the new environmentalism" in psychoanalysis. It is the theoretical core for the turning to a closer scrutiny of the impact of object relation on development, and of the ego aspect of object relation, in addition to the earlier consideration of the developmental significance of the libidinal phases. Freud's tracing of internal to external danger situations points in the same direction. All this together opened the way to a fruitful integration of data of direct child observation. This is the second step, after the detailed study of anxiety and defense, which went beyond Freud's earlier expectation that it is primarily through the study of psychoses that essential insights into the functions of the ego will be gained.

The reorientation to the problem of anxiety was, of course, a pivotal point in Freud's third phase of ego psychology: the ego was recognized as the only seat of anxiety, and Freud developed "this series: anxiety—danger—helplessness (trauma)" (1926a). The varieties of anxiety could be correlated with the dependences of the ego, from the id, from the superego, from the external world, and the typical sequence of danger situations could be traced. Not only is all this well known: I cannot discuss it in any detail here. But what I must mention is that Freud's concept of the danger signal again adds a new dimension to his ego concept. The danger signal is certainly the best studied example, and one of the most important, of what seems to be a very general feature of the ego: its capacity for anticipation. This, together with the idea of the ego's command of the pleasure-unpleasure principle, sheds new light also on repression and, in a way, also on the relation of the pleasure and reality principles. These formulations, too, would have been unthinkable on the basis of the preceding theories.

Through the danger signal, the ego appears dynamically to be in a more significant role than had previously been attributed to it. Freud drew attention to an underrating of the power of the ego that he had found in analytic writings—while often before he had warned against overemphasizing it. Economically, he spoke of the thought processes, and soon afterwards the ego processes in general, working, not with instinctual energy, but with a modified form of energy, called sublimated or desexualized. This seems to me a rather radical re-evaluation of the economic role of the ego. Topographically, the unconscious functioning of important parts of the ego is emphasized, which then allows us definitely to assign the mechanisms of defense their true place in mental structure. The unconscious nature of the resistances, discovered long before, can now be systematically accounted for, and ego resistances are clearly set apart from other forms of resistances.

Though they drew, of course, on his psychopathological experience, Freud's structural propositions covered the mental life, and its development, of the normal as well as the pathological individual. It has long since been recognized what the study of the normal owes to pathology, but it is also true that in order to understand neurosis and its etiology, we have to understand more completely the psychology of the healthy person, too. We can say that Freud's understanding of specific ego functions and their normal development, of the normal demarcation lines of the psychic systems, and so on, helped him to achieve a better insight into neurosis also. Generally, the difference between normality and neurosis is regarded as less marked in analysis than outside it. Also we consider defense in itself as not necessarily pathogenic. At any rate, if the ego's defense against instinctual danger does lead to neurosis, this is so because "of an imperfection of the psychic apparatus" (1926a). The instances in which protective measures, in themselves normal, can turn into disease have recently been described as the cause of a great number of illnesses, which are then termed "diseases of adaptation" (Selye, 1950). I think Freud would have enjoyed this late re-encounter with physiology.

We can say that Freud's structural hypotheses represent the closest and most systematic approximation to his early aim of a general psychology. The implications of this for a synthesis of psychoanalytic thought with other fields of knowledge have so far been only partly realized. Again, Freud's works on the ego in this third phase were considered by some, at least for a time, as excessively "theoretical," or at least more theoretical than his earlier ones. I think that never in his work—or, to be quite correct, hardly ever—did Freud lose the felicitous equilibrium between the keen consideration of fact and the devising of "good" concepts and hypotheses. Of course, he was never shy of theorizing. But the level of abstraction in some of his meta-psychological papers of the middle period is higher than, let us say, in *Inhibitions, Symptoms and Anxiety.* We may, then, well wonder from where the impression of excessive theorizing stems. It may happen that when one has worked with a given set of hypotheses for a long time they interpenetrate with fact finding in such a way that their hypothetical character is no longer clearly recognized. Highly abstract concepts, as for instance "libidinal cathexis" or others, are then used in a descriptive way by many, not in an explanatory way as they are meant to be used. But in new concepts the hypothetical implications are realized as such. About the allegedly speculative character of his ego psychology Freud wrote, in the *New Introductory Lectures* (1932), that for this impression "the character of the material itself is responsible, and the fact that we are not accustomed to dealing with it."

Of course, there is also the historical fact that in those years which were, in spite of all, years of his greatest creativity, Freud developed three comprehensive theories simultaneously. There was, in addition to his new ideas on psychic structure, the introduction of aggression as a primary drive on the same level as sexuality—and neither of these theories is more speculative than are many others in analysis; they are interrelated in more than one way. But there are also the far-reaching biological speculations on Eros and the death instinct. These differ from the two other theories, which are part of empirical psychology, in their sweep, and also in their difficulty of validation. The three theories are not always considered separately, and the speculative character which Freud himself attributed to the Eros-

Thanatos theory might have cast its shadow on the two others. It is highly interesting that at the same time when Freud, on the level of biological speculation, tried to account for the "phenomena of life" by the interplay of the two primordial drives, he *accentuated* for the purposes of empirical psychology the relative independence of the noninstinctual forces of the ego. Obviously, we are confronted here not only with two different terminologies, but also with two different levels of theory formation. It is not always easy to see clearly what refers to one and what to the other, though their distinction is essential. That the difference between the empirical and the speculative theories of drives should be made apparent by using a different nomenclature was suggested recently by Lampl-de Groot (1956) and by Lantos (1955).

Though Freud's ego theory in its third phase was incomparably more systematic than his previous approaches to the subject, he was far from considering it as completed. We find additions and reformulations in his last papers, especially in one of his greatest, "Analysis Terminable and Interminable" (1937a), and in the *Outline* (1940a). In these, the concept of the ego is not basically altered, although new dimensions are added to it, and the trend toward attributing to the ego greater independence and greater biological significance is enhanced. I will give two examples: the introduction in the former paper of inherited characteristics of the ego seems a radically new departure, if we compare it with what Freud had said on the subject as late as *The Ego and the Id*. In the *Outline,* self-preservation is described as a function of the ego—while it is said that it is neglected by the id; which, by the way, clarifies also the difference between the id of the human being and the instincts of the animals.

May I close by telling you that in my experience, which is no doubt the experience of many others, the understanding of psychoanalysis is greatly enriched the closer we come to a grasp of Freud's constant struggle for a conceptualization fit to account for the peculiarities of the material with which he was confronted. To make it coherent and to eliminate, as far as possible, its contradictions, he had to devise his own conceptual tools, and the formulations and reformulations discussed today are actually but a part of this effort, which ended only with the ending of his life. Freud (1932) spoke of his endeavor to "introduce the right abstract ideas," and said "we are constantly altering and improving them." We learn from his effort what is possible and what is fruitful in coping with the demands which psychoanalytic experience makes on our thinking. We wonder how it fell to Freud to make his great discoveries; we also wonder how he developed the new tools to extract their fullest meaning. Gregor Mendel's discovery of the laws of genetics was without doubt momentous. But the ways in which he dealt with his discoveries were, in principle, known and comparatively simple. Freud's psychological research method could not build on methodological models, hallowed by tradition, as is the case in other fields. In scientific psychology there was hardly anything, at least in the time of Freud's beginnings, that he used or, for that matter, could have used to uncover and deal with the phenomena he was the first to perceive. With Freud, even his creativity as a discoverer did not surpass his creativity in devising concepts and hypotheses that fit his observational material and direct research to meaningful questions. Among great scientists there are those who confront the world with strikingly new facts; but there are also those who not only demonstrate new facts but also teach the world to look at them in an entirely new way, thereby also changing the forms or modes of our thinking. There are only a few in our time whom we would put into this second category. But there is no doubt that Freud is among them.

CHAPTER 15

Comments on the Scientific Aspects of Psychoanalysis

(1958)

I N THIS lecture I will examine the body of facts and theories we call psychoanalysis from a point of view not altogether widely discussed in our literature. We all consider psychoanalysis, among other things, a science. It is, however, not always clearly understood to what degree and in what respects this statement is true, nor is it always easy to say what are the distinctive formal and methodological characteristics of this science. If the analyst is often shy of discussing such questions with representatives of other, more highly systematized and methodologically more firmly established fields of science, this may well be due to the rather forbidding difficulties to explain to these others even comparatively simple aspects of analytic method or content. But it is also true that not many of us give much thought to such matters, and that with even fewer it is in the foreground of their interest and work. This is undoubtedly the result of a characteristic feature of psychoanalysis as a profession which is a union of practical with scientific activities, and of the

---

This paper and the following one, though they were, as lectures, addressed to very different audiences, have the general topic and the outline in common. Thus some overlapping could not be avoided. I decided nevertheless to publish them both in this collection, because in each one a number of points are made which are not presented in the other.

development of our profession. It easily leads to what E. Kris (1947) has called a lack of "trained clarifiers" of the kind we find in the physical sciences. But I think that progress in the clarification of our hypotheses, and systematization, and the consideration of methodological principles is no less important in analysis than in other sciences. The possibility fully to extricate their meaning from our observations depends on it. Later I shall briefly speak about attempts in this direction, coming, in part, from outside professional analysis. It is true that hypotheses used in our work can be tested, for instance, experimentally. Still, this statement is not generally true. Moreover, the function of these propositions in the context of analysis as a whole is unquestionably very hard to evaluate from an extra-analytic viewpoint. Because of these circumstances, I am convinced that the major part of this work of clarification and testing will fall to the analysts' lot.

As so much of every aspect of psychoanalysis has originated in the work of Freud, I may briefly comment here on what he felt about its scientific character. Freud has been decried because of his narrow scientism, because of his positivism—and equally often because of rather opposite tendencies which some writers thought to discover in his work, for instance, a bent toward metaphysical speculation, or even mysticism; he has been called a rationalist and an irrationalist, a humanist and an antihumanist. Such judgments, though often primarily aimed at his philosophy, or at what some people believed his philosophy to be, imply as a rule also judgments of analysis. In spite of this great variety of partly antithetical evaluations, it should be clear to every student of his works that Freud had early in his life developed a strict belief in the scientific methods of thinking and that this belief continued unshattered till his end. The word "belief" here points to his conviction that reliable and testable knowledge can be ascertained in no other ways but those of science. It is equally clear that in what we might call his "cautious optimism" he expected rational thinking to have the power of slow, gradual expansion. Finally, there is no doubt that for him psychoanalysis meant the conquest, for scientific study, of human behavior in the broadest sense; a field that in its essentials had never before been touched by scientific exploration. He thought, as many psychoanalysts do, that even the therapeutic aspect of analysis would in the long run be overshadowed by its importance for a science of man. This primacy of scientific aims and the responsibilities vis-à-vis the rules and procedures of scientific thinking that go with it have become essential in the development of psychoanalysis—in contradistinction to other psychological schools, though they have grown, in part, in the same soil. Neither with Jung, nor Adler, nor Rank do we find the same dedication to scientific method, or the unquestioned readiness to submit to its demands, nor do we find there the same energetic and consistent endeavor to wrestle with the untold difficulties our subject matter forces us to face.

Precisely because of his sense of responsibility toward the demands of scientific thinking, Freud never denied, or disowned, or passed over the imperfections of psychoanalysis as a science. After a visit Einstein had paid to him, he wrote to a friend (Jan. 11, 1927): "He has had the support of a long series of predecessors from Newton onward, while I have had to hack every step of my way through a tangled jungle alone. No wonder that my path is not a very broad one and that I have not got far in it" (Jones, 1953-57, 3:131). We have the right to disagree with the last sentence. But this passage clearly shows that Freud was very far indeed from considering psychoanalysis a closed or completed, or, in many respects, even a satisfactory system. Being well aware of the many white spots on the map of analysis, he did not believe "to have all the answers"—a notion about the state of analysis occasionally met with inside and outside of it. Freud was fully aware of the need for reformulation of many aspects of psychoanalysis, and of the tentative character of some of his statements. Also, concerning an important aspect of analysis he stated that one cannot yet deal with it without introducing "uncertain assumptions and unproven guesses." But he did not doubt the superiority of analysis over all other approaches to a psychology of personality in explaining not only the phenomena he had been the first to discover, but in explaining also an ever broader sector of human behavior in general.

We know today (from the letters to W. Fliess) that the field this science was meant to cover was, not only in Freud's later years but from his beginnings, psychology in the most comprehensive sense. It was never meant to be limited to the study of pathological phenomena, though even today psychoanalytic psychology is sometimes presented as "theory of neurosis." I want to emphasize, then, Freud's very broad conception of psychoanalysis as a science, despite the fact that his first decisive insights were gained through the study of neurosis and despite the fact that this study has remained in the center of our therapeutic work. What actually happened was that Freud in learning to understand neurosis uncovered at the same time the essential features of mental functioning in general: conflict, defense, dynamic unconscious processes, etc. His broad approach was foreshadowed in his "Project for a Scientific Psychology" and explicitly stated in *The Interpretation of Dreams.* But he often said that he obviously could not approach all parts of psychology at the same time; moreover, the fact that he had not, or only cursorily, approached a subject, he maintained, should not be misconstrued as meaning that he did not appreciate its importance. Actually, even today not all the implications of this comprehensive conception have been worked out and the process of broadening and reformulation continues. What, then, is the field of analysis?

The question is somewhat obscured by the idea, mentioned before and occasionally found both inside and outside analysis, that it is somewhat like a closed system. This is a very simple, but a very un-Freudian approach. The need for growth and development is already implied in the very outline Freud gave us. Everything we can focus on and explain with its conceptual tools, and its method, is part of it —as long, of course, as it is not contradicted by observation or another more reliable theory. We may also, if we prefer, make a distinction between "actual" and "potential" analysis—the latter, as I said before, probably comprising its application to every chapter of psychology. I may add here that also another attempt at broadening our conception of psychoanalysis as a science has become more or less accepted. We would no longer limit it to what has its immediate origin in the use of the analytic method in the analytic situation. We include work in applied analysis, in various fields of medicine, social science, and so on. Also the use of psychoanalytic concepts and hypotheses in the direct observation of children is today recognized as part of scientific analysis.

Psychoanalysis is richer in theoretical complexities than any other approach to psychology, though the complexities of some physical sciences may be greater. This complex theorizing in analysis is, I think, dictated by the special features of its subject matter. It can stand any comparison with physical sciences as to its originality and ingenuity and particularly as to the unique combination of logical and imaginative power of its creator. Still, some of our terms are ambiguous. The hypotheses are frequently not clearly differentiated as to their closeness to observation, or as to the degree to which they have been confirmed. The level of systematization is, in general, comparatively low, in spite of efforts to remedy this state of affairs. The suggestion, made by many, to achieve a higher degree of clarification and systematization by reformulating psychoanalytic theory according to newer developments in biology or physics might occasionally be helpful—as has been the borrowing of such model by Freud. But such suggestions too often ignore the special conditions in our field and, more generally, the fact that the use of such borrowings has to be checked in every case as to its fruitfulness in the field into which they are transplanted. In addition, simply to translate our experience into the language of a field that appears somehow more tangible (as is the case, e.g., with brain physiology) but about which (as certainly was the case with brain physiology) we know even less, is not always feasible or fruitful. And recently suggestions for a renewed collaboration of psychoanalysis with the study of the brain abound. These are questions not only of a theory of science—as which they are commonly presented—but also of, if I may say so, practical considerations with regard to a given science in a given stage of its development. The methodological demands on science are generally made from the vantage points of its most advanced field. It will not always prove profitable to apply them rigidly or literally to a beginner among sciences, as analysis is. It is not wise to limit, in the beginning, the field to those parts than can easily be approached in a methodologically unobjectionable way (see also Rapaport, 1958). In many instances, methodological considerations had to be postponed. But I may also mention that some hypotheses, rather questionable from the viewpoint of a philosophy of science, have in the case of analysis proved their heuristic value.

It is difficult to describe clearly, in logical terms, what is generally called "clinical research." The fact that the analysts' observations are made in a clinical setting has, in more ways than one, determined also the development of the scientific aspects of analysis. That much is obvious. What is less obvious—it has, as a matter of fact, never been systematically studied—is the comparative scientific potential of the various ways of clinical approach. It would be worth while to examine this question more closely. On the other hand, clinical work seems, in a certain sense, often more "scientific" in analysis than in many other clinical fields. I state this only as an impression, but it is certainly one shared by many. The problem has a variety of aspects. There are, first of all, the great case histories of Freud in which the scientific problems are explicitly stated and which usually combine the presentation of his clinical findings with the discussion of the theoretical (and often also technical) problems involved. They show the constant mutual promotion of observation and theoretical thinking at work. But this style of his case histories has, one could say, remained unique. It has only rarely been imitated, and hardly ever successfully.

There is, then, this second factor. Findings in analysis have been presented in very different ways. There are the reports on "pure" observations (mostly, as we shall see, only comparatively "pure"), more frequent in the earlier years of analysis, though they are not entirely absent today. But the insight into relations of a dynamic, or genetic, or structural nature is more in the foreground than the reporting of isolated data. The placement of the data with respect to mental functioning and its vicissitudes has become the immediate concern not only of the theoretician. That is, the observations are viewed also from the angle of our theoretical knowledge, as validations or invalidations of a hypothesis and in the most fortunate circumstances as crucial experiments. The analyst is thus no longer like a naturalist who discovers and describes a new flower or a new animal. Explanatory concepts enter the picture, and there are several levels of them. Some are still comparatively close to observation, while others are far removed from overt behavior and from immediate experience. This development in analysis has its parallels in the development of other sciences. Once lawlike propositions on the structure of neuroses, on the instinctual drives, on typical phases of development, and so on, had been formulated, our knowledge of mental processes and their interactions became less tenuous and many hypotheses became less tentative in character. The analyst learned to feel more secure, more at home with them, and the corresponding concepts entered more and more the reporting of clinical material. This is indeed a characteristic feature of clinical discourse in analysis, in contradistinction with many other branches of clinical work. It shows the theoretical training of the analyst and his scientific interest; it shows above all a relation of fact finding and theory, imposed by our subject matter and typical of analysis.

Reviewing a great number of analytic papers or lectures, you find certain distinct types as to the ways in which the clinical and theoretical aspects are combined. There is of course the classical type in which clinical material is presented, compared with earlier findings, and classified, and then searched for theoretical implications. Other papers, though clinical in appearance, actually set out to prove or illustrate a hypothesis which is the main concern of the author; it may be presented as such, or it may be presented as derived from the clinical data, while in reality the latter are mere illustrations of the thesis and not its origin. There are many other types and the subject would no doubt deserve a special study.

The case of hypothesis preceding observation is, of course, an entirely legitimate procedure (Hartmann, Kris, Loewenstein, 1953) which has played a considerable role already in Freud's beginnings (and plays an analogous role in other fields). Predilections for certain forms of thinking or presentation appear in a continuum, from the case in which what looks like a clinical contribution is actually directed by thinking on a high level of abstraction, to the other extreme at which an essay formulated in terms of theory is actually closely geared to observation. Obviously, this is also one result of the impossibility to present in a paper, or even in a book, all the observational data gathered in analysis. Thus abbreviations become necessary. What one calls "clinical" and "theoretical" presentations in analysis are divergent styles of abbreviation. In this paper, I merely wish to demonstrate that due to specific features of the psychoanalytic approach the demarcation line of clinical and theoretical work is often not easily traceable. These circumstances may also help to explain why it is that in analysis complex and imaginative construction may be presented in data-language, or clinical language, as well as in concept-language or theoretical language. This is indubitably so, and the statement of these facts implies, of course, no criticism. But this state of affairs, characteristic of psychoanalysis, poses a problem in communication. Every reading of psychoanalytic literature asks of the reader a labor of reconstruction if he wants to view it in its aspect as a scientific contribution: what was the background in terms of observables? What are the hypotheses, either presupposed by the author, or deducible from his work?

We cannot expect to find in every analyst the beautiful harmony between theoretical, clinical, and technical insight and skill which was the hallmark of one genius. As we find individual preferences for one aspect, a certain degree of specialization is natural enough. But it is still true in analysis—and this again is different in other fields—that "good theory" cannot be written without broad clinical experience and that every clinical understanding presupposes knowledge in theory. The full meaning of clinical findings can only be developed in the framework of theory. Therefore, as I said, clinical work is generally permeated by hypotheses, as, for instance, not even the simplest statement concerning unconscious processes could be made without them. This example shows that what I am describing here is not an accidental occurrence but directly traceable to a basic feature of analysis.

There is, in this, of course, also an element that can easily become, and not infrequently has become, a handicap to scientific work in analysis, and this is another reason why I mention it in this context. That is, the hypotheses may interpenetrate with fact finding in such a way that their hypothetical character is not always clearly recognized (Hartmann, Kris, Loewenstein, 1953). Highly abstract hypothetical constructs (as libidinal cathexis, etc.) are then reported in a descriptive sense, as data of observation. Such a procedure induces confusion in both clinical practice and theory. If the hypotheses are not, as they should be, spelled out as such, they cannot be tested by further research. Second, that constructs are sometimes described as findings may well be one of the reasons (though certainly not the only possible one) why certain "findings" cannot be confirmed by other observers. This factor makes it particularly desirable in psychoanalytic research—it is, of course, a principle of every science—that if there is construction, we indicate how it has been arrived at; that is, our hypotheses should be as clearly and as explicitly stated as possible, in order that their relations with others become apparent and that they may be checked by further work. This level of scientific work has not yet been reached in all aspects of analysis, but it has been achieved in some, as a result mainly of a more meticulous study of the theoretical assumptions we bring to bear on our material.

This is the point at which to refer to the problem of interpretation. I do not mean here interpretation as part of our therapeutic technique, but rather as a cognitive tool. Loewenstein has spoken recently about its different aspects (1957). Now, interpretation is tentative explanation, therefore close to hypothesis. Here, too, we find different levels which we could distinguish as "deep" and "superficial"—in analogy to, but not identical with, the meanings these terms have in technique. Interpretation may be just the pointing to common elements in a sequence of associations and thus establishing a connection. On another level of cognitive interpretation, a great number of data, by far transcending the immediate givens of a situation, and a considerable amount of hypothetical thinking have to be introduced, in order to come to a conclusion. Here we meet again the problem of the ratio of observational and hypothetical elements I discussed before. It would be quite wrong, in analysis, to expect a simple correlation between this ratio and the scientific value of an interpretation. Experience decides against this easy answer. Interpretations introducing even a great many variables often prove superior—if they are based on an adequate constructive power of the analyst who integrates his knowledge and theoretical thinking. Fortunately, in analysis "deeper" insight is often truer insight too. This is another aspect which analysis shares with the theoretically highly developed sciences.

Due to the pervasive nature of the genetic aspect in analysis, the reconstruction of early childhood experiences or situations is of essential interest in this connection. We have learned how to gear theoretical expectations to observables in "predicting the past." It works beautifully, as far as we can suppose that the structure of the mental apparatus and the laws governing it are not too different at the stage we are reconstructing from their more familiar later stages—and if enough experiential checks are available. Both these conditions are not fulfilled in dealing with the preverbal stages of development. Hence our extrapolations referring to that stage have mostly a rather tenuous character. What appears as evidence is of necessity often but a reflection of the hypotheses we introduced; such extrapolations are implied in their points of departure. Given the paramount interest of analysis in these preverbal developments, it is imperative that they be studied also by every other method at our disposal. This has been done in direct child observation by psychoanalysts, by investigations that are analytic as to concepts and hypotheses without using the analytic method. The concepts devised for later stages of development not always being sufficient, it has become one of the main endeavors, especially of ego psychology today, to find concepts which fit reconstructive data as well as data of direct observation and which facilitate their interrelation. Freud's reformulation of the theory of anxiety, emphasizing the genetic role of external danger, made this broadening of the field of psychoanalysis possible. Later concepts, of the conflict-free sphere, of the ego apparatuses, of primary autonomy, and so on, point in the direction of such a unifying theory, which includes the direct study of both maturation and development in the scope of psychoanalysis.

If there is some discontent, outside of analysis but often also shared by psychoanalysts, as to the relation of facts to theories, this can certainly not be attributed to a lack of data. The amount of the data available to the experienced analyst is rather overwhelming. In this respect, too, analysis leaves every other approach to a psychology of personality far behind. It is sometimes argued that psychoanalysis has actually studied only a comparatively small number of cases. But this argument misses the point. In every individual case we often gather hundreds of data pertinent to a problem in question, contiguities in free associations or other observed regularities. That is, every clinical "case" is actually hundreds of cases, scientifically speaking. Or, rather, we can say that for every "case" there is often a great wealth of instances in which every single hypothesis that comes into play can be tested. And our technique is constantly based on predictions of future responses.

This wealth of data is growing, but it is not always easy to impart this knowledge, to make it intersubjective—though, of course, some ways of communication in teaching or professional contacts of other kinds have been worked out.

On the other hand, our demands on clarification and systematization of theory have remarkably increased. The recent paper by Rapaport and Gill (1959) is an important step in this direction. Still there are, as I said before, broad sectors of our theories in which this clarification and systematization, insight into the relations between various aspects of theory, distinction between confirmed and nonconfirmed parts of it, between hypotheses close to observation and hypothetical constructs have not yet been achieved. This is mainly due to the fact that, compared to other branches of psychology, we work in analysis with a quite unusual number of variables; and in the last instance to the nature of the subject matter that is in the center of psychoanalytic interest.

There are some other general features of analysis which counteract an easy "scientification" (if you will excuse this term) and which it is good to keep in mind. Each one of these would deserve a thorough investigation.[1] But for the purpose of this lecture I have to abbreviate and to simplify a highly complex subject. The data gathered in psychoanalytic observation are primarily behavioral data. And the aim is clearly the explanation of human behavior—though in a broader sense than at least the older schools of behaviorism would have found acceptable. These data, though, are interpreted in analysis in terms of mental processes, of motivation, of meaning. Our concepts of mental processes are usually more than one step removed from behavioral data—and, as I may mention right here, also from immediate experience. The remoteness from the behavioral aspect is one reason why an objective, or maybe we should better say intersubjective, testing of analytic propositions becomes in most instances an arduous task. Hence the conviction of many analysts that these propositions can be tested only in the analytic situation itself. This, again, is often but not always true.

In analysis, as in other fields, investigation obviously proceeds in different layers. There is a chiefly descriptive aspect to it. There is

---

[1] Some of them are discussed in greater detail in Chapter 16.

one level, still close to observation, but already going beyond it in one or another respect. Then there is the level of theoretical discourse. The relations between these levels can well be studied in psychoanalytic case histories. Many of the most important concepts are explanatory in nature, e.g., the concept of unconscious mental processes, of libido, of cathexis and many others (Hartmann, 1927; Feigl, 1949; Frenkel-Brunswik, 1954). This element was essential in making a comprehensive psychology of personality possible.

As I said, this characteristic of analytic discourse often removes it rather far from overt behavior and from immediate experience. The frequent remoteness from the subjective experience has been deplored by some; yet, given the kind of conceptual tools analysis uses, it would hardly be otherwise (see also Wisdom, 1953). The problems of "subjectivity" and "objectivity" are posed in analysis in a way somewhat different from the usual one in that we attempt an objective study also of the psychological factors accounting for subjectivity. I may add, though it might not appear to the point in the context of this presentation, that in the course of analysis the new insights the patient gains by way of objectivation can be gradually integrated, in a secondary way, also in his immediate experience.

We find the explanatory character, the comparative remoteness from the descriptive level, in many main aspects of analytic thinking. It means, among other things, that elements of behavior, similar in a descriptive sense, may be considered dynamically or genetically as rather different, and vice versa. We encounter this problem, of course, also in other fields of science, but hardly to the same extent in other branches of psychology. As this level of conceptualization is often met even in clinical work, readers not used to this style of thinking will often experience a feeling of discomfort.

As to individual clinical observations versus the formulation of lawlike propositions, I want to say the following: one works in analysis between the extremes of two attitudes. One atttiude would, for the sake of closeness to colorful clinical experience, let the wealth of phenomena stand unformed and insufficiently connected; and another one would force precociously their variety into the procrustean bed of too narrow theorizing (Hartmann, 1929). On the other hand, critics of analysis are often not aware of the wealth of observations on which it rests; but they also frequently misjudge the role of theory in it. Theoretical concepts (as libido, the mental systems, etc.) are then discussed as if they were meant in a descriptive sense.

While the position of psychoanalysis to behaviorism is, in a general way, clear, we become naturally interested in the question: what, then, is its position vis-à-vis the introspective schools of scientific psychology? I do not want to stress the obvious, namely that analysis is to a large extent based on introspection, nor the difficulties which arise in an attempt to make an introspective psychology scientific in the usual sense of the term. I rather want to say that this difficulty has in this case partly been overcome by the theories of analysis which lead to generalizations and objectivation beyond immediate experience, and in turn to hypotheses which are accessible to testing. I think our experience bears out the point that it is only by the introduction of hypotheses on different levels, and sometimes on a high level of abstraction, that the full meaning of the observables can be gathered, which means above all that predictions become possible.

Today, nobody would consider science a mere summary of facts; also, the role of imagination in science has come to be clearly recognized in our days (Einstein and others). But it is not too well known how far imagination based on self-observation can contribute to hypothesis formation in the field of psychology. It probably plays a considerable role with what one is wont to call "intuitive" psychologists. According to Freud, such "intuitions" are the result of mostly preconscious observation and induction. While hunches, guesses, unaccountable insights, or intuitions are likely to play a role in the formation of hypotheses in other fields, too, it is possible—though not sufficiently explored—that in psychology those based on self-observation are often an important element, which could mean that some aspects of mental processes can be approached in this way. That this possibility is increased if the objectifying devices of the psychoanalytic method are brought to bear on it, I have said before. Also one should not overrate the degree to which nonchecked self-observation is relevant in psychoanalytic thinking. But it is striking that there are thinkers who seem to have the capacity of developing, without systematic and controlled observation, hypotheses that are later confirmed by way of induction; also of course that among those thinkers who have abundantly written, on the basis of their "intuition," about human behavior, we find only some who have this capacity. It might well be that in psychology this kind of capacity for fruitful hypothesizing plays a different and more important role than in other fields. I certainly do not want to overestimate the merits of uncontrolled guesses. But I point to this because it could become a fascinating object for the study of creative thinking in psychology, and one that only psychoanalysis could dare to approach. Where conclusions, later confirmed, have been arrived at on grounds of scanty observations which one would consider an insufficient basis for induction, it is conceivable that in those cases self-observations of yet unknown breadth and complexity might have been one determining factor. The possibility that self-observation may have this function does not, of course, obviate the necessity to check systematically such apparent "intuitions" with every available method.

It is very likely that in the work of Freud and other analysts such unaccountable insights have occurred. If so, it is clear that, certainly with Freud, his striving for scientific discipline, his patient accumulation of observational data, and his search for conceptual tools to account for them have kept their use under control. Many subjects approached in analysis, had, before Freud, been studied by so-called intuitive psychology only. But he was wont to oppose psychoanalytic psychology to intuitive psychology, and the development psychoanalysis has taken bears out this point. Still the relation between the cues used and theory is no doubt a rather complex one in psychoanalysis. This consideration leads us back to what I said before about this relationship. I do not think that concept formation in analysis differs in principle from concept formation in science in general (see Hartmann, 1927). But the complexity of the theoretical structure and the fact that validation, at least as to some of its aspects, is extraordinarily difficult, pose problems which are not always clearly understood and have not always been solved in a satisfactory way.

Suggestions to translate psychoanalytic theory into the language of operationism have been made repeatedly (Ellis, 1956; and others). But such attempts have not gone very far. Moreover, the nature of the special problems with which analysis has to deal was not always sufficiently realized. On the other hand, I may at least mention here that Flew (1956), facing some of these special problems with which psychoanalysis is confronted, has come to the conclusion that "these peculiarities are such as to ensure that their central and basic place in psychoanalysis must give this discipline a logical status different from, though not of course for that reason either inferior or superior to, that of sciences concerned with things other than human beings, and even from that of sciences concerned with less distinctly human aspects of human beings."

I pointed before to that constant use of predictions and their checking which is an essential part of the technique of psychoanalysis. However, this refers mostly, though not exclusively, to hypotheses still comparatively close to observation. But beyond this level, a great number of constructs figure in analysis for explanatory and predictive purposes and for the direction of further research. The "logical gap" (Einstein) between the level of constructs and observation, very obvious in modern physics, is apparent also in the less highly systematized fields like psychoanalysis. Its constructs originate, in the last instance, in observation, to which we have to add the legitimate role of imagination in theory formation (to which I referred before). It is, of course, difficult to assess their comparative distance from the data of observation in analysis and in other fields, but we will agree that essential aspects of psychoanalytic theory are rather far removed from clinical observation. Freud and some other analysts were not shy of theorizing. It was felt, in analysis, that too puritanic an attitude toward the introduction of hypotheses, or toward the introduction of complex hypotheses, had not proved and could not be expected to be beneficial to the development of scientific psychology. A great number of hypotheses were, then, introduced, in cognizance of their function, and accepted, modified, or rejected according to the usual criteria. They were not to be in contradiction with experience and with each other, and had to prove their explanatory value. For some levels of theorizing the acceptance of "good" and rejection of "bad" hypotheses appeared to be comparatively easy; but this is certainly not true of all levels of theory, neither in analysis, nor in other sciences. I may say here that the complexity of the theoretical structure of psychoanalysis seems to me not just a theorizing for theory's sake. Despite opposite and rather generally shared demands for simplification, this complexity may be a necessary and fruitful response to the demands a more comprehensive conception of personality makes on our thinking today. Historically it is true that in psychology before Freud a definite distrust of theory prevailed; and this attitude is still apparent in various aspects of social science. As to the present stage in analysis there is no doubt that it is a stage of growing complexity. All attempts at simplification, of which there are many, at a concentration on only one aspect at the expense of others, had to be paid for by a severe limitation of the explanatory reach and the predictive value of analysis. It is possible that the optimal relation between complexity of theory and explanatory fitness differs in different stages of the development of a theoretical system. Thus one may hope, possibly even expect, that at some future time we may reach a decidedly more beautiful and satisfactory stage, when simple formulations will become of equal or superior value (see Chapter 11).

It is partly due to this intricate interdependence of variables that the problem of quantification, difficult enough to approach in some other fields of psychology, seems even more inaccessible in psychoanalysis. Obviously, measurement which has been defined as "the business of pinning numbers on things" (S. S. Stevens) is not equally easy in every field of science. We compare the strength of impulses, the tenacity of resistances, the impact of rational tendencies, etc., we infer from the strength of a resistance the force of repression; but one cannot measure these factors. It may be that "more, less, greater than, fewer of, increase or decrease in, etc., may be used more profitably" than numeration (Brower, 1949). One can measure overt behavior, or physiological processes in the central nervous system, etc., but not mental processes in the sense we use the term in analysis. We assume relationships between the former and the latter, thus an approach to measurement by way of the former is not unthinkable. Often "processes that are difficult to measure may be studied in behavioral as well as in physical sciences by analyzing the frequency, duration, and degree of their interference with a more easily measured process" (Lindsley, 1957). Actually, though, these connections are in our case always highly complex and have mostly not been sufficiently clarified. Quantification is possible and has been widely achieved in nonanalytic branches of psychology as to those psychological processes which are, viewed from the vantage point of a psychology of personality, of a peripheral nature. They may, since analysis moves toward a general psychology, become more important than they have previously been also in psychoanalysis proper. Still, I have to remind you at this point of what I said before of the relative remoteness of the factors predominantly considered in analysis from this aspect of psychology, which means that the translation from the language suitable for this aspect into the one dominant in analysis is no easy matter; it has been tried, though, with respect to certain problems and has proved feasible.

There is no doubt, of course, that systematization in science can, in principle, benefit from measurement. But it is possible that at the present stage of development of psychoanalysis, measurement at all costs, as some want to have it, considering the variables only from the angle of our capacity to measure them, would sacrifice an essential aspect of analytic research.

Despite what I just said about measurement, in regard to psychoanalysis, quantification is implied in many analytic concepts, in the "force" of the drives, in the "strength" of the ego, in the principles of regulation, etc. As a matter of fact, we find this quantifying concept formation even at a level of hypothesis formation comparatively close to clinical observation. We trace the vicissitudes of cathectic charges from one dream element to another, or from an instinctual tendency to a symptom. This introduces an element of coherence into our psychological hypotheses. Of course, such a quantifying concept formation without possibility of measurement poses a problem and this problem has been widely discussed. I will not go into it any further here, beyond saying that I do not consider this procedure logically unacceptable.

It is obvious that the endeavor to validate psychoanalytic hypotheses by all means suitable to the purpose is welcome in analysis as it might help toward a clarification of its theories. Experimental work, outside of the analytic situation, with this purpose in mind has also been done by analysts themselves, of which I shall quote two examples. Certain psychoanalytic ideas concerning the use and meaning of symbols could be confirmed extra-analytically by Roffenstein (1923) and by Betlheim and Hartmann (see Chapter 17). Recently, Fisher (1954, 1956, 1957) has validated some aspects of Freud's ideas on perception, imagery, and dreams, and has in other respects suggested modifications of analytic theory.

Direct observation of psychotic patients confirmed on a large scale what Freud had inferred about the characteristics and main contents of primary processes. Indirect validations of psychoanalytic propositions have become available as a consequence of their use in psychology, anthropology, etc., since the demarcation line between analysis and neighboring fields has become less strict than it had been before. Such studies are often an incidental profit from studies frequently not primarily aimed at validation. To give you again an example, I remind you of G. Klein's (1954) investigation of the impact of needs (thirst, in his case) on cognition, and on the influence of "cognitive styles" on it. This problem of the interaction of needs (taken as representing drives) and cognition (a function of the ego) is, of course, close to the center of analytic interest. "Cognitive styles" have been described, and their explanation has been attempted, e.g., in Freud's presentation of the problems of obsessive thought. Among the studies of the motivation-cognition problem I may also mention the work of Frenkel-Brunswik (1949).

There exists, as you all know, an extensive literature on experiments in animals and in man that aim at the testing of psychoanalytic hypotheses, or hypotheses derived from analysis.[2] These studies have so far not decisively contributed toward a reformulation of psychoanalytic theory. But it is true that the best of them lead us to a better insight into certain difficulties inherent in our field and may lead us to renewed efforts to strive for better formulations of our hypotheses, sharper definitions, and greater systematic coherence. Early criticisms of analysis often gave the impression that those stumbling blocks could easily be overcome, but for the disinterest or the ineptness of the analysts. If one were to let those critics do the theorizing, everything could be comfortably arranged according to the best available standards. This approach was entirely ignorant of the specific characters of our subject matter and of the complexities encountered by every method that seriously strives for an explanation of personality. It entirely overlooked the essential insight that hypotheses are primarily tools, to be adapted to the demands of a given field. To accept these directions and warnings would have meant, for the analysts, to become "acceptable" in the sense of methodological standing—but also to pay for it by accepting a disastrous curtailment of the reach and the depth of his work. Fortunately, this brand of criticism has somewhat receded today. Still even now it sometimes needs emphasizing that this understanding of hypotheses as tools,

---

[2] This point, too, is treated somewhat more explicitly in Chapter 16.

a principle widely accepted in every science, leads to the conclusion: that in a considerable part of our field scientific progress can be expected in the first line from those who are not only able to judge the logical nature of such tools, but also to test their fruitfulness in actual psychoanalytic work.

The achievement of greater clarification and systematization, then, still rests primarily on the analysts themselves. But every step in this direction might well, in turn, increase also the potential relevance for this process of contributions coming from outside psychoanalysis.

I will conclude this lecture, which was mainly on method and theory, with a practical suggestion. Speaking of the scientific aspects of analysis, one should really also speak of the analyst as a scientist. If what I said is true, namely, that the methodological development of analysis will mainly rest on the work of the analysts themselves, one would hope them to be prepared for this additional task. It has often been said that his personal analysis endows the student with the degree of objectivity essential for scientific work. But such statements, while not actually false, are incomplete. The personal analysis is certainly a prerequisite for that kind of work, but is not in itself sufficient. Obviously, there are also questions of gifts and of interests involved—but they do not concern us here. My point is rather that as the logic of experimentation or of statistical work is taught in other fields, there is something—as a matter of fact, very much— that is teachable and learnable about the special methodological aspects of psychoanalysis as a science and one would wish that our curricula will find it possible to include opportunities for such studies.

CHAPTER 16

Psychoanalysis as a Scientific Theory

(1959)

WHEN some forty-five years ago Freud (1913) wrote for the first time about the philosophical interest in analysis, his main point was that philosophy could not avoid taking fully into account what he then called "the hypothesis of unconscious mental activities." He also mentioned that philosophers may be interested in the interpretation of philosophical thought in terms of psychoanalysis—adding, though, here as elsewhere, that the fact that a theory or doctrine is determined by psychological processes of many kinds does not necessarily invalidate its scientific truth. Since then, the knowledge of human behavior and motivation we owe to analysis has greatly increased, has become much more comprehensive but also more specific; and this development has certainly influenced not only social science, anthropology, and medicine, but also philosophy in a broad sense. Yet this does not mean that analysis can "answer" what one usually calls philosophical problems, though it leads to looking at them from a new angle. Some of its potentialities in this respect have been made use of only rather scantily so far. I am thinking, for example, of its possible contribution toward a better understanding of ethical problems. The interest psychoanalysis may have for philosophers has clearly two aspects: it resides partly in the new psychological findings and theories of analysis, but also in certain questions of methodology raised by Freud's and other psycho-analysts' approach to the study of man.

In speaking of psychoanalysis one often refers to a therapeutic technique. One may also refer to a method of psychological investigation whose main aspects are free association and interpretation; or, finally, to a body of facts and theories (Freud, 1923b). In this last sense, we would certainly consider as psychoanalytic any knowledge gained directly by Freud's method of investigation; but many of us would today consider analysis to include related procedures such as the application of psychoanalytic insights to data of direct child observation, a field which has grown in importance in the last two decades. Of the three aspects just mentioned, it is the method of exploration that has undergone the least change; it is commonly used in a situation defined by a certain set of rules and referred to as the psychoanalytic situation or the psychoanalytic interview. The therapeutic technique has been repeatedly modified, and psychoanalytic theory has gone through a series of more or less radical modifications, by Freud and by others. I want to emphasize that the inter-relations among these three aspects are, in analysis, a central topic—though in the context of this presentation I can refer to them only occasionally.

The theories of psychoanalysis follow principles of systematization, as do theories in other fields. Freud, however, did not speak of analysis as a "system," but rather accentuated its unfinished character, its flexibility, and the tentative nature of a considerable part of it. Actually, adjustments and reformulations of various aspects of theory have repeatedly become necessary. There are chapters such as the psychology of the dream, of libidinal development, of anxiety, and of symptom formation, that have been more systematically worked out than others. Psychoanalysis is obviously far from being a closed system of doctrines, though it has sometimes been represented as such. Also, though some fundamental tenets of psychoanalysis are accepted by all (Freudian) analysts, agreement on all of them is obviously lacking.

There is in analysis a hierarchy of hypotheses as to their closeness to observation, their generality, and the degree to which they have been confirmed. It appears that a neater classification as to these points and a higher degree of systematization (considering the different levels of theorizing) than exist today would not only facilitate my task in discussing psychoanalysis as a scientific theory but also clarify the standing of analysis as a scientific discipline. Promising efforts in this direction have been made and are being made by analysts and also by nonanalysts, but as yet no complete and systematical outline drawn from this angle is available; a recent work by David Rapaport (1958) comes close to performing this task. This is probably the reason, or one of the reasons, that in more or less general presentations of psychoanalysis references to its history abound, and the reader will forgive me if they do in this paper too, at least in its first part. I shall mostly refer to the work of Freud, because most of the more general theories of analysis have their origin in it, and because he is in many ways more representative of psychoanalytic thinking than anybody else.

Historical explanations are often substituted for a system; an attempt is made to clarify the function of propositions in their relation to others by tracing their place in the development of analysis. Also, without such historical reference it happens over and over again that analytic hypotheses are dealt with on one level, so to say, which belong to different phases of theory formation, and some of which have actually been discarded and replaced by others. Again, because of the comparatively low level of systematization, I think it is true that even today a thorough knowledge of at least some chapters of analytic theory cannot be acquired without knowledge of its history (see Chapter 4).

From the beginning, explanations of human behavior in terms of propositions about unconscious mental processes have been an essential part and one characteristic feature of psychoanalysis. I may, then, start by introducing Freud's concepts of unconscious processes. He makes a distinction between two forms of unconscious mental activity. The one, called preconscious, functions more or less as conscious activities do. It is not conscious, in a descriptive sense, but can become conscious without having to overcome powerful counterforces. Where such overcoming of resistances is necessary, as is the case with repressed material, we speak of unconscious processes in the stricter, the dynamic, sense of the word. The dynamic impact of these unconscious processes on human behavior—and not only in the case of mental disease—is one main tenet of Freud's theory of unconscious mental activities.

There is rather wide agreement that conscious data are insufficient for the explanation of a considerable part of behavior, and particularly of those aspects that were first studied in analysis. However, its critics have repeatedly claimed that the introduction of unconscious processes is superfluous. The explanation needed could be stated, or should be sought for, in terms of the more reliable data of brain physiology. The question here is not just whether, and why, explanations based on such data would be per se more reliable, nor why psychological hypotheses about mental processes ought not to be introduced in explaining human behavior. We have also to consider the fact that, given the actual state of brain physiology, many and even comparatively simple aspects of behavior of the kind we are dealing with in analysis cannot be explained. To rely on brain physiology alone would mean to renounce explanation of the greatest part of the field that psychoanalysis has set out to explain. Or, if one should insist on attempting an explanation on physiological grounds, the resultant hypotheses would of necessity be considerably more tenuous and more speculative even than psychoanalytic hypotheses are suspected to be by its critics today.

Freud, well trained in the anatomy and physiology of the brain, actually started out by attempting to devise a physiological psychology that could provide him with concepts and hypotheses to account for his clinical insights (1895). But beyond a certain point this approach proved of no use. He was thus led to replace it by a set of psychological hypotheses and constructs; and this step represents probably the most important turning point in the history of psycho-analysis. It was the beginning in analysis of psychological theory, the heuristic value of which he found to be greatly superior—a point that, I think, has been corroborated by its subsequent development.

But it is true that even after this radical turn in his approach Freud held on to the expectation, shared by many analysts, that one day the development of brain physiology would make it possible to base psychoanalysis on its findings and theories. He did not think this would happen during his lifetime, in which he proved to be right. In the meantime certain, though limited, parallels between analytic propositions and discoveries in the physiology of the brain have become apparent. Also, the usefulness of some psychoanalytic hypotheses for their field has been recognized by at least some repre-sentatives of brain research (Adrian, 1946). As to the psychology of unconscious processes, I think it can be said that Freud in developing that part of analysis was much less interested in the ultimate "nature" or "essence" of such processes—whatever this may mean—than in finding a suitable conceptual framework for the phenomena he had discovered.

While Freud, after the first years of his scientific work, relin-quished the attempt to account for his findings in terms of physiology, it is nevertheless characteristic of some of his psychoanalytic theoriz-ing that he used physiological models. He was guided by the trend in German physiology which has been designated as the physicalist school (Bernfeld, 1944), whose representatives were, among others, Helmholtz and Bruecke, the latter being one of Freud's teachers. Certain aspects of the psychology of neurosis, for example, led him to introduce into psychoanalysis the concept of regression (to earlier stages of development), which had been used in the physiology of his day; this concept, though, acquired new meaning in the context in which he used it. Also, in making "function" the criterion for defining what he called the mental systems (ego, id, superego), Freud used physiology as a model. But this no longer implies any correlation to any specific physiological organization (Hartmann,

Kris, Loewenstein, 1946). The value of such borrowings or analogies has, of course, to be determined in every single instance by confronting their application with tested knowledge (data and hypotheses). Physiological models (also occasionally physical models, as is obvious, for instance, in Freud's concept of a "mental apparatus") have been used also by other psychoanalysts (see, for example, Kubie, 1953) in order to illustrate certain characteristics of mental phenomena or to suggest a new hypothesis. The use even of metaphors need not of necessity lead into muddled thinking once their place in theory has been clearly delineated. The danger that earlier implications of those model concepts might impair their fruitful use in the new context of psychoanalysis has on the whole been successfully avoided (Hartmann, Kris, Loewenstein, 1946).

The broadening of the scope of psychology that came about as the consequence of the inclusion of propositions about unconscious mental processes meant, first of all, that many aspects of a person's life history that had never been explained before—and that, as a matter of fact, one had not even tried to explain—could be accounted for in terms of the individual's experience and dispositions. Causation in the field of personality is traceable only at its fringes without this broadening of theory. Freud was a strict determinist and often stated that to fill that gap in earlier psychological approaches, partly because of which the study of personality had been unsatisfactory, was one of his primary aims in developing analytic theory. More recently it has been said, by the mathematician von Mises (1939), that the observations correspond rather to statistical than to causal relations. I may mention at this point that this interest is the causation of mental phenomena included, quite naturally, also the interest in what we call the genetic viewpoint, since Freud's attention had been drawn to many facts of early childhood which had been unknown, and regularities in the relationships between early childhood situations and the behavior of the adult had become apparent. For Freud, the investigation of highly complex series of experience and behavior, extending over long periods of time, soon moved into the center of interest.

Developmental research was to become equally important for psychoanalytic theory and practice. It is significant that the reconstructive approach in analysis led not only to the discovery of a great wealth of childhood material in every individual case, but also to the ascertainment of typical sequences of developmental phases. The genetic approach has become so pervasive, not only in psychopathology but also in psychoanalytic psychology in general, that in analysis phenomena are often grouped together, not according to their descriptive similarities but if they have a common genetic root (oral character, anal character). It was only much later that this predominance of a genetic conceptualization was counterbalanced by a sharper distinction between genesis and function, to which I shall shortly return in speaking of the structural point of view.

Here I want to add that while I just spoke of the study of the individual's "life history," it would be misleading (though it actually has been done) to classify this aspect of analysis as a historical discipline. This misinterpretation may be traceable to its comparison with archaeology, which Freud occasionally uses. It is true that most analytic knowledge has been gained in the psychoanalytic interview and that the concern with developmental problems refers primarily to the history of individuals. But this should not obfuscate the fact that the aim of these studies is (besides its therapeutic purpose) to develop lawlike propositions which then, of course, transcend individual observations.

At this point I should like briefly to summarize the role of psychoanalysis as a psychology of motivation, still bearing in mind that psychoanalysis takes into consideration the interaction of the individual with his environment, as well as his so-called "inner-psychic" processes. And I have to present to you, at least briefly, a discussion of what, in analysis, we call "metapsychology," a term that signifies not (as it might seem) that which is beyond psychology altogether, but simply those psychological investigations that are not limited to conscious phenomena, and that formulate the most general assumptions of analysis on the most abstract level of theory. Metapsychology is concerned also with the substructures of personality, the ego, the id, and the superego which are defined as units of functions. The id refers to the instinctual aspect, the ego to the reality principle and to the "centralization of functional control" (to borrow a term from brain physiology). The superego has its biological roots in the long dependency on the parents and in the helplessness of the human child; it develops out of identifications with the parents; and it accounts for the fact that moral conflict and guilt feelings become a natural and fundamental aspect of human behavior. The structural formulations, referring to the distinction of ego, id, superego, have several theoretical and clinical advantages. The most important is probably that the demarcation lines of the three systems, ego, id, superego, are geared to the typical conflicts of man: conflicts with the instinctual drives, with moral conscience, and with the outside world. The paramount importance for neurotic *and* normal development of these conflicts, and of the ways to solve them, was one of the earliest discoveries of Freud and has remained central in psychoanalytic practice and theory ever since.

Critics of analysis often tend to underrate the wealth of individual data on which it is built. On the other hand, it also happens that the theoretical nature of concepts like libido is not fully realized; for example, libido is often identified with sexual experience, or as a mere generalization of some observable connections.

In the beginnings of psychoanalysis (even after the importance of unconscious processes had been realized), Freud still adhered more or less strictly to associationism. But when he found conflict to be a primary motivating force of behavior, and specifically an important etiological agent in neurosis, he gradually developed the concept of mental tendencies and purposive ideas. Psychoanalysis became a psychology of motivation, the motives being partly, but not generally, considered in analogy with those consciously experienced. There originated the idea of wishes, in certain circumstances warded off by defensive techniques. He discovered the role of repression and later of other defense mechanisms, like projection, isolation, undoing, and so on. The consideration of mental processes from this angle of synergistic or antagonistic motivating forces is what has been known since as the dynamic aspect of psychoanalysis. The systematic and objective study of conflict has remained one of its essential aspects and has proved a necessary and fruitful avenue to the explanation of human behavior. This was a second bold step in the development of psychoanalysis. The importance of "conflict" had, of course, been known in religious and philosophical doctrines and in literature, but scientific psychology before Freud had had no means to approach the subject.

The dynamic factors involved in both sides of a conflict were, for some time, rather poorly defined. It was, then, again primarily data of analytic observation that led to the realization of the importance of the instinctual drives among the motivating forces. I am referring here to Freud's discovery of infantile sexuality. This discovery was, at the time, considered by many as the product of revolting imagination; today, it can easily be confirmed in every nursery.

Even at the period when instinctual motivation seemed to be pretty much ubiquitous, the basic fact of conflict was not overlooked. Self-preservative instinctual drives were, at the time, thought of as the opponents of sexuality. Besides this, the concept of overdetermination, referring to the multiple motivation of all human behavior, continued also through the phase in which motivation was, on the level of general theory, nearly always considered instinctual.

Again, to fit it to his field of observation Freud had to modify the concept of "instinct" commonly used in other fields. His term, in German, *Trieb,* in English, "instinctual drive," or "drive," is certainly not identical with what one refers to as the instincts of lower animals. His concept of drives had to prove its usefulness with respect to human psychology. Here, the sources of the drives are of much less importance than their aims and their objects. The lesser rigidity of the human drives, the comparatively easy shift of the aims, the freeing of many activities from a rigid connection with one definite instinctual tendency, the comparative independence from and variety of possible response to outer and inner stimuli have to be taken into account in considering the role of the drives in human psychology. Still, the psychoanalytic theory of instinctual drives is broad enough to show also many impressive parallels with the findings of a modern school of zoologists (ethologists).

The concept of a continuity of this driving force allows the consideration of a great variety of mental acts from the angle of their investment with drive energy. Furthermore, in this way it is possible to understand the close relationship of many mental processes which, looked at from the surface, would appear to be entirely heterogeneous. The capacity for displacement or transformation into various kinds of human activities; the motivational role traceable through, and specific on, all levels of man's growth from birth to maturity; their central role in typical conflicts; and the fact that they involve relations to human objects—these are some of the psychologically essential aspects of the psychoanalytic concept of human drives. According to Freud, sexuality and aggression are, among all the drives one could describe, those that come closest to fulfilling the demands psychoanalysis makes on a concept of drives.

The concept of mental energy was then elaborated in the sense that it is the drives that are the main sources of energy in what Freud calls the "mental apparatus." However, a strictly quantifying approach to these energic problems has so far not been developed. Or rather: while it is possible to speak of a greater or lesser degree of, let's say, a resistance (against the uncovering of some hidden material), we have no way of measuring it. To account for the difference in the unconscious and the conscious (and preconscious) processes Freud postulated two forms of energy distribution, conceptualized as, respectively, primary and secondary processes. The primary processes represent a tendency to immediate discharge, while the secondary processes are guided by the consideration of reality. This distinction is again both theoretically significant and clinically quite helpful. The thesis that behavior is to be explained also in terms of its energic cathexis is what we call, in analysis, the economic viewpoint.

The regulation of energies in the mental apparatus is assumed to follow the pleasure principle, the reality principle (derived from the pleasure principle under the influence of ego development), and a tendency to keep the level of excitation constant or at a minimum. There are parallels to this in hypotheses formulated by others, and again the use of physical and physiological models played a role in the Freudian concepts.

The three aspects of psychoanalytic theory I have mentioned so far—the topographical (conscious–preconscious–unconscious), the dynamic, and the economic (energic)—represent Freud's first approach to what he called "metapsychology." It is postulated that a satisfactory explanation of human behavior includes its consideration in relation to all aspects of metapsychology. The "meta" in this term points to a theory going "beyond" the investigation of conscious phenomena. The word, generally accepted in psychoanalysis, has proved misleading for many outside analysis. Actually, as I mentioned before, "metapsychology' 'is nothing but a term for the highest level of abstraction used in analytic psychology.

A fourth aspect of metapsychology, called structural, was explicitly stated considerably later, though it was implicit in earlier theoretical thinking on mental conflicts. The forces opposing the drives in typical conflict situations, warding them off and forcing them to compromise formations (of which the neurotic symptom may serve as an example), are today conceptualized as an essential aspect of what we call the ego. At the core of this concept formation is the recognition of the relevant differences between instinctual tendencies which strive for discharge, and other tendencies that enforce postponement of discharge and are modifiable by the influence of the environment. This means, of course, that the dynamic and economic viewpoints can no longer be limited to the vicissitudes of instinctual drives. Also the original concept of a defensive ego had to be broadened to include in the ego those nondefensive functions of the mental apparatus that are noninstinctual in character. Many of these are not, or not necessarily, part of the conflictual set-up; we call them today "the nonconflictual sphere of the ego" (Hartmann, 1939a). Here belong (though they too may be involved in conflict, without, however, originating in it) perception, thinking, memory, action, and so on. It is likely that in man not only instinctual factors are in part determined by heredity, but also the apparatus of the ego underlying the functions just mentioned. We speak of the primary autonomous functions of the ego. It is true that analysis is, due to its method, directly dealing with environmental factors and with reactions to them, but this has never implied a denial, in principle, of heredity. It is in this sense that we speak of a drive constitution, and today also of constitutional elements in the ego, and of the role of maturational factors in the typical sequence of developmental phases.

To those functions that we attribute to the ego belongs also what one can call the centralized functional control which integrates the different parts of personality with each other and with outer reality. This function (synthetic function or organizing function) is in a way similar to what, since Cannon, we call homeostasis, and may represent one level of it.

The ego is, then, a substructure of personality and is defined by its functions. The instinctual aspect of personality is today conceptualized as the id. Through the development of the ego it becomes possible that the pleasure principle, dominant in the realm of the instinctual drives, can be modified to that consideration of reality, in thinking and action, that makes adaptation possible and is termed, as I said before, the reality principle. Through recent work, the relation between adaptation to outer reality and the state of integration of inner reality has become more accessible. This development in psychoanalytic theory has thus led to an improved understanding of man's relations to his environment, and to the most significant part of it, his fellow men—which is, however, not to say that the sociocultural aspects of mental functions and development had been overlooked in earlier analysis. Psychoanalysis, in contradistinction to some other schools of psychology, has never been confined exclusively to the consideration of "inner-psychic" processes; it has always, and by no means accidentally, included the consideration of the individual's interactions with the environment. At any rate, the study of object relations in human development has more recently become one of the most fruitful centers of analytic interest ("new environmentalism," Kris, 1950b). Ego psychology represents a more balanced view of the biological and the social and cultural aspects of human behavior. We may say that in analysis cultural phenomena are often studied in their biological context and significance, and biological phenomena in relation to the sociocultural environment (see Chapter 14). But this aspect will be discussed more fully later.

Some of the functions of the ego have, in the course of development, to be wrested from the influence of the drives. Gradually, they then reach, through a change of function, a certain degree of independence from instinctual origins and of resistance against reinvolvement with the drives (secondary autonomy—see Hartmann, 1939a; and Chapter 7). A similar concept, though less specific in relation to psychoanalytic propositions, has been introduced by G. Allport (1937). This relative independence of the ego is also energically conceptualized, with respect to the sources of energy at the disposal of ego functions. The necessity more clearly to distinguish function from genesis is one of the main implications of the structural viewpoint.

The third unit of functions, considered a substructure of personality, is called the superego. To it we attribute the functions of self-criticism, conscience, and the formation of ideals. The acceptance of moral standards is considered a natural step in ontogenesis. Moral conflict and the guilt feelings that are an expression of it are, from the time when the superego has been instituted, one fundamental aspect of human behavior. The superego has a biological root in the comparatively long dependency and helplessness of the child of the human species, which also means increased importance of the parents for its development. The superego develops out of identification with them, to which, in subsequent layers of development, identifications with others are added. Also obvious in its genesis is a sociocultural factor, which accounts for an important segment of tradition formation. The acceptance of certain moral demands, the rejection of others, the degree of severity of the superego, and its capacity to enforce its demands can very frequently be traced in clinical investigation.

Structural hypotheses are in many ways more comprehensive than earlier formulations of partly the same problems. They have also a considerable value in clinical thinking, because they are particularly fit to account for what has remained dominant in clinical work, that is, the various forms of typical conflict situations. Actually, as I said before, the demarcation lines of those units of functions, or systems, or substructures of personality are so drawn that they correspond to the main conflicts of man, which we now describe as conflicts between ego and id, superego and ego, and ego and reality. It was in this respect that Freud found the older topographical model, the layer model (conscious–preconscious–unconscious), rather disappointing, though in other respects it still retains a certain degree of significance. Defenses as well as drives can be unconscious; thus differences between conscious and unconscious processes cannot be used to account for these conflicts.

I thought it advisable to begin by giving a picture of certain fundamentals of psychoanalytic theory, and of the degree of its comprehensiveness, by indicating at least some of its dimensions, and also the relations between different parts of these theories. Its comprehensiveness means also its actual or potential importance in many neighboring fields. My survey shows also at least some of the points at which questions can be raised from the viewpoint of a philosophy of science. There would have been an alternative to the way of presentation I chose. I could have shown how, in the analysis of a symptom or a dream, our observations lead to anticipations, and how the various levels of our conceptual tools are brought to bear on them; also, how in this process theoretical thinking is constantly brought back to the observables. But this alternative would inevitably demand the introduction of a great number of variables and a discussion of the analytic method and the analytic situation much broader than I am able to give here. Of course, a sector of psychoanalytic propositions can be tested outside analysis, and some have been tested in this way; but it is still true that it is, in the field of analysis, extremely difficult to assay the suitability of the hypotheses for the purposes for which they have been primarily devised without the use, in the analytic situation, of the analytic method.

Since its beginnings analysis has struggled for a system of concepts fit to account for the peculiarities of the subject matter it had to deal with. Freud spoke of his endeavor to "introduce the right abstract ideas" and said, "We are constantly altering and improving them." This work has continued; nevertheless, not all concepts used are equally well defined. The distinction between independent, intervening, and dependent variables is often not clearly drawn. Also the different degress of confirmation of the various parts of the complex network of psychoanalytic hypotheses are frequently not made apparent in analytic writings. Actually, there are many reasons for the lack of methodological strictness we often find in analysis. Some of them are encountered in every theoretical approach to the central aspects of personality. In addition, there is the fact that for psychoanalytic research there were no traditional methodological models available that could be used in its service; the differences in content as well as in method prevented a borrowing in this respect.

Freud had a firsthand knowledge of experimental method and was thoroughly steeped in the philosophy of science of the great *Naturforscher* of his day. He was fascinated by the theories of evolution, which left their imprint on his thinking, and, of course, there must have been other factors in the intellectual climate of his "formative years" that influenced his development as a scientist. The heuristic character and value of hypotheses were well known to him, as well as the role of basic concepts and postulates. Though Freud was certainly not primarily interested in the philosophy of science, it is still true, and it has often been said by psychoanalysts and recently also by others (Frenkel-Brunswik, 1954), that his "sophistication" in this respect was much greater than early reactions to his work would let one realize. But we have to consider that logical clarification is not usually found in the early development of a science and is often not the work of the great explorers (Hartmann, Kris, Loewenstein, 1946). It is only more recently that it has become, in the case of analysis, a subject of particular interest to a great number of workers.

Psychoanalysis was, of course, "new" not only because of its conceptual language, its method, and the methodological problems it posed, but "new" also as to content. The reorganization of commonly accepted knowledge, as a consequence of new data having been found and new modes of thinking having been introduced, and of the replacement of old scientific, or old common-sense, or socialized, "truths" by the new ones, is mostly a slow and often a difficult process. In analysis, such new insights, which do not only add to our knowledge but also force upon us a revision of old ways of thinking, abound. There is also the additional difficulty that some (not all) of its discoveries could be made only under specific conditions (the analytic situation); and known facts often appeared in confrontation with such discoveries in a different light. On the other hand, looking at these discoveries from outside analysis, it seemed difficult to "place," if I may say so, these unexpected and apparently improbable insights, their real connections with other factors being hardly understood. Attitudes toward demands for reconsideration of what had appeared to be safely anchored knowledge do not of course always observe the lines of logical thinking. Psychoanalysis has systematically studied—has, indeed, to study in every single clinical case—this problem, that is, the conditions for the capacity or incapacity to observe new phenomena in the realm of psychology and to think rationally about them. At any rate, once the shock the content of Freud's discoveries had represented to his contemporaries had somewhat subsided, people started to take them more seriously and even to attribute to them a certain amount of scientific standing. This process of rehabilitation of analysis was then fortified by the confirmation of psychoanalytic findings in medicine and child psychology, and through the proven usefulness of analytic hypotheses in these fields, as well as in anthropology, and in other social sciences. This naturally led to a different evaluation of the psychoanalytic method, too, which was at the origin of these discoveries, and of the psychoanalytic theories of which these hypotheses were a part.

It is not surprising that the newness and the scope of the psychoanalytic findings and theories made changes of concepts and the introduction of new hypotheses imperative. In his tentative formulations, Freud occasionally did not even disdain to take models of motivation from common-sense psychology. But to these common-sense elements, confronted with new facts and subjected to analytic conceptualization, mostly rather uncommon sense has accrued. It also seems, from the perspective of a few decades of empirical work, that quite a few methodologically questionable formulations have proved their heuristic value. Given the state of the psychology of personality, risks as to the development of the method as well as of hypothesis formation had to be taken. One could not limit the field to those parts that could already be handled in an unobjectionable way. Knowing the inherent difficulties of the subject matter, one may well be inclined to postdict that without the courage and impetus of a genius this most comprehensive attack on the explanation of human behavior that we call analysis could hardly have come about.

I said before that even today some logical uncertainties persist. The methodological demands made on science, the signposts which indicate which routes are open and which prohibited, which ways are likely to lead to dead ends, are generally geared to the logically best-developed branches of science. These we rightly admire as models of methodological clarity (which is not to deny that even there methodological controversies arise). Progress in physics, or in biology, has repeatedly led to demands on psychoanalysis for reformulation of its theories in accordance with these developments in other sciences. In principle there is no reason why such borrowings could not enrich the tools or the clarity of analytic thinking, as has happened with other models. But this question is less one of the theory of science than of the, we could say, "practical" needs of a specific science—the empirical question of the fitness of certain elements of logically well-structured sciences for other less developed fields. There is also, of course, the question of the necessarily different conditions in different fields. There is the need to outline a fruitful methodological approach to the less systematized sciences, to allow maximal productivity on a given level of insight into the relations between fact and hypothesis and according to the degrees of formal organization.

Before discussing in a more general way the relations between data and theories in psychoanalysis, I next shall speak of one of the inherent difficulties of our field. Every psychologist is confronted with the problem of how knowledge of the mental processes of others can be achieved. (I am not speaking here of the possibility of knowing another person's subjective experience.) As to our own mental processes some do—and some don't—refer to "self-experience." For those who do, a further difficulty is introduced if, as is the case in psychoanalysis, self-experience is accepted in principle, but its cognitive value remains in doubt. That is, it is a question of further investigation as to what is the indicative value of a given element of self-perception in terms of mental process. Looked at from this angle, analysis can be termed a systematic study of self-deception and its motivations. This implies that thinking about our own mental processes can be found to be true or false. There is in analysis, as you know, the concept of "rationalization," to give you an example. While self-experience is obviously an important element in analysis, its theories, as I said before, transcend this level of discourse.

The lawlike propositions of metapsychology are not formulated on the level of self-experience. Generally, Freud's views on introspection have not always been clearly appreciated. They are, though, evident already in the kind of psychoanalytic thinking that is comparatively close to observational data, as in Freud's ideas on the psychopathology of everyday life (1901). In a slip of the tongue, for instance, when, in place of a word we consciously intended to use, another one, not consciously intended, appears, we use the behavioral aspect in evaluating the psychological situation—we use it, that is, in taking the word actually spoken as an indication of an unconscious motivation that takes precedence over the conscious one.

The data gathered in the psychoanalytic situation with the help of the psychoanalytic method are primarily behavioral data; and the aim is clearly the exploration of human behavior. The data are mostly the patient's verbal behavior, but include other kinds of action. They include his silences, his postures (F. Deutsch, 1952), and his movements in general, more specifically his expressive movements. While analysis aims at an explanation of human behavior, those data, however, are interpreted in analysis in terms of mental processes, of motivation, of "meaning"; there is, then, a clear-cut difference between this approach and the one usually called "behavioristic," and this difference is even more marked if we consider the beginnings of behaviorism rather than its more recent formulations.

As to the data, it is hard to give, outside the analytic process itself, an impression of the wealth of observational data collected in even one single "case." One frequently refers to the comparatively small number of cases studied in analysis and tends to forget the very great number of actual observations on which we base, in every individual case, the interpretations of an aspect of a person's character, symptoms and so on.[1]

By keeping certain variables in the analytic situation, if not constant, as close to constancy as the situation allows, it becomes easier to evaluate the significance of other variables that enter the picture. The best-studied example of this is what is called the "passivity" of the analyst, in contradistinction to the considerably more pronounced activity of the psychotherapist. This is not to claim that psychoanalysis is an experimental discipline. However, there are

[1] Thus every single clinical "case" represents, for research, hundreds of data of observed regularities, and in hundreds of respects.

336 ·

situations where it comes close to it. At any rate, there is sufficient evidence for the statement that our observations in the psychoanalytic situation, set in the context of psychoanalytic experience and hypotheses, make predictions possible—predictions of various degrees of precision or reliability, but as a rule superior to any others that have been attempted in the psychology of personality. Due to the emphasis on the genetic viewpoint, many predictions are what has been called "predictions of the past" (Hartmann and Kris, 1945), that is, reconstructions of the past which can often be confirmed in astonishing detail (Bonaparte, 1945). One obvious limitation of our predictive potential is, of course, the great number of factors determining, according to psychoanalytic theory, every single element of behavior —what Freud has termed "overdetermination." Still, our technique is constantly directed by tentative predictions of the patient's reactions. Also, studies in developmental psychology by means of direct child observation, such as have been conducted by E. Kris and other psychoanalysts (M. Kris, 1957), are guided by the formulation of expectations and their checking in individual cases. Here I just want to point to one way in which psychoanalytic hypotheses can be used vis-à-vis individual cases and how they may be confirmed in experience. I may mention here that problems of validation of psychoanalytic hypotheses ought not to be equated, as has too often been done, with the problem of therapeutic success.

A further difficulty results from the fact that psychoanalytic theory must also deal with the relation between observer and observed in the analytic situation. There are personality layers, if you will excuse this term, that in the average case the observed cannot reach without the help of the observer and his method of observation. But the insight of the observer ought not to be confused with the insight of the observed. Some of these problems belong in a theory of psychoanalytic technique. But there is also the problem of the "personal equation" (see Chapter 6; E. Kris, 1950b). The field of observation includes not only the patient but also the observer who interacts with the former ("participant observation"). The interaction of analyst and analysand is accounted for in the theories of transference and countertransference. As to the potential handicaps of observations traceable to the mental processes of the observer, they are subject to the constant scrutiny of the analyst. Some such handicaps of psychological observation can certainly be eliminated by the personal analysis of the observer, and this is one of the reasons that a didactic analysis is an essential element in the training of our students of analysis. Thus, what I want to say here is not that in the psychology of personality objectivity is impossible. It is rather that psychoanalysis has discovered potential sources of error and found a way to combat them.

Distortions of self-observation as well as of observations of others that occur as consequences of instinctual pressure are clinically easily traceable, and can be accounted for by analytic theory. To one aspect of this problem we find a close analogy in the behavior of animals: the "world" of the hungry animal is different from the "world" of the same animal in heat. In man, following structure formation, the situation is more complex. How much we can perceive psychologically with respect to ourselves and others, and how we perceive it, is also determined by defensive and other functions we attribute to the ego; and the superego, too, can influence our perceptive range and lead to distortions. The influence of central personality factors— needs, desires, affective states—on perception in general (not just of the psychological field) has also been experimentally demonstrated; and how, despite this, "objective" perception is possible is an object of special study (G. Klein, 1958). The questions of objectivation and of "testing of reality," as Freud called it, are also accounted for in psychoanalytic theory and lead again to the concept of degrees of ego autonomy that I mentioned before.

The body of analytic theories on the "mental apparatus" must include, as an essential sector, hypotheses fit to explain the distortions of psychological observation. No doubt this involvement of the observer and the potential sources of error of his perception and judgment represent an added difficulty in analytic clinical practice and research. But it is well known that even in other fields, and often to a troubling degree, this problem plays a role. However, this complication we are confronted with in analysis is an essential feature of certain aspects of human behavior rather than a result of imperfections of the state of psychoanalytic theory. There is, as I have said, also a psychologically fruitful side to these same complexities that have led to some methodological discontent. Corrections of at least some distortions of psychological observation and thinking are within the reach of our method. In the so far most comprehensive study of Freud's development, his biography by Ernest Jones, the role of his self-analysis in the unfolding of his thought has been emphasized. Now, self-analysis has this function only in exceptional cases; but we have similar experiences in great numbers from the analysis of others. In a more diluted way, this correction of blind spots can occasionally even be achieved outside analysis, as a consequence of changing attitudes toward certain factors that are essential for a psychology of personality.

It is very likely that in the work of Freud and other analysts so-called "intuitions" have played a role. But it is clear that, certainly in Freud, his striving for scientific discipline, his patient accumulation of observational data, and his search for conceptual tools to account for them have reduced their importance to a stimulus factor in the formation of psychoanalytic theories. Many subjects approached in analysis had before Freud been studied by so-called intuitive psychology only. But he was wont to oppose psychoanalytic psychology to intuitive psychology, and the development psychoanalysis has taken bears out this point. Still the relation between data and theory is no doubt a rather complex one in psychoanalysis. There are the cases in which, mostly in the beginning, he approached a problem with what he called "a few psychological formulae," that is, tentative hypotheses, whose heuristic value must be determined. To give you one example: certain clinical observations on hysterical patients had been made by Breuer before Freud, and also by Janet. But these discoveries were viewed from the angle of dynamic unconscious processes of conflict and defense only by Freud. It was with him and not with the others who had made similar observations that they opened the way to the understanding of mental conflict in general, which was later found to be an essential factor in normal and abnormal development. Here the introduction of fruitful hypotheses was decisive for the scientific momentum of a discovery (Chapter 14). It led to an integration of the observed facts and also to the discovery of new facts. It is true in psychoanalysis as elsewhere that theories cannot be considered as mere summaries of observations. Actually, "the storehouse of pre-existing knowledge influences our expectations" and often "preconscious expectations . . . direct the selection of what is to be registered as observation and what seems to require explanation" (Hartmann, Kris, Loewenstein, 1953, p. 16). It is also obvious in psychoanalysis that the psychological investigator "must know that every step of his progress depends on his advances in the sphere of *theory,* and on the conceptual consistency, breadth and depth reached therein" (K. Lewin, 1926, p. 78).

In dealing with new observations and often new hypotheses it has become unavoidable to redefine the meaning of many concepts in analysis and to add new ones. Some concepts that have meaningfully been used, e.g., in studying the psychology of lower animals in experimental situations, are less fit if we deal with human behavior. Also, concepts common in everyday usage, in medicine, in philosophy, had to be redefined for psychoanalytic purposes. I mention this here, because it has sometimes made interdisciplinary communication more difficult. Thus, as I said before, the concept of instinctual drives has been radically modified. And there are redefinitions, in analysis, also of the concepts of libido, of anxiety, and others. To this, I may quote W. Heisenberg's statement (1952) that "the transition . . . from previously investigated fields to new ones will never consist simply of the application of already known laws to these new fields. On the contrary, a really new field of experience will always lead to the crystallization of a new system of scientific concepts and laws."

The analyst's observations are made in a clinical setting. The psychological object is studied in a real-life situation: the patient comes to another person, the analyst, in the hope of being freed from limitations of his capacity for work and his enjoyment of life, imposed by changes in his personality that are considered pathological but remediable. This means readiness for hundreds of hours of work and for being confronted with his life history, with parts of his personality that have been repressed, and, generally, with many surprising and often unpleasant insights into his mental processes. In the therapeutic situation, motivations are mobilized that help to combat the natural resistance against objective scrutiny of one's self. Such motivations can hardly be expected to be available outside a real-life situation; actually the many attempts outside of analysis to create, for purposes of investigation, situations meant to mimic situations of real life have not lead very far. This point, then, refers chiefly to the superiority of analysis in making data available and creating a readiness for their observation.

On the other hand, it is good to remember Freud's reactions when after years of experimental work he decided to follow his research interests in the clinical field (and the quite similar reactions we meet today in young scientists turning to psychoanalysis). "He [Freud] confessed to a feeling of *discomfort*. He who had been trained in the school of experimental sciences was writing what read like a novel. Not personal preferences, he said, but the subject matter forced such a presentation on him" (Kris, 1947). He was confronted with a mostly unexplored field, with human motivations, human needs and conflicts. "Everywhere," he said later, "I seemed to discern motives and tendencies analogous to those of everyday life." Some concepts of common-sense psychology, which, as I said before, were tentatively applied, had to be redefined, though the terms were sometimes retained. Thus common-sense psychology soon proved insufficient; nor could the scientific psychology of his day and its methodology be of great help. Freud had only what he called a "few formulae," or hypotheses, to guide him. But it was only after the special and the more general theories of analysis had been developed that the full meaning could be extracted from the clinical data he had gathered.

There is always something ambiguous about the meaning of "clinical research" in general. There exists, so far as I know, no really satisfactory presentation of the subject in terms of the philosophy of science. I just want to say here a word about Freud's case histories. Every one of his comprehensive case histories is at the same time a study in psychoanalytic theory. I mention them at this point because they show the constant mutual promotion of observation and hypothesis formation, the formation of definite propositions which make our knowledge testable, and the attempts to validate or invalidate them.

Another aspect of the clinical origins of psychoanalytic theory is the fact that more was found, in the beginning, about pathological than about normal behavior. The etiology of neurosis was studied before the etiology of health, though psychoanalysis has, in principle, always aimed at a comprehensive general psychology. Also, as I mentioned, more became known, in the first attempts to deal with the field, about the instinctual drives, especially about sexuality and its development, than about the forces opposing the drives in the typical ego-id conflicts. This, however, has changed in the last two or three decades, and thus analysis has today come closer to what it always was intended to be, though not every aspect and not every implication of its very comprehensive conceptual frame have so far been actually developed.

In clinical work, one is used to being guided by signs and symptoms in forming an opinion concerning the presence or absence of a pathological process. But the question of the significance and the use of signs for purposes of explanation is, of course, logically of much wider relevance. Different meanings can be attributed to the terms sign, signal, expressive sign, symbol, and so on, and these differences are important also in psychoanalysis. However, I do not propose to deal with this problem here. Suffice it to say that a considerable part of psychoanalytic work can be described as the use of signs—a series of associations, a dream, an affect vis-à-vis the analyst

—as indications of mental processes. In this sense one speaks of the psychoanalytic method as a method of interpretation (Hartmann, 1927; Bernfeld, 1932; Loewenstein, 1957). This has both a cognitive and a therapeutic aspect. They partly coincide, that is, in so far as a therapeutic agent of foremost significance in analysis is making the patient aware of, and capable of integrating, previously unconscious and, through defense, split-off processes. Some of those signs, for example, some of the symbols we find in dreams, have a rather ubiquitous meaning, while the interpretation of others requires a closer scrutiny of the individual under observation. At any rate, there are many situations in which the relation between a sign and what it signifies becomes easily recognizable, for instance, in the associations immediately following the observation of some detail of behavior. In others, various levels of theory have to be introduced to explain the connection. Such sign systems are used today not only in the psychoanalytic situation but also in the study by analysts, by means of direct observation, of child development. Many childhood situations of incisive significance for the formation of the adult personality have a low probability of direct manifestation. One tries to learn about the sign function of data of child behavior for a recognition of the central, and often unconscious, development that we know from the psychoanalytic interview (see Chapter 6). At this point it is possible, or even likely, that a misunderstanding may occur of what I have said about a low probability of manifestation outside analysis of certain processes investigated in analysis. I want, then, to add explicitly that this was not meant to be a general statement. Many phenomena first studied in the analytic situation could later be studied also in the direct observation of psychotics, in so-called applied psychoanalysis, or in the direct observation of children. What I want to emphasize in this context is that the comparative study of reconstructive data and data of direct observation of children can, on the one hand, lead to the confirmation of analytic propositions; on the other hand it can lead to the formulation of more specific hypotheses.

The essential importance of constructs for the coherence of the psychoanalytic system (or whatever we choose to call it) can be gathered already from the brief outline I have given in the first part of this discussion. Theories, or hypotheses of a different order, connect them with observational data. That these constructs, which are introduced because of their explanatory value, cannot be directly defined in terms of observational data, but that inferences from the constructs can be tested by observation, has long been known in psychoanalysis (Hartmann, 1927). Still, some of these constructs seem particularly suspect to many critics of analysis. An occasional lack of caution in the formulation of its propositions, or Freud's liking for occasional striking metaphors, has led to the accusation against analysis of an anthropomorphization of its concepts. But in all those cases a more careful formulation can be substituted which will dispel this impression.

There is, then, the question whether and in what sense such constructs are considered "real"; and, more specifically, the question has often been asked whether and in what sense Freud considered constructs like libido, the "system unconscious," and the substructures of personality in the sense of structural psychology, as real. He said that the basic concepts of science form the roof rather than the foundation of science and ought to be changed when they no longer seem able to account for experience; also that they have the character of conventions. But he certainly thought that what he meant to cover by these basic concepts had effects which could be observed. He was in no danger of confusing concepts with realities; he was a "realist" in a different sense. He does not seem to have thought that "real" means just "the simplest theoretical presentation of our experiences," but rather that those basic concepts pointed to something real in the ordinary sense of the word.

It is quite possible that Freud, as Frenkel-Brunswik (1954) has said of "scientists of great ingenuity," sometimes proceeded "from observation directly to hypothetical constructs and . . . derived the intervening variables later." But it is also evident from Freud's work that he by no means always spelled out the ways in which he had arrived at the formulation of his constructs. It is hard to say in a general way under what conditions a direct transition from data to constructs would seem legitimate or fruitful. It has been suggested by Ellis (1950) that "where intervening variables are of a limited usefulness in scientific theorizing, hypothetical constructs take in the widest range of relevant phenomena, and lead to a maximum success in the prediction and explanation of behavior."

It is obvious that among the intervening variables "dispositional concepts" play a significant role in analysis. The term "mental disposition" has actually been used in analysis, but the same kind of concept is often also covered by different terms. It has been pointed out (Hartmann, 1927) that the concept of "latent attitudes" used by Koffka and others comes rather close to psychoanalytic thinking. The term mental tendency is ubiquitous in psychoanalysis, and many of these tendencies, as mentioned before, are understood to be not manifest but in the nature of a disposition.

Speaking now of the series independent–intervening–dependent variable, I want to quote a passage from Rapaport (1958) about a significant aspect of intervening variables in analysis. He clearly states the point I have in mind: "Let us assume that an aggressive drive is our independent variable and overt behavior toward an (actual or thought) object our dependent variable. It will be noted that in a certain subject at certain intensities of the drive we will observe aggressive behavior (in deed or thought) toward the object, at other intensities we will observe no overtly aggressive behavior but rather excessive kindness (reaction formation). In other subjects at certain intensities the aggressive behavior will be diverted from the object to other objects (displacement) or upon their own self (turning round upon the subject), or will be replaced by ideas and feelings of being aggressed by the other (projection). In these observations the defense of reaction formation, displacement, turning round upon the subject, projection, etc., will be conceptualized as intervening variables."[2] Here let me remind you of what I said before, that the explanation of manifest behavior presupposes in every single case the consideration of a great number of variables. The statement, current in analysis, that the same manifest action, attitude, fantasy may have different "meanings" (that is, may be the result of the interaction of different tendencies) has often been misunderstood. It has been said that it opens the door to bias or arbitrary interpretation. This argument seems to neglect the point I have just made. What the psychoanalytic approach has shown is a complex interdependence of a variety of factors, and of patterns of factors. I may mention too, in this context, that working with unilinear causal relations alone has not always proved satisfactory. The essential fact of interdependence of mental functions does not always allow a clear-cut answer to the question of which variable has to be considered as independent and which one as an intervening variable. A stimulus from the outside world will sometimes be considered an independent variable, but in another context also an instinctual tendency or an autonomous tendency of the ego (Rapaport, 1958). We came across this problem of relative independence in speaking of the secondary autonomy of the ego, but it has a much wider significance in psychoanalytic psychology.

Turning now to the validation of psychoanalytic hypotheses, I shall follow Kris (1947) in distinguishing validations in analysis from validations outside of it. To begin with the former, I may repeat that the amount of time spent in the study of any single individual is vastly greater, and the wealth of data considerably richer, than in any other clinical set-up. This alone would make the use of the analytic method in the analytic situation the *via regia* to the psychology of personality. In this setting, data do appear which are not, or not easily, accessible to other methods. This asset as to fact finding has, of course, a disadvantage in another respect: an observation an analyst makes may seem entirely credible to another analyst

---

[2] This passage is quoted from the original draft of this paper, and was slightly altered in the published version.

who possesses the necessary experience, an interpretation quite convincing, while the same observation may appear hardly credible, the same interpretation highly improbable or artificial, to one who approaches the field with a different method and in a different setting. For the analyst, one constant angle of his work is the observation of data and of sequences of data, the tentative interpretations (in search of the common elements in such sequences), and the checking of his interpretations against the subsequent (and past) material. It is safe to say that the greater part of evidence for the psychoanalytic propositions still lies with this work.

To broaden the reach of intersubjective validation beyond the relatively small group of workers in psychoanalysis, and also for teaching purposes and for comparing different techniques, the recording of interviews has been recommended by many (Kubie, 1952) and practiced by some. More recently, records of analytic interviews were submitted to other analysts, who were asked to predict the developments in subsequent sessions (Bellak, 1956). Such studies are likely gradually to attract a greater number of research workers, but, for the present, their potential contribution to the scientific status of analysis cannot yet be estimated.

As to the genetic propositions of analysis, the direct observation of children not only has become a rich source of information, but has also given us the possibility to make our hypotheses more specific and to check their validity. A great number of Freud's hypotheses on childhood could be confirmed by direct observation of children. But to validate more completely our genetic propositions, "systematic observations of life histories from birth on" are necessary. "If the longitudinal observation in our own civilization were to be systematized and the study of life histories were to be combined with that of the crucial situations in Freud's sense, many hunches might be formulated as propositions, and others might be discarded" (Hartmann and Kris, 1945).

The literature on experimental research, both in animals and in man, devised for the purpose of testing propositions derived from psychoanalysis has become very extensive. It has been repeatedly reviewed (Sears, 1943; Kris, 1947; Benjamin, 1950; Frenkel-Brunswik, 1954; and others), and I do not think I should go into it in any detail here. The following remarks are, then, random remarks and do not attempt to be in any way systematic. The classical animal experiments of Hunt, Levy, Miller, Masserman are probably known to many of you. Many of the animal experiments were conducted with considerable insight and great skill. Where the experimental set-up is adequate, the frequency of "confirmation" is impressive. Or, as Hilgard (1952) states, "It has been possible to parallel many psychoanalytic phenomena in the laboratory. When this is done, the correspondence between predictions according to psychoanalytic theory and what is found is on the whole very satisfactory."

Of course, we would not expect that every psychoanalytic proposition can be tested in animal experiments (Frenkel-Brunswik, 1954). But there are also definite limitations to so-called "experimental psychoanalysis" in the human. It appears difficult (though it has been attempted occasionally) to study "real" conflicts with the tools that "experimental psychoanalysis" has at its disposal (Hartmann and Kris, 1945; Kris, 1950b). And I may insert here that even experimentation that tends to remain close to "life situations," as does the work of K. Lewin, Dembo, Zeigarnik and others, is not quite free from those limitations.

A rather harsh criticism of Sears' "Survey" has been voiced by Wisdom (1953). But also with others who do not share his point of view, a certain amount of dissatisfaction has become apparent (A. Freud, 1951b; Rapaport, 1958; Kubie, 1952). Sometimes in those experiments the hypotheses tested were not psychoanalytic propositions at all, though the author had meant them to be. Sometimes they were taken over literally from psychoanalytic writings, but the context in which they appear in analysis, and thus their function, were not sufficiently considered; thus the results had to be ambiguous. It also happened that, looked at from the vantage point of analysis, experiments could be considered as validations of certain points in analysis, though not of those the author had in mind. In evaluating the results of "experimental analysis," there is, in addition, the perspectival character of every method to be considered, highlighting certain aspects and throwing others into the shade. Every method implies a selection, and data are being centered in different ways, depending on our approach (Chapter 6; Rapaport, 1958). That is, an analysis of the methods used, and an attempt to correlate them, becomes of prime importance.

On the whole, this field of research has not so far decisively contributed toward a clarification or systematization of psychoanalytic theory. As a rule, these studies do not go beyond what has been demonstrated in analysis before (Hilgard, 1952; Kubie, 1952); they have often neither achieved new insights nor stimulated research. But, at their best, they have a value as confirmatory (or nonconfirmatory) evidence. Apart from this, they have greatly contributed to bridging the gap between psychoanalysis and other psychological disciplines. Also, "experimental psychoanalysis" continues to expand, and there is the possibility that certain drawbacks of its beginnings will be overcome.

Another source of potentially fruitful contacts is the confrontation of psychoanalysis with learning theory. Thus Dollard and Miller (1950) have attempted "to give a systematic analysis of neurosis and psychotherapy in terms of the psychological principles and social conditions of learning." They concentrate their study on Freudian principles, and the theorist of analysis, though often disagreeing, will profit from this and similar ventures.

This review of experimental checking of psychoanalytic hypotheses is admittedly a sketch only. But even if it were not, even if I had given the full picture, it would remain beyond doubt that the main body of evidence rests not on these studies but on the wealth of empirical data gathered by the analytic method in the analytic situation. The task better to define his concepts, to work toward a higher level of clarification and systematization of his hypotheses, rests, in the main, still with the analyst. This is, of course, far from saying that attempts at validation using extra-analytical methods, or criticisms originating in points of view different from those of analysis, are not to be welcomed by analysts. It is to be hoped, though, in the interest of sound interdisciplinary communication, that these criticisms, more than has often been the case in the past, will be based on a close familiarity with the methods of analysis, with the special nature of its subject matter, and with the role theorizing has played and plays in its development.

PART II

CHAPTER 17

On Parapraxes in the Korsakoff Psychosis

(1924)

I F WE start out from the general view that there is a close relationship between organic-cerebral and psychic mechanisms, it
seems justified to raise the question whether the psychologically
well-described and well-known processes of repression, displacement,
and condensation have their counterpart in the realm of organic
disorders. There have been attempts to clarify problems of organic
brain disorders from the psychological point of view; we will refer
here only to the studies of Pick (1913), Pötzl (1917), and Schilder
(1922). The latter two, bringing psychoanalytic considerations to
bear on their data, were able to demonstrate mechanisms in aphasia
that may be considered related to repression. We have set ourselves
the task of testing, by means of learning experiments, the efficacy
of this approach on those parapraxes (that is, substitute formations)
which are part of the memory disorder of the Korsakoff psychosis.

The psychological studies of the Korsakoff syndrome have set
themselves the task of analyzing its most striking symptom, namely,
the impaired registration[1] of recent impressions. They did so by ex-

---

This paper was written with Stefan Betlheim. Notes signed D.R. are by the translator, David Rapaport.

[1] "Registration" here translates *Merkfähigkeit,* often used in the German literature
in contrast to *Erinnerungsfähigkeit* ("recall-ability"); cf., for example, Kohnstamm
(1917).—D.R.

periments, which in the negative sense established and circumscribed the defect, and in the positive sense demonstrated whatever traces such recent impressions left. We are indebted to Brodmann (1902) and Gregor (1907, 1909) for the experimental proof that the learned material is not lost in the Korsakoff psychosis but, as Gregor puts it, is demonstrable by means of Ebbinghaus's saving procedure. Several observers before him had already been impressed by the fact that experiences during the psychosis which were apparently forgotten would occasionally re-emerge even after surprisingly long time intervals.

We can therefore assume that even in this very severe organic disorder experience is not annihilated, but only its reproduction is inhibited in a manner so far unknown. Schilder (1924) demonstrated the same for the epileptic twilight state. But we do not know how the traces of these experiences are represented; nor do we have thorough investigations of the relationship between the content of the patient's impressions and his distorted reproductions. There are only a few hints to the answer to this question: Gregor observed that in learning a series of words, any word learned may be replaced by one related to it by content or by clang association and that occasionally associative fusions (Müller and Pilzecker, 1900) occur.[2] He also observed that the distortion often reveals a "tendency· to the trivial." Not infrequently one encounters the view that the missing memory is replaced by "any" other at "random." According to some investigators (Mönckemöller, 1898; Grünthal, 1922; and others), the content of confabulations is taken from the everyday life of the patient; other investigators emphasized the fantastic character of these confabulations. How much and what form of recent experience and recent learning can be demonstrated in confabulations has been little explored. It is known that delirious experiences frequently re-emerge in the form of confabulations.

We started out by comparing material learned with its distorted

---

[2] The phenomenon described as "associative fusion" is analogous to the Freudian concept of condensation.

reproduction. Besides some neutral bits of prose and a poem, we had the patients learn brief stories of crudely sexual content. Since the distortion by psychic influences of objectionable and particularly of sexual imagery and thoughts has been particularly well investigated in the analysis of dreams and neurotic symptoms (Freud), we expected to get an answer to some of our questions by using such short stories as learning material.

It goes without saying that only meaningful material could be used for our purpose. We chose the following bits of prose:

I. Rabbi Moir, the great teacher, sat on the Sabbath in the school instructing the people, while at his home his two sons were struck by lightning and died.

II. (a) A young girl went for a walk in the fields all alone. A young man came, attacked her, and threw her to the ground. The girl struggled, but it was no use. The man pulled up her skirts and pushed his stiff organ into her vagina. After the intercourse he fled, leaving the crying girl lying on the ground.

II. (b) A young man attacked a young girl, pulled up her skirt, and pushed his stiff organ into her vagina.

III. When the mother left the house, the father locked himself up in a room with his daughter, threw her on the bed, and raped his own child.

These stories were read to the patients who were then asked to reproduce them. Help was given when needed. Even though we were of the opinion that those mechanisms which we will demonstrate in the reproduction of learned material are also demonstrable in spontaneous confabulations, we chose not to investigate the latter because it seemed hardly feasible to establish the exact relationships between experiences and their elaborations in spontaneous confabulations.

To avoid tiresome repetitions, we will use a few easily understandable signs. For instance: "IIb 3 times +" means that the story

IIb was reproduced after three presentations without error. "+ 1 time" means that the story in question was read once again.

A complete publication of the very extensive case histories does not seem feasible. We will give here only extracts.

CASE 1. M.R., a divorced woman, age twenty-seven, was admitted to the psychiatric clinic on February 16, 1924, with the following information. On February 8 she was delivered after a pregnancy of normal length. In the last few days before delivery her orientation became impaired and she did not remember the delivery itself. According to a close girl friend, the patient had been drinking for many years, mainly brandy, and especially heavily in the last few months. Allegedly, she had never before become psychologically conspicuous.

On admission the patient was restless, fearful, and poorly oriented. She showed a marked disturbance of registration (a test word and a three-digit number were forgotten within one minute) and a definite tendency to confabulate. A superficial intelligence test showed no disturbance of comprehension and judgment. Somatic findings: pupils normal, nystagmus on fixating in every direction. Tremor of the upper extremities, patellar-reflex absent on both sides. Achilles reflex weak on both sides. Paresis of all extremities, severe in the lower and milder in the upper. No signs of nerve degeneration. Musculature and nerve trunks of all extremities painful on pressure. Dulled cutaneous sensitivity, lowering of tactile, pain, and temperature sensitivity, particularly in the lower extremities. Spinal fluid: Pandy, Nonne-Apelt, Goldsol, Wassermann, Meinecke negative. Serum Wassermann negative.

In the next few days the patient showed signs of mild delirium, a slight clouding of consciousness, mild motor restlessness, and primarily optic, occasionally acoustic, and perhaps even tactile hallucinations. At times she was anxious, saw frogs and snakes in her bed, a child between her thighs, and was afraid that she would crush it. Memory of the delivery could not be elicited. These states of delirious excitement repeated themselves with the same content through several days and then abated completely.

The patient then became lucid. Her mood was at first very labile, and the registration defect striking. In her spontaneous confabulations her family played an important role. She had no awareness of or insight into either her psychological or her somatic condition. At times the patient put forth her confabulations with great certainty—indeed, the doubting listener was met by a supercilious smile; at other times, often soon afterward and for the same confabulations, the patient assumed the attitude healthy people take toward their daydreams, that is, she did not seem to take them seriously. At this point learning experiments were initiated, using both neutral and crudely sexual material. The patient's attention and will to learn were highly variable.

February 28. After seven repetitions, Story I was reproduced correctly except for minor errors.

February 29. I, 4 times +.

March 3. On being asked for the story, she related: "Two daughters of the Rabbi died, namely, their heads were chopped off." She said she had read this story at home.

March 8. (What was the story you were told?) "About Abraham and Isaac and Abraham's sons." (Anything else?) "The two sons of Abraham died and Isaac was very sick." On repeated questioning: "About Nathan the Wise, he was deported from the country, and then he taught the people."

After three presentations the meaning of IIa was reproduced in abbreviated form, but it was clear that the patient fully understood its content. A few minutes later, but without a new presentation of IIa: "A young gentleman found a young girl lying in the field. He pulled up her skirts and misused her and pushed the knife into her vagina." When asked why she was talking about a knife, she said: "You said that he had a knife!" After three more readings: "On the edge of a field a young girl knelt and cried. . . ." (What else?) "About a young hunter. She ended up in a cloister." + 1 time:

"On the edge of a field a young gentleman found a young girl. He pulled up her skirts and wanted to misuse her. But she struggled and he didn't succeed. My cousin also told me about it." After one reading of IIb: "A youngster saw a young girl lying down and pushed the vagina-knife into her shear."[3] When the sex stories were read, the patient was by no means bashfully defensive, but on the contrary, showed a certain pleasure in the content.

March 9. (The first story?) "Something about Isaac, I don't know any more." Later: "I have read myself about Sabbath in the Bible."

March 10. (Story?) "That about Nathan I have written down once before. About Isaac, how was that . . . just suddenly. . . ."

March 11. IIb, 1 time +.

March 12. When asked about the story read the day before: "Don't know. . . . It comes to my mind in bits. . . ." (Young man?) "He knifed her. It was her brother." (Knifed whom?) "The sister." (What else?) "The brother, the other Abraham was his name. . . . Mother said I should tell the Catechist not to question me so much!" During these days the patient addressed one of us constantly as teacher or Catechist, and the other as a merchant from her neighborhood and thought that she was being taught religion. On the same afternoon: (The story?) "I don't know." (Young man and young girl?) "They get married in the end."

March 13. IIb, 1 time: "He pulled up her stiff skirt. . . ." (What else?) "I can't." IIb, 1 time. Suddenly very anxious: "Doctor, could you not look out the window, my sister-in-law got wounded!" (Where?) "On the head!" (How?) "They shot at her. . . . A soldier went after her, he jumped on a train and wanted to knife me."

March 14. She claimed to be fourteen years old, in the sixth grade,

---

[3] The translation does not convey the distortions so striking in the original German. The story phrase was: "sein steifes Glied in ihre Scheide"; the word *Glied* ("organ") was symbolically replaced by *Messer* ("knife"). Then, we may speculate, the adjective *steif* ("stiff") did not fit and was replaced by *schneidend* ("cutting"). Finally interchanging *Scheide* and *schneidend* resulted in: "Scheidemesser in die Schneide," which seems to change the vagina into a cutting instrument.—D.R.

and considered the investigator her teacher. After one reading, III is repeated correctly but not verbatim. After the second and third readings it was strongly distorted (in spite of help) and the objectionable parts disappeared completely. After the fourth reading: (as the mother left the house . . .) "The father locked himself in with the daughter." (What then?) "Then he broke the dishes." + 1 time. (About whom is this story?) "About the Holy Mary."

March 15. (Tell the story! As the mother left the house . . .) "The doctor locked himself up with the younger sister." (She laughs. What else?) "The teacher locked himself up with the daughter. . . ." (Go on!) "Next time."

March 17. III was correctly reproduced after three presentations; then it was read again: (What did I tell you?) "I heard that they brought the cows and tied the bull up with a velvet ribbon." When asked to tell it again: "When the mother left the house she took the rope and wanted to hang the servant. A father drowned and then they found him alive."

March 24. Story I was slowly read to her; she recognized it only upon hearing the words "by lightning" and then finished it correctly.

March 28. (Told you about a Rabbi?) I, +.

April 28. The patient was mostly in a good mood, humorous and jocular. The somatic status was by and large unchanged. When asked whether she was told about a rape, the patient answered in the affirmative and reproduced the story correctly with some help. I + III, 1 time +.

May 5. Only mild disturbance of registration. No confabulation. The patient was oriented in space and time. She was amnesic for the entire time of her pregnancy, for the delivery, and for her first four weeks at the clinic.

July 19. The symptoms of polyneuritis had considerably receded. Psychologically the patient was entirely lucid, but had an amnesia for her pregnancy and delivery which could not be lifted even by narcohypnosis (Dr. Schilder). I, 1 time +. IIb, 1 time +.

CASE 2. A woman, age forty-eight, was transferred on April 7, 1924 from the medical department to the psychiatric clinic. Two months previously she had collapsed in the street and had had a mild paresis of the left upper and lower extremities ever since. On admission to the clinic the patient was restless and showed a marked impairment of registration and a pronounced inclination to confabulation. Signs of delirium became prominent in the first few days.

Neurological findings: pupils enlarged, react sluggishly to light and convergence. Motor cranial nerves normal. No nystagmus. Mild paresis in the left upper extremity. No spasms. In the lower extremities no paresis, no spasms. Deep reflexes present, evidence of nerve degeneration on both left and right. Left ankle clonus. No Babinski. Parkinsonlike tremor in the left leg. On attempting to walk or stand the patient immediately fell backward. Sensation undisturbed. Fundi normal. Spinal fluid: Nonne-Apelt, Pandy, Goldsol, and Wassermann negative. Cell count 5. Serum Wassermann negative. The right hand grasped constantly toward objects held out to the patient. No aphasic or apraxic disorder.

Learning experiments similar to those with Case 1 were begun.

April 11. I was reproduced after three presentations meaningfully but not verbatim. The patient confabulated about every element of the story.

April 14. IIa, 1 time: "A young girl went across the field, a young man went down the stairs. He let the young girl fall down and pulled up her skirts and stuck his slanted knee,[4] where did he stick it?" + 1 time: "A young girl went over a road, there came a young man, the girl stumbled, he let the girl stand there crying and shouting." (Why did she cry?) "I told you she fell down the stairs." + 1 time: "A young girl went on a stairway, she slipped and stumbled." IIb, 2 times: "A young man ran down the stairs and the girl

---

[4] Some of the instructiveness of the German version is lost in the translation. *Steifes Glied* ("stiff organ") is transformed by substituting *Knie* ("knee") for *Glied* and replacing *steif* by *schief*, meaning "skewed," "slanted," etc. *Schief* replacing *steif*, however, has also the connotations of crooked, unfair, crippled.—*D.R.*

fell and broke her knee." IIb, + 1 time. The contents were fully comprehended.

April 15. (The story I told you?) "Two girls went up a stairway, two boys went after them, they married the two girls, because one was pregnant and the other went home." IIb, 3 times: "Now I will tell it exactly. Two girls went across a field, one of them was pregnant, then they went up the stairway, then the young doctor threw one of the girls down, pulled up her skirt and examined her."

April 16. (The story?) "Two young men and two young ladies ran up the stairs. When the two men ran up they stopped and stuck their slanted knees into the vagina."

April 17. IIb, 1 time: "Two girls who hopped over a stairway, jumped off the stairway, and the two boys jumped up again, the girl has fallen and he pulled up her little skirt. When he saw that she was pregnant, he married her. What I am afraid of is only to be looked at from the side. When the man hears me say that, he will say: That's what you do while I am in the insane asylum. I have never been stuck in such a sickness." (What kind?) "Well, clap! They can threaten me as long as they want to that they will cut off my tongue and dig out my eyes! I have done nothing wrong." Pictures presented to her were well apperceived in whole and in detail. The patient talked much, joked readily, and made a show of superiority.

April 19. The patient was completely lucid. "People think perhaps I want to be Empress, out of envy . . . but I could become one." (Emperor?) "Well, I think Wilhelm the 28th."

April 28. IIb, 1 time +. Shortly after, she was requested to repeat it. "A man meets a young girl in the field, he attacked her and stuck his crooked[5] finger into her vagina. When he saw that the girl became a mother, he married her." Somatic status unchanged.

May 5. The patient stated that she did not want to drink coffee because there was poison in it. Her statements on the events of the

[5] "Crooked" translates *krumm.—D.R.*

last few days and hours and on the duration of her stay at the clinic were completely false, and were elaborated in the manner of confabulations. When asked about the stories she had been told: "They were innocuous, about two girls and a boy." (What else?) "Two girls hopped down a stairway and the boys."

May 8. Death. Autopsy (May 9): Old mitral endocarditis with insufficiency and some stenosis. Cystitis and pyelitis calculosa. High-grade edema of the leptomeninges and of the brain. Chronic internal hydrocephalus. Microscopic study not yet available.

CASE 3. M.P., a woman, age forty-nine, admitted to the psychiatric clinic on June 5, 1924. Patient had been drinking heavily for fifteen to twenty years, allegedly up to 1½ liters of rum daily. She had been bedridden for a week. She was disoriented and asserted she had lunched the day before with Chancellor Seipel, and expressed similar other ideas.

On admission the patient was disoriented as to time and place. She was in a good mood and jocular. Questions put to her as well as perceptions were completely forgotten in a few minutes; confabulatory activity was very rich. Somatic status: tremor of tongue and fingers, pupils react poorly to light. Paresis of the upper and lower extremities; could neither stand nor walk. The muscles and nerve trunks of all extremities painful on pressure. Patellar and Achilles reflexes absent on both sides. No pyramidal signs. No nerve degeneration phenomena.

June 13. The patient was very distracted and at first rejected the learning experiment. Every statement of hers was embellished with confabulations. IIb, 8 times. She did not reproduce it correctly even once and the distortions were extreme. Yet the numerous reproductions showed that the patient did comprehend the meaning of the material. Her comprehension (upon superficial examination) seemed generally good.

June 14. IIb, 1 time: "A young man and a young girl are together . . . the need . . . the organ in Number 4." (Number 4?) "Well, that I do not know."[6] After repeated reading: "A young man has an affair with a young girl and stuck therefore organ Number 4. . . ." (Number 4?) "That's what I would say." After yet another repetition: "A young man gave me four cigarettes and I will take the four cigarettes; it is hidden as soon as I got it."

June 20. Death.

The cardinal symptoms of the Korsakoff psychosis are demonstrable in all these cases. The first two cases also showed initially signs of delirious confusion. Cases 2 and 3 died after a few weeks of observation without the psychosis having subsided, whereas the first patient has already been at the clinic for five months, and for the past few weeks has neither confabulated nor shown disturbances of registration. However, her amnesia for her pregnancy and delivery as well as for the first weeks of her stay in the hospital has persisted. It is not without interest that the child, for whose birth the patient is amnesic and whose existence she denies even when she is directly told of it, appeared as a hallucination in the delirious phase—the child in the bed between the thighs (cf. Bonhöffer, 1901). In Cases 1 and 3 the etiological factor appears to be chronic alcoholism, which expresses itself neurologically in the polyneuritis. In Case 2 neither the anamnesis nor the clinical picture nor even the autopsy gives definite information as to etiology; the internists suspected uremia as the etiological factor.

Upon superficial examination comprehension seemed undisturbed in all three cases. (Compare, however, Gregor, 1909; and Gregor and Römer, 1907). The attitude toward confabulations was variable: at times they were put forth with great seriousness and deep conviction, and at other times in a playful and detached way, or even in the manner normals look upon their daydreams. It seems to be significant that we found no correlation between registration disturbance and confabulatory tendency. It is justifiable to assume that

[6] Note the fragmentation of the sentence. The German *Glied* has a more direct reference to the male sex organ than the English "organ."—D.R.

impairment of registration tends to facilitate the emergence of subjective material, which in turn may render the retention of external impressions difficult; nevertheless, these disorders seem to run two rather independent courses. Episodes of humorous criticism intermingled with phases of depression were common to all three cases and were very clear even in the case whose anamnesis offers no clue of an alcoholic etiology. Case 2 showed fleeting megalomanic ideas. The perseveration of parapraxes, noted by several authors, was particularly striking in Cases 1 and 2. To these we shall return later on. We can also corroborate Pick's (1915) observations regarding the unfaltering insistence upon obviously contradictory statements. Self-references became strikingly prominent in these patients so that even experiences of others communicated to them were immediately treated as belonging to their own person.

Our experiments encountered the same difficulties, rooted in the nature of the Korsakoff psychosis, which have been observed by previous investigators: fluctuation of attention, little inclination to learn the material offered, even to the point of refusal, and finally a peculiarly irregular alternation between remembering and forgetting so that a memory apparently lost suddenly appears, while one that was just there disappears. In our first two cases, traces of the learned material were demonstrable by means of Ebbinghaus's saving procedure. In the third case a systematic learning of bits of prose, however short, could not be accomplished. We found no significant difference between innocuous and objectionable material in the number of repetitions necessary for learning. The following are examples of distorted reproductions of an innocuous story. (Case 1. I, March 8): "About Abraham and about Isaac and about Abraham's sons," and on the same day: "About Nathan the Wise, he was expelled from the country and then taught the people."[7] Here a word of the story, "Rabbi Moir," is replaced by one which is associatively related to it and belongs to the same sphere. We must remember that the mecha-

[7] The translation falls short of the perseverative word play of the original: "expelled" translates *aus dem Lande gewiesen,* and "taught" translates *unterwies.—D.R.*

nism is the same here as in "normal" forgetting, with the exception that we can demonstrate—as Freud (1901) has shown—that in most of these cases there is a psychological motivation underlying the distortion. Our findings on the reproduction of objectionable material were similar except that substitute formations also occurred; for example (Case 2, IIa, April 15): "The two girls went up a stairway, two boys went after them, they married the two girls, because one was pregnant and the other went home." Similarly, Case 1 (IIa, March 8) replaces the words: ". . . stuck his stiff organ into her vagina" by ". . . pushed the knife into her sheath." When asked why she talked about a knife, the patient said: "You said that he had a knife." The rape scene several days later: "He knifed her"; and at another time: "They shot at her." Another example (Case 3, IIb, June 14): the words, "stiff organ," are replaced by "cigarette," etc. Here the parapraxes are related to the learned material as a symbol is to what it symbolizes. Therefore, objectionable phrases are replaced by words familiar to us as typical symbols from dream analysis and other sources. (To climb stairs, to knife, to shoot, are symbols for intercourse: knife and cigarette are penis symbols.) Our conclusions are based on typical ubiquitous symbols, of which there are but few, and not on those symbolizations in which there is a broader range of individual variability, because the latter cannot be evaluated without thorough analytic study of the life history of the patient. By this procedure we also hope to forestall the objection—rooted in a misunderstanding of the theory of symbolism—that since in psychoanalysis every idea of an object may be interpreted as a symbol, the demonstration of symbols in our cases has no value as proof. Climbing stairs as a symbol seems especially significant to us because it is clearly unexplainable by a conscious wish for distortion. Significantly, the symbolic distortions occurred frequently just before or just after a correct reproduction (without further readings).

Distorting in order to rob the story of its objectionable character and render it harmless is present not only in the symbol formations but also in additions and substitute formations. In reproducing IIa

(March 8) patient 1 said: "But she struggled and he didn't suc-ceed"; or patient 2 gave a happy ending to the story: "They married the girls, because one was pregnant." A greater resistance to learning crudely sexual stories than to learning harmless ones was found only in patient 3 and even there only in the beginning when it took the form of bashful rejection. We want to add that even when the dis-torted reproduction contained apparently random actual percepts there was often a deeper relationship determining the choice of that perception material. It has already been emphasized that parapraxes often stubbornly perseverate. To us it seems that this was true of symbolizations to an even greater extent.[8] The stair-climbing in Case 2 may serve as an example because it was retained in nearly every reproduction, while other elements of the reproductions varied. We find this somewhat analogous to the stubborn persistence of neurotic symptoms due, according to Freud's conception, to the circumstances that they are sustained by both the repressing and the repressed tendencies—from both sides, as it were. Thus we have demonstrated that in learning experiments the undoubtedly organically anchored registration disorder of the Korsakoff psychosis leads to substitute formations. Some of these are the result of displacement onto asso-ciatively related ideas within the same sphere and others are related to the idea learned in the same fashion as is a symbol to what it symbolizes. This relationship is familiar from the analysis of para-praxes, dreams, neurotic symptoms, and schizophrenic thinking. We cannot further discuss here the characteristics which distinguish the two kinds of distortion process described. But we want to emphasize that in our experiments only the crudely sexual material underwent a symbolic disguising process. This observation is in keeping with the teachings of psychoanalysis concerning the close relationship of drive life and symbolic thinking and with the considerations that lead psychoanalysis to call symbolic thinking "the language of the unconscious," as well as with Schilder's theory (1920) in which

---

[8] This is in good harmony with Kogerer's (1920) finding that in the Korsakoff psychosis dreams are often better retained than real experiences.

symbols are considered preparatory stages of thought development. The process which in our cases led to symbolic distortions we must consider organically founded, but its effects must be described as analogous to repression, though the nature of this process is unknown.

As an aside we should like to mention that since our findings are derived from experiments, the method of which is independent of psychoanalytic postulates, they may be considered experimental verifications of the validity of certain Freudian symbol interpretations. In this respect they are related to investigations on the mode of representation of sexual material presented to hypnotic subjects in posthypnotic dream suggestions. Schrötter (1911) and Roffenstein (1923) reported positive results (derived from such investigations) confirming Freud's interpretation of dream symbols.

We have already indicated that in the Korsakoff psychosis and in epileptic twilight states the memory traces are retained; however, their reproduction must be considered hampered by an organic process. Apparently, the difference between such amnesias and the so-called "functional" ones is that the psychological genesis of the latter is demonstrable, while in the former an unknown organic factor takes its place. Whether the "registration" of the memory trace takes the same course in both cases cannot be decided with certainty. Schilder's (1924) work undoubtedly supports this assumption. He has shown that in several important types of organic amnesias impressions apparently forgotten may be brought to consciousness in deep hypnosis in the very form in which they were experienced. He studied amnesias following epileptic twilight states and attempts at suicide by hanging. The amnesias following the latter were convincingly shown by Wagner-Jauregg (1889) to be organically determined.

This brings us to the question: how are we to conceive of the representation of memory traces in our cases? The most obvious assumption would be that the original impressions are retained undistorted and their emergence in symbolic disguise is to be ascribed to an organic reproduction-inhibiting factor. But there is another assumption that cannot be lightly dismissed, namely that in certain cases and for certain contents even the registration of the memories may take place in symbolic form. Again we must recall the theories of Freud who was the first to assert that on early levels of development the symbol and what it symbolizes are identical.

That the memory disorder of the Korsakoff syndrome is organically founded is conceded by all investigators (excepting only Moebius). But one can assume, as Bonhöffer (1901) did long ago, that there is also a functional factor and that only its interaction with the organic-cerebral factor yields the total psychological picture of the Korsakoff syndrome. The functional factor of the memory disorder seems clearest in posttraumatic cases. Even if we consider the functional factor secondary, it is permissible to assume that in our cases too, psychologically demonstrable tendencies make use of organically preformed distortion mechanisms. The aim of our investigation was to demonstrate through the study of symbolic distortions how the deliberate application of psychological insight affords a partial glimpse into the operation of these organic mechanisms.

CHAPTER 18

Understanding and Explanation

(1927)

W E UNDERSTAND the content of a statement. We understand the proof of the Pythagorean theorem, the structure of a sculpture or a musical composition. We understand an action arising out of a decision, and the heated defense which follows an insult. A Weltanschauung may be understandable to us an an expression of weakness or insecurity, while another may be understandable as an expression of overflowing vitality in the individual who holds it. We may understand one person's enthusiastic response to an experience as appropriate, whereas in another it impresses us as inauthentic; and, indeed, in still other cases the same way of reacting may appear wholly incomprehensible. Behind a person's rational façade, the interrelation of his language and actions may be understandable in terms of certain instinctual tendencies. We can understand a neurotic symptom as the gratification of instinctual

---

"Verstehen und Erklären" (which is the original title) was first published as a chapter in a book on the basic concepts and theories of psychoanalysis. This chapter deals with a school of psychology (*verstehende Psychologie*) looked at from the point of view of psychoanalytic findings and hypotheses. That school has never had as much influence on American and British psychologists and psychiatrists as it did, at least at the time, on German psychology (and psychiatry). Nevertheless, I consider it advisable to publish in this volume a translation of "Verstehen und Erklären." There is the fact that thoughts originating in the work of Dilthey, Jaspers, Spranger do occasionally appear in the literature of this country too. But I decided on this republication above all because it seems to me that in this critical comparison of psychoanalysis and *verstehende Psychologie* some aspects of the method and concept formation of the former gain considerably in explicitness and clarity.

drives; a self-inflicted injury may be understood as arising from guilt feelings and a tendency toward self-punishment. A dream symbol is understood as the representation of an unconscious process, and so forth.

Here we must immediately set forth a basic distinction pertaining to the term "understanding." Rickert (1921a, p. 429) distinguishes understanding as "grasping an irreal meaning-structure" from understanding as "grasping real psychic being." He equates understanding (involving other minds) in the latter sense with sympathy (*Nacherleben*), and so labels it. But irreal meaning-structures, such as the meanings of words, the contents of judgments, etc., by no means represent processes "taking place in time in the noncorporal life of particular individuals," and must therefore be excluded from the subject matter of psychology. Max Weber (1921, p. 2) makes the same distinction when he speaks of "rational" and "sympathetic" evidence of understanding. We also find the issue discussed by Simmel (1921, p. 38).

The concept of understanding which refers to the connection between meaning-structures divorced from their actualization in real events is basically no more pertinent for psychology than it is for any other discipline. That is to say, we understand the content of a judgment about what is mental in the same way as we understand judgments about other things. And that which we thereby understand is a meaning, and not a mental process. One might wish to say that signification, meaning, and sense must have a special relationship to the mental, since it is mental processes which "bear" them. But this would be to forget, first, that a work of art, for example, which can certainly also be an object in the material world, has a meaning, and that its meaning is for us (objectively) understandable; and, second, that psychology, as a reality science, must sharply delimit its subject matter from all meaning-structures not having the attribute of real being.

To be sure, this is not to say that understanding in this first sense is of no use in knowing other minds. It is through the meaning and sense of words and sentences that we may be led to the mental processes in the one who communicates. That which is revealed through language and writing, along with expressive movements and gestures, forms the most important bridge to knowledge of another self. This is also true of the conditions in the analytic situation. Most important elements of psychological knowledge of the mental life of our patients, upon which we build our conclusions, are communicated through statements—and thus through the meaning-content of judgments—which we understand "rationally." That psychoanalysis accords, above and beyond this, attention to what is unintentionally expressed by the patient needs no further comment here.

When a patient in analysis relates his experiences to us what we first of all rationally understand is the meaning of a spoken communication, which refers to a mental state. But if we entertain doubt as to the truthfulness of what he is saying (e.g., because of something we observe in his facial expression), or if we seek to ascertain what motives may make this presumed insincerity understandable, then understanding in the second sense in involved.[1] In both cases one can speak of an interpretation based on signs.

Two things, however, can be meant by the term "sign." Husserl (1921) distinguishes between sign as "signal" and "expression"; "Every sign is a sign of something, but not every sign has a 'meaning,' a 'sense' which is expressed along with the sign" (Vol. 2, p. 23). Signs, as signals, do not express anything, even though they point to something. "This is the sense in which a stigma is the sign of a slave, and a flag the sign of a nation." One speaks of signals, then,

---

[1] The translation of *Verstehen,* and particularly of its adjective, *verstehende,* raises special problems. Both are here translated by "understanding." It is used here only in this second sense in which it refers to the way in which we represent to ourselves subjective states of mind. Understanding in its ordinary and wider usage has from here on been rendered by such words as "comprehending" or "grasping."

I question the translation of *Verstehen* as "meaning" and *verstehende Psychologie* as "the psychology of meaning" or of "meaningful connection," which Hoenig and Hamilton use in their recent translation of Jaspers (1963). The reasons for this will become clear further along in the paper.

when "some object or state of affairs whose existence is actually known indicates the existence of certain other objects or states of affairs, so that the conviction as to the being of the one is experienced as the motive (in fact, as a nonunderstandable motive) for the conviction as to, or belief in, the being of the other" (p. 25).

In contrast to signals, there are meaningful signs, expressions. Every statement, all discourse is expression. Gestures and facial expressions "with which we involuntarily, and not with the purpose of communication, accompany our discourse" are, on the other hand, according to Husserl, not meaningful signs but mere signals. They are not expressions in the consciousness of the speaker, they "have no genuine meaning." In contrast to this narrower conception of expression, Allers (1925) has rightly, and in agreement with everyday language, used this term also when "an explicit communicative intention is lacking in the speaker, but through the investment of meaning by observers a signification is apprehended in the various outward appearances of the speaker." The term "expression" is thus suitable also for those cases in which we understand a mental process on the basis of comportment or expressive movements and gestures.

In psychoanalytic interpretations both kinds of signs play a role: analysts interpret at times signals and at other times expressions. There is, however, a broad middle ground where the relegation to one or the other class of signs can be quite uncertain. Thus we find side by side certain symbolic representations, some of which may be classified as expressive phenomena (in the wider sense described above), and some of which function only as signals. In the first group, for example, might be a patient's rubbing movements as expressive of a masturbatory wish (and in similar cases it is sometimes also admissible to assume an unconscious tendency to communicate). In the second category, we might find, say, wood as a symbol of latent dream thoughts which refer to the female genitals, an instance which, in any event, does not present us with a *prima facie* meaningful connection. I want to add that according to psychoanalytic theory, there are always also other than meaningful relationships between symbol and symbolized—namely, those involving regular laws and corresponding to causal connections. This view, and its experimental verification, is a topic which will occupy us later.

The concept of psychological understanding as a means by which we can directly know what goes on in the mind is one we have already encountered in the writings of Dilthey (1924). We learned that proceeding from what he considers the necessary unfruitfulness of explanatory psychology in its application to the humanities, he opposes to it a descriptive psychology which presents "the uniformly appearing components and connections of every developed human psyche in their own context, which is not inferred but immediately experienced." In understanding mental processes we proceed from the context of the totality "which is experientially given," and: "We explain by purely intellectual means, but we understand through the working together of all our emotional powers." Elsewhere we find: "We explain nature, but we understand the mind." By means of hypotheses and deductions we unify our experiences of the material world, but in the psychic realm such interrelation "is given in the actuality of experiencing." The science of mind can "not penetrate beyond that which is given of and in itself in inner experience."

What Dilthey's way of thinking gives us is a vigorous emphasis on description as opposed to explanation and therewith the roots of later phenomenological psychology. For Dilthey, the sphere of description embraces mental interrelationships no less than mental states. But it is immediately apparent that such description is severely limited on all sides—with reference, that is, to gaps in self-knowledge, the unconscious, and physiological processes. And where concrete representation is asked for, Dilthey, too, must avail himself of psychological constructs.

A further essential characteristic of his psychology is the sharp contrast he draws between natural and mental events and between the corresponding approaches that have to be used in order to gain knowledge about them. With respect to the material world, connections are established by means of thought processes, whereas structural connections in the mind are directly experienced (*erlebt*). In addition, that which "effects" the transition from one mental state to another is considered part of what is directly experienced (*erlebt*). Causal connections would therefore already be given in the act of experiencing (*Erleben*).

As opposed to this, let us here merely cite—without going further into the matter—the remarks of Ebbinghaus (1896): "The greatest and most important connections which, for definite reasons, we claim exert most influence upon the psychic life do not lie directly before us as facts but are, rather, established by us." Structural connections are, as Ebbinghaus rightly says in his critique of Dilthey, not experienced but inferred.

The task of a phenomenological psychology—and Dilthey opened up the way to its constitution as a separate discipline—consists, according to Jaspers, in "directly presenting to ourselves the mental states which our patients really experience, observing them with respect to their kind and species, carefully delimiting them, and differentiating them by well-defined terms" (1920, p. 31).

It would, perhaps, have been better had this movement continued to be known as "descriptive" psychology, since the term "phenomenology" in this context can lead to confusion and to an unjustifiable equation with Husserl's phenomenology. But since the term has become entrenched, I want to make it clear that I am using it in Jaspers' sense.

Psychoanalysis advocates, as opposed to Dilthey's overestimation of mere description, the right of psychology to explain and construct hypotheses. It maintains that the task of psychology, as of other natural sciences, is the study of mental processes and of the laws regulating mental activity. It thus opposes Dilthey when he says that the construction of hypotheses is basically inappropriate to the subject matter of psychology. Furthermore, psychoanalysis claims that phenomenological research is only one condition, though an essential one, for the fulfillment of its task. Psychoanalysis has long since transcended the limits which Dilthey set to explanatory psychology. Many spheres of "higher mental activity" which he considered to be inaccessible to "constructionist methods" have also been unlocked by experimental methods, and psychoanalysis has come to see the most essential processes of the human mind from the causal point of view. It is Dilthey's lasting achievement that he demanded the systematic understanding of the "overwhelmingly rich reality" of mental life. However, that a natural-science psychology is useless in the solution of this task is a dated view rooted in the conditions existing at the time when explanatory psychology was in its infancy.

Every systematic approach, including that which deals with the mind, must clearly recognize the discrepancy between experiencing and knowing—a discrepancy which Dilthey hoped to avoid in his "descriptive and analytic" psychology but which obtains for both descriptive and explanatory disciplines. At any rate, those who reject the latter approach must no longer base their rejection on its uselessness in coming to grips with complex psychic processes.

What is, for Dilthey, the nucleus of human personality which is inaccessible to explanatory, but not to descriptive psychology? "Satisfaction of drives, the attainment and preservation of pleasure, joy, and fulfillment, the warding off of that which diminishes, oppresses, and constricts. This is what welds the play of our perceptions and thoughts with our voluntary actions into structural connectedness. A complex of drives and emotions, this is the center of mental structure . . ." (1924, p. 206). We must, therefore, say that the very thing which, for Dilthey, is the center of the personality is precisely what has become the particular subject matter of psychoanalysis which uses the methods of the natural sciences.

In fact, Dilthey did not clearly delimit the boundaries between what is to be accessible to understanding as opposed to explanation. But it is apparent that what he had in mind, basically, were the complex processes of the psyche. Since the problem of understanding encompasses the question of what the justification for and limits of a natural-science psychology are, it is clear that it has to become an essential issue for psychoanalytic methodology. It is true that psychoanalysis works—to a far greater degree than other schools of scientific psychology (I disregard those which derive from psychoanalysis)—with psychological connections that are also understandable. The question thus becomes: what methodological significance does psychoanalysis accord to psychological understanding? What value, from the analytic standpoint, does understanding have for knowledge of the mind? First, however, let us turn to the theories of Jaspers who has further developed Dilthey's line of thought.

He first distinguishes between static and genetic understanding: "In many cases we understand directly how one psychic event emerges from the other. We understand the anger of someone attacked, the jealousy of a deceived lover, the acts and decisions that spring from motives. In phenomenology we represent to ourselves a number of isolated qualities or states, and the understanding that accompanies this has a *static* quality. Where we grasp the emergence of one thing from another our understanding has a *genetic* quality. In static understanding (phenomenology), we attain, as it were, a cross-section of the mental; in genetic understanding (*verstehende* psychopathology), a longitudinal section" (1920, p. 19).

Psychological phenomenology and its corresponding mode of attaining knowledge, static understanding, are rather alien to the specific questions asked by psychoanalysis. On the other hand, I have already stated that the results of phenomenological psychology are a necessary foundation upon which explanatory psychology builds, and that such results, when they are firmly established, may also be used in psychoanalytic research. I heartily subscribe to Kronfeld's view (1920, p. 394): "Phenomenology is a preliminary approach necessary for any psychological theory which seeks to explain phenomena (genetically); it is a preliminary approach in the same sense that any psychological ontology is. It is on the one hand the precondition for the formation of the theories, and on the other hand it demands such theories; otherwise it remains essentially incomplete."

Genetic understanding can best be clarified in its relation to

Jaspers' theory of mental connections. Lipps (1909, p. 42), in contrast to Dilthey, already made a clear distinction between causal connections, which exist only for the intellect, and "directly experienced" connections. Now Jaspers sharply contrasts understanding and explanation, those connections which are understandable and those which are causal. As we have already heard: "We sink ourselves into the psychic situation and understand genetically by empathy how one psychic event emerges from another"; but "by repeated experience that a number of phenomena are regularly linked together, we explain causally" (1920, p. 170). Making this distinction, Jaspers sets himself apart from Dilthey's conception of understanding. For the latter believed that even causal connections in the mental sphere fall within the field of immediate experience. For Jaspers, genetic understanding meets its limitations in relation to three areas: phenomenological data, purely rationally understandable contents, and extraconscious mechanisms.

Many of those connections which psychoanalysis has brought to our attention are without doubt genetically and sympathetically understandable.[2] The relationships, discovered in analysis, between instinctual impulses and instinctual behavior are understandable, and so are repressions and some reaction formations. What we experience directly here is that one mental state emerges from another. However, the goal of psychoanalysis is not the understanding of the mental, but rather the explanation of its causal relationships. I have already referred to this, and will come back to it again. I said that mental connections discovered by psychoanalysis are, to be sure, often also understandable, but this is not the essential issue for analytic theory. Some authors have nevertheless misunderstood psychoanalysis and regarded it as though it were a branch of the school of psychological understanding. It is therefore imperative clearly to set forth the main position of psychoanalysis in relation to this school.

[2] "Sympathetic experience" here translates *Nacherleben,* which is, literally, after-experience, the attempt to reproduce in one's own experience what someone else has experienced.

The expression "meaning (or rather, understandable) connection" may refer either to a particular kind of connection or to a particular way of knowing it. Kronfeld (1920, p. 359) has rightly pointed out that in Jaspers' work both meanings of the term merge. Thus, Jaspers (1920, p. 171) can say: "In the natural sciences we find causal connections only, but in psychology our bent for knowledge is satisfied also with the comprehension of quite a different sort of connection." But in many other places he regards understanding as a particular method by which mental objects are grasped and which, as a method, is contrasted with explanation. A further ambiguity of Jaspers' doctrine lies in the fact that while, on the one hand, causal explanation is, in principle, supposed to encounter limits nowhere, he, on the other hand, actually limits it to regularities which are non-meaningful (nonunderstandable). He says: genetic understanding "is the subjective, self-evident comprehension of mental connections from within, so far as they can ever be grasped in this way, [but explanation is] the objective demonstration of connections, effects, and ruling principles which cannot be understood and are only explicable by cause and effect" (p. 173). One again and again gains the impression that Jaspers recognizes a causality which proceeds from the physical to the mental, but not one that proceeds from the mental to the mental. But if causal explanation is to be excluded from the sphere of the understandable (although elsewhere Jaspers turns about and says that understanding is only something extra added to explanation), then such phrases as "We genetically understand how one psychic event emerges from another" are rather misleading. For then our genetic understanding would be, not the comprehension of an actual emergence, but merely the establishing of an experience of emergence, and this experience does not require that the elements constituting the experienced connection be objectively connected.

"The experience of connections is not identical with the connections between what is experienced" (Koffka, 1912, p. 6; see also Kronfeld, 1920, p. 383). The experience of a connection can, as any other experience, be an object for phenomenological observation. On the other hand, it can also be investigated by explanatory psychology with respect to its conditions, development, etc. But what can this lived experience tell us about *actual* mental connections? What knowledge can it give us? How can experiencing itself contain within it the criterion for the real givenness of mental connections?

At this point we meet—in so far as the understanding of fellow human beings is involved—the general problem of knowing the minds of other persons. I cannot here present a detailed discussion of the various theories which seek to solve this problem, theories, for example, of analogical reasoning, empathy, or Scheler's "theory of perception" which Binswanger, among others, has adopted. I will simply refer the reader to the critiques of Scheler's theory put forth by Rickert and Kronfeld. For Jaspers, psychological understanding also signifies an empathetic understanding and, according to him, knowledge of another person's mental states and connections therefore involve empathy. Empathetic understanding "leads us . . . right into the mental connections themselves."

If, then, empathy is supposed to be a tool of psychological knowledge, wherein lies the criterion of its validity? Not, surely, in the empathetic experience itself. For, in the first place, empathy is no more than a means by which another person's mental processes become accessible (*zur Gegebenheit bringen*). Empathy is supposed to bring forth certain experiences which are analogous to those of the other person, but in itself it contains, of course, no guarantee as to its own reliability or validity. One cannot speak of knowledge here without there taking place somewhere along the way an act of thinking, putting one thing in relation to another. Moreover, the nature of empathetic experience is still poorly understood, and its value in knowing other minds is still quite uncertain. The initial task would be to establish—as W. Baade (1915) has attempted—an evaluation of such experiences with regard to their possible contributions to psychological knowledge. In Baade's view, and in his terminology, the most valuable among them "are those based on representation and not capable of assimilation."

Jaspers, however, appeals to the "self-evidence"[3] which is supposed to be as much an element of psychological understanding as it is of rational knowledge. When a connection is understood by us, "our experience is one of immediate evidence. . . . The evidence of genetic understanding is something ultimate" (p. 171). Now, it is unquestionably proper to speak of "evidence" with regard to rational understanding; but it is at best highly doubtful that we can transfer the notion of evidence to the sphere of psychological understanding. The importance which evidence has in logic and mathematics it can never have in the area of a reality science. For it is precisely not realities which are involved in the subject matter of logic and mathematics. But, be that as it may, I do not wish to place too much stress upon this objection and will proceed to use the term "self-evidence" in the way Jaspers understands it. In this regard, however, it must immediately be said that what is important for scientific psychology is not so much the self-evidence of understanding as its value for psychological knowledge. And Jaspers provides us with no criterion which would distinguish between self-evident understanding which leads to correct judgments, and self-evident understanding which leads to error. That, however, is precisely what is required if self-evident understanding is to be a means of gaining knowledge and if the theory of understandable connections is to mean more than the mere establishing of the experience of evidence.

It is obvious that the most serious errors can occur if we allow ourselves to be guided solely by the self-evidence of psychological understanding when we judge a psychological connection. For example: we meet a man who appears to be strong and in good health and who abhors and fights anything sickly, weak, or half-hearted.

---

[3] "Self-evidence" translates the German *Evidenz*. It has a strictly subjective meaning, the inner sense of conviction or certainty. To distinguish it from its objective sense (e.g., evidence as used in a courtroom or an empirical experiment) we have used the rather clumsy noun "self-evidence."

The man's own health and well-being make this attitude understandable; we experience this meaning-connection as directly self-evident. But now, let us assume, we "get to know the man better," and we learn from him or from someone else that he suffers from a serious defect which he is loathe to admit, and which has until now remained concealed from us, and that he is basically not only in very poor health but psychologically also a very insecure person. Now, too, we understand, and the connection between the man's own weakness and insecurity and his abhorrence of these things in others is clear to us, and the insight into this connection is accompanied by an experience of self-evidence. We should not think of this example as merely an exception. Everyone encounters such cases in his daily life. We must then say: the experience of self-evidence has deceived us; or: self-evidence opposes self-evidence and the decision as to truth or falsity obviously cannot be derived from self-evidence. The understandable connection has, in a concrete case, proved to be a pseudo connection. But it is precisely the exposing of such pseudo connections which plays so great a role in psychoanalysis. And, as I shall further elaborate, it is primarily the psychology of unconscious processes which forces us to cast a highly distrustful eye upon the reliability of understanding.

That one can err in judging another person is by no means a new discovery. And the proponents of understanding psychology of course realize this as well as anyone. But it is for us to establish that the self-evidence of understanding too cannot protect us from such deceptions. There apparently remains one way out: recourse to what is self-evident not to the average man but to those with a genius for *Menschenkenntnis,* that is, to the "psychology" of some writers and philosophers. But this way out soon reveals its inadequacy when one considers—and this can be seen in hundreds of ways—how difficult it would be to single out (except maybe for some rather meaningless banalities) any evident connection which is not contradicted in the works of another "intuitive" psychologist. For this reason alone the recourse from the average man to the insightful psychology of brilliant personalities is unacceptable as a criterion of validity for the self-evidence of understanding. In any case, it is out of the question as a scientific method.

I may add here: it is simply not true that while genetic understanding may in isolated instances go astray, it maintains its validity in the average case. On the contrary, there are self-evidently understandable connections of which it is very doubtful whether they have even a single corresponding actual connection.

Let us go one step further and consider those cases in which we understand mental developments or reactions as arising from character traits and experiences though this connection does not actually exist. In these cases the self-evidence of understanding becomes a veritable well-spring of deception. For it is precisely the experience of self-evidence which prevents us from pushing ahead to the real connections. In judging mental structures it is harder for us to detach ourselves from self-evidently understood connections than from a particular hypothesis which is not accompanied by the experience of self-evidence. It is just the self-evidence of understanding which tempts us to hasty generalization and to neglect of the circumstances peculiar to the individual case. Here lie dangerous sources of error for every "understanding" psychology—at least in so far as it strives to be a reality science and seeks to say something about real mental events.

The tenaciousness with which prescientific thought holds on to certain psychological maxims which are hardly ever confirmed by experience is in part a result of their self-evidence. The association of possible ways of thinking or acting with certain personality types occurs very often, not on the basis of induction, but on the basis of understandability. Statements like: as a "good person," or as a "devout Catholic," or as an "honorable," "honest" character, etc., he "must" decide in such a way, or he "could not possibly" have done anything else—statements of this sort persist even when actual experience teaches that "the good man" or "the devout Catholic" in fact seldom or never decides in such a way, and almost always or even always acts in a different way. It is, for the most part, self-evident understanding—aside from the question of hidden valuations which are also often at the root of it—which is responsible for making unwarranted interconnections.

We understand, not only others, but naturally our own self as well. Indeed, self-understanding is probably the primary function upon which the understanding of others is based. It must therefore immediately be established that while the objections to empathy as a source of knowledge do not apply to self-understanding, all that was said about the unreliability of the experience of self-evidence with respect to knowledge of real mental connections holds true here as well. Psychoanalytic data and even everyday observation teach us that even here the experience of a connection is far from accurately reproducing the actual mental connection. Psychoanalysis cannot, therefore, base its decision for or against assumptions about these connections in the last instance upon the presence or absence of psychological insight experiences in its patients—something which most of its critics, including such knowledgeable ones as Roffenstein (1922),[4] demand of it.

But self-understanding as a tool of knowledge suffers, in addition, from a handicap which is not—at least not to the same extent—involved in our understanding of other persons. Psychoanalysis has demonstrated beyond all doubt that our consciousness invariably shows us only a part of our total personality, only a segment of the structure of our mental life. A great deal (from the standpoint of explanatory psychology, perhaps the most essential) remains concealed from us: it is unconscious, and only certain highly developed

[4] After the completion of this chapter, Roffenstein's clear and thoughtful book on the problem of psychological understanding was published (1926). His critique of psychological understanding as a means of gaining knowledge coincides largely with mine. However, he then proceeds to draw specific conclusions with regard to—or better: against—the psychoanalytic psychology of unconscious mental life, conclusions which, in my opinion, can certainly not be derived from his fundamental premises. On the contrary, I would maintain that it is precisely psychoanalysis which is the science he demands; that is to say, a science which proceeds inductively and is rooted in biology.

techniques enable us to lift this portion of our personality into consciousness. The obstacles to this are greater with regard to ourselves than with other persons. Only the theory of mental dynamics clearly shows us how the dynamic interaction of conflicting mental tendencies determines which mental processes may penetrate into consciousness and be apperceived.

The result of such a point of view is: distrust of the objectivity of self-experienced motivational connections. In line with this thought psychoanalysis has, through systematic, genetically directed investigations, made significant and well-established new discoveries. Precisely here, however, lies one of the most powerful causes of that emotional rejection of psychoanalysis which has brought it many enemies (quite apart from those who oppose it on purely theoretical grounds), namely: the opinion that "mental processes are in themselves unconscious and only reach the ego and come under its control through incomplete and untrustworthy perceptions— . . . *the ego is not master in its own house*" (Freud, 1917b, p. 143). Freud rightly believes that this "narcissistic injury" constitutes a serious emotional stumbling block for anyone who attempts to delve more deeply into the problems dealt with by psychoanalysis. This fundamental mistrust of pseudo connections, which so frequently arise from self-understanding and falsify the picture of one's own personality, is certainly not the exclusive property of psychoanalysis. Nietzsche's psychology in particular is permeated by this "mistrust," and in this respect, as well as others, we can regard psychoanalysis as the systematic grounding and legitimate development of Nietzsche's "intuition."

We also "understand" it when a person "will not own up to" certain instinctual impulses, wishes, predilections, and aversions. And here, then, is the point at which understanding, as it were, cancels itself: we understand how in certain cases self-understanding must lead to pseudo connections.

Affective elements also play a role in our efforts to reach through understanding true judgments concerning mental connections in other persons. These affective elements may both facilitate and inhibit this endeavor. They can be rooted in one's affective attitude toward the person concerned, or in the affective attitude toward certain regions of the mind; in both cases—and for the moment I am speaking only of cognitive inhibitions—affective elements can lead to the experience of pseudo connections which conceals the actual ones. This is why every practicing psychoanalyst is himself required to undergo analysis. That is to say, it has been demonstrated that "blind spots" (Stekel) in the knowledge of other people's psyche often occur in those areas which the analyst has not entirely succeeded in integrating into the totality of his own personality.

The question as to why a person derives his behavior from false assumptions, why he is blind to certain qualities, why he does not admit to having certain wishes, why his image of himself is falsified by understandable but pseudo connections, why, in general, self-understanding here is still less reliable than the understanding of others—this question leads deep into the psychoanalytic theory of instinctual drives. That something very significant is at issue here was clearly seen by Nietzsche (1882, Book I, 44): "However important it may be to know the motives according to which mankind has really acted hitherto, perhaps the *belief* in this or that motive, and therefore that which mankind has assumed and imagined to be the actual mainspring of its activity hitherto, is something still more essential for the thinker to know."

It has not, of course, escaped Jaspers' attention that in certain cases understood and actual connections are disparate. "In any given case the judgment of whether an understood connection is real does not rest on its self-evident character alone. It depends primarily on the tangible facts (that is, on the verbal contents, cultural factors, people's acts, ways of life, and expressive gestures) in terms of which the connection is understood, and which provide the objective data. All such objective data, however, are always incomplete" (1920, p. 172). That is doubtless true, but it is not enough. For what Jaspers refers to are only degrees of sympathetic understanding—though, in this case, degrees of its completeness, but not levels of the experience of self-evidence. We must add that even in those cases in which "what is understood is based on the objective data of expressive gestures, verbal utterances, and behavior," this understanding, if it is not controlled by inductive reasoning (which, among other things, must take into account also the relationship to the unconscious mental processes), can and often must lead to false connections. Our objections to the reliability of self-understanding have made that quite clear. Only by establishing laws and analyzing individual cases on the basis of these laws can we decide whether or not a relationship actually obtains between various psychical data.

Jaspers believes that his "understandable connections" correspond to the conceptual forms which are known as "ideal types." This notion of ideal type is defined by him in the following way: "Ideal types are constructs of a coherent whole which we envisage on the occasion of our experiences but do not owe to experience; rather they are constructed in an *a priori* way from a few given presuppositions" (1920, p. 338). What point of view governs this "construction" remains unclear in his writings. This definition of the ideal type in its relation to understanding is far removed from the original conception of understanding which we found in Dilthey: "construction" takes the place of the "directly experienced connection." Furthermore—and this was our point of departure—in Jaspers' work, we find this ideal-type determination of understandable connections side by side with another kind, which equates genetic understanding with the sympathetic experience of one thing emerging from another. As we cited above: "By entering into the sphere of the mind, we understand genetically the way in which the mental emerges from the mental." From the very nature of understandable connections as ideal types, however, it follows "that they carry no empirical significance" (p. 338). But then, can such a construct have any other purpose than that of making possible a meaningful ordering of actual mental connections? And if the understandable connections "are the standard by which we assess real, individual cases," in what sense, then, can understanding be called a cognitive tool?

When actuality corresponds to the ideal type, there the demands of knowledge are "peculiarly satisfied" (p. 338). That, too, is correct, but again it is misleading. For we have this peculiar experience not only in such cases but also when we are faced with pseudo correspondences, that is to say, those cases which, as I have emphasized, cannot be disregarded as "exceptions." I said, in fact, that it is just the self-evidence of understanding which tends to deceive us about the actual mental connections. Since the "peculiar satisfaction" of which Jaspers speaks can tell us nothing about the reality or probable reality of the connection, we must then demand that the cognitive value of understanding as an ideal type be carefully examined in its application to actual experience. But where such an understandable connection—whether it be termed "sympathetic" or a "construction" or something between the two—does not stand the test of experience, where it leads to errors and also cannot function as a standard, there it loses any significance for a reality science of psychology.

If understandable connections are concepts of the kind one calls "ideal types," then they are neither true nor false: they are "means of expression and description" (terminological tools: *Ausdrucksmittel der Darstellung*). Jaspers explicitly rejects the demand that understandable connections must be tested empirically. In this way, of course, there remains the unanswered question: what is the scientific value, then, of pointing out these connections?

Jaspers borrowed the concept of ideal type from Max Weber. The latter, however, clearly states that "the understanding of connections [must] as far as possible still be controlled by the customary methods of causal ascription before any self-evident interpretation is taken as a valid 'understandable explanation'" (1922, p. 404). Further on he writes (p. 413), "'Meaningful' interpretations of concrete behavior as such are initially of course ..., no matter how self-evident, only hypotheses of connections. They require the same kind of practical verification as any other hypothesis, and in principle by the same means. They become useful hypotheses for us only when we can assume a measure (which varies with the individual case) of 'plausibility' that (subjectively meaningful) motivation networks are present." The self-evidence of interpretation implies nothing about the actual connections: ". . . no matter how meaningful a self-evident interpretation as such may appear to be, it cannot on this account alone claim to be a causally valid interpretation. In itself it must remain only an especially plausible hypothesis" (1921, p. 4). Here the logical character of the ideal type is—more sharply and more consistently than in Jaspers—defined and established as a construct. Such "thought pictures" bring particular relationships and processes together into "conceptual contexts." "As to content, these constructs have the character of a utopia which is to be reached by the conceptual intensification of certain elements of reality" (1922, p. 190). "Ideal type" concepts are valuable either heuristically or as means of description. Their purpose is to "sharpen our judgment with respect to classification" (1922, p. 190) and to guide the formation of hypotheses. On the other hand, without the demonstration "that what can be assumed to be a theoretical construct also in some degree corresponds to an actual course of events," even the most evident connection "would be worthless for the knowledge of real action" (1921, p. 5).

One must not—as Kronfeld does—reject Max Weber's theory of ideal types as a "clumsy logical patchwork." It seems to me that his singling out and clear methodological delineation of his concept of "ideal types" is of inestimable value for history and sociology. It seems questionable to me, however, whether it can successfully be applied to psychology—quite apart even from the lack of clarity attaching to Jaspers' efforts. Here Binswanger (1922, p. 301) has rightly seen the danger of a psychological rationalism wherein rationally interpretable behavior would be applied to the mental as an ideal type and made the starting point in any representation of it. But Weber, in any case, does not err in these respects. He sharply delimits his "understanding" sociology from any possible psychological method. Jaspers, too, circumvents the difficulty by extending the self-evidence of the ideal types to the nonrational, to the sphere of what, psychologically, is only empathetically understandable. Nevertheless, because of the particular kind of self-evidence which distinguishes rational from irrational understanding, a method which does not recognize the criterion of empirical evidence still runs the risk cited by Binswanger.

The difficulties and internal inconsistencies of Jaspers' theory of understandable connections should not blind us to its great historical significance. More than any other theory, it led psychopathologists to reflect upon the methodological basis of their science. Even Jaspers' attempt to demarcate this approach from those schools of psychology that are part of natural science instructed and enriched the proponents also of the latter. The decisive turning toward the inner experience of the patient, toward the psychological characteristics of form and content of the psychoses was the basis upon which evolved an investigative approach which yielded results in many important modern psychiatric studies (in the work of Jaspers himself, and that of Kurt Schneider and Mayer-Gross, among others). This deeper penetration into the content of and the internal connections in psychoses is, despite all methodological distinctions, what Jaspers' school and psychoanalysis have in common—the great difference, though, I repeat, being that for psychoanalysis the experience of the patient (be it of states or processes) is the starting point of scientific work and not, as it is for "understanding" psychology, the goal.

If we now view the relation between understandable and causal connections from the standpoint of the actual psychological connection, we come to the following conclusion: understanding (in the sense of sympathetic experience [*Nacherleben*] of actual mental events) encounters its necessary limits in two facts of psychic life: in the unconscious life of the mind, and in those processes which we group together under the name of "somatic intrusion" (Schilder). No psychology can dispense with the assumption of an "unconscious" describable in a manner similar to conscious mental states and associations. A disputable point can be whether this unconscious is recognized as a part of the mind or is referred to the physiological sphere. I shall discuss both alternatives below, and for the time being will let this issue remain unresolved. The indisputable fact which concerns us here is that the interconnections of consciousness exhibit gaps, and that one can speak neither of a real continuity of the stream of consciousness nor of a closed causal network in the sphere of consciousness.

We have yet to show how psychoanalytic data made it imperative for psychology to free unconscious processes from the shadowy realms to which most psychological theories had exiled them, and to grant the unconscious processes a dominant place in the life of the mind. The supposition that unconscious connectives are to be introduced only where consciousness exhibits gaps hardly does justice to the facts. These gaps are, indeed, what first necessitates the introduction of unconscious processes and makes this introduction most plausible. But a more penetrating look into the psychology of the unconscious has taught us that even where some continuity of consciousness exists, unconscious forces nevertheless continually influence (feed) experience whether of special mental events or of their connections.

Unconscious connections as well as unconscious influences upon conscious states and processes are, however, not experienced (*erlebt*) and therefore cannot be sympathetically experienced (*nacherlebt*). They evade the sympathetic understanding of others just as they evade self-understanding. If we accept psychoanalytic theory according to which unconscious forces ubiquitously and effectively influence psychic life, if we grant that psychoanalysis has gained its findings by reliable means (see Hartmann, 1927, Chapter 5), then the sphere in which sympathetic understanding (*nacherlebendes Verstehen*) is possible is of necessity severely limited. Understanding can give us an accurate picture of mental connections only where we do not have to assume the existence of unconscious links; and it can give us an approximately accurate picture where these links play no essential role. There is an inference which we must draw from the assumption of the unconscious (and this is an unavoidable assumption): it is that the limits of understanding can be determined only after an investigation into the mental connections which actually obtain. The fallibility of an understanding psychology will be variously judged depending upon the significance which one attributes to the unconscious mind. From the standpoint of psychoanalysis, this fallibility must necessarily be very great.

There are several alternatives. In the first place, the actual connection may not be represented in the subject's experience; or there is no experience whatsoever of a connection. We are then accustomed to saying that our own thoughts are "strange," our decisions "puzzling," our actions "incomprehensible." Such instances are even more significant for psychopathology.

In the second place, the (mental) cause of a mental event is not present in the subject's experience, but in its place one finds understandable relationships to circumstances that accompanied the event. The best and most often cited example of this is posthypnotic suggestion. Here the hypnotist's instructions, which are the cause of the particular actions, are forgotten, excluded from consciousness. But in the subject's experience there arises another connection—it "occurred to him," or he "suddenly wanted"—from which he sees his actions as emerging: that is to say, an understandable connection which in no way coincides with the actual process. This example is an unusually clear representative of an immense number of other analogous processes.

Third, the actual connection may be mirrored in experience, but incompletely so that only a part of the real process is understood—indeed, the most essential aspect often remains concealed. Many affective reactions to events belong here; and so do the direction and strength of our instinctual impulses whose persistently effective early history is, indeed, for the most part unconscious; furthermore, all those processes that are codetermined by the laws of association and reproduction, laws that in themselves are not understandable. When, on the basis of introspection, a person attributes his "bad mood" to a recent disappointment, his happiness to some good news he has just received, or understands his liking for someone as motivated by that person's good nature or beauty or cleverness, then, as a rule, a partial cause is correctly ascertained. But when we look at it analytically we may find that perhaps the degree of the affective reaction, or the timing, or the qualitative tone seem inappropriate. And we may be able to show that forgotten experiences, concealed wishes, or repressed hostility have had a hand in influencing the nature and the degree of the person's reaction. Or, on the basis of what we know about the ontogenesis of instinctual life, we may be in a position to trace someone's choice of object to earlier (unconscious) fixations. But the motivation of his choice which he has carefully ascertained by introspection represents the connection in a patchy way, and ignores what is obviously most essential. However, it is often possible, with the help of inductive laws of behavior, to complement and, to a degree, correct the understandable connections. We may, quite generally, say: the effect of every experience is codetermined by the individual's past; in his subjective experience, however, this effect is only incompletely mirrored.

The second circumstance which in principle makes it impossible to substitute, as it were, sympathetic understanding for explanation concerns the influence of the somatic upon the mental. The assumption of a closed system of psychic causality is, as I shall presently show, consistent only on the basis of the metaphysical hypothesis of a universal psychophysical parallelism. If one rejects this hypothesis, one's conception of mental connections must somehow account for the process of "somatic intrusion."

The execution of a planned action can be modified under the influence of narcotic intoxication. Moods, feelings, activities, and tempo are characteristically influenced by somatic conditions. The aftereffect of experiences is dependent upon the intensity, duration, and quality of intervening physiological processes. Here I can only mention the far-reaching connection between physiological developmental processes and typical variations in mental structure, as well as the area of the organic psychoses. In all of these cases, the somatic influences do not undo the web of understandable connections. What takes place is, rather, that the causal connections are covered by pseudo connections. The factor that determines—or at least code-termines—the existence (*Dasein*) and being-thus (*Sosein*) of action and moods is the effect of somatic intrusion; but the understandable connection contains nothing of this, or nothing that is essential; and it lets it appear that actions, moods, etc., emerge from understandable connections.

In addition, even the interference of brain processes need not necessarily impair the understandability of one experience emerging from another. This must be emphasized as opposed to Jaspers' position because he sets up the understandability or nonunderstandability of connections as a criterion for distinguishing the process psychoses. Moreover, since the demarcation of the understandable varies from observer to observer, a classification from this point of view can never be unambiguous. Psychological understanding is an ability which varies from individual to individual and which can, as also Jaspers rightly stresses, be improved with practice.

I do not want to overemphasize the fact of somatic intrusion. Psychoanalysis itself has shown that it is still admissible to apply psychological concepts where previously explanations would have been based solely on physiological processes. And it would certainly be incorrect to say that the demonstrable and presumed effects of the somatic upon the mental endanger the status of psychology as an independent science. But whatever weight one assigns to it, the influence of the organic upon the mental is a fact. Next to unconscious processes, it is the most important factor which leads to the necessary disparity between the understandable and causal connections. For this reason alone understanding can never be *the* method of psychology. On the other hand, neither the unconscious nor somatic intrusion limits explanation as a method.

Here one should also mention the possibility of broadening the concept of understanding. One also speaks of understanding when the connections are rooted in or lead via the unconscious. What is meant is that a person's actions can be understood from his fundamental orientations or goals even when he himself is not conscious of this connection, even when his actions are codetermined by unconscious instinctual attitudes, or in some other way determined by processes not represented in consciousness. Jaspers speaks here of "as-if" understood connections. One understands the connection as if it were experienced as such. From a logical point of view, this "as if" understanding constitutes a compromise between empathetic understanding and hypothesis. It is thus far removed from the original concept of sympathetic understanding.

Nor should this type of understanding be taken to involve an "intuition" of emergence (*Auseinanderhervorgehens*) of the sort upon which Binswanger's theory of understanding is based (for Binswanger [1922, p. 290], understanding is "the intuition of a real succession of qualities"). A good many of the causal psychoanalytic connections are also understandable in this second sense. But no one would maintain that it is possible to look at and watch, say, the transition from anal erotism to avarice or pedantry.

In this extended sense of understanding, assumptions are made about the presence of certain mental states on the basis of knowledge of other understandable connections, and these assumptions make understanding possible. Thus, we are dealing with constructs which are thought of as analogous to the subjectively experienced connection; experienced connections are generalized, extended to what is not experienced, and made the schematic foundation for the interpretation of mental events.

At one of its extremes, understanding psychology (in this sense) takes the following form: interest in mental processes recedes in favor of interest in the objective meanings which these processes convey. We see, then, a search for interpretable meaning which must ultimately transcend not only the limits of consciousness but also the limits of the mental as such—in order finally to reach the sphere of objective mind. Understanding becomes more and more an interpretation of meaningful contexts. Whether an interpretation is admissible or not is eventually decided by the possibility of assigning it a place in the order of "intellectual" (*"geistig"*) contexts. With this, understanding ceases to represent a psychological method. For here we no longer recognize what we have come to know as psychological understanding—we are in the realm of understanding symbols and meanings. It is obvious that such a mode of interpreting the mental cannot see or cannot take into account the fact of somatic intrusion.

But I think we cannot assume general understandability and on that arbitrary premise exclude nonunderstandable determinants. Second, I want to mention in this context that the task of empirical psychology is precisely to represent the processes of psychic life, without letting, e.g., concepts of "value" and valuational "meaning" intrude into its presentation; values come within its purview only to the extent that human thought or will is oriented to them.

It is essential that psychological research maintain the distinction between psychological and rational understanding. Only the former can be spoken of as a psychological procedure and it is extremely important for psychologists and psychopathologists to know when they are dealing with the one or with the other. Even everyday clinical experience—not to mention the methodological demand for conceptual purity—necessitates this distinction, and Kurt Schneider (1922) is quite right in pointing out that the equivocations which attach to the ambiguity of the word "understand" can also be disastrous for specific problems of psychiatry.

The teleological interpretive schema which characterizes Adler's "individual psychology" (1912, 1920) also leads to neglect of the somatic factor, and for this psychology the distinction between consciousness and unconsciousness becomes irrelevant. Nevertheless, Adler still remains in the sphere of psychology and does not go beyond the psychical into the sphere of irreal meaning. His interpretation remains a psychological procedure.

Psychoanalysis, although it has extended the limits of the mental further than its scientific predecessors, does not deny the influence of the somatic. Its conception of instinctual drive is rooted in the organic, and with the help of this concept it has sought to link psychical with biological processes. Freud (1905) emphatically stressed the organic side of his concept of instinctual drive. Further indications of this orientation are the emphases psychoanalysis puts on phylogenesis, constitution, the physiological processes underlying puberty and climacterium, and in general on somatic developmental processes, as well as its theory of libido. The recognition and systematic clarification of somatic intrusion, the effect of bodily processes upon libido organization are important problems in psychoanalytic theory.

When psychoanalysis interprets an action or a symptom as an instinctual gratification, although the patient is not conscious of this connection, it may in a certain sense be permissible to refer to this interpretation as a classification in a "meaningful" context. But to say this is not to have said what for psychoanalysis is most essential. It was not the meaningfulness of instinctual behavior originating in instinctual impulses which led psychoanalysis to broaden the concept of instinctual drives and to attribute to them a basic function in mental life. The decisive factor was that this assumption made it possible to find lawfulness and order in mental life where previously all psychology had groped in the dark. In a word: the psychoanalytic formulations according to which instinctual processes play a fundamental role in mental life must be accorded the dignity of a fruitful hypothesis.

Psychoanalysis seeks to explain the experience of connections in the same sense that it seeks explanation of any other experience. Where the scope of psychology has been widened by new and systematic observation in analysis and where these have led to contradictions with the experiences of connection, then it is these latter—however evident they may be—which fall by the wayside. The Freudian theories of the unconscious are a powerful arbiter of the self-deceptions which originate in self-evident understanding. And the struggle against psychoanalysis is not least of all a revolt of driving forces, which are behind these evidential experiences, against control by the natural sciences.

Psychoanalysis has acquainted us with a great many experiences of connection which had previously escaped recognition by psychology. Today, these connections are understandable; but some of them have not always been understood: an eye for understanding connections can indeed be trained. Above all, that method of analogy on which the analytic interpretation of unconscious processes is based (see Hartmann, 1927, Chapter 5) has enormously broadened our knowledge of mental connections. It is not surprising if such psychoanalytic connections are also understandable. They are, after all, carried over from the psychology of conscious life to the unconscious, and essentially correspond to the empathizable sequence of instinctual impulse and actions. But, as I said earlier, this can give us no grounds for regarding psychoanalysis as an "understanding" method, for this sequence is not only empathetically understandable, it is at the same time one of the most important causal connections in the mind.

This point of view is of more general significance. For the sequence of instinctual drive and instinctual action is not, of course, the only understandable connection which at the same time can be viewed as causal. There are causal connections also between decision and action, between insult and defense, between the death of someone near and the ensuing mourning, between the offensive character of a desire and its repression, between the repression of a wish and its realization in disguise, etc. In all these cases we find not only understandable but also causal sequences—and even prescientific thought had already been familiar with some of these. The basis of such prescientific connections was constantly examined, complemented, and corrected by psychoanalysis—and also often rejected. In this way it established laws which it then carried over, as hypotheses about possible mental connections, to psychic realms as yet unknown. The importance of analytic assumptions is not based on a "higher self-evidence" which would characterize them in contradiction to the propositions of other schools of psychology. One need only compare, for example, the psychoanalytic conception of mourning or jealousy with other current explanations. One cannot speak here of a higher degree of understandability. It is the need to explain existing facts which compelled psychoanalysis to develop these hypotheses.

Many psychoanalytic concepts—and not unimportant ones—do not point at all to understandable connections, e.g., elements of the psychoanalytic theory of dynamics and energetics. Many mechanisms with which Freud has acquainted us, i.e., condensation and symbolism, are as such not understandable (what is meaningful in these cases is only the content reference), nor are the biologically envisaged concepts of fixation and regression. If we still need to prove that psychoanalysis should not be classified as an "understanding" psychology, we may point out the following: an understanding of the unconscious in analogy with consciously experienced connections is of course conceivable. But such an approach could by itself never lead to the assumption that in the unconscious we find specific ways of working which we do not find in consciousness (Freud, 1915b). This assumption is comprehensible only when it is made clear that its value lies in its explanatory power, that it is a theoretical construct.

What most psychoanalysts reject in Adler's psychology is in no way based on the latter's lack of understandability; it is not, in this sense, a matter of one interpretive scheme against another. Rather, the rejection of Adler's psychology is caused by his avoidance of the biological, and his abandonment or neglect of what we call mechanisms—these, however, constitute elements of analytic theory which are, at least in part, not "understandable."

We have already noted that in the history of psychoanalytic theory assumptions have repeatedly been discarded, not because they ran counter to meaningful interpretation, but because they did not stand the test of increased empirical data. Thus, when the original trauma theory (as an explanatory principle of the neuroses) proved to be inadequate, Freud felt compelled to trace the determinants of his patients' neuroses to their childhood, and in this way discovered infantile sexuality. But interpretations based on traumatic experience had also been understandable, and it is not at all possible to say that the current analytic view of the etiology of neurosis has a higher degree of "self-evidence" than the earlier trauma theory.

Psychoanalysis has been reproached for seeking to understand too much. In light of the above considerations, this might mean that it has too widely staked out the area within which mental processes may be resorted to for explanatory purposes. It is hard to decide if the reproach is justified or not. A method which would allow us to draw a sharp line, in particular instances, between unconscious and organic processes does not exist today. In this area, too, psychoanalysis represents a beginning. But these difficulties do not argue against the assumption of unconscious psychic processes, for the necessity of this assumption is well anchored in other respects. But one thing must be realized: even where psychoanalytic literature makes a conscious effort to apply the psychologically demonstrable connections of instinctual processes to the organic-biological sphere, this does not involve an understanding method illicitly overstepping the boundaries of its field of applicability. It rather represents an (at least logically) unobjectionable attempt to use the knowledge of certain primitive psychological mechanisms as hypotheses with respect to organic-biological events. Whether such an attempt can be fruitful, and where the limits of its applicability are, can be decided only by empirical data, which for the most part are still lacking.

We can thus refute the view, first expressed by Jaspers (1913), that psychoanalysis "is actually an understanding psychology and does not provide us with causal explanations." I may add here that in reading Binswanger's work, one also has the general impression that he claims Freudian theories for understanding psychology—though, to be sure, his concept of understanding is quite different from that of Jaspers.

Schilder (1923) refuses to distinguish between causal and understanding connections. For him, there are genuine and pseudo connections, and, in his view, the genuine connections are at the same time also causal. This does not resolve the difficulty which, as we have noted, rests in the fact that understanding itself furnishes us no means of distinguishing genuine from pseudo connections. But on the basis of this conceptualization in which genuine understanding connections are identical with causal connections in the psychical sphere, the psychoanalytic method could also be termed understanding, as long as this term means nothing else than psychologically explanatory.

It is difficult to comprehend why those who have themselves worked with the analytic method should harbor any misunderstanding concerning the status of psychoanalysis as a natural science. Those whose acquaintance with psychoanalysis derives exclusively from reading the literature may have been led to such misunderstandings by the Freudian nomenclature. Freud does not, for example, always clearly differentiate between "meaningful" and "causally determined." This is due to the fact that those psychical determinants which Freud always encountered in his analysis of parapraxes, dreams, and neuroses may also turn out to be "meaningful." The result was: connections of the understanding sort reach beyond the limits of consciousness. This is also the sense in which Freud uses, e.g., the expression "unconscious motivation," or he speaks of the "meaning" of neurotic symptoms. But the interpretation of symptoms always remains for Freud the establishment of the causal mental nexus (of which the relationship between instinctual drive and instinctual gratification is a prototype). Freud leaves no doubt that he considers this relationship to be a causal one. If, therefore, a symptom is, in Freud's terminology, considered to be "meaningful," this simply refers to the possibility of assigning it a place in the (causal) relationships of the mind. When Freud shows that dreams are "meaningful," he intends to say that they have their foundation in unconscious (though analogous to conscious) and often meaningful thought-connections on the basis of which the apparently absurd manifest content can be explained with the aid of our knowledge of dream mechanisms.

Freud explicitly stressed that the assumptions of psychoanalysis are hypotheses, and that the method of psychoanalysis is a method of the natural sciences. In the same way he stressed that the truth or falsity of analytic theories can be decided only on empirical grounds. There should thus remain no doubt as to how Freud intended his terms to be understood.

Our critique of psychological understanding has thus confirmed that psychoanalysis is a natural science not only in its manner of conceptualization, as has been shown earlier (see Hartmann, 1927, Chapter 1), but also in the scientific goals it sets itself—namely, the knowledge of laws and regularities. Judgments as to the existence or nonexistence of connections are, in psychoanalysis, only inductively demonstrable. And again one has to reject the reproach that psychoanalysis—unlike understanding psychology—tends to simplify. Moreover, this can be a fault only from the standpoint of understanding, not from the standpoint of a natural-science theory. As Jaspers rightly says, understanding psychology could never lead to the formation of theories, but explanatory psychology must do just this, regardless of whether the inductively established connections are also understandable.

Psychoanalysis is, therefore, an inductive science of the connections between complex mental structures. Its propositions are obtained empirically and have to be verified empirically. The inductive basis of its knowledge is slim compared to that of the physical sciences, and its accessibility to experimental verification is fraught with difficulties. But where such experiments have been performed, the results have supported analytic theories. Parenthetically, all the possibilities existing in this regard have by no means been exhausted. These difficulties are not due to the unfitness of the analytic method, but involve obstacles which today must be overcome by every psychology which seeks to study mental life in what has been called its "full content."

Until now we have neglected one point of view which has frequently induced investigators to turn to the understanding method.

Understanding, in contrast to explanation, appears "to penetrate into the inner connections" (Spranger, 1924, p. 3). But we must recall that at the outset of our investigation into the scientific status of psychoanalysis we came to the conclusion that no scientific psychology is capable of preserving in its concepts the lived immediacy of its primary material, and that any psychology has to sacrifice to its scientific goal the illusion of that "deeper penetration" into its subject which belongs to immediate experience.

In its place we gain definitive systematic knowledge. If someone should here think of "resignation," I would say that the scientific approach in psychology, as in other fields, implies "resignation" only from the point of view of the experiencing person. This view, by the way, attributes to primitive man—he "understands," in an animistic manner, also changes of inanimate nature—a "deeper penetration" into natural phenomena (not in the sense of a deeper experience but in that of deeper, more penetrating knowledge) than is possible by means of the scientific approach. For this reason alone this view is hardly tenable.

The principle of causality is also applicable to the sphere of the mind. I said before that one should not, as also Schwarz (1925) has done, oppose understanding as *the* method of psychology to the causal explanation of processes in nature by limiting causality to the quantifiable, and by characterizing it as "the specific category of concepts in physics." For the principle of causality is not limited to causal equations. The kind of "teleological" interpretation, which is also used in psychoanalysis, and, above all, in Adler's individual psychology, in which mental processes are understood in terms of their goals which may either be set consciously, or are unconscious—all this does not contradict a causal explanation. To view a process within a teleological framework can generally in biology be a valuable methodological principle—"the indication of the totality of relationships, of purposiveness facilitates the first causal connection between parts and whole" (M. Hartmann, 1925, p. 24).

In summary: we have rejected understanding as *the* method of psychology, have indicated its limitations, and have shown why it must become a source of error for psychological knowledge. We then showed that such error can be avoided only by reliance upon inductive proof. These statements should not be construed to imply the worthlessness of understanding for psychology. Many understandable connections (including the "as-if" understandable connections) are, as I mentioned before, actually causal connections. We must not forget that the emergence of a voluntary action from an act of will is the paradigm not only of the understanding connection but also of the causal relationship. The concept of causality, however—and this is the crucial point—has freed itself from its origin in the experience of causality. This subjective experience no longer is a valid criterion of causal connections. Understanding connections are, as hypotheses, in many ways indispensable, but their validity must in every case be established empirically. No psychology of the more complex aspects of the mind can fully dispense with understanding. But as long as it is a science, it must not use understanding without having established the limits of its reliability. To ascertain these limits and thereby to determine the sphere within which understanding and causal connections coincide is one of the essential tasks of psychoanalysis.

CHAPTER 19

An Experimental Contribution to the Psychology of Obsessive-Compulsive Neurosis

On Remembering Completed and Uncompleted Tasks

(1933)

THE QUESTION as to whether and how completion or interruption of tasks, wishes, and thoughts influences their recall has been discussed for some time in the special area of the psychology of dreams. W. Robert wrote in 1886: "The causes [of dreams] are always the same: the resumption of sensory impressions which have not been worked through intellectually or an uncompleted mental activity. . . . Dreams are precipitations of thoughts nipped in the bud. . . . Something that has been fully thought through never produces dreams; only something that dwells unfinished on someone's mind or passes casually through one's mind can do so." The author interprets his observations in terms of a theory which ascribes to dreams a tension-reducing function: dreams have healing power, they are a safety valve of the mind; ". . . a human being deprived of the possibility to dream would have to become mentally disturbed after some time because large amounts of unfinished and undigested thoughts and of shallow impressions would accumulate in his brain.

Under their impact, whatever must be incorporated into memory in a finished and completed form would be smothered."

Y. Delage (1891) places even stronger emphasis on this very viewpoint. He bases his theory on the following observations: "As a rule, ideas which occupied the mind during waking do not come back in dreams"; and "An impression can produce a dream only if the mind has turned away from that impression almost immediately after having received it or due to absent-mindedness at the moment of perception. This distraction of the mind may assume such an extent that the perception was completely unconscious to the point where it left no trace in memory. It is understandable that in that case the dream appears to be entirely a spontaneous formation."

Delage presents the following theoretical contructs for the classi-fication of these findings: "Every sensation, every idea contains a certain amount of energy which it spends in investing the thought. When our attention is diverted from it the energy consumption stops; the smaller this consumption, the more energy remains avail-able. During sleep attention is neither directed by the will nor diverted by new sensations, and we are left to our old impressions which arise from a state of temporary inhibition, and each one with its remaining amount of energy tends to resume its interrupted development." The unresolved impressions form "set springs" (*"des ressorts tendus"*) and "there can be more force in a little tightened spring than in a bigger one which has almost resumed its position of inertia. . . . In short, our impressions are accumulators of energy." From this statement the author derives a piece of advice concerning the avoidance of nightmares: "If you fear their flow, it is wise to discharge them before falling asleep."

We present an example from Delage's work which is of special interest for our further considerations because in this illustration the "incompleteness" is represented by an obsessive fear: "One of my cousins, a young man with a very nervous temperament, frequently goes hunting with his younger brother. Sometimes a vivid impression crosses his mind like a bolt of lightning at the moment of pulling the trigger: isn't his brother in his line of fire? But since his brother is right at his side, safe, and in no danger, the thought disappears immediately. At night he often dreams that he killed him while hunting. Once the danger was real, not for the brother but for an old woman whom the hunter had not seen. The shot passed right above her head. This time the emotion was terrible. All day long he did not stop thinking of it, and in the evening they spoke about nothing else at home. That incident he never saw in a dream."

It is known that Freud (1900) partially corroborated the observations underlying the above theoretical constructs and wove them into his theory of dreams. He mentioned Robert as well as Delage. To be sure, in the over-all structure of Freud's theory of dreams the aforementioned observations play a minor and not a central part. Thus we read in *The Interpretation of Dreams:* "The unconscious prefers to weave its connections round preconscious impressions and ideas which are either indifferent and have thus had no attention paid to them, or have been rejected and have thus had attention promptly withdrawn from them" (p. 563). And a few pages earlier: "There is no need to underestimate the importance of the psychical intensities which are introduced into the state of sleep by these residues of daytime life, and particularly of those in the group of unsolved problems. It is certain that these excitations continue to struggle for expression during the night; and we may assume with equal certainty that the state of sleep makes it impossible for the excitatory process to be pursued in the habitual manner in the preconscious and brought to an end by becoming conscious" (p. 554f.). But in order to enter a dream any waking thought must connect itself with a repressed infantile wish. Freud states in relation to the question whether unresolved wishes can have the function of instigating dreams: ". . . children's dreams prove beyond a doubt that a wish that has not been dealt with during the day can act as a dream-instigator. But it must not be forgotten that it is a *child's* wish, a wishful impulse of the strength proper to children. I think it is highly doubtful whether in the case of an adult a wish that has not been fulfilled during the day would be strong enough to produce a dream" (p. 552).

We cannot pursue this thought any further here. It must suffice for our purposes to have indicated what importance contemporary dream theory attributes to the reproduction of uncompleted material.

Pötzl (1917) conducted tachistoscopic experiments in which he exposed pictures at speeds of 1/100 seconds. He was able to demonstrate in the majority of cases (for nine out of twelve subjects) that these pictures presented during the day exerted a clear-cut influence on the formation of the manifest dream of the following night. Immediately after the pictures were exposed, everything the subjects could indicate with reference to their perceptions was recorded. A second protocol contained the corresponding associations of the day. A comparison with the dreams of the following night showed that those elements of the pictures which were not contained in the protocols appeared faithfully reproduced in their details and clearly recognizable in the dream—in other words, those which apparently remained entirely unnoticed during the tachistoscopic exposure and which also had not occurred to the subjects afterwards. Pötzl "found that there exists a relationship of exclusion, owing to which whatever has been mentally formed as a Gestalt is excluded from subsequent development so that only parts of the original excitation can develop and whatever has developed into a Gestalt loses the power to act further" (p. 117).

Malamud and Linder (1931) later reported similar experiments using partially modified hypotheses. These authors proceeded from the following train of thought. When elements of a situation are not perceived or are forgotten and when these same elements can then be shown to be associated with specific repressed excitations appearing in the dreams of the following night, the mechanism of this kind of forgetting or nonperceiving can then be understood. The results of the experiments showed that some elements of the pictures appeared which had been omitted in the description of what had been perceived during the exposures. These elements which had been omitted in the protocols seemed to stand in some specific relationship to former experiences and frequently to the subjects' central conflicts. But it appears that experiences of the day preceding the dream can influence the results in so far as these experiences connect with complex elements.

Allers and Teler's work (1924) touches also to some degree upon our problem. These authors were looking for an answer through experimentation to the question whether "unnoticed" material could be demonstrated to have an influence on our conscious thought processes. Their experimental method was the following: the tachistoscopic exposure of pictures was 4/100 sec., which was considerably longer than in Pötzl's experiments; protocols about the subjects' perceptions and association tests were obtained on the following day; besides neutral stimulus words the list contained words which referred to those elements in the pictures which did not appear in the protocols. "The results of these experiments are: under the influence of suitable stimulus words, pictorial 'representations' appear in the interval between stimulus and response word; although not mentioned in the description given by the subject immediately after the exposure, and not recognized either then or thereafter as having been seen earlier, i.e., as having been components of the originally exposed pictures, these 'representations' are nevertheless elements of the perceptual manifold presented" (p. 141). In the opinion of the authors, the selection of what is perceived is determined by the factor of "word-nearness," the nameability of individual components, because in view of the experimental instructions the subjects are set to reproduce them.

Contrary to Pötzl's dream experiments, the clearly perceived elements of the pictures always stood out in the reports of these subjects. I shall not discuss to what degree this may be related to the peculiarities of the process of dreaming. Allers and Teler believe that the difference in results may be attributed to the difference in exposure time.[1]

Zeigarnik (1927) dealt with the problem of the effect of current needlike tensions on certain forms of recall. This research was part of a more extensive series of experiments conducted by Kurt Lewin concerning the psychology of action and emotion. An answer was sought to the question how recall of activities interrupted before their completion is related to recall of completed tasks. Each subject was given some tasks to be completed and some which were interrupted before completion. To exclude possible differences due to the characteristics of any given task, the tasks were distributed among the subjects in such a way that each task was interrupted as often as it was completed.

The ratio of the retained uncompleted (RU) to the retained completed (RC) activities is a measure of the preference of one of these groups in retention over the other. Lewin and Zeigarnik demonstrated that, on the average, the uncompleted tasks were recalled about 90 per cent better than the completed ones; i.e., the arithmetic mean of $\frac{RU}{RC}$ is 1.9.

The authors gave the following theoretical explanations of their findings: "At the time when a subject forms the intention to execute the task on the basis of the instructions a quasi need is produced which by itself strives for the completion of the task. Dynamically speaking, this process corresponds to the genesis of a tension system which aims at relaxation. Completion of the task then means discharge of the system, relaxation of the quasi need. When a task is interrupted there remains a tension residue; the quasi need is not satisfied." The reason for better recall of unfinished activities thus lies in the continuation of a "quasi need." Recall here plays the role of an indicator of the needlike tension.

[1] Recent research has considerably advanced the study of some of the problems touched upon in the introduction to this paper. For a survey of the newer literature, see Charles Fisher (1960).

This theoretical formulation of the facts reminds us of the dynamic-energetic concepts of psychoanalysis and of the "set springs" referred to by Yves Delage. Zeigarnik writes: "How such tensions will express themselves in the apparently quite different process of recall can be derived only from a general theory of psychic dynamics, which would first of all have to decide whether the process of recall is concerned simultaneously with the discharge of individual tensions." Such a general psychodynamic theory exists—the psychoanalytic one—which can explain the dynamic relationship between certain classes of experiences and recall. Freud (1920) proceeds from the observation that the dreams of persons with traumatic neuroses lead them again and again back to the situation of the accident. This fact obviously contradicts the pleasure-seeking and unpleasure-avoiding tendency, which is otherwise a useful guide of far-reaching applicability for the explanation of psychic relationships. We are dealing here with a result of what Freud called repetition compulsion. The traumatic neurosis is understood to be the consequence of a breach in the stimulus barrier, and the dreams of those suffering from traumatic neurosis "are endeavouring to master the stimulus retrospectively, by developing the anxiety whose omission [at the time of the trauma] was the cause of the traumatic neurosis" (1920, p. 32). The repetition factor in children's play must be understood from the same point of view. Here too recall serves the mastery of experiences. Children's play is a "process of assimilation through repetition" (Waelder, 1932). These two examples demonstrate cogently how the process of recall can operate in the service of tension discharge. However, we must not forget that the psychoanalytic concept of repetition compulsion does not include every repetition in the psychic realm.

Zeigarnik's experiments further demonstrated that differences in the interpretation of the request for recall influence the will to recall and thereby also the ratio of RU to RC. Moreover, subjects who can be considered to have a relatively impulsive character showed a particularly high predominance of RU over RC. The $\frac{RU}{RC}$ ratio is higher in children than in adults. "The more uncontrolled a person's needs are, the less he can renounce need gratification; the more 'childlike' and natural he is in the experiment, the stronger is his tendency to a preponderance of uncompleted actions." The $\frac{RU}{RC}$ ratio remains very constant in individual subjects. Finally, the decisive issue concerning the ratio of recall is the internal completion of the task and not its external termination.

Schlote (1930) has rechecked Zeigarnik's experiments. He found that "the unfinished activities assumed a preferred position in relation to the finished tasks in so far as the activity which corresponds to an uncompleted task shows a tendency to return to consciousness when an opportunity arises; and this return occurs much faster and with greater certainty than is the case with completed tasks. Naturally this preferred position must express itself also in better retention due to the effectiveness of such a tendency." Schlote, who closely follows the psychological formulations of Ach, recognizes only the effectiveness of the determining tendencies directed toward goal realization as the cause of better retention of incompleted tasks. I cannot discuss here Schlote's objections to Lewin's concept of quasi needs, and to his method, and in part to the results of Zeigarnik's experiments.

The subject matter of the experiments reported below is the recall of completed and uncompleted activities by obsessive-compulsive neurotics. For several reasons, it seemed to me of interest to investigate the behavior of obsessive-compulsive neurotics with respect to this question. Various authors have correctly emphasized that incompleteness or inability of closure is characteristic of the thinking of obsessive-compulsive neurotics. This quality of their thought processes in particular gave rise to the expectation that the "tension systems" might in their case act differently from the way in which they act in normals, and that this difference might be verified experimentally. Thus some light might be thrown also on the tendency toward repetition, which is a well-known but not yet fully understood characteristic of obsessional neurosis. Recently Federn (1930) correctly pointed out that this tendency toward repetition occurs— I should like to add the qualification: in part—on this side and not beyond the pleasure principle, and that it must therefore not be equated with the repetition compulsion as this term is commonly used in psychoanalysis. Yet the effect of true repetition compulsion is unmistakable in obsessional neurosis.

The method follows that reported by Zeigarnik (1927). The subjects were given the following tasks: (1) to write down a poem; (2) to model a head from plasticine; (3) to draw a flower vase; (4) to write an address in printed letters; (5) to draw a plan of Vienna; (6) to combine pairs of cardboard triangles from among a larger number of such triangles into quadrangles; (7) to prick holes at a given distance inside a square; (8) to cross out all letters "l" and "n" in a sentence; (9) to compose a meaningful sentence of four words; (10) to count backwards from 90 to 49; (11) to multiply 5457 x 6337; (12) to write down ten cities whose names begin with "L"; (13) to solve a matchstick problem; (14) to cut out a spiral from a piece of paper; (15) to make a package; (16) to write down three names each beginning with the letter "k" of famous men, works of art, cities, animals, and plants; (17) to solve a puzzle; (18) to draw a cube which stands on one corner; (19) to continue a started honeycomb pattern; (20) to put together a postcard cut into pieces; (21) to pick out needles of a specific kind from a larger quantity; (22) to arrange strips of paper according to length; (23) to braid; (24) to write down ten nouns without either "e" or "r."

One half of the tasks were carried out to completion; during the other tasks the subject was interrupted before completion. Tasks completed by the first subject were interrupted for the next subject, etc. Only spontaneously recalled tasks were used for the calculation of the results (for the reasons for this procedure, see Zeigarnik, p. 39).

First the experiments were carried through with a control group of five healthy subjects. I could confirm in all cases Zeigarnik's findings of a preponderance of RU over RC. The ratio $\frac{RU}{RC}$ was 1.75, 1.50, 1.43, 1.25, 1.50 for the five healthy subjects respectively, with a mean of 1.48. Yet these scores are considerably lower than those reported by Zeigarnik. I do not know what is responsible for this difference of our results in general. But perhaps it may be of interest to point out that subject IV who scored lowest has a somewhat autistic personality and a character which is close to the compulsive type. If this subject is disregarded in the calculation, the mean is raised to 1.55.

The same experiments were then made with nine obsessive-compulsive neurotics. The results are summarized in Table I.

TABLE I

Subject	RU	RC	$\frac{RU}{RC}$
I	9	10	.90
II	8	8	1.00
III	4	4	1.00
IV	7	5	1.40
V	8	8	1.00
VI	9	7	1.28
VII	6	7	.86
VIII	3	7	.43
IX	4	2	2.00
Mean	6.4	6.4	1.10*

$$*M \frac{RU}{RC} \neq M \frac{RU}{RC}$$

Whereas we obtained a mean $\frac{RU}{RC}$ ratio of 1.48 with the healthy subjects, we obtained a mean of 1.10 with the obsessive-compulsive subjects. *Obsessive-compulsive neurotics recall uncompleted activities hardly better than completed ones.*

The extraordinarily high ratio score obtained by subject IX stands out in this series, but this subject's behavior during and after the experiment did not provide an explanation. One may wonder whether the idea the subject formed concerning the subsequent enumeration of the tasks played a role. Zeigarnik's experiments demonstrated that subjects for whom the enumeration means a mere narration obtain generally a higher $\frac{RU}{RC}$ ratio than those who consider the enumeration a memory test. Subject IX belongs, however, to the latter group—a circumstance giving the appearance of irregularity with regard not only to the ratio but also the small number of remembered tasks ($RU + RC = 6$). Subjects I, V, and VIII also belong to this type who considers the enumeration as a memory test. For them, the sums of RU and RC are 19, 16, and 10 respectively, with a mean of 15. If subject IX, however, is included, a mean of 12.9 is obtained as compared to a mean of 13 for the representatives of the other type (both means for $RU + RC$). In this case, there is then little difference between the mean $\frac{RU}{RC}$ ratios (1.08 as compared to 1.11).

Thus the two groups differ less from each other than in Zeigarnik's experiments with normal subjects; evidently the interpretation of the enumeration as a memory test does not, for the obsessive-compulsive neurotics, play a significant role in the framework of their total attitude toward the experiments. We must also remember that, according to Zeigarnik, the difference of $\frac{RU}{RC}$ for the two groups arises mainly as a result of differences in the RC scores which approach the RU scores more in one case than in the other (see p. 37). On the other hand, our obsessive-compulsive subjects did (on the average) not obtain very different RU and RC scores.

All subjects regarded the experiment as an intelligence, aptitude, or diagnostic test. They believed it served to determine "whether my mind has suffered" (subject II); "whether I am normal" (subject IV); "you doubt my intelligence!" (subject III); "it is like fingerprints for criminals" (subject VI); "it is like at an employment agency" (subject VIII); "it has to do with a psychotechnical test" (subject VII). Subjects I, V, and IX said: "Intelligence test."

Subjects I, II, IV, V, and VII stated spontaneously that the investigation made them "nervous." Subject V said: "I am so excited. I have feelings of anxiety and my heart beats faster as if it would jump out of my body from all that fear."

Zeigarnik found that the "excited" subjects in her group of healthy individuals did not have better recall of uncompleted tasks. Our obsessive-compulsive subjects who obviously "became nervous" during (and because of) the experiment did not show any—or more correctly, any significant—decrease in the $\frac{RU}{RC}$ ratio. The ratio is 1.03 for our "nervous" subjects as compared to 1.18 for those subjects who did not show or report any "nervousness" in this sense during or after the experiment. In view of the difficulties involved in delineating somewhat reliably this factor of "becoming nervous," I am not attributing any great significance to the difference between Zeigarnik's and our results.

The majority of our subjects spontaneously reported afterwards that they had the feeling of having performed poorly, or of having been generally incapable, or that they doubted the correctness of their solutions of the tasks (subjects II, III, VII, VIII, IX). Subject VIII said: "I am never sure the first time . . . surely I did not do well!" and subject IX: "I have the feeling I should have done better!" and subject VII: "Did I do it right? It is certainly all wrong!" Such remarks were also made after the individual tasks. Occasionally the subjects voiced the intention to resume the task.

Zeigarnik's investigations showed that a number of subjects experienced certain tasks as unfinished, although they were "objectively" completed; furthermore, that some subjects were dissatisfied with their performances even on subjectively completed tasks. These tasks were *better retained* than the remainder of finished tasks. We have seen that such behavior constitutes the rule among obsessive-compulsive subjects. These findings would thus agree with the fact that the RU and RC scores of obsessive-compulsive neurotics differ less from each other than those of normals. However, if we compare those subjects who reported dissatisfaction with their performance with the rest of the group, no significant differences appear (1.06 and 1.14, respectively). Of course, it is easily possible that such criteria as "dissatisfaction with the performance" were not adequately expressed in the reports of our subjects. Zeigarnik explains the fact that completed tasks with which her subjects were dissatisfied were better retained than other completed tasks by saying that "the subject is subjectively in a situation similar to that of having been interrupted. The need to repeat the task develops in the subject." I want to emphasize that subjective incompletion of a task and the tendency for repetition must be recognized as influences upon recall.

What is the situation concerning this "need to repeat" with respect to our subjects? With this question we return to the psychology of obsessive-compulsive neurosis. The tendency to repeat plays an important role in the symptomatology of the majority of our subjects: the compulsion to rip open again what has been sewn (subject I), always to turn around in the street (subject II), to do everything twice (subject IV) etc.; other symptoms were obsessional doubt and indecision. I do not want to enter here upon the remainder of the symptoms. If the cases in which these symptoms played a predominant role (they are only partially identical with those who reported dissatisfaction with their performance) are compared with others in which these symptoms are less evident, the first group shows a considerably lower value for the investigated ratio than does the latter group (.93 as compared to 1.43). It clearly is large enough to deserve our attention. It clearly speaks in favor of the tendency to repeat and of the subjective sense of incompletion influencing recall.

It was particularly Friedmann (1920) who placed the factor of incompleteness of or inability to complete a thought process in the center of a theory of obsessive-compulsive neurosis. Obsessional thoughts, according to his theory, are supposed to be the consequence of the logical impossibility of completing doubts, worries, expectations.

Because of Freud we know today more about the structure and genesis of obsessive-compulsive neurosis, though this disease is still "unconquered as a problem" (Freud). We also have better insight into the nature of compulsive repetitions. The part played by the "repetition compulsion" (in its narrow sense) in obsessive-compulsive neurosis is obscure; but here we must disregard also the little we know so far about its role as a fixating factor in repression and its relationship to the destructive drives, which move so strongly into the foreground in obsessive-compulsive neurosis (Federn, 1930). I do not want to discuss here the psychoanalytic theory of obsessional thinking and of obsessive-compulsive neurosis in general, and refer the reader to two recently published, excellent books which treat this subject in detail (Nunberg, 1932; Fenichel, 1931). I mention only some of the well-established findings which are closely related to our subject matter. We can understand the compulsion to execute two opposed actions immediately after each other (diphasic symptoms) on the basis of what many analyses have taught us: one of these actions represents a drive gratification and the other a defense against the drive impulse. The obsessive-compulsive neurotic's belief in magical "omnipotence of thought" explains (together with our knowledge about the drive structure of these neurotics) his inhibition of thought; the magic procedure of "undoing," which is characteristic of this disease, enables us partly to understand compulsive repetitions. The tendency to undo "may perhaps account for the obsession for *repeating* which is so frequently met with in this neurosis and the carrying out of which serves a number of contradictory intentions at once. When anything has not happened in the desired way it is undone by being repeated in a different way; and thereupon all the motives that exist for lingering over such repetitions come into play as well. As the neurosis proceeds, we often find that the endeavour to undo a traumatic experience is a motive of first-rate importance in the formation of symptoms" (Freud, 1926a, p. 120). The repetition is aimed at weakening or canceling the magical significance of an action. If, however, the obsessive-compulsive neurotic's strict superego was not satisfied with the details of the repetition, then further repetitions follow. The magical world of the obsessional neurotic and his hypercathexis of thought processes—which are related to his typical regression and to the restriction of his activities (activity equals destruction)—also are responsible for his endeavor to blur the differences between what actually happened and what possibly might have happened, between what has been done and what he has thought.

Now we understand why, for the obsessive-compulsive neurotic, the character of "completedness" of an action remains subjectively relative, and where the "need to repeat" originates. This is also the source to which the peculiarity of the results obtained with the obsessive-compulsive subjects can be attributed. Here we see the factors which find their expression in the altered structure of their "quasi needs."

We are now confronted with the question in which way we have to think of "quasi needs" as dependent on *true needs*. Obviously for any general psychodynamic theory it will be decisive to what degree its concepts can do justice to the *dynamically decisive* driving forces. It seems to me that my investigations demonstrate that Lewin's dynamics is in need of—and is capable of—being complemented by a more comprehensive theory of drives. In view of the manifold correspondences of concepts and content, I consider it very promising to make the attempt to base Lewin's psychology upon psychoanalytic dynamics of drives and affects. However, to prove in detail the fruitfulness of this attempt would mean to go beyond the scope of this paper.

CHAPTER 20

Psychiatric Studies of Twins

(1934-1935)

T HE problem of the formative powers of Anlage and environment has perhaps been less objectively clarified and more passionately debated in characterology than in any other field of science. Two viewpoints are diametrically opposed to each other. One camp attempts to derive all lawfulness and development of personality from hereditary factors neglecting all or almost all environmental factors. Characterology is considered to be a branch of genetics. The members of the opposite camp understand man, so to speak, "from the outside." They present the Anlagen as some almost unspecific material which obtains its shape only thanks to environmental influences. The most extreme representatives of this trend know hardly any limits to the optimistic expectations which they attach to establishing a rational order of environmental factors.

Both sides decree with great certainty what is endogenous in char-

The following is a translation of parts of a study dealing with identical twins, published in two sections in the *Jahrbücher für Psychiatrie und Neurologie,* 50 (1934) and 51 (1935). The original contained both the clinical data (based on observations of ten pairs of identical twins) and their theoretical discussion. The version presented here includes mostly the latter, with particular reference to the characterology of identical twins. Its relevance to certain aspects of psychoanalytic theory led me to the decision to include these parts of the original paper in this volume. Without listing here the recent literature on twin psychology, I want to point out that during the last years psychoanalysts have made many contributions to this field. As a consequence, a number of points I discussed in my paper, often in a tentative way, have come closer to a solution.

acter development and what is not without possessing so far the necessary basis for such inductions. Frequently one gets the impression that the authors only seemingly fight about empirical findings, while in reality preconceived ideas collide. Also one must not overlook the fact that considerations derived from a philosophy of life and even political considerations frequently play a decisive part in the choice of one's orientation. Moreover, certain professional (therapeutic, educational, eugenic) factors may dictate one's approach.

The majority of scientists assumes, however, a mediating view, as an example of which I want to mention here only Stern's convergence theory (1919): "External and internal factors, past and environment participate simultaneously in any real existence [*Sein*] and activity [*Tun*] of an individual. These factors do not act in opposition to each other or in some indifferent, inorganic parallelism but in a manner in which they require and promote each other in such a way that one is inconceivable without the other. Certainly one can and even must often isolate in one's mind which respective roles internal and external factors play in the expression of a given personality characteristic. But this isolation is merely a conceptual one; in reality we find in man no qualities, no action, no phenomenon, in brief, no characteristic, psychological, physical or neutral, which could be said to be inborn or acquired. Hence the misleading question 'Is this or that characteristic inborn or acquired?' ought finally to be rejected and to be replaced by the only appropriate question '*How much of this characteristic* is congenital and *how much* is acquired?' The either-or position is always incorrect; the both-and position is always correct." Not only acts but also dispositions underlie convergence. The individual participates in all convergence processes as an entity. Finally, convergence theory emphasizes particularly the necessity not of only ordering external and internal factors according to their relative importance but also investigating them with regard to their qualitative structure. Thus some methodological clarification has been reached, but a concrete direction for research has not yet been indicated.

Stern's convergence theory reverts to an idea which—at least in its fundamental aspects—had already emerged in the theory of neurosis. Freud (1916-17) speaks of "complementary series" (*Ergänzungsreihen*), a term which covers the following: "From the point of view of causation, cases of neurotic illness fall into a *series,* within which the two factors—sexual constitution and events experienced, or, if you wish, fixation of libido and frustration—are represented in such a way that where one of them predominates the other is proportionally less pronounced. . . . In the intermediate cases in the series, more or less of the disposing factor (the sexual constitution) is combined with less or more of the injurious impositions of life" (p. 303f.). Psychoanalysis does not deny the importance of Anlagen for the formation of personality and neurosis; but psychoanalysis assumes a special position with respect to this problem in so far as this theory places for methodological reasons experiential factors in the forefront. Hereditary predispositions cannot be studied directly by the psychoanalytic method but present themselves to the latter, so to speak, "by exclusion" as the unresolved residue after the experiences and reactions of a person have been brought to light in all their developmental details. Thus methodology requires first an analysis of the experiential aspects but does not in advance deny the determining power of hereditary predispositions.

Psychoanalysis was not chosen haphazardly here as an example. As a matter of fact, characterology owes to it and also to medical psychology in general some important impetus. Its problems lead again and again into the area of characterology; but I believe that, on the other hand, characterology requires roots in a biological conceptualization of man such as medical psychology has developed. Even representatives of humanistic (*geisteswissenschaftlich*) characterology like Utitz (1925) always appreciated the great methodological and substantive gains which characterology owes to medical thought. Different directions were taken by characterologies derived from philosophies of life and by the value characterologies of philosophers, the attempts of *verstehende Psychologie*[1] and of the phenomenological school to understand the personality, and finally by the powerful edifice of Klages's metaphysics of character (1928). While the psychology of personality is indebted to these schools for some important contributions and basic insights, a detailed discussion of their tenets is beyond the scope of this paper.

Purely descriptive cross-sections can rarely supply much information about character structure. Characterological concepts must necessarily go beyond what is in conscious awareness, and also beyond a mere description of behavior. It must be the aim of the psychology of personality to discover the laws of character development. This requires the construction of explanatory concepts. Here too the most promising path is genetic analysis. Even the problem of classifying character traits or personalities can be solved only partially on the basis of pure description, for phenomenologically "similar" behavior may have dynamically or genetically very different meanings and vice versa. A summarization of traits in accordance with their descriptive similarities therefore does not always coordinate actually homologous formations. In this manner we cannot, or only with difficulty, grasp the coexistence of "contradictory" character traits in one and the same individual; and it becomes just as difficult to understand the frequently only insignificant symptomatic weight of "identity" of characteristics in different people. Such an approach cannot offer any verdict concerning the durability or the modifiability of personality traits or concerning their respective compatibility or mutual exclusion (Hartmann, 1929). Hence we must go back to dispositions, to thresholds of responsiveness, and structures. Kronfeld (1920) declares similarly: "True personality research must go beyond mere descriptive typology."

This has actually been the road taken by medical characterology. In this context I must mention Kretschmer's (1918) attempt at a psychiatric theory of personality based on criteria of impression-

[1] See Chapter 18.

ability, retention, intrapsychic activity, and conductivity, and Ewald's (1924) psychiatric characterology. The conceptual approach of psychoanalytic characterology must also be mentioned here because of its dynamic and dispositional formulations. Even an opponent of psychoanalysis like Hoffmann (1928) clearly emphasized the need for a "drive- and aim-oriented personality theory." Of course, important differences exist also: psychoanalytic personality theory differs, for example, from Ewald's attempt above all in its refusal to resort from the beginning to conceptualizations based on something organic (as the explanatory principle). Psychoanalytic characterology distinguishes itself from all other personality theories of this kind primarily through its much greater emphasis on developmental factors (simultaneously as the basis for the derivation of character traits and for their classification). Yet, medicine as a point of departure and the emphasis on biological data create after all on both sides a strong bridge.

The problem of personality structure has undoubtedly sometimes been viewed in medicopsychological literature from too lopsided a somatic perspective. It was assumed that a scientific approach to personality needs must eventually work with concepts referring to the soma. This is certainly an error. There is nothing in the nature of psychic processes that would exclude a scientific approach. Pure description is by no means more essentially the way of dealing with the characteristics of psychic processes than with other subject matters; the descriptive method may rather represent in psychology and psychiatry merely a certain developmental stage of these sciences. Of course, in principle there exists no contradiction between a psychological and an organic approach; the contradiction begins only when one inquires what character, insanity, etc., "really are." I do not want to discuss this question now. What is of importance here is that medically oriented characterology too has no valid reason for avoiding psychological conceptualizations. Such an avoidance equals a short cut from the character to its organic-biological foundations, a short cut which, in view of our presently insufficient knowledge of psychosomatic relations, endangers the empirically quite weak bridge of such correlations.

At this point the best known correlation of physique and character, namely that of Kretschmer, should at least be mentioned. As in all similarly oriented attempts, this is a *classification* (*Zuordnung*), and it would be quite erroneous uncritically to "identify" body types with character types. Kretschmer did not succumb to this error. He himself states that the "inner reasons" for the psychophysical connections are still to be investigated. Perhaps Kretschmer's coordination in particular leads us a step beyond the simple formula "physique-character." There may exist, as Ewald thinks, a true functional relationship between the pyknic body type and even temperament (possibly also cyclothymic psychosis). These coordinations may be presented in very different ways. I remind the reader of the idea of a purely reactive relationship between character, neurosis, etc., on the one hand, and physique or organic function (in particular, organ inferiority) on the other (Adler, 1912). No doubt such reactive relations do exist in the area of character; but I do not believe that the discovery of these connections has solved the problem. Their relations are not the developmentally decisive factor for the neuroses (or even for the character). The above train of thought was to serve us here only as an illustration of a problem which no personality theory must overlook whatever its methodological starting point may be.

Whether one places the psychic or the somatic foundations of character in the foreground, in either case, both directions are in principle open to research: the path via the analysis of the environment and that via biogenetics. Hoffmann (1926) who consistently took the latter path designates as the aim of biogenetic characterology the isolation of genetically independent single Anlagen (basic genetic elements) in heredity and the uncovering of the manner in which its structural connections form the psychologically unique individual. All such attempts—which have certainly already produced some valuable results—imply the often-stated proposition that the environment cannot "bring out" in a personality what was not there first as Anlagen. In my opinion, such a formulation rather confuses than clarifies the issue. The problem lies precisely in this "bringing-out-in-the-personality." If we equate character with "basic genetic elements" (*"genischen Radikalen"*), then this statement becomes self-evident. But most characterologists agree that such a conceptualization raises serious objections. If character is defined as usual (e.g., as "the person seen from the perspective of his or her strivings" [Utitz, 1925]), then "person" is no longer merely the sum or the "structural union" (*"Strukturzusammenschluss"*) of Anlage elements but is formed by all previous "convergence processes." In other words, "all empirical convergence processes unfold between groups of conditions which themselves are already results of convergences" (Stern, 1919).

Biogenetic character analysis compares the characterological phenotype of a person with the characterological phenotypes of the members of his family. Such a method is certainly possible, but it must count upon many sources of errors. Conclusions from such a comparison to the heredity of personality traits would be cogent only if it had first been proven that paratypical factors cannot play a decisive part in this connection. However, this proof is missing; and quite apart from this, a biogenetic character analysis can be expected to bear fruit only after it has uncovered the basis character elements in ontogenesis.

Too far-reaching constructs must be avoided. Only a detailed analysis of personality development can supply clues as to "primary" versus "secondary" ontogenetic factors. It is always dangerous merely to proceed—like Pfahler (1932), for example—from a series of "basic functions" assumed to be innate conditions of mental processes in terms of kind and intensity (e.g., for Pfahler: attention, perseveration, affective responsiveness, vital energy), and to attempt to derive all phenotypic personality traits from the meeting of these basic functions with the environment. Such an attempt is precarious, first of all, because there is no real evidence to the effect that any "basic functional structure" remains unchanged throughout the process of development; furthermore, because the "derivation" of character and temperamental traits from that structure must remain constructive as long as the development of the concrete forms of behavior has not been actually observed through all evolutional stages. When, for example, the tendency to be consistent and exact is claimed to be an "unavoidable response" of all persons who show narrow, fixating attention and strong perseveration, or when the "busy-body" type is explained on the basis of strong vital energy, weak affective responsiveness, greatly fluctuating attention, and little perseveration—then one cannot avoid the impression that such a view misses the essential developmental psychological relations which a biologically oriented psychology ought to emphasize. This should at least partly be considered in connection with a point of view of more general importance: It is possible to delineate a developmental psychological construct by formal criteria (C. Bühler, 1930); but individual deviations from the schema of such a construct, the relative importance of the phases for the life of a given individual, the succession of phases, etc., can be clarified only by a study of the content. Such a study concentrates on the direction of concrete tendencies in the developing personality and relates this direction to concrete objects of desires, rejections, etc. Thus strivings which are determined by their content can only very imperfectly be derived from purely formal premises; and one cannot concentrate upon the content of psychic processes without carefully analyzing the environmental situations.

I mention in this connection again the conceptual approach of psychoanalytic personality theory (Freud, 1932). I presented my position with respect to the methodological prerequisites and possibilities of that psychoanalytic personality theory in an earlier work (Hartmann, 1927).

Three groups of factors which form man "from the outside" can be distinguished: "(1) The nonhuman nature: light, air, and water, food, soil, climate, fauna, and flora; (2) fellow humans: relatives and acquaintances, friends and enemies, inferiors and superiors, teachers and pupils; (3) man-made culture: government and law, art and science, transportation and commerce, class and profession" (Stern, 1919). A circumscribed part of these environmental influences has been particularly clearly investigated by Hellpach (1921) who also includes somatic aspects. Thus he could demonstrate (e.g., on the Frankish face) that the facial bone structure is not so definitely fixed by heredity as had been presumed, but that it is shaped by temperament and environmental characteristics, and that language plays an essential part in this process (cf. Gruhle, 1924). When we now attempt to arrange the "external factors" enumerated above in accordance with their actual influence upon the formation of the individual, it becomes obvious that we must attribute the decisive influence to the (affective) relations to fellow humans.

From many (perhaps from most) studies of the relative influence of Anlage and environment upon character formation one gains the impression that the hypothesis which is to be proven forms already part of the basic assumptions underlying the study, while there is not yet any scientific certainty to support that hypothesis. In other words, we are still at the beginning of a development whose end the authors believe to hold already in their hands. Under these circumstances we are entitled to expect some answer from the twin-study method. The possibilities it opens can be of particular use in this area if we do not limit ourselves to determining whether or not a given trait (in the phenotype) appears in one or both twins—which would, of course, be sufficient for a biogenetic analysis of certain diseases—but also observe the growth of the personality by means of the interaction between heredity and environment. This is, after the aforesaid, of prime significance. Hence we must give a special place within this over-all problem to the study of monozygotic twins in their early age. Unfortunately, so far very few reports have been published on this important subject.

I would like to refer here at least briefly to two investigations which are more detailed than is usually the case in the literature. Hahn's (1926) observations concern female adolescent twins whose general behavior was originally quite different. But in the course of their development they grew more and more similar due to a specific configuration of experiences. Since the two girls had earlier grown up under different influences, their original differences might, Hahn concludes, be explained on the basis of environmental influences. These twins, however, differed to a considerable extent also physically which may have been due to rickets. At any rate, we must be careful in our evaluation of the results because it could not be established with certainty whether or not the twins were really identical. In the second study, H. Meyer (1929) very thoroughly investigated two pairs of adolescent female identical twins. Following Lange, the author summarizes her impressions as follows: "one must look for the factors which are responsible for the existing differences not among psychic influences or among genetic conditions but among patent external damages."

Lange (1929) himself found on the basis of his research with (adult) practically healthy monozygotic twins that there is not the degree of conformity which Galton and others after him had assumed to exist, but that identical twins "must most frequently be very much alike in the deeper layers of their beings even if the visible differences are quite striking." Lassen (1931) investigated the "social and moral character traits" of a larger number of twins. She used the questionnaire method. Her subjects were mainly teachers and in some cases also parents. She found that identical twins are more similar than fraternal twins in terms of their moral and social behavior as measured by all characteristics investigated in this study.

The material about the intelligence of twins is already very extensive. Some earlier studies suffer from the fact that they compare same-sex twins with opposite-sex twins and not identical with fraternal twins. Hence the results cannot be utilized without reservations. Furthermore, according to Peters's (1925) findings, same-sex ordinary siblings (who are not twins) generally differ less in mental achievement than opposite-sex siblings. We are indebted to von Verschuer (1930) for a study which is free from this methodological mistake and which investigated not only the heredity of intellectual abilities in general but also the inheritance of different types of intelligence. His study is based on Rorschach protocols. Siemens (1924), Weitz (1925), and others reported earlier on concordances[2] and differences in school records of twins. Frischeisen-Köhler's recent research (1930) indicates that environmental influences (during school age) are most marked in girls during grades seven to nine and in boys during grades eight to nine. School achievement of identical twins showed much concordance. Bouterwek's (1932) studies yielded the same results. This author emphasizes serious illnesses of only one twin in his explanations of differences in behavior. I have discussed these questions in greater detail in another paper (Hartmann, 1933).

The characterological twin studies by Lottig (1931a) deserve our special interest. This is so far the only detailed publication about personality inventories of practically normal twins; in addition, it comprises a great amount of material. The author based his classification of "character traits" (character is here understood in the widest sense) on that of Klages (1928), who distinguishes "substance" (*Stoff*), "kind" (*Artung*), and "construction" (*Gefüge*) (matter, quality, structure). Of the numerous very important findings of this study I want to emphasize only the following: monozygotic twins showed very extensive concordance in terms of "substance" (memory, learning ability, concepts, etc.), somewhat less extensive concordance in terms of "kind" (drives, interests, etc.), and still clearer differences concerning "construction" (types of psychic processes, speed, moods, etc.). Concordance is in all three areas significantly greater in monozygotic than in dizygotic twins.

The question of whether behavioral differences in monozygotic twins are more clearly discernible in intelligence, temperament, or character is, however, still much under discussion. Such a comparison must encounter special difficulties. First of all, it is well known that

---

[2] Concordance refers to the correspondence of specific traits.

it is not easy to determine "intelligence" on the basis of intelligence tests. Furthermore, in testing intelligence character attitudes are probably often unintentionally tested too. Finally, different authors draw the line between character and temperament in different ways and often not very clearly. For example, Ewald (1932) expresses himself as follows: "one could say . . . with a grain of salt: that there is drive (or better "impulse" [*Drang*]), and how much of it, is a matter of temperament, into which direction the drive moves, is a matter of character." Such a conceptualization expresses clearly enough the interdependence of the two aspects of personality. In the analysis of my observations[3] I therefore never placed great emphasis on the distinction between traits of temperament and those of character. Like those of Lottig, my findings indicate that the behavior of monozygotic twins differs more in the area of character and temperament (in a narrower sense) than in the sphere of intelligence. I shall revert to this point in my discussion of my own results. The otherwise very informative observations of monozygotic twins who were raised separately (Muller, 1925; Newman, 1929, 1932) have not brought forth any unambiguous results concerning this issue. [. . . .]

It is impossible to come to any definitive conclusions because we have too few follow-up studies of separately raised identical twins and the investigations of their characters are too superficial. But the reach of paratypical factors can already be envisaged. The maximal extent of this reach has certainly not yet been delineated in the investigations published so far, since external factors were not extremely diverse in these cases. Newman concludes from his investigation of only three pairs of twins that the first and second pairs show on all tests, and the third pair shows on all tests but one, differences twice as great as those in monozygotic twins raised together and at least as much difference as dizygotic twins raised together. This seems to indicate that the influence of different environments upon identical

---

[3] These observations were reported in Parts I and II of the original paper and are not included in this translation.

heredity approximately equals the influence of identical environment upon different Anlagen. This is only a preliminary judgment. Newman adds that further experiences may require corrections, and states in another publication that Anlage is about twice as noticeable as environment. But we do not want to place too much weight upon either quantitative finding.

With regard to the problem of the relative modifiability of intelligence traits on the one hand and character and temperament traits on the other, some of Newman's observations agree with Muller's case in which the latter found greater differences in the character sphere; but other cases of Newman showed the opposite so that we cannot yet consider this discussion closed.

I want to emphasize that Newman's reports do not seem to indicate a clear-cut parallelism between "identical" and "different" environment and more or less concordance. There also exists no clear parallelism between differences in education and differences in intelligence or, for example, between variant socioeconomic environments and dissimilarities of temperament and character. Thus, in two pairs, one of which showed considerable educational differences while the other showed considerable differences in socioeconomic environment, there was both times greater variance in intelligence than in personality factors. This should not surprise us. We know that essential environmental factors are regularly missed in an ordinary anamnesis and that the concepts "school" or "social background (*milieu*)" encompass only a fraction of the actually effective environmental influences.

Hence, in the discussion of my own observations on twins I never speak of "identical environment." But I want to hint at least briefly at this issue, because it plays some part in the conclusions of many authors. Even Newman uses in his discussion the concept of "identical" or "similar" environment when, for instance, education, social background, profession coincide or resemble one another. Bouterwek argues in the same fashion, and Pfahler makes the judgment: "It is a commonly observed fact that two siblings who are raised in exactly the same atmosphere become entirely different personalities: one causative world—two different characters." Yet, the "parental situation" is never "identical" for siblings. This must be underlined also with respect to Hoffmann (1928) who believes that divergent development in children of the same parents is completely incomprehensible without recourse to Anlage. If one knows how fundamentally different the actually effective environment (thus, above all, the relation to parents and siblings) can be for children from the same family, one cannot support arguments which are based on such statements.

At this point we can continue a train of thought which I touched upon in my introduction: we cannot assume that a difference in the degree of similarity of mental traits in identical and fraternal twins is entirely reducible to idiotypical factors. A. and M. Holub (1933) recently also accepted this view. I explained this viewpoint by the tendency of identical twins to identify with each other. It is well known that on the average the characters of monozygotic twins show greater correspondences than those of dizygotic twins; but the derivation of this difference is by no means entirely clear. Since it is known that identification processes play an important role in character formation, one must be particularly cautious in this respect in personality studies of twins. Hence I limited myself to reporting observations of the personalities of identical twins.[4]

In the following summary of the results of my own observations[5] I deem it appropriate to emphasize those factors which relate to control of reality on the one hand and to control of instinctual drives on the other, i.e., everything concerned with socialization, professional life, sexuality, marriage, etc. We know today that these forms of behavior tell us frequently more about the structure of the per-

[4] For the report of these observations, see Parts I and II of the original paper.

[5] The original paper reports on ten pairs of identical twins (labeled I to X). I to III were psychotic, IV feeble-minded, V to VIII were "normal" adults, IX and X "normal" children. The part of the paper presented here is mainly based on the observations of V to VIII, but in some contexts I also refer to I to IV and to IX and X.

sonalities under investigation than we can learn from weighing one individual trait against another. Lange (1933) says the same when he states as a methodological directive for twin studies on normal subjects: "The original character is decisive in crucial moments of existence [*An den Wendepunkten des Daseins entscheidet das ursprungliche Wesen*]."

Let us begin with profession. The two pairs of twins aged nine must here, of course, be disregarded. Three of the remaining four pairs consist of twins who differ in their professions. If vocational training is included, the careers of twins VII and VIII separate during puberty and those of twins VI after the first Bar examination. Only our twins V do not different from each other in this respect. I want to emphasize that these findings disagree with other data reported in the psychological literature on twins, according to which the vocational choices of twins are mostly identical. Our twins differ also at least partially in their vocational interests and with regard to the central or peripheral importance their profession has within the total structure of their personalities. Occasionally (e.g., in pair VI) there are also important differences in the way in which they pursue their studies.

In pairs VI and VIII the twins belong to different social groups. The twin on the socially "lower" level is in both cases not quite satisfied with his position. The respective twin of VIII explicitly gives as the reason for his dissatisfaction his brother's greater success. The social position of twins V coincided like their life history in general. Twins VII occupy an intermediary position, but they too do not differ significantly from each other with respect to social level.

Some kind of difference between the twins can be noticed in each of the four pairs concerning their attitudes toward fellow humans. One of the two has always "greater difficulties in making contacts." Pairs VI and VIII show more obvious dissimilarities, while these very twins have in their social behavior many characteristics in common. Thus twins VI resemble each other in their pronounced status consciousness, and twins VIII in their congenial behavior and their being well liked by their colleagues. Twins V and VII are similar in some forms of social behavior and different in others. In no case can one speak of complete unlikeness. Twins V are both definite egotists. The less sociable of twins VI is at the same time the more altruistic one. Twins VIII do not differ much on the dimension egotism-altruism. Of the two adolescent pairs (which we can include in this comparison) one twin is more egotistic, the other more helpful in one pair; one more awkward in making contacts than the other in the second pair.

Concerning sexual behavior the available anamneses are of course incomplete. Our material offers approximately the following picture. The nature and the degree of the psychic crisis of puberty differ somewhat in twins VII and to a much greater extent in twins VIII where a neurosis in one of them complicates the situation. I shall come back to this matter. Concerning physical pubertal changes, all four pairs are conspicuous for their late development. I do not believe that one can make a general statement on the basis of these findings. They require further checking on a larger population, but the possibility of a connection of these findings with their being twins cannot be ruled out. Furthermore, it is noteworthy that twins V and VIII have definitely weak sexual desires, while those of twins VII are not strongly developed. The psychological factor of the twin relationship may also play some part. Both twins of pairs V, VI, and VIII practiced pubertal masturbation during the same period of time. Twins VI are clearly different in their sexual behavior. Until the age of twenty both were very much attached to their mother and very distant to other women. The attitude of one of them changed then, he became sexually less selective and now takes his relations with members of the opposite sex rather lightly. The twins themselves attribute this change to some sexual disappointment.

Concerning attitudes toward marriage I first want to distinguish only between "married" and "unmarried." We then find concordance in pairs V and VI. We may also include here pair VIII of which one twin has been married for a year and the other is presently engaged.

There is a difference between the twins of pair VII. If we include psychological attitudes toward the question of marriage, we find that twins V both present the same reasons for their rejection of marriage. In pair VI one twin wishes to have a family and children, while the other one does not seem to have such desires. Not only is one twin of pair VII married and the other not, but they also differ in their attitudes toward everything concerning marriage. If we include the prepsychotic personalities of the psychotic twins and the severely retarded twins, the picture does not change very much. One twin of pair I is married, the other is single. Both twins IV remained unmarried. (For the last pair we must take into consideration that they are both imbeciles.) The twins whose psychoses began before puberty must, of course, be disregarded here.

I have so far described how monozygotic twins differ from and resemble each other in dealing with certain tasks. Much concordance obviously exists concerning attitudes toward career, marriage, etc., but it does not go quite as far as some "concordance enthusiasts" believe. I have, however, so far neglected a very important issue which also belongs in this discussion of the mastery of drives, reality, etc., namely, the problem of neurosis.

Let us begin with the prepsychotic states of twins I, II, and III. One twin of pair I suffered during the eight years preceding the onset of the schizophrenic process (subsequent to a psychic trauma) from hysterical attacks. Twins III are reported to have "always been nervous." Neurotic signs which develop during a prepsychotic phase cannot simply be equated with other forms of neurosis. We do not yet know very much about the clinical and psychological meaning of prepsychotic neuroses and may learn more about this problem too from comparative studies of larger populations of twins. Often prepsychotic "nervousness" may presage the impending psychotic process. I cannot assume this to be the case for twins I. There is little to be said about the picture of the prepsychotic neurosis of twins I. It is in no way different from other hysterical attacks. However, the prepsychotic "nervousness" of twins III, which is further complicated by a number of strange characterological traits (cf. Hartmann and Stumpfl, 1930), impresses me rather as schizoid psychopathy than as true neurosis. The retarded, nonpsychotic twins IV had both suffered from typical childhood neurosis, which, however, was much more pronounced in one of them.

Turning now to the "practically normal" twins we do not find any reference to neuroticisms in the anamneses of twins V, but we must remember that in general little was known about their history. One of twins VI suffered between ages four and seven from phobias of darkness, ghosts, and burglars; his brother's symptoms, as far as they existed at all, were much less pronounced. The onset of the neurosis (darkness and ghost phobias, sleep disturbances, slight compulsive symptoms) was somewhat later in twins VII who both had had neurotic symptoms but noticeably differed with regard to their intensity. The sister who had been more neurotic in childhood recently showed again neurotic traits. Nothing is known of a childhood neurosis in twins VIII. But one of them suffered from a neurosis from age fourteen to the end of puberty: he became oversensitive, distractible, excitable, and enuretic; during the same period a diagnosis of stomach neurosis was made. His brother had no neurotic symptoms either then or later. Only one twin of each of the two adolescent pairs suffered from an infantile neurosis (onset age four for IX and age seven for X). The respective symptoms were timidity, oversensitivity, and excitability in the first case; and anxiety, insomnia, vomiting, and tic in the latter.

Our first reaction to these findings may be astonishment about the fact that—except for one pair with a very incomplete anamnesis—among these pairs of "practically normal" twins there is none without at least one twin who at least temporarily had had neurotic traits. Unfortunately Lange (1929) did not publish any details of his investigations with "normal" identical twins (except for the group of criminals). But his summary contains a statement which agrees with my findings to a certain degree. He writes about his observations on "healthy" identical twins: "We cannot find a single one whose mental life was not somehow damaged." My records contain mainly infantile and pubertal neuroses. Thus, our reaction will be less strong if we remember that childhood neuroses are counted among the kind of borderline states between normalcy and pathology which afflict an extremely large number of people. A statistical definition of "mental health" would perhaps even discount these symptoms and not regard them as pathological. If, however, we start with a concept of normalcy, then it is justified to consider these symptoms as pathological. I cannot state that this frequent incidence of childhood neuroses in monozygotic twins should simply be related to the twin relationship as long as we have no comparative studies about their possible special character or about possible differences in intensity. Nevertheless it must be admitted that such a connection is conceivable.

The next factor of interest is the extent of dissimilarity particularly concerning neurotic symptoms. We saw that only one twin among the first three pairs seemed to have a clear-cut neurosis (the hysterical woman of pair I). Both retarded twins gave evidence of neurotic symptoms during childhood, but the neurosis of one of them was much more serious. Differences in the intensity of neurosis were apparent also in twins VI and VII. Only one twin of pair VIII had a pubertal neurosis; there is, therefore, a difference between these two brothers even concerning the feature "neurosis." The same applies to the infantile neuroses of only one twin each of pairs IX and X. Complete concordance could be assumed only for twins V (absence of all neurotic symptoms), but in their case the above-mentioned objection arises. (I want to point out, in view of my further discussion, that in six cases out of seven, the neurotic or more neurotic twin was at the same time the more stubborn one.)

After what I just said one may wonder how much importance one should attribute to variant behavior among twins of whom one had a severe and the other a mild childhood neurosis. The answer to this question must depend on whether one considers childhood neurosis, as I do, as something afflicting the majority of men— including those who are healthy later on—or whether one considers it as an exceptional event of considerable pathognomonic significance.

So far few twin studies of pathology have been published which could be used for research concerning the etiology of neuroses. Some viewpoints and facts can be found in Weitz (1925), Löwenstein (1928), Hartmann and Stumpfl (1928), and Lottig (1931b). Lange's research (1933) speaks in favor of considerable paravariability of hysteria; but he also offered examples demonstrating astonishing concordance even in details of symptomatology. We also do not yet have a clear picture concerning obsessional-compulsive neurosis. There are so far no reports on psychological twin studies of infantile neuroses.

From the material collected I gained the impression that dissimilarities in neurotic symptomatology of identical twins are not only frequent but that neurotic symptoms are among the psychic characteristics of greatest variability. I shall now turn from the subject of neurosis to a discussion of intelligence, character, and temperament of our twins. I shall return to the possible connections between neurotic and characterologic dissimilarities in twins in my conclusion.

The traits which are usually combined under the heading of intelligence show far-reaching concordance. These findings correspond to those of several authors. There is concordance between memory, perception, and comprehension most of the time. The same can be said of school achievement. Occasionally school marks show a higher concordance even than achievement. It happens, of course, that one twin is intellectually a little further developed than the other or that more noticeable differences appear in one or the other grade. However, in none of the cases can one speak of significant differences. Among these cases I did not find such considerable differences in intelligence as I did in a pair of twins who later on became psychotic (Hartmann and Stumpfl, 1933). I have already pointed out that one must always take the possible effects of personality differences into consideration when one encounters differences in intelligence.

For most "talents," too, there is predominantly concordance. There were no clear artistic talents among the cases I studied. Both twins are either very, or moderately, or not at all musical. In this respect, too, one can observe now and then minor differences (e.g., in twins IX). Yet these differences are never as great as in the aforementioned twins who became psychotic. In this area the most frequent dissimilarity appears (in the majority of cases) in talent for drawing even in those twins of whom neither is left-handed. Differences in dexterity are also not rare.

Among qualities of character and temperament and among interests we find all shadings from the most striking resemblance to quite strong differences. Lottig reported particularly great concordance in "substance" of character, somewhat less in "kind," and still less in "construction" (following Klages), as we have seen. As stated above, I could corroborate the preponderant similarity of "substance" (comprehension, memory, etc.) as compared to other aspects of personality. The problem of the relative paravariability of the other aspects of personality is not easily solved. My observations make it questionable whether qualities of temperament ("construction") actually vary more than so-called "character traits." Though my data, too, indicate noticeable deviations in the area of temperament (twins VI and VIII, and during certain periods IX), some dissimilarities in character in a narrower sense impressed me even more. In relation to "interests," there were great variations between concordances and nonconcordances which are hard to explain. This concept combines psychologically very diverse tendencies many of which certainly count among the derivative peripheral forms of human behavior.

I used as an auxiliary method for the investigation of similarities and differences also the study of handwriting. I considered it appropriate to use the "blind" method, which means that the expert had no knowledge of the origin of the material or of the hypotheses underlying the study. The trained graphologist and colleague of mine (Dr. W. Marseille) who was kind enough to supply me with the analyses was presented with thirteen handwriting samples of which ten stemmed from five pairs of identical twins. I shall present the reports elsewhere. At this point, I want only to remark that

Marseille discussed in his reports of four pairs of twins the possibility that the handwritings of the corresponding twins were those of one and the same person; he also noticed a large degree of correspondence in the handwritings of the fifth pair. But I do not want to enter here upon the various problems raised by this part of the investigation. So far only few detailed reports on handwritings of monozygotic twins exist. The amount of concordance which I have found in my material seems quite unusual (Lange, 1929; Lottig, 1931a; Kockel, 1931).

In the evaluation of differences in behavior we must also take into consideration that a characteristic may appear clearly in one twin and even more clearly in the other. In other cases a characteristic is "present" in one and "absent" in the other. Concerning the meaning of "presence" or "absence" of the characteristics in question, we must refer to a general psychology of personality. Such distinctions (whether or not someone has a good memory; whether or not someone is courageous, ambitious, stubborn; in some cases also whether or not someone is neurotic) depend on all kinds of classificatory principles which I do not propose to analyze in detail. For purposes of an empirical study without an underlying theory of personality (or neurosis), it seems most appropriate to proceed from average scores which must then be evaluated as far as possible with respect to such factors as sex, age, social position, etc.

Among the character traits which differ in the subjects I noticed again and again one group which comprises approximately the following characteristics: orderliness (pedantry), cleanliness, stubbornness, handling of money, ambition and vanity. Differences in orderliness, stubbornness, and stinginess were, however, especially pronounced and most frequently demonstrable.[6] Sometimes these traits were present in both twins, but much more strikingly so in one of them as indicated above; in other identical twins I found rather large discrepancies between their behavior.

[6] These traits correspond to the "anal character" described by Freud (1908a).

For reasons which I shall discuss in a moment, these findings seem to me to be of empirical and methodological importance. Hence, I shall list here individually all twin pairs which belong in this category. I shall begin with those twins who later on became psychotic, although I have only few data on which to base an answer to this question.

Twins I are among those subjects whose anamnesis covering the prepsychotic phase is unfortunately only very cursory, but they too show dissimilarity concerning stubbornness.

Twins II gave already in childhood evidence of rather clear differences. One sister is stubborn, hard, withdrawn; the other, suggestible and ambitious.

Twins III are reported both to have been stubborn. Details are unknown.

Twins IV (severely mentally retarded) differ from each other also in this respect: one of them is more stubborn and pedantic than the other who is more concerned with cleanliness and is thriftier and more ambitious. Apart from the neurosis of one of them, these are the most essential differences observed between these twins.

Twins V are both thrifty, stubborn, and clean, but one of them is more orderly almost to the point of being pedantic. I should like to de-emphasize this discrepancy because the more pedantic twin is an epileptic.

Twins VI differ as follows: one is more stubborn, only the other one is pedantic and thrifty. The difference between them is very impressive, but it is not equally pronounced in all three traits. Both twins are stubborn, but one of them much more so. Thriftiness and orderliness appear, however, only in one of them. Apart from differences in sexual behavior this is the most decisive distinguishing factor encountered in these twins.

Twins VII differ also with respect to these traits but their distribution is another one. The sister who was more stubborn in childhood is still so and handles money more rationally. The other shows more orderliness and cleanliness. Except again for one single other characteristic, differences are most marked in regard to their respective attitudes toward money.

Twins VIII differ with respect to the traits under consideration in the following way: all these traits are found together and more pronounced in one of them. He is thriftier, more pedantic, more stubborn, and also pettier than his brother. But the difference is not sharp. Rather, the characteristics are more accentuated in one of them. As indicated earlier, these twins show more pronounced dissimilarity in terms of temperament.

In twins IX (the first of the nine-year-old pairs) one is more stubborn; the other, more orderly, more hot-tempered, and more egotistical.

Twins X show very obvious differences. One sister is more stubborn and orderly, but cannot hold on to money, while the other is thriftier and more ambitious. These differences are marked. This pair shows, moreover, other clearly pronounced differences.

Thus we evidently have here a cluster of traits subject to a large degree of paravariability (with due consideration of the small number of cases). I have noticed in this connection that this cluster is composed of traits to which psychoanalytic characterology has paid particular attention (cf. Freud, 1908a). As I briefly mentioned earlier, psychoanalysis emphasizes in its study of character development identification (with parents, siblings, etc.) on the one hand and sublimation processes on the other. The latter are considered to function as reaction formations against early infantile phases of drive development. The traits here under consideration (stubbornness, pedantry, thriftiness) are considered to result from such reaction formations.

The observations reported above show, however, that the traits which form this cluster are to a large extent independent of one another. Only in a single case (VIII) do we find all these traits more pronouncedly in one twin than in the other. Among the other pairs, one of these traits is always predominant in one twin and another trait of this cluster in the other twin. This separation goes astonishingly far. In one case the generally cleaner and more orderly sister is less orderly in her handling of money; in another case one twin is more pedantic, but the other handles money more carefully and is cleaner, etc.

These facts seem to me important for the following reason: "understanding"[7] characterologies which classify personality traits according to their understandable relationships can never do justice to such a far-reaching independence of forms of behavior which appear to be "similar." The data which I obtained from the twins make the existence of such an independence appear very probable, although they do not actually prove it. This is another argument in favor of individual analyses of the characterology in identical twins, the need for which I have already emphasized above. Such individual analyses are probably going to overthrow a number of past ideas about principles of classification of personalities.

I believe that the best way to do justice to the facts consists in introducing the concept of *substitution*[8] of those traits (stubbornness, pedantry, thriftiness). A simple reflection tells us that studies of the pathology and the psychology of twins represent the best method of investigating the possible substitution of diseases, character traits, etc. One can, for instance, investigate by means of twin studies whether the subcategories of schizophrenia or of manic-depressive psychosis can substitute for each other in the hereditary process. I may also mention here an observation I made (together with Stumpfl, 1933) on schizophrenic twins one of whom (already before becoming psychotic) had been highly talented in music, while the other was an excellent chess player. Here too the differentiation of a common factor could be envisaged.

I want to emphasize this train of thought because the findings to which I have drawn attention may serve as a model for characterological twin studies and for the possibilities they open up in general. We should then have to look for the character Anlagen in some

---

[7] See Chapter 18.

[8] This concept also includes the idea that, given the same Anlage, specific traits can substitute for each other.

primitive biological factors of the vital-psychic layers whose differentiation into character *traits* of the phenotype would be caused paratypically. The various possible outcomes of such a process of differentiation could then developmentally substitute for one another. It is, of course, inexact to state in a general way that experiential factors condition the selection among the traits which can possibly appear on the basis of the Anlage (of a cluster of traits). The totality of all other psychic and somatic Anlage factors must also be taken into consideration. The cluster of traits discussed here serves only as an illustrative example, because my data brought it to the surface. Further research is certainly going to uncover similar clusters of character traits. [. . . .]

My data do not seem to corroborate the existence of a correlation between low physical resistance (as far as it can be ascertained from the anamneses) and neurosis. On the other hand, at least some cases show a relation to the peculiarities of the family situation. This fact was already mentioned in the discussion of the different pairs of twins. "Feeling older" than the other twin, predominant identification with the father or with the mother, differentiation into a more "masculine" and a more "feminine" attitude may also play some part.

Besides, considerable differences in personality did not (or not always) imply that only one twin suffered from severe physical illnesses (or did so more frequently and more intensely). But another relationship imposed itself. The three pairs of which only one twin had a neurosis (VIII, IX, X) are also those into whose personality development we could gain some deeper insight; in one pair a clearer differentiation appeared only after puberty and the others were adolescents. These pairs are also among those who show relatively sharp differences in the personality structures of the two respective twins.

In these cases, I believe, the growth of character and temperamental differences out of the neurosis (or out of the factors which underlie its development) can be clearly observed. We shall have to wait for confirmations of this idea by other investigators and by further research. Such differences may, of course, partially or totally disappear again in the course of development. At any rate, in the course of my observations I frequently had the experience that extensive differences in the personalities of monozygotic twins, whenever they could be followed up in detail during their development, were related to their neurotic pathology. These findings may be considered to be more generally relevant to studies of twins if we remember how common infantile neuroses are, a fact that both my material and other authors have demonstrated. Thus it could be assumed that there exists a close relationship between differences concerning the feature "neurosis" (including its form, intensity, and course) and those concerning the character and temperament of identical twins. (We have seen how frequently monozygotic twins differ with regard to the feature "neurosis.") But perhaps a different hypothesis would be better and still in agreement with my findings: Among those paratypical factors which collaborate in the development of character and temperament the factors which underlie neuroses must be recognized as important.

The findings reported above have led to this conclusion. The step beyond it, toward a twin study of the etiology of neurosis, must be left to another series of observations.

Bibliography

Ach, N. (1905), *Über die Willenstätigkeit und das Denken*. Göttingen: Vandenhoeck & Ruprecht.

———— (1910), *Über den Willensakt und das Temperament*. Leipzig: Quelle & Meyer.

———— (1921), *Über die Begriffsbildung*. Hamburg: Buchner.

Adler, A. (1912), *The Neurotic Constitution*. New York: Dodd Mead, 1930.

———— (1920), *The Theory and Practice of Individual Psychology*. New York: Harcourt, Brace, 1940.

Adrian, E. D. (1946), The Mental and the Physical Origins of Behaviour. *Int. J. Psycho-Anal.*, 28.

Alexander, F. (1923), The Castration Complex in the Formation of Character. *Int. J. Psycho-Anal.*, 6.

———— (1933), The Relation of Structural and Instinctual Conflicts. *Psychoanal. Quart.*, 2.

Allers, R. (1925), Begriff und Methodik der Deutung. In: *Psychogenese und Psychotherapie körperlicher Symptome*, ed. O. Schwarz. Berlin: Springer.

———— & Teler, J. (1924), On the Utilization of Unnoticed Impressions in Associations. In: *Preconscious Stimulation in Dreams, Associations, and Images. Psychological Issues*, Monogr. 7. New York: International Universities Press, 1960.

Allport, G. (1937), *Personality*. New York: Henry Holt.

Alpert, A. (1949), Sublimation and Sexualization. *The Psychoanalytic Study of the Child*, 3/4.*

Angel, A., *see* Katan, A.

Arlow, J. A. (1952), Discussion of Dr. Fromm-Reichmann's paper. In: *Psychotherapy with Schizophrenics*, ed. E. B. Brody & F. C. Redlich. New York: International Universities Press.

Axelrad, S. & Maury, L. M. (1951), Identification as a Mechanism of Adaptation. In: *Psychoanalysis and Culture*, ed. G. B. Wilbur & W. Muensterberger. New York: International Universities Press.

Baade, W. (1915), Über die Vergegenwärtigung von psychischen Ereignissen durch Erleben, Einfühlung und Repräsentation, sowie über das Verhältnis

---

* *The Psychoanalytic Study of the Child*, currrently 18 Vols., ed. R. S. Eissler, A. Freud, H. Hartmann, M. Kris. New York: International Universities Press, 1945-1963.

der Jaspersschen Phänomenologie zur darstellenden Psychologie. *Z. Neurol. & Psychiat.*, 29.

Bak, R. C. (1939), Regression of Ego-Orientation and Libido in Schizophrenia. *Int. J. Psycho-Anal.*, 20.

———— (1943), Dissolution of the Ego, Mannerism and Delusion of Grandeur. *J. Nerv. & Ment. Dis.*, 98.

———— (1954), The Schizophrenic Defence against Aggression. *Int. J. Psycho-Anal.*, 35.

Bellak, L. & Smith, B. (1956), An Experimental Exploration of the Psychoanalytic Process. *Psychoanal. Quart.*, 25.

Bender, L. (1947), Childhood Schizophrenia: Clinical Study of 100 Schizophrenic Children. *Amer. J. Orthopsychiat.*, 17.

Benjamin, J. (1950), Methodological Considerations in the Validation and Elaboration of Psychoanalytical Personality Theory. *Amer. J. Orthopsychiat.*, 20.

Beres, D. & Obers, S. J. (1950), The Effects of Extreme Deprivation in Infancy on Psychic Structure in Adolescence. *The Psychoanalytic Study of the Child*, 5.

Bergler, E. (1945), On a Five-Layer Structure in Sublimation. *Psychoanal. Quart.*, 14.

Bergman, P. & Escalona, S. K. (1949), Unusual Sensitivities in Very Young Children. *The Psychoanalytic Study of the Child*, 3/4.

Bernfeld, S. (1931), Zur Sublimierungslehre. *Imago*, 17.

———— (1932), Der Begriff der Deutung in der Psychoanalyse. *Z. angew. Psychol.*, 52.

———— (1944), Freud's Earliest Theories and the School of Helmholtz. *Psychoanal. Quart.*, 13.

———— (1946), An Unknown Autobiographical Fragment by Freud. *Amer. Imago*, 4.

———— (1949), Freud's Scientific Beginnings. *Amer. Imago*, 6.

———— (1951), Sigmund Freud, M.D., 1882-1885, *Int. J. Psycho-Anal.*, 32.

———— (1953), Freud's Studies on Cocaine, 1884-1887. *J. Amer. Psychoanal. Assn.*, 1.

———— & Bernfeld, S. C. (1952), Freud's First Year in Practice, 1886-1887. *Bull. Menninger Clin.*, 16.

Betlheim, S. & Hartmann, H. (1924), Über Fehlreaktionen bei der Korsakowschen Psychose. *Arch. Psychiat.*, 72.

Bibring, E. (1936), The Development and Problems of the Theory of Instincts. *Int. J. Psycho-Anal.*, 22, 1941.

———— (1937), On the Theory of the Therapeutic Results of Psycho-Analysis. *Int. J. Psycho-Anal.*, 18.

Binswanger, L. (1922), *Allgemeine Psychologie*. Berlin: Springer.

Bibliography

Bleuler, E. (1911), *Dementia Praecox or the Group of Schizophrenias*. New York: International Universities Press, 1950.

Bonaparte, M. (1945), Notes on the Analytical Discovery of a Primal Scene. *The Psychoanalytic Study of the Child*, 1.

Bonhöffer, K. (1901), *Die akuten Geisteskrankheiten der Gewohnheitstrinker*. Jena: Fischer.

Bornstein, B. (1955), In Panel on Sublimation, reported by J. A. Arlow. *J. Amer. Psychoanal. Assn.*, 3.

Bouterwek, H. (1932), Ein Beitrag zur Zwillingspädagogik. *Arch. Rassen- & Gesellschaftsbiol.*, 26.

Breuer, J. & Freud, S. (1895), Studies on Hysteria. *Standard Edition*, 2.

Brierley, M. (1932), Some Problems of Integration in Women. *Int. J. Psycho-Anal.*, 13.

———— (1944), Notes on Metapsychology as Process Theory. *Int. J. Psycho-Anal.*, 25.

———— (1947), Notes on Psychoanalysis and Integrative Living. *Int. J. Psycho-Anal.*, 28.

———— (1952), Review of D. Rapaport, "Organization and Pathology of Thought." *Int. J. Psycho-Anal.*, 33.

Brodmann, K. (1902), Experimentelle und klinische Beiträge zur Psychopathologie der polyneuritischen Psychose. *J. Psychol. & Neurol.*, 1.

———— (1904), Experimentelle und klinische Beiträge zur Psychopathologie der polyneuritischen Psychose. *J. Psychol. & Neurol.*, 3.

Brower, D. (1949), The Problem of Quantification in Psychological Science. *Psychol. Rev.*, 56.

Brun, R. (1946), *General Theory of Neurosis*. New York: International Universities Press, 1951.

Bühler, C. (1930), *Kindheit und Jugend*. Leipzig: Hirzel.

———— (1954), The Reality Principle. *Amer. J. Psychother.*, 8.

Bühler, K. (1929), *Die Krise der Psychologie*. Jena: Fischer.

———— (1930), *The Mental Development of the Child. A Summary of Modern Psychological Theory*. New York: Harcourt, Brace.

———— (1934), *Sprachtheorie*. Jena: Fischer.

Buytendijk, F. J. J. (1955), Über den Schmerz. *Psyche*, 9.

Bychowski, G. (1943), Disorders in the Body Image in the Clinical Picture of Psychoses. *J. Nerv. Ment. Dis.*, 97.

———— (1952), *Psychotherapy of Psychosis*. New York: Grune & Stratton.

Cannon, W. B. (1932), *The Wisdom of the Body*. New York: Norton.

Delage, Y. (1891), Essai sur la théorie du rêve. *Rev. Scientifique*, 48.

Deri, F. (1939), On Sublimation. *Psychoanal. Quart.*, 8.

de Saussure, R. (1950), Present Trends in Psychoanalysis. *Congrès International de Psychiatrie, Paris 1950*, 5. Paris: Presses Universitaires de France.

Despert, J. L. (1940), A Comparative Study of Thinking in Schizophrenic Children and in Children of Preschool Age. *Amer. J. Psychiat.*, 97.

——— (1941), Thinking and Motility Disorder in a Schizophrenic Child. *Psychiat. Quart.*, 15.

Deutsch, F. (1952), Analytic Posturology. *Psychoanal. Quart.*, 21.

Deutsch, H. (1937), Absence of Grief. *Psychoanal. Quart.*, 6.

——— (1944), *Psychology of Women*, 1. New York: Grune & Stratton.

Dewey, J. (1922), *Human Nature and Conduct*. New York: Henry Holt.

——— (1939), *Theory and Valuation*. Chicago: University of Chicago Press.

Dilthey, W. (1924), Ideen über eine beschreibende und zergliedernde Psychologie. *Gesammelte Schriften*, 5. Leipzig: Teubner.

Dollard, J., Doob, L. W., Miller, N. E., & Sears, R. R. (1939), *Frustration and Aggression*. New Haven: Yale University Press.

——— & Miller, N. E. (1950), *Personality and Psychotherapy*. New York: McGraw-Hill.

Dorer, M. (1932), *Historische Grundlagen der Psychoanalyse*. Leipzig: Meiner.

Dorsey, J. (1943), Some Considerations on Psychic Reality. *Int. J. Psycho-Anal.*, 24.

Durfee, H. & Wolf, K. M. (1933), Anstaltspflege und Entwicklung im ersten Lebensjahr. *Z. Kinderforsch.* 42/43.

Ebbinghaus, H. (1896), Über erklärende und beschreibende Psychologie. *Z. Psychol. Neurol. Sinnesorg.*, 9.

Eidelberg, L. (1940), Instinctual Vicissitudes and Defense against Instincts. *Studies in Psychoanalysis*. New York: International Universities Press, 2nd ed., 1952.

Einstein, A. (1950), *Out of My Later Years*. New York: Philosophical Library.

Eissler, K. R. (1953), Notes upon the Emotionality of a Schizophrenic Patient and Its Relation to Problems of Technique. *The Psychoanalytic Study of the Child*, 8.

Ellis, A. (1950), An Introduction to the Principles of Scientific Psychoanalysis. *Genet. Psychol. Monogr.*, 41.

——— (1956), An Operational Reformulation of Some of the Basic Principles of Psychoanalysis. In: *The Foundations of Science and the Concepts of Psychology and Psychoanalysis*, ed. H. Feigl & M. Scriven. Minneapolis: University of Minnesota Press.

Erikson, E. H. (1940), Problems of Infancy and Early Childhood. *Cyclopedia of Medicine, Surgery and Specialties*. Philadelphia: Davis.

Ewald, G. (1924), *Temperament und Charakter*. Berlin: Springer.

——— (1932), *Biologische und "reine" Psychologie im Persönlichkeitsaufbau, Prinzipelles und Paralleles (Temperament und Charakter, II. Teil); zugleich ein Beitrag zur somatologischen Unterlegung der Individualpsychologie.* Berlin: Karger.

Bibliography

Federn, P. (1929), The Ego as Subject and Object in Narcissism. *Ego Psychology and the Psychoses.* New York: Basic Books, 1952.

————— (1930), The Reality of the Death Instinct, Especially in Melancholia. Remarks on Freud's book *Civilization and Its Discontents. Psychoanal. Rev.,* 19, 1932.

————— (1936), On the Distinction between Healthy and Pathological Narcissism. *Ego Psychology and the Psychoses.* New York: Basic Books, 1952.

————— (1938), The Undirected Function in the Central Nervous System. *Int. J. Psycho-Anal.,* 19.

Feigl, H. (1949), Some Remarks on the Meaning of Scientific Explanation. In: *Readings in Philosophical Analysis,* ed. H. Feigl & W. Sellars. New York: Appleton-Century.

Fenichel, O. (1931), *Hysterien und Zwangsneurosen.* Vienna: Internationaler psychoanalytischer Verlag.

————— (1941), *Problems of Psychoanalytic Technique.* New York: Psychoanalytic Quarterly, Inc.

————— (1945), *The Psychoanalytic Theory of Neurosis.* New York: Norton.

Ferenczi, S. (1924), *Thalassa: Theory of Genitality.* New York: Psychoanalytic Quarterly, Inc.

Fisher, C. (1954), Dreams and Perception. *J. Amer. Psychoanal. Assn.,* 2.

————— (1956), Dreams, Images and Perception. *J. Amer. Psychoanal., Assn.,* 4.

————— (1957), A Study of the Preliminary Stages of the Construction of Dreams and Images. *J. Amer. Psychoanal. Assn.,* 5.

————— (1960), Introduction to *Preconscious Stimulation in Dreams, Associations, and Images. Psychological Issues,* Monogr. 7. New York: International Universities Press.

Flescher, J. (1951), *Mental Health and the Prevention of Neurosis.* New York: Liveright.

Flew, A. (1956), Motives and the Unconscious. In: *The Foundations of Science and the Concepts of Psychology and Psychoanalysis,* ed. H. Feigl & M. Scriven. Minneapolis: University of Minnesota Press.

Foulkes, S. H., *see* Fuchs, S. H.

French, T. (1936), Learning in the Course of a Psychoanalytic Treatment. *Psychoanal. Quart.,* 5.

————— (1937), Reality and the Unconscious. *Psychoanal. Quart.,* 6.

————— (1941), Goal, Mechanism and Integrative Field. *Psychosom. Med.,* 3.

————— (1945), The Integration of Social Behavior. *Psychoanal. Quart.,* 14.

Frenkel-Brunswik, E. (1949), Intolerance and Ambiguity as an Emotional and Cognitive Personality Variable. *J. Personal.,* 18.

————— (1954), Psychoanalysis and the Unity of Science. *Proc. Amer. Acad. Sci.,* 53.

Freud, A. (1936), *The Ego and the Mechanisms of Defense.* New York: International Universities Press, 1946.

―――― (1945), Indications for Child Analysis. *The Psychoanalytic Study of the Child*, 1.

―――― (1949), Aggression in Relation to Emotional Development: Normal and Pathological. *The Psychoanalytic Study of the Child*, 3/4.

―――― (1951a), Observations on Child Development. *The Psychoanalytic Study of the Child*, 6.

―――― (1951b), The Contributions of Psychoanalysis to Genetic Psychology. *Amer. J. Orthopsychiat.*, 21.

―――― (1951c), Negativism and Emotional Surrender. Paper read at the 17th International Psycho-Analytical Congress, Amsterdam.

―――― (1952), The Mutual Influences in the Development of Ego and Id. *The Psychoanalytic Study of the Child*, 7.

―――― (1954a), Psychoanalysis and Education. *The Psychoanalytic Study of the Child*, 9.

―――― (1954b), In: Problems of Infantile Neurosis: A Discussion. *The Psychoanalytic Study of the Child*, 9.

―――― & Dann, S. (1951), An Experiment in Group Upbringing. *The Psychoanalytic Study of the Child*, 6.

Freud, S. (1887-1902), *The Origins of Psychoanalysis, Letters to W. Fliess*. New York: Basic Books, 1954.

―――― (1895), Project for a Scientific Psychology. *The Origins of Psychoanalysis, Letters to W. Fliess* (1887-1902). New York: Basic Books, 1954.

―――― (1896), Further Remarks on the Neuro-Psychoses of Defence. *Standard Edition 3.**

―――― (1900), The Interpretation of Dreams. *Standard Edition*, 4 & 5.

―――― (1901), The Psychopathology of Everyday Life. *Standard Edition*, 6.

―――― (1905), Three Essays on the Theory of Sexuality. *Standard Edition* 7.

―――― (1908a), Character and Anal Erotism. *Standard Edition*, 9.

―――― (1908b), 'Civilized' Sexual Morality and Modern Nervous Illness. *Standard Edition*, 9.

―――― (1909), Notes upon a Case of Obsessional Neurosis. *Standard Edition*, 10.

―――― (1911a), Formulations on the Two Principles of Mental Functioning. *Standard Edition*, 12.

―――― (1911b), Psycho-analytical Notes upon an Autobiographical Account of a Case of Paranoia (Dementia Paranoides). *Standard Edition*, 12.

―――― (1911-15 [1914]), Papers on Technique. *Standard Edition*, 12.

―――― (1913), The Claims of Psycho-Analysis to Scientific Interest. *Standard Edition*, 13.

―――― (1913-14), Totem and Taboo. *Standard Edition*, 13.

* *The Standard Edition of the Complete Psychological Works of Sigmund Freud*, 24 Vols., translated and edited by James Strachey. London: Hogarth Press and the Institute of Psycho-Analysis, 1953-

Bibliography

———— (1914a), On Narcissism: An Introduction. *Standard Edition,* 14.

———— (1914b), On the History of the Psycho-Analytic Movement. *Standard Edition,* 14.

———— (1915a), Instincts and Their Vicissitudes. *Standard Edition,* 14.

———— (1915b), The Unconscious. *Standard Edition,* 14.

———— (1915c), Repression. *Standard Edition,* 14.

———— (1916-17), *A General Introduction to Psychoanalysis.* New York: Garden City Publ. Co., 1943.

———— (1917a [1915]), A Metapsychological Supplement to the Theory of Dreams. *Standard Edition,* 14.

———— (1917b), A Difficulty in the Path of Psycho-Analysis. *Standard Edition,* 17.

———— (1919), "A Child is Being Beaten." *Standard Edition,* 17.

———— (1920), Beyond the Pleasure Principle. *Standard Edition,* 18.

———— (1921), Group Psychology and the Analysis of the Ego. *Standard Edition,* 18.

———— (1923a), The Ego and the Id. *Standard Edition,* 19.

———— (1923b), Psycho-Analysis. *Standard Edition,* 18.

———— (1924a [1923]), Neurosis and Psychosis. *Standard Edition,* 19.

———— (1924b), The Economic Problem in Masochism. *Standard Edition,* 19.

———— (1924c), The Dissolution of the Oedipus Complex. *Standard Edition,* 19.

———— (1924d), The Loss of Reality in Neurosis and Psychosis. *Standard Edition,* 19.

———— (1926a), Inhibitions, Symptoms and Anxiety. *Standard Edition,* 20.

———— (1926b), The Question of Lay Analysis. *Standard Edition,* 20.

——— (1927), Letter to Marie Bonaparte. In: *The Life and Work of Sigmund Freud,* 3 by E. Jones. New York: Basic Books, 1957, p. 131.

———— (1930 [1929]), Civilization and Its Discontents. *Standard Edition,* 21.

———— (1932), *New Introductory Lectures on Psychoanalysis.* New York: Norton, 1933.

———— (1936), A Disturbance of Memory on the Acropolis. *Collected Papers,* 5. London: Hogarth Press, 1950.

———— (1937a), Analysis Terminable and Interminable. *Collected Papers,* 5. London: Hogarth Press, 1950.

———— (1937b), Constructions in Analysis. *Collected Papers,* 5. London: Hogarth Press, 1950.

———— (1937-39), *Moses and Monotheism.* New York: Vintage Books, 1955.

———— (1940a [1938]), *An Outline of Psychoanalysis.* New York: Norton, 1949.

———— (1940b [1938]), Splitting of the Ego in the Defensive Process. *Collected Papers,* 5. London: Hogarth Press, 1950.

Friedmann, M. (1920), *Über die Natur der Zwangsvorstellungen und ihre Beziehungen zum Willensproblem.* Wiesbaden: Bergmann.

Fries, M. & Lewi, B. (1938), Interrelated Factors in Development. *Amer. J. Orthopsychiat.,* 8.

Frischeisen-Köhler, I. (1930), Untersuchungen an Schulzeugissen von Zwillingen. *Z. angew. Psychol.,* 37.

Frumkes, G. (1953), Impairment of the Sense of Reality as Manifested in Psychoneurosis and Everyday Life. *Int. J. Psycho-Anal.,* 34.

Fuchs, S. H. (1936), Zum Stand der heutigen Biologie. *Imago,* 22.

Geleerd, E. R. (1946), A Contribution to the Problem of Psychoses in Childhood. *The Psychoanalytic Study of the Child,* 2.

Glover, E. (1931), Sublimation, Substitution and Social Anxiety. *Int. J. Psycho-Anal.,* 12.

———— (1935), A Developmental Study of Obsessional Neurosis. *Int. J. Psycho-Anal.,* 16.

———— (1943), The Concept of Dissociation. *Int. J. Psycho-Anal.,* 24.

———— (1947), Basic Mental Concepts. *Psychoanal. Quart.,* 16.

———— (1949), *Psychoanalysis.* New York & London: Staple Press.

Greenacre, P. (1954), In: Problems of Infantile Neurosis: A Discussion. *The Psychoanalytic Study of the Child,* 9.

Gregor, A. (1909), Beiträge zur Psychopathologie des Gedächtnisses. *Mschr. Psychiat. & Neurol.,* 25.

———— & Römer, H. (1907), Beiträge zur Kenntnis der Gedächtnisstörung bei der Korsakowschen Psychose. *Mschr. Psychiat. & Neurol.,* 21.

Grinker, R. R. (1954), *Psychosomatic Research.* New York: Norton.

Groos, K. (1901), *The Play of Man.* New York: D. Appleton.

Gruhle, H. W. (1924), Konstitution und Charackter. *Naturwissenschaften,* 12.

Grünthal, E. (1923), Zur Kenntnis der Psychopathologie des Korsakowschen Symptomenkomplexes. *Mschr. Psychiat. & Neurol.,* 53.

Hahn, R. (1926), Persönlichkeitsstudien bei einem 8jährigen Zwillingspaar. *Z. Kinderforsch.,* 32.

Hart, H. (1948), Sublimation and Aggression. *Psychiat. Quart.,* 22.

Hartmann, H. (1927), *Die Grundlagen der Psychoanalyse.* Leipzig: Thieme.

———— (1929), Über genetische Charakterologie, insbesondere über psychoanalytische, *Jb. Charakterol.,* 6.

———— (1933), Über Zwillingsforschung in der Psychiatrie. *Wien. Med. Wschr.,* 83.

———— (1939a), *Ego Psychology and the Problem of Adaptation.* New York: International Universities Press, 1958.

———— (1939b), Psycho-analysis and the Concept of Health. *Int. J. Psycho-Anal.,* 20.

Bibliography

———— (1934-1935), Psychiatrische Zwillingsstudien. *Jb. Psychiat. Neurol.,* 50 & 51.

———— (1944), Psychoanalysis and Sociology. In: *Psychoanalysis Today,* ed. S. Lorand. New York: International Universities Press.

———— (1947), On Rational and Irrational Action. In: *Psychoanalysis and the Social Sciences,* 1. New York: International Universities Press.

———— (1948), Comments on the Psychoanalytic Theory of Instinctual Drives. *Psychoanal. Quart.,* 17.

———— (1950a), Comments on the Psychoanalytic Theory of the Ego. *The Psychoanalytic Study of the Child,* 5.

———— (1950b), Psychoanalysis and Developmental Psychology. *The Psychoanalytic Study of the Child,* 5.

———— (1950c), The Application of Psychoanalytic Concepts to Social Science. *Psychoanal. Quart.,* 19.

———— (1951), Technical Implications of Ego Psychology. *Psychoanal. Quart.,* 20.

———— (1952), The Mutual Influences in the Development of Ego and Id. *The Psychoanalytic Study of the Child,* 7.

———— (1953), Contribution to the Metapsychology of Schizophrenia. *The Psychoanalytic Study of the Child,* 8.

———— (1954), In: Problems of Infantile Neurosis: A Discussion. *The Psychoanalytic Study of the Child,* 9.

———— (1955), Notes on the Theory of Sublimation. *The Psychoanalytic Study of the Child,* 10.

———— (1956a), Notes on the Reality Principle. *The Psychoanalytic Study of the Child,* 11.

———— (1956b), The Development of the Ego Concept in Freud's Work. *Int. J. Psychol-Anal.,* 37.

———— (1958), Comments on the Scientific Aspects of Psychoanalysis. *The Psychoanalytic Study of the Child,* 13.

———— (1959), Psychoanalysis as a Scientific Theory. In: *Psychoanalysis, Scientific Method, and Philosophy* (The Second Annual New York University Institute of Philosophy), ed. S. Hook. New York: New York University Press.

———— (1960a), *Psychoanalysis and Moral Values.* New York: International Universities Press.

———— (1960b), Towards a Concept of Mental Health. *Brit. J. Med. Psychol.,* 33.

———— & Kris, E. (1945), The Genetic Approach in Psychoanalysis. *The Psychoanalytic Study of the Child,* 1.

———— ———— & Loewenstein, R. M. (1946), Comments on the Formation of Psychic Structure. *The Psychoanalytic Study of the Child,* 2.

———————————— (1949), Notes on the Theory of Aggression. *The Psychoanalytic Study of the Child*, 3/4.

———————————— (1951), Some Psychoanalytic Comments on "Culture and Personality." In: *Psychoanalysis and Culture*, ed. G. B. Wilbur & W. Muensterberger. New York: International Universities Press.

———————————— (1953), The Function of Theory in Psychoanalysis. In: *Drives, Affects, Behavior*, ed. R. M. Loewenstein. New York: International Universities Press.

———— & Loewenstein, R. M. (1962), Notes on the Superego. *The Psychoanalytic Study of the Child*, 16.

———— & Stumpfl, F. (1928), Ein zwillingspathologischer Beitrag zur Frage: Idiotypus, Paratypus und Neurose. *Wien. Med. Wschr.*, 78.

———————————— (1930), Psychosen bei eineiigen Zwillingen. *Z. Neurol. & Psychiat.*, 123.

Hartmann, M. (1925), *Biologie und Philosophie*. Berlin: Springer.

Heisenberg, W. (1952), *Philosophic Problems of Nuclear Science*. New York: Pantheon.

Hellpach, W. (1921), Das fränkische Gesicht. *Sitzungsberichte der Heidelberger Akademie der Wissenschaften*, 1.

Hendrick, I. (1942), Instinct and the Ego during Infancy. *Psychoanal. Quart.*, 11.

———— (1943), Work and the Pleasure Principle. *Psychoanal. Quart.*, 12.

———— (1946), *Facts and Theories of Psychoanalysis*. New York: Knopf.

———— (1951), Early Development of the Ego: Identification in Infancy. *Psychoanal. Quart.*, 20.

Hermann, I. (1929), Das Ich und das Denken. *Imago*, 15.

———— (1936), Sich Anklammern—Auf Suche Gehen. *Int. Z. Psychoanal.*, 22.

Hilgard, E. (1952), Experimental Approaches to Psychoanalysis. In: *Psychoanalysis as Science*, ed. E. Pumpian-Mindlin. Palo Alto: Stanford University Press.

Hitschmann, E. (1947), The History of the Aggression-Impulse. *Samiksa*, 1.

Hoffer, W. (1949), Mouth, Hand and Ego Integration. *The Psychoanalytic Study of the Child*, 3/4.

———— (1950), Development of the Body Ego. *The Psychoanalytic Study of the Child*, 5.

———— (1952), The Mutual Influences in the Development of Ego and Id: Earliest Stages. *The Psychoanalytic Study of the Child*, 7.

Hoffman, H. (1926), *Das Problem des Charakteraufbaus*. Berlin: Springer.

———— (1928), *Charakter und Umwelt*. Berlin: Springer.

Holt, R. R. (1962), A Critical Examination of Freud's Concept of Bound vs. Free Cathexis. *J. Amer. Psychoanal. Assn.*, 10.

Holub, A. & Holub, M. (1933), Zur Frage der Charakterentwicklung bei Zwillingen. *Int. Z. Individ.-Psychol.*, 11.

Bibliography

Husserl, E. (1921), *Logische Untersuchungen.* I: Prolegomena zur reinen Logik. II: Untersuchungen zur Phänomenologie und Theorie der Erkenntnis. Halle: Niemeyer.

Isakower, O. (1938), A Contribution to the Pathopsychology of Phenomena Associated with Falling Asleep. *Int. J. Psycho-Anal.,* 19.

Jackson, E. B. & Klatskin, E. H. (1950), Rooming-In Research Project: Development and Methodology of Parent-Child Relationship Study in a Clinical Setting. *The Psychoanalytic Study of the Child,* 5.

James, W. (1890), *The Principles of Psychology.* New York: Dover, 1950.

Jaspers, K. (1913), "Kausale" und "verständliche" Zusammenhänge zwischen Schicksal und Psychose bei der Dementia Praecox (Schizophrenie). *Z. Neurol. & Psychiat.,* 14.

———— (1920), *Allgemeine Psychopathologie,* 2nd ed. Berlin: Springer.

Jokl, R. (1950), Preservation of Sublimation in Classical Psychoanalytic Procedure. *Bull. Menninger Clin.,* 14.

Jones, E. (1913), The Attitude of the Psycho-Analytic Physician towards Current Conflicts. *Papers on Psycho-Analysis.* London: Ballière, Tindall & Cóx, 3rd ed., 1923.

———— (1924), *Social Aspects of Psycho-Analysis.* London: Williams & Norgate.

———— (1936), Psycho-Analysis and the Instincts. *Brit. J. Psychol.,* 26.

———— (1941), Evolution and Revolution. *Int. J. Psycho-Anal.,* 22.

———— (1953-57), *The Life and Work of Sigmund Freud,* 3 Vols. New York: Basic Books.

Kanner, L. (1943), Autistic Disturbances of Affective Contact. *Nerv. Child,* 2.

———— (1949), Problems of Nosology and Psychodynamics of Early Infantile Autism. *Amer. J. Orthopsychiat.,* 19.

Kardiner, A. (1945), *The Psychological Frontiers of Society.* New York: Columbia University Press.

Katan, A. (1937), The Role of "Displacement" in Agoraphobia. *Int. J. Psycho-Anal.,* 32, 1951.

Katan, M. (1953), Schreber's Prepsychotic Phase. *Int. J. Psycho-Anal.,* 34.

Klages, L. (1928), *Grundlagen der Charakterkunde.* Leipzig: Barth.

Klein, G. (1954), Need and Regulation. In: *Nebraska Symposium on Motivation,* ed. M. R. Jones. Lincoln: University of Nebraska Press.

———— (1958), Cognitive Control and Motivation. In: *Assessment of Human Motives,* ed. G. Lindzey. New York: Rinehart.

Klein, M. (1923a), The Role of the School in the Libidinal Development of the Child. *Contributions to Psycho-Analysis.* London: Hogarth Press, 1948.

———— (1923b), Infant Analysis. *Int. J. Psycho-Anal.,* 7.

———— (1930), The Importance of Symbol-Formation in the Development of the Ego. *Int. J. Psycho-Anal.,* 11.

———— (1932), *The Psycho-Analysis of Children.* London: Hogarth Press.

———— (1947), Notes on Some Schizoid Mechanisms. *Int. J. Psycho-Anal.*, 28.

———— (1948), *Contributions to Psycho-Analysis, 1921-1945.* London: Hogarth Press.

Kockel, H. (1931), Handschriftenstudien bei Zwillingen. *Dtsch. Z. ges. & gericht. Med.*, 18.

Koffka, K. (1912), *Zur Analyse der Vostellungen und ihrer Gesetze.* Leipzig: Quelle & Meyer.

Kogerer, H. (1920), Beitrag zur Psychologie der Gedächtnisstörungen. *Allg. Z. Psychiat.*, 76.

Kohnstamm, O. (1917), Über das Krankheitsbild der retro-anterograden Amnesie und die Unterscheidung des spontanen und des lernenden Merkens. *Mschr. Psychiat. & Neurol.*, 41.

Kretschmer, E. (1918), *Der sensitive Beziehungswahn.* Berlin: Springer.

———— (1931), *Körperbau und Charakter.* Berlin: Springer.

Kris, E. (1934), The Psychology of Caricature. *Psychoanalytic Explorations in Art.* New York: International Universities Press, 1952.

———— (1941), The "Danger" of Propaganda. *Amer. Imago,* 2.

———— (1947), The Nature of Psychoanalytic Propositions and Their Validation. In: *Freedom and Experience,* ed. S. K. Hook & M. R. Konwitz. Ithaca, N.Y.: Cornell University Press.

———— (1950a), On Preconscious Mental Processes. *Psychoanalytic Explorations in Art.* New York: International Universities Press, 1952.

———— (1950b), Notes on the Development and on Some Current Problems of Psychoanalytic Child Psychology. *The Psychoanalytic Study of the Child,* 5.

———— (1950c), Introduction to *The Origins of Psychoanalysis, Sigmund Freud's Letters to Wilhelm Fliess.* New York: Basic Books, 1954.

———— (1951a), The Development of Ego Psychology. *Samiksa,* 5.

———— (1951b), Opening Remarks on Psychoanalytic Child Psychology. *The Psychoanalytic Study of the Child,* 6.

———— (1952), *Psychoanalytic Explorations in Art.* New York: International Universities Press.

———— (1955), Neutralization and Sublimation: Observations on Young Children. *The Psychoanalytic Study of the Child,* 10.

———— & Speier, H. (1944), *German Radio Propaganda.* London, New York, Toronto: Oxford University Press.

Kris, M. (1957), The Use of Prediction in a Longitudinal Study. *The Psychoanalytic Study of the Child,* 12.

Kronfeld, A. (1920), *Das Wesen der psychiatrischen Erkenntnis.* Berlin: Springer.

———— (1928), Fragestellungen und Methoden der Charakterologie. In: *Konstitution und Charakter,* ed. M. Hirsch. Leipzig: Kabitsch.

Kubie, L. (1948), Instinct and Homeostasis. *Psychosom. Med.,* 10.

———— (1952), Problems and Techniques of Psychoanalytic Validation and

Bibliography

Progress. In: *Psychoanalysis as Science,* ed. E. Pumpian-Mindlin. Palo Alto: Stanford University Press.

———— (1953), Some Implications for Psychoanalysis of Modern Concepts of the Organization of the Brain. *Psychoanal. Quart.,* 22.

Lampl-de Groot, J. (1947), Development of the Ego and Superego. *Int. J. Psycho-Anal.,* 28.

———— (1956), Psychoanalytische Trieblehre. *Psyche,* 10.

Lange, J. (1929), Leistungen der Zwillingspathologie für die Psychiatrie. *Allg. Z. Psychiat.,* 90.

———— (1933), Zwillingsbildung und Entwicklung der Persönlichkeit. *Naturwissensch.,* 21.

Lantos, B. (1955), On the Motivation of Human Relationships. *Int. J. Psycho-Anal.,* 36.

Lashley, K. S. (1938), Experimental Analysis of Instinctual Behavior. *Psychol. Rev.,* 45.

Lassen, M.-Th. (1931), Zur Frage der Vererbung "sozialer und sittlicher Charakteranlagen" (auf Grund von Fragebögen über Zwillinge). *Arch. Rassen- & Gesellschaftsbiol.,* 25.

Lasswell, H. (1930), *Psychopathology and Politics.* Chicago: University of Chicago Press.

Levey, H. (1939), A Critique of the Theory of Sublimation. *Psychiatry,* 2.

Lewin, K. (1926), Comments Concerning Psychological Forces and Energies, and the Structure of the Psyche. In: *Organization and Pathology of Thought,* ed. & tr. D. Rapaport. New York: Columbia University Press, 1951.

———— (1935), *A Dynamic Theory of Personality.* New York: McGraw-Hill.

———— (1936), *Principles of Topological Psychology.* New York: McGraw-Hill.

Lindsley, E. O. (1957), Operant Behavior During Sleep: A Measure of Depth of Sleep. *Science,* 126.

Loewald, H. W. (1951), Ego and Reality. *Int. J. Psycho-Anal.,* 32.

Loewenstein, R. M. (1950), Conflict and Autonomous Ego Development During the Phallic Phase. *The Psychoanalytic Study of the Child,* 5.

———— (1956), Some Remarks On the Rôle of Speech in Psycho-Analytic Technique. *Int. J. Psycho-Anal.,* 37.

———— (1957), Some Thoughts on Interpretation in the Theory and Practice of Psychoanalysis. *The Psychoanalytic Study of the Child,* 12.

Lottig, H. (1931a), *Hamburger Zwillingsstudien.* Leipzig: Barth.

———— (1931b), Zwillingsstudien zur Frage der psychopathischen Reaktionsbreite. *Deutsch Z. Nervenh.,* 117-119.

Lowenfeld, H. (1944), Some Aspects of a Compulsion Neurosis in a Changing Civilization. *Psychoanal. Quart.,* 13.

Löwenstein, O. (1928), Muskeltonus und Konstitution. Experimentelle Zwillingsuntersuchungen zur Kenntnis der psychophysischen Konstitution. *Mschr. Psychiat. & Neurol.,* 70.

Mahler, M. S. (1952), On Child Psychosis and Schizophrenia: Autistic and Symbiotic Infantile Psychoses. *The Psychoanalytic Study of the Child,* 7.

———— & Elkisch, P. (1953), Some Observations on Disturbances of the Ego in a Case of Infantile Psychosis. *The Psychoanalytic Study of the Child,* 8.

———— Ross, J. R., Jr., & Fries, de Z., (1949), Clinical Studies in Benign and Malignant Cases of Childhood Psychosis (Schizophrenia-Like). *Amer. J. Orthopsychiat.,* 19.

Malamud, W. & Linder, F. E. (1931), Dreams and Their Relationship to Recent Impressions. *Arch. Neurol. & Psychiat.,* 25.

Mannheim, K. (1935), *Man and Society in an Age of Reconstruction.* New York: Harcourt, Brace, 1940.

Menninger, K. A. (1938), *Man Against Himself.* New York: Harcourt, Brace.

———— (1942), Love Against Hate. New York: Harcourt, Brace.

———— (1954), Psychological Aspects of the Organism Under Stress, Parts I and II. *J. Amer. Psychoanal. Assn.,* 2.

Meyer, H. (1929), Studien an Jugendlichen Zwillingen. *Z. Neurol. & Psychiat.,* 120.

Meynert, T. (1884), *Psychiatrie.* Vienna: Braumüller.

Mönckemöller, O. (1898), Casuistischer Beitrag zur sogenannten polyneuritischen Psychose. *Allg. Z. Psychiat.,* 84.

Morris, C. (1938), The Foundation of the Theory of Signs. *Encyclopedia of the Unified Sciences.* Chicago: Chicago University Press.

Müller, G. (1911), Zur Analyse der Gedächtnistätigkeit und des Vorstellungsverlaufes. *Z. Psychol.,* Suppl. Vol. 5.; Suppl. Vol. 8, 1913; Suppl. Vol. 9, 1917. Leipzig: Barth.

———— & Pilzecker, A. (1900), Experimentelle Beiträge zur Lehre vom Gedächtnis. *Z. Psychol.* (suppl. Vol. 1). Leipzig: Barth.

Müller-Braunschweig, K. (1925), Desexualization and Identification. *Psychoanal. Rev.,* 13, 1926.

Muller, H. J. (1925), Mental Traits and Heredity. *J. Hered.,* 16.

Murphy, G. (1947), *Personality.* New York: Harper.

Murphy, L. B. (1944), Childhood Experience in Relation to Personality Development. In: *Personality and the Behavior Disorders,* ed. J. McV. Hunt. New York: Ronald Press.

Myers, C. S. (1945), The Comparative Study of Instincts. *Brit. J. Psychol.,* 36.

Newman, H. H. (1929), Mental and Physical Traits of Identical Twins Reared Apart. *J. Hered.,* 20.

———— (1932), Mental and Physical Traits of Identical Twins Reared Apart; Case V, Twins "B" and "D"; Twins Ada and Ida. *J. Hered.,* 23.

Nietzsche, F. (1882), Joyful Wisdom. *The Complete Works of Friedrich Nietzsche,* ed. O. Levy. New York: Macmillan, 1924.

Bibliography

Nunberg, H. (1920), On the Catatonic Attack. *Practice and Theory of Psychoanalysis.* New York: International Universities Press, 1960.
———— (1928), Problems of Therapy. *Practice and Theory of Psychoanalysis.* New York: International Universities Press, 1960.
———— (1930), The Synthetic Function of the Ego. *Practice and Theory of Psychoanalysis.* New York: International Universities Press, 1960.
———— (1932), *Principles of Psychoanalysis.* New York: International Universities Press, 1955.
———— (1937), Theory of Therapeutic Results of Psychoanalysis. *Int. J. Psycho-Anal.,* 18.
———— (1939), Ego Strength and Ego Weakness. *Practice and Theory of Psychoanalysis.* New York: International Universities Press, 1960.
Orr, D. W. (1942), Is There a Homeostatic Instinct? *Psychoanal. Quart.,* 11.
Panel: Theories of Psychoanalysis (1949), reported by E. Kris. *Bull. Amer. Psychoanal. Assn.,* 5.
Parsons, T. (1950), Psychoanalysis and Social Structure. *Psychoanal. Quart.,* 19.
———— & Shils, E. (1951), *Toward a General Theory of Action.* Cambridge: Harvard University Press.
Peters, W. (1925), *Die Vererbung geistiger Eigenschaften.* Jena: Fischer.
Pfahler, G. (1932), *Vererbung als Schicksal.* Leipzig: Barth.
Piaget, J. (1937a), Primary Factors Determining Intellectual Evolution from Childhood to Adult Life. *Factors Determining Human Behavior.* Cambridge: Harvard University Press.
———— (1937b), *The Construction of Reality in the Child.* New York: Basic Books, 1954.
Pick, A. (1913), *Die agrammatischen Sprachstörungen.* Berlin: Springer.
———— (1915), Beiträge zur Pathologie des Denkverlaufes beim Korsakoff. *Z. Neurol. Psychiat.,* 28.
Pious, W. L. (1949), The Pathogenic Process in Schizophrenia. *Bull. Menninger Clin.,* 13.
Pötzl, O. (1917), The Relationship Between Experimentally Induced Dream Images and Indirect Vision. In: *Preconscious Stimulation in Dreams, Associations, and Images. Psychological Issues,* Monogr. 7. New York: International Universities Press, 1960.
Rank, B. (1949), Aggression. *The Psychoanalytic Study of the Child,* 3/4.
———— & MacNaughton, D. (1950), A Clinical Contribution to Early Ego Development. *The Psychoanalytic Study of the Child,* 5.
Rapaport, D. (1950), On the Psycho-Analytic Theory of Thinking. *Int. J. Psycho-Anal.,* 31.
———— ed. (1951), *Organization and Pathology of Thought.* New York: Columbia University Press.
———— (1958), *The Structure of Psychoanalytic Theory: A Systematizing Attempt. Psychological Issues,* Monogr. 6. New York: International Universities Press, 1960.

——— & Gill, M. M. (1959), The Points of View and Assumptions of Meta-psychology. *Int. J. Psycho-Anal.*, 40.

Redl, F. & Wineman, D. (1951), *Children Who Hate.* Glencoe, Ill.: Free Press.

Redlich, F. C. (1952), The Concept of Schizophrenia and Its Implications for Therapy. In: *Psychotherapy with Schizophrenics,* ed. E. B. Brody & F. C. Redlich. New York: International Universities Press.

Reich, W. (1933), *Character Analysis.* New York: Orgone Institute, 1945.

Ribble, M. (1943), *The Rights of Infants.* New York: Columbia University Press.

Richter, C. (1941), Biology of Drives. *Psychosom. Med.*, 3.

Rickert, H. (1921a), *Die Grenzen der naturwissenschaftlichen Begriffsbildung.* Tübingen: Mohr, 3rd & 4th ed.

——— (1921b), *Kulturwissenschaft und Naturwissenschaft.* Tübingen: Mohr, 4th and 5th ed.

Robert, W. (1886), *Der Traum als Naturnotwendigkeit erklärt.* Hamburg: H. Seippel.

Roffenstein, G. (1922), Zum Problem des Unbewussten. *Z. ges. Neurol. & Psychiat.*, 80.

——— (1923), Experimentelle Symbolträume. *Z. ges. Neurol. & Psychiat.*, 87. Translated in part in: *Organization and Pathology of Thought,* ed. D. Rapaport. New York: Columbia University Press, 1951.

——— (1926), *Das Problem des psychologischen Verstehens. Ein versuch über die Grundlagen von Psychologie, Psychoanalyse und Individualpsychologie.* Stuttgart: Püttmann.

Róheim, G. (1943), Sublimation. *Psychoanal. Quart.*, 12.

Rosen, V. (1953), On Mathematical "Illumination" and the Mathematical Thought Process. *The Psychoanalytic Study of the Child.*, 8.

Rosenfeld, H. (1947), Analysis of a Schizophrenic State with Depersonalization. *Int. J. Psycho-Anal.*, 28.

——— (1950), Note on the Psychopathology of Confusional States in Chronic Schizophrenias. *Int. J. Psycho-Anal.*, 31.

——— (1952), Notes on the Psycho-Analysis of the Super-Ego Conflict of an Acute Schizophrenic Patient. *Int. J. Psycho-Anal.*, 33.

Schilder, P. (1920), Über Gedankenentwicklung. *Z. Neurol. & Psychiat.*, 59.

——— (1922), Bemerkungen über die Psychologie des paralytischen Grössen-wahns. *Z. Neurol. & Psychiat.*, 74.

——— (1923), *Medical Psychology.* New York: International Universities Press, 1953.

——— (1924), Zur Psychologie epileptischer Ausnahmezustände (mit beson-deren Berücksichtigung des Gedächtnisses). *Allg. Z. Psychiat.*, 80.

——— (1938), *The Image and Appearance of the Human Body.* New York: International Universities Press, 1950.

Schlote, W. (1930), Über die Bevorzugung unvollendeter Handlungen. *Z. Psychol.*, 117.

Bibliography

Schmideberg, M. (1938), After the Analysis. . . . *Psychoanal. Quart.*, 7.
Schneider, K. (1922), Versuch über die Arten der Verständlichkeit. *Z. Neurol. & Psychiat.*, 75.
Schrötter, K. (1911), Experimentelle Träume. *Zbl. Psychoanal.*, 2.
Schur, M. (1961), Animal Research. 4. Discussion: A Psychoanalyst's Comments. *Amer. J. Orthopsychiat.*, 31.
Scott, W. C. M. (1948), Some Embryological, Neurological, Psychiatric and Psycho-Analytic Implications of the Body-Scheme. *Int. J. Psycho-Anal.*, 29.
Sears, R. (1943), Survey of Objective Studies of Psychoanalytic Concepts. *Soc. Sci. Res. Council Bull.*, 51.
Selye, H. (1950), *Stress*. Montreal: Acta.
Selz, O. (1913), Die Gesetze der produktiven Tätigkeit. *Arch. Psychol.*, 27.
——— (1922), *Zur Psychologie des produktiven Denkens: eine experimentelle Untersuchung*. Bonn: Cohen.
Siemens, H. W. (1924), *Die Zwillingspathologie*. Berlin: Springer.
Simmel, G. (1921), *Die Probleme der Geschichtsphilosophie*. Leipzig: Duncker & Humblot, 4th edition.
Spitz, R. A. (1945), Hospitalism: An Inquiry into the Genesis of Psychiatric Conditions in Early Childhood. *The Psychoanalytic Study of the Child*, 1.
——— (1950), Relevancy of Direct Infant Observation. *The Psychoanalytic Study of the Child*, 5.
——— & Wolf, K. M. (1949), Auto-erotism. *The Psychoanalytic Study of the Child*, 3/4.
Spranger, E. (1924), *Psychologie des Jugendalters*. Leipzig: Quelle & Meyer.
Sterba, R. (1930), Zur Problematik der Sublimierungslehre. *Int. Z. Psychoanal.*, 16.
——— (1934), The Fate of the Ego in Analytic Therapy. *Int. J. Psycho-Anal.*, 15.
——— (1942), *Introduction to the Psychoanalytic Theory of Libido*. New York: Nervous & Mental Disease Publishing Co.
Stern, W. (1919), *Die menschliche Persönlichkeit*. Leipzig: Barth.
Strachey, J. (1953), Note in the *Standard Edition*, 7, p. 156. London: Hogarth Press.
Sullivan, H. S. (1953), *The Interpersonal Theory of Psychiatry*. New York: Norton.
Székely, L. (1951), Die Realität in der Auffassung Freuds. *Theoria*, 17.
Utitz, E. (1925), *Charakterologie*. Charlottenburg: Pan-Verlag R. Heisse.
von Mises, L. (1944), The Treatment of "Irrationality" in the Social Sciences. *Philos. phenomenol. Res.*, 4.
von Mises, R. (1939), *Kleines Lehrbuch des Positivismus*. The Hague: van Stockum & Zoon.
von Verschuer, O. (1930), Erbpsychologische Untersuchungen an Zwilligen. *Z. ind. Abstamm. & Vererbungslehre*, 54.

Waelder, R. (1929), *Psychological Aspects of War and Peace.* New York: Columbia University Press, 1939.

———— (1930), The Principle of Multiple Function. *Psychoanal. Quart.,* 5, 1936.

———— (1932), The Psychoanalytical Theory of Play. *Psychoanal. Quart.,* 2, 1933.

———— (1936a), Bedeutung des Werkes Sigmund Freuds für die Sozial- und Rechtswissenschaften. *Revue internationale de la théorie du droit,* 10.

———— (1936b), The Problem of Freedom in Psycho-Analysis and the Problem of Reality-Testing. *Int. J. Psycho-Anal.,* 17.

———— (1951), Structure of Paranoid Ideas. *Int. J. Psycho-Anal.,* 30.

Wagner-Jauregg, J. (1889), Über einige Erscheinungen im Bereiche des Zentralnervensystems, welche nach Wiederbelebung Erhängter beobachtet werden. *Jb. Psychiat. & Neurol.,* 8.

Weber, M. (1921), *Wirtschaft und Gesellschaft.* Tübingen: J. C. B. Mohr. English translation by T. Parsons: *The Theory of Social and Economic Organization.* New York: Oxford University Press, 1947.

———— (1922), *Gesammelte Aufsätze zur Wissenschaftslehre.* Tübingen: J. C. B. Mohr.

Weil, A. P. (1953a), Certain Severe Disturbances of Ego Development in Childhood. *The Psychoanalytic Study of the Child,* 8.

———— (1953b), Clinical Data and Dynamic Considerations in Certain Cases of Childhood Schizophrenia. *Amer. J. Orthopsychiat.,* 23.

Weiss, E. (1950), Reality and Reality Testing. *Samiksa,* 4.

Weiss, P. (1949), The Biological Basis of Adaptation. In: *Adaptation,* ed. J. Romano. Ithaca: Cornell University Press.

Weitz, W. (1925), Studien an eineiigen Zwillingen. *Z. klin. Med.,* 101.

Wexler, M. (1951), The Structural Problem in Schizophrenia: Therapeutic Implications. *Int. J. Psycho-Anal.,* 32.

Winnicott, D. W. (1953), Transitional Objects and Transitional Phenomena. *Int. J. Psycho-Anal.,* 34.

Wisdom, J. (1953), *Philosophy and Psycho-Analysis.* New York: Philosophical Library.

Wittels, F. (1943), Struggles of a homosexual in pre-Hitler Germany. *J. Crim. Psychopathol.,* 4.

Zeigarnik, B. (1927), Über das Behalten von erledigten und unerledigten Handlungen. *Psychol. Forsch.,* 9.

Zilboorg, G. (1930), Affective Reinterpretation in the Schizophrenias. *Arch. Neurol. & Psychiat.,* 24.

———— (1941), The Sense of Reality. *Psychoanal. Quart.,* 10.

———— (1943), Psychiatry as a Social Science. *Amer. J. Psychiat.,* 99.

Bibliographical Notes

CHAPTER 1 was originally published in the *International Journal of Psycho-Analysis*, 20:308-321, 1939.

CHAPTER 2 was originally published in *Psychoanalysis Today*, ed. S. Lorand. New York: International Universities Press, 1944, pp. 326-341.

CHAPTER 3 was originally published in *Psychoanalysis and the Social Sciences*, 1:359-392. New York: International Universities Press, 1947.

CHAPTER 4 was originally published in *The Psychoanalytic Quarterly*, 17:368-388, 1948.

CHAPTER 5 was originally published in *The Psychoanalytic Quarterly*, 19:385-392, 1950; it was reprinted in *The Yearbook of Psychoanalysis*, 7:81-87. New York: International Universities Press, 1951.

CHAPTER 6 was a contribution to the Panel on "Psychoanalysis and Developmental Psychology," held at the Annual Meeting of the American Psychoanalytic Association, Detroit, April 29. It was originally published in *The Psychoanalytic Study of the Child*, 5:7-17. New York: International Universities Press, 1950.

CHAPTER 7 was read at the Annual Meeting of the American Psychoanalytic Association, Montreal, May, 1949. It was originally published in *The Psychoanalytic Study of the Child*, 5:74-96, 1950. New York: International Universities Press, 1950.

CHAPTER 8 was read at the Midwinter Meeting of the American Psychoanalytic Association, New York, December, 1948. It was published in *The Psychoanalytic Quarterly*, 20:31-43, 1951.

CHAPTER 9 was read at the Symposium on "The Mutual Influences in the Development of Ego and Id," held at the Seventeenth Congress of the International Psycho-Analytical Association, Amsterdam, August 8, 1951. It was published in *The Psychoanalytic Study of the Child*, 7:9-30. New York: International Universities Press, 1952.

CHAPTER 10 was a contribution to the Symposium on "Theory of Schizo-phrenia," held at the Eighteenth Psycho-Analytical Congress, London, July, 1953. It was originally published in *The Psychoanalytic Study of the Child*, 8:177-197. New York: International Universities Press, 1953.

CHAPTER 11 was part of a panel discussion on "Problems of Infantile Neurosis," held by the New York Psychoanalytic Society and Institute at Arden House, New York, on May 8, 1954. It was originally published in *The Psychoanalytic Study of the Child*, 9:31-36. New York: International Universities Press, 1954.

CHAPTER 12 was the Introduction to the Panel on "Sublimation," held at the Midwinter Meeting of the American Psychoanalytic Association, New York, December 4, 1954. It was originally published in *The Psychoanalytic Study of the Child*, 10:9-29. New York: International Universities Press, 1955.

CHAPTER 13 was read at the Freud Centenary Sessions of the Hampstead Child-Therapy Clinic, London, May 4, 1956. It was originally published in *The Psychoanalytic Study of the Child*, 11:31-53. New York: International Universities Press, 1956.

CHAPTER 14 was read at the Freud Centenary Meeting of the British Psycho-Analytical Society, May 5, 1956; it was also read at the Midwinter Meeting of the American Psychoanalytic Association, December, 1956. It was originally published in the *International Journal of Psycho-Analysis*, 37:425-438, 1956.

CHAPTER 15 was the A. A. Brill Lecture of the New York Psychoanalytic Society, March 25, 1958. It was originally published in *The Psychoanalytic Study of the Child*, 13:127-146. New York: International Universities Press, 1958.

CHAPTER 16 was a contribution to the Proceedings of the Second Annual New York University Institute of Philosophy, New York, March 28-29, 1958. It was originally published in *Psychoanalysis: Scientific Method and Philosophy. A Symposium,* ed. S. Hook. New York: New York University Press, 1959; also New York: Grove Press and London: Evergreen Books, 1960, pp. 3-37.

CHAPTER 17 was first published in German as "Über Fehlreaktionen bei der Korsakowschen Psychose." It was written together with S. Betlheim. The English translation by David Rapaport appeared first in *Organization and Pathology of Thought,* ed. D. Rapaport. New York: Columbia University Press, 1951, pp. 288-307.

CHAPTER 18 was originally published as Chapter 3, "Verstehen und Erklären," of *Die Grundlagen der Psychoanalyse.* Leipzig: Georg Thieme, 1927, pp. 36-61. It is here published in English for the first time.

Bibliographical Notes

CHAPTER 19 was originally published as "Ein experimenteller Beitrag zur Psychologie der Zwangsneurose. Über das Behalten erledigter und unerledigter Handlungen." *Jahrbücher für Psychiatrie und Neurologie,* 50:243-278. It is here published in English for the first time.

CHAPTER 20 was originally a part of "Psychiatrische Zwillingsstudien," which appeared in *Jahrbücher für Psychiatrie and Neurologie,* Vol. 50, 1934, and Vol. 51, 1935. It is here published in English for the first time.

Author Index

Ach, N., 411, 446
Adler, A., 87, 245, 288, 299, 395, 398, 402, 424, 446
Adrian, E. D., 322, 446
Alexander, F., 133, 238, 446
Allers, R., 372, 408-409, 446
Allport, G., 123, 152, 222, 330, 446
Alpert, A., 237, 446
Angel, A., see Katan, A.
Aristotle, 43, 63
Arlow, J. A., 199, 446, 448
Axelrad, S., 255, 446

Baade, W., 379-380, 446
Bak, R. C., 186, 206, 447
Bellak, L., 347, 447
Bender, L., 183, 447
Benjamin, J., 348, 447
Bentham, J., 242
Beres, D., 163, 447
Bergler, E., 238, 447
Bergman, P., 170, 204, 447
Bernfeld, S., 216-217, 270, 282, 322, 343, 447
Bernfeld, S. C., 447
Betlheim, S., vii, 315, 353-368, 447
Bibring, E., 72, 86, 135, 159, 270, 447
Binswanger, L., 379, 388-389, 394, 399, 447
Bleuler, E., 448
Bonaparte, M., 337, 448
Bonhöffer, K., 363, 368, 448
Bornstein, B., 213, 230, 448
Bouterwek, H., 429-431, 448
Brandt, L. W., vii
Brentano, F., 278
Breuer, J., 233, 275-277, 339, 448
Brierley, M., 132, 175, 203, 216, 220, 226, 448
Brodmann, K., 354, 448
Brody, E. B., 446, 461
Brower, D., 314, 448
Bruecke, E., 322

Brun, R., 78, 448
Bühler, C., 83, 246, 426, 448
Bühler, K., 189, 222, 448
Buytendijk, F. J. J., 264, 448
Bychowski, G., 167, 194, 448

Cannon, W. B., 85, 291, 329, 448

Dann, S., 163, 219, 451
Darwin, C., 276
Delage, Y., 405-406, 410, 448
Dembo, T., 348
Deri, F., 237, 448
de Fries, Z., 188, 459
de Saussure, R., 255, 448
Despert, J. L., 183, 449
Deutsch, F., 336, 449
Deutsch, H., 124, 210, 449
Dewey, J., 44, 449
Dilthey, W., 369, 373-377, 386, 449
Dollard, J., 349, 449
Doob, W. L., 449
Dorer, M., 271-275, 449
Dorsey, J., 266, 449
Drever, J., 76
Durfee, H., 162, 449

Ebbinghaus, H., 354, 364, 374, 449
Eidelberg, L., 172, 449
Einstein, A., 259, 276, 299, 310-312, 449
Eissler, K. R., 188, 449
Eissler, R. S., 446
Elkisch, P., 459
Ellis, A., 312, 345, 449
Erikson, E. H., 108, 246, 449
Escalona, S. K., 170, 204, 447
Ewald, G., 423-424, 430, 449

Fechner, G. T., 85, 273
Federn, P., 126, 153, 412, 417, 450
Feigl, H., 309, 449, 450
Fenichel, O., 147, 171, 225, 232-234, 237, 417, 450

Ferenczi, S., 144, 248, 450
Fisher, C., 315, 409, 450
Flescher, J., 237, 450
Flew, A., 312, 450
Fliess, W., 245, 270, 280, 284, 288, 300
Forel, A., 76
Foulkes, S. H., *see* Fuchs, S. H.
French, T., 43, 116-117, 450
Frenkel-Brunswick, E., 309, 316, 332, 344, 348, 450
Freud, A., ix, 13, 30, 44, 99, 106, 111-112, 115-116, 123-124, 144-145, 149, 156-158, 162-164, 172, 177-178, 186-187, 190, 199, 207-213, 219-221, 238, 245, 253, 256, 283, 348, 446, 450-451
Freud, S., ix *et passim*
  bibliographical references to, 448, 451-452
  case histories of, 284, 302, 342; *see also* Schreber case, Wolf Man
  concept of "principles," 84-86
  concept of unconscious processes, 305, 320-321
  development of ego concept of, 113-117, 268-296
  evaluation of his work, 298-300
  influence of Herbart and Nietzsche on, 273-274
  influence of Meynert on, 274-275
  interest in philosophy of science, 332-333
  knowledge of experimental methods, 332, 341
  phases in development of psychoanalytic theory, 280-284
  scientific aim of, 104
  use of "meaningful," 400
Freud quoted:
  on analysts, 6
  on anxiety, 88, 128
  on attention cathexis, 173
  on censorship, 136-137, 254
  on character, 440, 442
  on complementary series, 421
  on countercathexis, 132-133
  on defense, 124, 138-140
  on disposition to conflict, 133, 165, 175, 198
  on dream, 406-407, 410
  on ego, 39, 107, 113-116, 156-157, 166, 384
  on ego working with desexualized energy, xii-xiii, 170, 222-224, 226, 227
  on emendation of theory, 141
  on free aggression and conflict, 133, 165, 175, 198
  on frustration, 199
  on group psychology, 31, 51, 95
  on helplessness of infant, 22, 73, 81, 161, 255, 291
  on hereditary core of ego, x, 120, 169, 205, 222
  on id, 107, 120, 156-157, 159, 166
  on indifferent energy, xiii, 227
  on infantile neurosis, 208-209
  on instinctual drives, 72-74, 396
  on mental functioning, 57, 241-243, 249
  on moral masochist, 27
  on narcissism, 126
  on neurosis and psychosis, 182, 184, 201
  on obsessional neurosis, 417-418
  on pleasure principle, 242-245, 249
  on psychoanalytic technique, 7, 67, 142-143, 148
  on psychosis, 182-183, 191, 193
  on reality principle, 39, 242-247
  on relation of psychoanalysis to sociological problems, 30-31
  on repression, 198-199, 235, 249
  on resistance, 133
  on result of analysis, 59
  on self-preservation, xiii, 82, 85, 119, 135, 168, 226, 250, 254
  on social factors in psychology and pathology, 25
  on sublimation, 128-129, 216, 220, 222-223, 228, 230, 237
  on thinking, 41, 115, 261
  on undifferentiated ego-id, 166
Friedmann, M., 416, 453
Fries, M., 121, 453
Frischeisen-Köhler, I., 429, 453
Frumkes, G., 266, 453
Fuchs, S. H., 13, 453

Galton, F., 428
Geleerd, E. R., 183, 453
Gide, A., 258
Gill, M. M., 308, 461
Glover, E., 6, 103, 118, 125, 139-140, 174, 204-206, 216, 224, 232, 237, 453

Goethe, J. W., 16
Greenacre, P., 207-208, 211-213, 453
Gregor, A., 354, 363, 453
Grinker, R. R., 211, 453
Groos, K., 89, 453
Gruhle, H. W., 427, 453
Grünthal, E., 354, 453

Hahn, R., 427-428, 453
Hamilton, 371
Hart, H., 226, 235, 238, 453
Hartmann, H., ix-x, 5, 10-11, 15, 39-41,
    50, 64-65, 80-83, 87, 97, 103, 112,
    116-124, 128, 147, 152, 160, 164-
    170, 178-179, 192, 195, 222, 226-
    227, 236, 242, 247-248, 252, 258,
    265, 304-305, 309-312, 315, 322-
    323, 328-330, 333, 337, 340, 343-
    348, 389, 397, 401, 419, 422, 426,
    429, 436-438, 443, 446, 447, 453-
    455
Hartmann, M., 402, 455
Hegel, G. W. F., 156
Heisenberg, W., 340, 455
Hellpach, W., 427, 455
Helmholtz, 322
Hendrick, I., 84-85, 116, 121, 170, 185,
    235, 455
Herbart, J. F., 273-274
Hermann, I., 186, 455
Hilgard, E., 348-349, 455
Hitschmann, E., 86, 455
Hoenig, 371
Hoffer, W., 105, 161, 167, 187, 455
Hoffman, H., 423-424, 432, 455
Holt, R. R., 233, 455
Holub, A. & M., 432, 455
Hook, S. K., 454, 457
Hunt, J. McV., 348, 459
Husserl, E., 371-374, 455-456

Isakower, O., 161, 456

Jackson, E. B., 162, 456
James, W., 456
Janet, P., 277, 339
Jaspers, K., 369-380, 385-389, 393-394,
    399-401, 456
Jokl, R., 218, 456
Jones, E., 3, 16, 86, 216, 235, 270-275,
    280-281, 291, 339, 452, 456
Jones, M. R., 456

Jung, C. G., 193, 281, 299

Kanner, L., 183, 456
Kardiner, A., 97, 456
Katan, A., 160, 190, 212, 456
Katan, M., 202, 456
Klages, L., 422, 429, 439, 456
Klatskin, E. H., 162, 456
Klein, G., 316, 338, 456
Klein, M., 109, 172, 183, 187, 198, 203,
    219-220, 226, 235, 266, 456-457
Kockel, H., 440, 457
Koffka, K., 345, 378, 457
Kogerer, H., 366, 457
Kohnstamm, O., 457
Konwitz, M. R., 457
Kretschmer, E., 422-424, 457
Kris, E., ix, 53-55, 60, 80, 87, 97-105,
    112, 121, 128, 131, 147, 162-163,
    166, 174, 177-179, 192, 195, 199,
    219-222, 226-234, 239, 270, 275,
    292, 298, 304-305, 322-323, 330,
    333, 337, 340-341, 346-348, 446,
    454-455, 457, 460
Kris, M., 109, 337, 457
Kronfeld, A., 376-379, 388, 422, 457
Kubie, L. S., 85, 323, 347-349, 457-458

Lampl-de Groot, J., 170, 178, 226, 295,
    458
Lange, J., 428, 433, 436-440, 458
Lantos, B., 295, 458
Lashley, K. S., 76-78, 458
Lassen, M.-Th., 428, 458
Lasswell, H., 458
Levey, H., 216, 458
Levy, D., 348
Levy, O., 459
Lewi, B., 121, 453
Lewin, K., 340, 348, 409-411, 418, 458
Linder, F. E., 407-408, 459
Lindsley, E. O., 314, 458
Lindzey, G., 456
Lipps, T., 377
Loewald, H. W., 245, 458
Loewenstein, R. M., 65, 80, 87, 97, 105-
    107, 112, 121, 128, 147-149, 166,
    179, 192, 195, 226-227, 257, 304-
    306, 322-323, 333, 340, 343, 454-
    455, 458
Lottig, H., 429-430, 438-440, 458
Lowenfeld, H., 57, 458
Löwenstein, O., 438, 458-459

Author Index

MacNaughton, D., 105, 190, 460
Mahler, M. S., 183-188, 459
Malamud, W., 407-408, 459
Malebranche, N., 82
Mannheim, K., 10, 55, 459
Marseille, W., 439-440
Masserman, J., 348
Maury, L. M., *see* Newman, L. M.
Mayer-Gross, W., 389
Mendel, G., 296
Meyer, H., 428, 459
Menninger, K. A., 85-87, 128, 170, 226-227, 459
Meynert, T., 274-275, 282, 459
Miller, N. E., 348-349, 449
Moebius, P. J., 368
Mönckemöller, O., 354, 459
Morgan, L., 76
Morris, C., 189, 459
Muensterberger, W., 446, 455
Müller, G., 354, 459
Muller, H. J., 430-431, 459
Müller-Braunschweig, K., 122, 459
Murphy, G., 75, 459
Murphy, L. B., 163, 459
Myers, C. S., 76-77, 459

Needleman, J., vii
Newman, H. H., 430-431, 459
Newman, L. M., vii, 255, 446
Newton, I., 299
Nietzsche, F., 274, 280-284, 384-385, 459
Nunberg, H., 7, 62, 117, 131, 139-140, 147-149, 164, 185, 195, 198, 235-236, 264, 417, 460

Obers, S. J., 163, 447
Orr, D. W., 85, 460

Parsons, T., 90-96, 266, 460, 463
Peters, W., 428, 460
Pfahler, G., 425, 431-432, 460
Piaget, J., 187-188, 255-257, 460
Pick, A., 353, 364, 460
Pilzecker, A., 354, 459
Pious, W. L., 195, 460
Pötzl, O., 353, 407-408, 460
Pumpian-Mindlin, E., 455

Rank, B., 105, 108, 178, 183-185, 190, 460

Rapaport, D., vii-ix, 131, 174, 203, 228, 233, 238, 255, 302, 308, 320, 345-349, 353, 358-364, 458, 460-461
Redl, E., 258, 461
Redlich, F. C., 185, 446, 461
Reich, W., 147, 461
Ribble, M., 163, 461
Richter, C., 86, 461
Rickert, H., 370, 379, 461
Robert, W., 404-406, 461
Roffenstein, G., 315, 367, 383, 461
Róheim, G., 221, 461
Römer, H., 354, 363, 453
Rosen, V., 221, 461
Rosenfeld, H., 195, 198, 461
Ross, J. R., Jr., 188, 459

Scheler, M., 379
Schilder, P., 167, 353-354, 366-367, 389, 399-400, 461
Schlote, W., 411, 461
Schmideberg, M., 6, 462
Schneider, K., 389, 395, 462
Schopenhauer, A., 274
Schrötter, K., 367, 462
Schur, M., 76, 462
Schwarz, O., 402, 446
Scott, W. C. M., 167, 462
Scriven, M., 449
Sears, R. R., 348, 449, 462
Sellars, W., 450
Selye, H., 462
Selz, O., 462
Shils, E., 92, 266, 460
Siemens, H. W., 429, 462
Simmel, G., 370, 462
Smith, B., 447
Socrates, 63
Speier, H., 55, 457
Spitz, R. A., 105-107, 118, 163, 173, 246, 462
Spranger, E., 369, 402, 462
Stekel, W., 384
Sterba, R., 146, 216-217, 232, 237, 462
Stern, W., 420-421, 425-427, 462
Stevens, S. S., 314
Strachey, J., 270, 280, 284, 451, 462
Stumpfl, F., 436-438, 443
Sullivan, H. S., 256, 462
Székely, L., 245, 462

Teler, J., 408-409, 446

Utitz, E., 421, 425, 462

von Mises, L., 43, 462
von Mises, R., 323, 462
von Verschuer, O., 428-429, 462

Waelder, R., 10, 41, 51, 90, 137, 183, 229, 410, 463
Wagner-Jauregg, J., 367, 463
Weber, M., 49, 370, 387-388, 463
Weil, A. P., 463
Weiss, E., 257, 463
Weiss, P., 167, 463

Weitz, W., 429, 438, 463
Wexler, M., 195, 463
Wheeler, W., 76
Wilbur, G. B., 446, 455
Wineman, D., 258, 461
Winnicott, D. W., 261, 266, 463
Wisdom, J., 309, 348, 463
Wittels, F., 463
Wolf, K. M., 162, 173, 449, 462

Zeigarnik, B., 348, 409-416, 463
Zilboorg, G., 195, 263, 463

Subject Index

Abnormal vs. pathological, 5
Abreaction, 150
Achievement, x, 239
  as criterion of health, 4-5, 8, 15
  of child, 173
Acting out, 27
Action, 173, 188, 329
  and social reality, 27, 92-93
  common-sense, 253
  development of, 39-41, 166, 173
  evaluation of, 382-383, 392, 396
  goals of, 39, 42-44, 49-51
  magic, 187
  means and ends, 43-51, 58-59
  psychoanalytic theory, 91-93
  psychology of, 37-68
  rational and irrational, 37-68, 90, 138;
    see also Rational behavior
  reality-syntonic, 202, 254
  recall of completed vs. uncompleted,
    409-418
  replacing direct motor discharge, 115,
    166
  theory of, 37-68
  utilitarian, 63-66, 135
Action research, 101
Activity, restriction of, 418
Adaptation, x, xiii, 22, 43-44, 56-61,
    290, 329
  and adaptedness, 167
  and ego strength, 139-140
  and instinctual drives, 80-81
  and maladaptation, 7
  and mental health, 4-18
  and neutralization, 236
  and preadaptedness, 246
  and reality principle, 252-253, 260;
    see also Reality
  and types of society, 28
  and synthesis, 16-17
  detour activity in, 9-13
  diseases of, 293
  impairment of, 28, 56-60

in neurotic and normal, 145
progressive and regressive, 10, 13, 59-
    60
state vs. process, 12, 15-17
to average expectable environment, 16
Adolescence, 44
Adultomorphism, and psychosomorphism,
    118
Advertisement, 32
Affect
  and instinctual drives, 73
  and values, 47-48
  in schizophrenia, 188
  role in judgments, 384-385, 391-392,
    see also Anxiety
Aggression
  aims, 87
  and civilization, 31
  and conflict, 133-134, 175
  and countercathexis, 131-134, 175-176,
    196-203; see also Countercathexis
  and organizing function, 62
  and social relations, 21
  and superego, 289
  and war, 24, 34
  as instinctual drive, 86-88, 294, 327
  changes in concept of, 215
  development of, 121, 210
  expression of, 24, 87
  in schizophrenia, 191
  in totalitarian society, 52-53
  neutralization of, xii-xiii, 87-88, 128-
    134, 163, 170-171, 175, 194-203,
    213, 226-230, 235-236; see also
    Neutralization
  parents' handling of child's, 36
  role in development, 105-161
  theory, 294
  unmodified, 133, 165, 175, 195, 198
  see also Self-destruction
Aggressivization, 122, 177, 190-192, 200-
    203, 213, 230
Aim inhibition, 73, 223

Aims
  ego vs. instinctual, 213
  ego-syntonic, 217
  libidinal, 160
  of ego, *see* Ego, aims of; Ego interests
  substitution of, 164, 217, 227-230
  see also Goals, Psychoanalytic technique
Ambition, 5, 440-443
Ambivalence, 31, 48
Anal phase, 108-109
Anlage, see Constitution, Endowment, Heredity
Animal, 295, 338-340
  compared to man, xii, 22, 77-79, 120, 162, 295
  experiments, 316, 347-348
  phobias, 31
  use of signal, 189
  see also Ethology, Instinct
Anthropology, 23-24, 31, 36, 95-97, 111, 315, 318, 334
Anthropomorphism, 234, 344
Anticipation, 40, 43, 115, 176, 188, 242, 245-247, 251, 292; *see also* Ego functions, anticipatory
Anxiety
  and libido, 128
  conditions, 212
  freedom from, 10-11, 67
  mastery of, 39-40
  real and neurotic, 144
  schizophrenic, 188
  signal, 40-41, 160, 164, 176, 250-251, 292; a biological necessity, 88-89; in schizophrenia, 188
  situations, 110-111; *see also* Danger situations
  social, 41
  social conduct as defense against, 27-28
  theory of, xii, 30, 114, 288-289, 292, 307, 319
  tolerance, 140
  see also Castration anxiety, Danger, Fear
Aphasia, 353
Art, 216-217, 221, 239, 370
  knowledge of artist's conflicts and fantasies does not explain his product, 221
Artistic activity, 13-14, 60; *see also* Creativity
Associationism, 153, 278, 325

Associative fusion, 354
Attention, 124-125, 173, 188, 273
Authoritarian system, 27
Autoerotism and narcissism, 126
Automatisms, xii, 76, 145
Automatization, 42, 254
Autonomy, 122, 145, 177, 246, 338
  and choice of defense, 106-107
  and neutralization, xiii, 229
  deficiency in primary, as etiologic factor in schizophrenia, 203-205
  degrees of, 218
  disturbances in development of, 178
  from genetic factors, xi
  functional, 152
  partial, ix, xiv, 295
  primary, xi, 119, 146, 151-152, 169, 178, 219, 229, 237, 307, 329
  secondary, xi-xiii, 64, 105-107, 123, 137, 146, 151-152, 176-178, 190, 204, 218-221, 229-230, 240, 330, 346
  see also Ego development
Avoidance, 6, 39, 125
  of pain (unpleasure), 249-251
  of reality, 253-254
  of unpleasant tasks, 12, 410

Behavior
  adapted and rational, 47
  alloplastic and autoplastic, 252
  and posthypnotic suggestion, 391
  automatized, 56-57, 254
  complexity of, 20-21, 35
  conforming and nonconforming, 258-259
  cross-section, 35, 41, 210-211
  cross-section vs. longitudinal view, 35, 210-211
  effect of physiological processes, 392-393
  evaluation of, 5-7, 34-35
  healthy and rational, 47
  instinctual, 76-79, 377, 396
  judgments about, 382-383, 392
  normal and pathological, 104, 138; *see also* Health, Normality
  reality-syntonic, 49-50, 92, 95, 129, 244, 254, 267
  sign function of, 102, 342
  social, 29-35
  structure of, 19-20

Behavior—*Continued*
variations in identical twins, 428-445
see also Action, Irrational behavior, Rational behavior
Behaviorism, 310-336
Biological viewpoint, 60-61
Biology, 22-23, 39, 44, 61, 70, 74, 82, 88-89, 117, 152, 167, 197, 269, 301, 396
psychoanalytic contribution to, 88-89
Bisexuality, 191, 205
"Blind spots," 339, 385
Body, a part of inner and outer world, 166-167; *see also* Infant
Body ego, 109, 121-122, 161, 169, 275
Body image, 121-122
Brain physiology, 117, 153, 169, 291-293, 321-325, 393

Castration anxiety, 110, 245
Catatonia, 198
Cathexis
and flight, 175
bound vs. free, 197, 233
changes in, 153, 220, 224-225
changes occurring in a field, 153
instinctual vs. neutralized, 187
libidinal, 219, 287-288, 294
mobility of ego, 203, 233
narcissistic vs. ego, 127, 231
of function vs. aim, 220-221, 229
of function vs. content, xii
of object representation vs. object-directed ego functions, 188
of self vs. ego, 192-193, 231, 287-288
verbal and thing, 149, 188-189
see also Countercathexis, Ego cathexis, Object cathexis, Psychic energy, Self
Causal explanations, *see* Explanations
Causality, principle of, 402-403
Censorship
between conscious and preconscious, 136-137, 254
between unconscious and preconscious, 136-137, 254
in dream, 280
Change of function, 123, 152, 221, 330
and social phenomena, 33, 44
Character, 115
anal, 103, 324, 440
analysis, 147
and physique, 424

compulsive, 28
development, 283-284; in identical twins, 419-445
formation, reactive, 176, 232-233
judgments about, 382-383
oral, 103, 324
type, 103, 112; *see also* Typologies
Character traits, 103, 382
concordance, in twins, 429-445
evaluation of, 5
reactive, 232-233
stability of, 35
substitution for each other, 443-444
Characterology, 419-445
psychoanalytic, 423, 442-444
Child
animal phobias in, 31
calcification of neurosis in, 211-212
cannot associate freely, 178
concept of reality, 245
conflict with reality, 288-289
direct observation, *see* Direct observation
dreams of, 406-407
evaluation of phase-specific reactions, 210-211
handling of toys, 173
play of, 410
pleasure in functioning, 83-84
regression in, 177, 190, 219
reversibility of recently acquired functions, 177
seduction of, 104
turning to outer world, 39
unusual sensitivities in, 204
ways of acquiring knowledge unavoidably lead to distortion of reality, 254-257
see also Development, Infant, Infantile neurosis, Objects, Psychosis
Child analysis, 100
Child rearing, 36, 111
Civilization
and aggression, 31
and education of child, 23
forms of, 26
of diverse epochs, 32, 95
process of, 10
Cleanliness, 440-443
Cognition, influence of needs on, 316
Cognitive styles, 316
Common sense, 253

Communication, 150, 189-190
 and knowledge of others, 370-372
 see also Language, Speech
Complementary series, 421
Compulsive neurosis, *see* Obsessional neurosis
Concept formation, 149-150
Concordance of character traits, 429-445
Condensation, 353-368, 398
Confabulation, 354-363
Conflict
 and free aggression, 133, 165, 175, 198
 and instinct, 78
 and mental health, 11-12
 and neurosis, 3-4, 26, 208-210
 and nonconflictual sphere, interdependence, 145
 between drives, 74
 differences between conscious and unconscious processes cannot account for, 331
 disposition to, 133-134, 165, 175, 198
 ego-id, xi, 11, 146, 164, 196, 289, 331
 ego-external world, 11, 34
 ego-superego, xi, 11, 146, 288, 331
 in psychosis, 182-184
 instinctual, and relation to reality, 17
 intersystemic, 138, 145
 intrasystemic, xi, 138-140, 145-146
 moral, 34, 325
 part of normal development, 7, 11-12
 phase-specific, 74, 109-110, 207, 210-212
 "real" and experimental, 348
 resolution, social factors in, 25-28, 35
 scientific study of, 277-278
 solution, factors influencing, 107, 123
 structure of neurotic, 148
 typical, 7, 11-12, 283, 325-327, 331
 with reality, 144-145, 184, 288-289, 331
 see also Autonomy; Ego, conflict-free sphere
Coordinating function, *see* Ego functions
Conscious (processes), 10-11, 21, 34-35, 136-137, 146-149, 254, 261-262, 321, 327, 331, 383-384, 390, 395, 400
Constitution, *see* Ego, Endowment, Heredity, Id, Maturation
Countercathexis, 160, 171-172, 196, 230
 and ego, 132, 145, 184-185, 228
 and fight, 175, 228, 232

and functional units, 145
and interpretation, 153
and neutralization, 171, 228-229, 235, 238
and repression, 185, 197
formation, 175-176
neutralized aggressive energy used in, 132, 175, 228-229, 235; *see also* Aggression, and countercathexis
used by ego vs. superego, 199
used in defense, 132, 196-203, 232, 235
Creativity, 13-14, 60, 216-217, 221, 224
Criminal, 19-20
Culture, 23-26, 35-36

Danger
 flight and fight, 125, 132-134, 175, 196
 relation of internal to external, 30
 signal, *see* Anxiety signal
 situations, 40-41, 55, 292; *see also* Fear
Daydream, 363
Death, reaction to, 64
Death instinct, 72, 294-295
Deaggressivization, 128-134
Defense, 115-116, 273
 aggressivized, 150
 analysis of, 152
 and ego strength, 138-140
 and neutralization, xiii, 107, 171, 232-235; *see also* Aggression, Countercathexis
 and postponement, 58, 170, 174-175; *see also* Reality principle
 and primary process, 219
 and reality testing, 201-203
 and resistance, 144, 150-152, 288, 292
 becomes independent aim, 44
 capacity for, 196-203
 changes in concept of, 215, 225-226, 284
 choice of, 106-107, 124-126, 151, 170, 197
 chronology, 106-107, 164, 170
 closing of eyelids in neonate as model of, 125
 development, 123-126, 165, 183
 genetic aspects, 151-152
 hereditary core, 169
 in obsessional neurosis, 417-418
 interpretation, 149-152
 intersystemic and intrasystemic aspects, 151-152

Defense—*Continued*
  modeled after instinctual pattern, 160
  models for, xi, 106-109, 124-125, 175
  normal, 293
  origin of, 124-125
  pathological vs. healthy, 12-13; *see also*
    Denial
  precursors, 106-107, 164, 170, 185,
    204
  preliminary stages, 106-109, 125
  primary autonomous, 185
  primitive, 151, 185
  quantitative and qualitative factor, 150-
    152
  relation to other ego functions, 151-
    152, 164-165
  reliance on reality as, 27, 39, 64-65
  sexualized, 150
  stability of, 175, 185
  structure of, in psychosis, 184-186, 191,
    194-203
  successful, 225-226
  twofold purpose of, 17
  types of, ix, 30
  unconscious, 278, 281, 288, 331
  use of countercathexis, 131-134; *see
    also* Aggression
  vulnerability, 204-205
  see also sub specific defense mechan-
    isms
Defusion, 195-197, 227
Deinstinctualization, 227-228
Delirious confusion, 354-363
Delusion, 178, 189, 201
Democracy, 33, 53
Deneutralization, and schizophrenia, 187,
  193-198
Denial, 266
  of outer reality, 201
  useful, 253
Dependence, of infant, 22-23, 73, 81,
  161, 255, 291, 325, 330
Depression, 6, 210
Desexualization, xii, 128-134, 192, 222,
  226; *see also* Neutralization, Sublimation
Development
  and adaptation, 59-60, 167
  and early bodily needs, 207-209
  and libidinal cathexis, 219
  and maturation, *see* Maturation
  and physiological growth, 168-170
  approaches to, xi, 161-162

biological and sociological concept of,
  16
change of pleasure conditions, 246-249
conflict-ridden vs. peaceful, 11-14, 34-
  35, 57; *see also* Autonomy
constant elements in, 24
cross-section vs. longitudinal, 160, 164,
  210-211
disparate, of drives and specific ego
  functions, 107, 108
environmentalist theory, 100, 109
general trend, 41
heredity-environment, 169, 419-431
id and ego aspects, 168, 172, 212
mutual influences of ego and id, 155-
  181
mutual interaction of ego and object
  relations, 105, 108, 163
normal, 7, 11-12, 293, 325, 340
one-sided theories, 100, 108-109
pathological and normal, 158, 208,
  325, 340
pathogenic interaction of drive and
  ego, 210
persistence of earlier phases, 213
phase characteristics and genetic determinants, 110-112
phase-specific vulnerabilities, 110-111,
  207, 212
predisposition to pathologic, 207
prestructural phases, 207
psychoanalytic theory of, 104-105, 155-
  181
same manifestation neurotic (cross-sec-
  tionally) and conflict solution (longi-
  tudinally), 210-211
theories of early, 101-112
theories by reduction, 112
trauma theory, 398-399
typical phases, 104-109, 161, 324
undifferentiated phase, 80-81, 117, 120,
  160, 166
variations of normal, 209
see also sub specific headings
Developmental psychology, 99-112, 172,
  192, 208, 225, 324, 334, 337, 425-
  427
Dictatorship, 33
Differentiation
  and integration, 80-83, 168, 175, 251
  and substitution, 444
  between libido and aggression, 195

Differentiation—*Continued*
individual differences in, 208
of ego and id, 22, 73, 80-81, 102, 119-120, 156, 184, 187, 196-198, 289; primary enmity, 115, 124, 158-159
and internal control, 174
and mental health, 4, 17-18
and neutralization, xiii-xiv, 128-134, 228-230; *see also* Aggression, Neutralization, Sublimation
and neutralized aggression, 87-88, 131-134
and pleasure principle, 250-252
and reality, 82, 114-115, 118-120, 145, 241-244, 258, 266; *see also* Reality principle
and self, 127-128, 279, 287-288
and self-preservation, xiii, 61, 80-86, 119, 168, 243, 247, 295
and social action, 90-91
and social behavior, 21
and social factors, 26
autonomy of, *see* Autonomy, Ego development
biological functions of, 117, 168, 290-291, 295
cathexis, xii, 126-128, 192-193, 203, 219, 231-233, 284, 287-288
collaborating with id, 164
conflict-free sphere, x, 34, 83-84, 107, 145-146, 164-165, 307, 328-329; *see also* Autonomy
control by conscious and preconscious, 10-11, 34
defined by functions, 273, 290
definition, 114
development of, *see* Ego development
development of Freud's concept of, 155-159, 268-296
disintegration, 193, 199
distortion, 205, 211
energetic aspects, 170-176
energies of, xii-xiv, 41, 127-134, 137, 170, 176, 194, 219, 222-230, 233, 236-240, 287, 330
fear of loss of, 11, 56
flexibility (plasticity), 11, 25, 81, 159
fragmented, 108, 179, 185
Freud's definitions of, 272-273, 277-279, 290
functions of, *see* Ego functions, **and** *sub* specific functions
genetic determinants of attitudes of, 176-177

individual differences in, 208
of ego and id, 22, 73, 80-81, 102, 119-120, 161-162, 165-167, 200, 208, 247, 291; reason for differences between instincts of animals and instinctual drives in men, 73, 80-81, 247
self-object, 102, 122, 165-166, 187, 200, 204, 246
structural, in man, 77-79, 120, 162, 247
Direct observation, x, xv, 48, 99-112, 116-118, 157, 160-162, 170, 178, 183, 204, 209, 222, 292, 301, 307, 319, 337, 343, 347
Displacement, 39-41, 78, 124, 353
and sublimation (neutralization), 217-225, 232, 235
primary- and secondary-process aspects, 172
promoting development, 160
Distortion
of reality, 254-256, 266
symbolic, 365-368
Dream, 152, 172, 177, 315, 319, 342-343
ego's contribution to, 280
experimental studies, 407-409
latent thought, 372
suggested hypnotically, 367
symbols, 365-367
tension-reducing function, 404-406
theory, 406-407, 410
Dynamic point of view, 225, 272, 278, 283, 289, 326-328

Economic factors, independence of, 30
Economic point of view, xii, 56-57, 191-196, 225, 234, 272, 289, 293, 327-328
Economics, 38, 90
Education, 19-20, 66, 105, 111
Ego
activities of, *see* Ego functions
aims of, 134, 160, 164, 197, 217, 221-223, 229-230, 234; *see also* Ego interests
and action, 39-45, 115, 121
and adaptation, 81-82, 115-116, 120
and external world, 24-26
and group psychology, 31
and instinctual drives, 80-88, 115, 118-

Ego—*Continued*
  hereditary core (endowment), x-xi, 23, 119-120, 156-157, 169, 204, 208, 222, 329; *see also* Ego apparatuses
  in psychosis, 183-191
  inhibitory apparatus, 174
  instinctualization of, 285-286
  mobility of cathexis, 203, 233
  modification, 24, 284
  needs of autonomous, 122
  partial concepts, 157
  precursors, 219-220, 230, 245
  primary disturbances of, 170
  primary energy, xiv, 227, 236, 240
  primitive, 167
  quantitative aspects, 4, 315
  relation to body, 169; *see also* Body ego
  relation to id, *see* Id; *see also* Differentiation
  relative independence of, ix, xiv, 295; *see also* Autonomy
  reservoir of neutralized energy, xii-xiv, 128-134, 194, 229-230, 233, 287
  sociocultural influences on, 291
  sources of energy of, 130, 219, 236-240, 330
  splitting of, 146, 198
  structural approach increased stature of concept, 292-295
  switching operations of, 234
  unconscious part, 34, 149
  use of aggressive energy against id, 176
  use of irrational factors, 10, 13
  using id energy for its aims, 164, 221, 229-230, 234
  weakness of, 139, 194, 205, 258
  works with desexualized energy, xii-xiii, 170, 222-228
  see also Body ego, Ego psychology, Pleasure ego, Psychoanalytic theory, Reality ego
Ego apparatuses, xi, 121, 124, 167-168, 203-204, 307
  autonomous, 246; *see also* Ego, hereditary core of
  intact in schizophrenia, 190
Ego development, ix, xii-xiv, 23, 40-41, 63, 84, 117-126, 155-181, 185, 208-210, 229, 250-252
  and development of object relations, 105, 108, 163, 292

  and language, 190
  and libidinal cathexis, 219
  and libidinal phases, 160
  and postponement of discharge, xi, 115, 119, 125, 171
  and resistivity to object loss, 193-194
  and tendency to regress, 190
  aspects of early, 165-170
  autonomous, 40-41, 80, 105-109, 119-126, 130, 140, 172-173; *see also* Autonomy
  influence on typical phases, 161
  influenced by conflict, and influencing conflict solution, 102
  maturation in, 40-41, 121, 167-169, 329
  precocious, 60, 107-109, 125, 172, 204, 213
  retarded, 107-108
  role of apparatuses in, 121
Ego drives, 83, 86, 135, 285
Ego functions, ix-xv, 114-117, 139, 241-243, 273, 277, 292, 325, 328-330
  and degree of neutralization, 228-229, 233-234
  and primary and secondary processes, 233
  and psychoanalytic technique, 144-146
  and self-representation, 220, 226
  anticipatory, 40, 188-190; *see also* Anticipation
  autonomous, *see* Autonomy, Ego development
  coordinating, 61-63, 115-117
  defect in schizophrenia, 184-191
  detour, 59-60, 115
  development, 250-252, 255, 285-286
  differential study, 107
  differentiating, 196, 202
  flexibility vs. stability, xii
  hierarchy of, xiii, 11, 138
  instinctualization of, 170, 192, 200, 217-220
  integrative, 11, 58, 62, 115-117, 145, 168, 236, 254, 264, 290-291
  interplay of adaptive and organizing, x
  mobility of cathexis, 233
  modeled after instinctual pattern, 160
  nondefensive, 227, 230-234, 328
  object-directed, xii, 131, 173, 187-188, 191-194, 231

Ego functions—*Continued*
  organizing, x, 10, 13, 62-63, 66, 86,
    115-117, 138, 145, 168, 236, 248,
    254, 329
  physiological and psychological data,
    168-169
  precocious development, 161, 172
  putting some functions out of action,
    xiii, 11, 56, 177-178
  redefinition, 186-187
  reversibility of, 176-177
  selective impairment in schizophrenia,
    190-191, 194, 202-203
  stability of, 176, 218-219, 229
  structuralization of, 134-135, 147; in-
    trasystemic, 145-146, 151
  superego interfering with, 48
  synthetic, 6-7, 13, 17, 61-62, 67, 86,
    115-117, 137-138, 145, 149, 168,
    196, 202, 236, 254, 264, 290-291,
    329
  vulnerability of, 204; of recently ac-
    quired, 219
  see also sub specific functions
Ego ideal, 195, 330
  and group psychology, 31
  and neutralization, 238-239
Ego interests, 32, 35, 43, 54-55, 90-91,
    135-139, 176, 286
  and structural theory, 134-139
  energic aspects, 137-138
  genesis, 64-66
  genetic determinants, 137
  structure of, 64-66
  terminology, 136
  see also Ego, aims of
Ego libido, 284-285
Ego nuclei, 118, 122
Ego psychology, xi, xiv, 4, 38, 100, 127,
    178-179, 241
  and concept of sublimation, 216, 221
  and observational data, 178-179; *see
    also* Direct observation
  and theory of development, 105-111
  and theory of motivation, 159
  balanced view of biological and social
    aspects, 330
  clinical implications, 144
  development of, 113-117, 156, 270-
    272, 278-294, 307
  impact on psychopathology, 117, 129,
    134
  implications for study of psychosis, 182

technical implications, 142-154
  see also Psychoanalytic theory
Ego strength, 11, 22, 67, 129, 139-140,
    212, 218, 258
  and autonomous (nonconflictual) func-
    tioning, 145, 177
  and intrasystemic structures, 146
Egoism, 135-138
  and narcissism, 286
Élan vital, 74
Embryology, 110
Empathy, 379, 394
Endowment
  in identical twins, 419-433
  instinctual, 23; *see also* Id
  see also Ego, Heredity
Enjoyment, as criterion of health, 8, 15
Environment
  search for appropriate, 252
  two concepts of "our real world," 261-
    264
  see also Development, Reality
Epilepsy, 354, 367
Eros, 291, 294
Ethology, 76, 327
Evolution, 166-167
Experiencing (*Erleben*), as means of ob-
    taining knowledge, 373-391
Experimental studies
  of dream, 315, 407-409
  of perception, 315-316, 338
  of recall of completed and uncom-
    pleted tasks in obsessive-compulsive
    neurosis, 404-418
  using stories of sexual content to test
    recall in Korsakoff, 355-368
  see also Psychoanalysis
Explanation and understanding (*Verste-
    hende Psychologie*), 369-403
Expressive movements, 336, 371-372

Family
  environment never identical for dif-
    ferent members, 431-432, 442-444
  structure of, 93
Fanaticism, 53
Fantasy
  and reality, 256, 265-266
  and social reality, 27, 93
  and sublimation, 221
  and total behavior, 30
  need satisfaction in, 39
  unconscious, 93, 221

Father
  and concept of reality, 245
  killing of, 31
Fear
  of dissolution of personality, 186
  of incompleteness, 405
  of losing object or object's love, 22
  of loss of control, 11
  of social environment, 41
  see also Anxiety, Danger, Ego
Feeding, 36
Field theory, 153
Fixation, 191, 203, 219, 392, 398
  and pathological development, 210-214
  ego aspect, 194
Free association, 11, 178, 307, 319
Free will, 10
Freedom, 10-11
Friendship, 21
Frustration, 23-25, 238
  and aggression, 199
  of early physical needs, 207, 211
  role in reality principle, 245-246
Function
  and genesis, 221-222, 324, 330
  change of, *see* Change of function
  see also sub specific functions
Future, 40, 251; *see also* Anticipation

Genital stage, 17, 59
Genetic point of view, xi, 21, 35, 93-94,
  103, 106-112, 222, 250, 283, 289,
  323
Genetics, 296, 419-432, 443-444
Goals
  of action, *see* Action
  organization and structure of, 39, 53-
  54, 57-58, 92
  "useful," 63-64
  see also Psychoanalytic technique, aims
Graphology, 439-440
Grasping, 121
Group psychology, 20-21, 31, 51-55, 95-
  97: *see also* Authoritarian system,
  Totalitarian system
Guilt feelings, 31-32, 132, 140, 199, 325,
  330, 370,
  unconscious, 42-44, 288

Health, x, 225, 381
  and capacity to suffer, 6
  etiology of, 145, 342
  evolutionary concept, 17
  not a statistical average, 4
  psychoanalytic concept of, 3-18, 47, 60,
  66, 145
  variations of, *see* Development, variations of normal
  see also Normality
Health neurosis, 6
Heredity, 23-25, 120, 169, 204-205, 222,
  329, 419-431, 442-444; *see also* Ego,
  Endowment, Id, Maturation
History, 31-38, 51, 95, 263, 272; *see also*
  Psychoanalysis
Homeostasis, 85, 291, 329
Hypnosis, 367, 391
Hysteria, 26, 339
  hypnoid, 277

Id
  aims, 136, 229-230
  and action, 42-45
  and external world, 24-26
  and instinctual drives, 79-83
  and social behavior, 21
  cathexis of, xii
  changes in, 159
  concept, 329
  development, 155-181
  ego serving aims of, 164, 221
  functions, xii, 114, 139, 325
  innate tendencies, 125
  relation to ego, xi, 157-159, 164, 176,
  183-184, 187, 221, 229-230, 234,
  239
  transformations of, 24-25
  see also Differentiation, Instinctual
  drives
Ideal types, 386-389
Ideology, 32
Identification, 21, 212
  and atypical development, 109
  and body control, 122
  and countercathexis, 203
  and group psychology, 31
  and object relations, 255
  and sublimation (neutralization), 222-
  225, 231, 235, 238
  and superego, 330
  in schizophrenia, 196
  in twins, 432
  primary, 186
  relation to instinctual drives, 160

Illness
  and health, concept of, 3-18
  denial of, 6-7
Imagination, 12
Incest taboo, 31
Individual psychology, 395, 398
Industrialization, 55
Infant
  impulse gratification and frustration in,
    23-24, 36
  influence of mother's absence, 107
  learning about body and its functions,
    122, 255
  primary responses, 246
  prolonged helplessness of, 22-23, 73,
    81, 161, 255, 291, 325, 330
  see also Child, Direct observation, Ob-
    jects
Infantile neurosis, 207-214
  etiologic factors in early and later
    phases, 208-209
  in twins, 436-438
Inhibition, 115, 217
  cognitive, 385
Insight, 253
Instinct (animal), xii, 70-71, 76-82, 120,
    162, 247, 295, 326
Instinct to master, 84
Instinctual drives (*Trieb*)
  aims of, 72, 134
  and action, 37-45, 49-51
  and defense, 58-59, 150-153
  and psychic structure, 79-86
  and social instinct, 32, 35
  and total behavior, 30
  changes in development of, 159
  constitution, 329
  development of, 72-75
  distinguished from instinct, xii, 70, 76-
    81, 120, 162, 247, 295
  dual theory of, 86-87
  fusion and defusion, 195-197, 227
  hereditary core, x, 222
  independent variable in development,
    105-106, 119
  mode of gratification, 23
  objects, 72-73
  psychoanalytic definition and concept,
    70-72, 326-327
  psychoanalytic theory of, 69-89, 114,
    283, 295, 396
  quantitative factor, 4, 140, 315
  role in behavior, 369, 384, 391

  sources of, 72-73
  specific features of psychoanalytic con-
    cept, 70-76
  study of, xv, 4, 21
  see also Aggression, Aims, Ego, Id, Li-
    bido, Psychic energy
Instinctual life
  glorification of, 9
  influence of cultural factors on, 30
Instinctualization, xi-xiii, 229; *see also*
    Aggressivization,   Deneutralization,
    Sexualization
Integration, 67, 81; *see also* Differentia-
    tion; Ego functions
Integrative function, *see* Ego functions
Intellectualization, 152
Intelligence, 45, 136
  and conflict, 102, 123
  and instinct, 76-77
  of twins, 428-438
Intentionality, 173, 247, 278
Intercourse, 177
Internalization, 41, 86, 115, 264
Interpretation, 148-149, 319, 343, 347
  based on signs, 371-372
  dynamics and economics, 150-151
  effect of, 152-154
  "principle of multiple appeal," 153-
    154
  sequence, 147-148
  side effects, 150-151
  structural aspects, 150-154
Intersystemic approach, 145, 151-152
Intersystemic conflict, *see* Conflict
Intoxication, 392
Intrasystemic approach, 145-146, 151-152
Intrasystemic conflict, *see* Conflict
Introjection, 124
Introspection, 310-312, 335-336, 392
Intuition, 310-311, 339, 381, 384, 394
Irrational, definition, 45-51
Irrational action, 37-68
Irrational behavior (phenomena), 21, 32,
    37-68
Isolation, 48, 124-125, 325

Knowledge
  and understanding of others, 259, 370-
    371, 381-386, 393
  criterion of validity of, 379-389
  means of obtaining, 373-387; *see also*
    Understanding

Knowledge—*Continued*
objective and conventional (social-ized), 257-260
ways of acquisition of, unavoidably lead to distortion of reality, 254-257
Korsakoff psychosis, 353-368

Language
acquisition, 149-150
and action, 369
and thinking, 255-256
development, 190
functions of, 189
in schizophrenia, 188-190
role, in psychoanalytic technique, 149-150, 154
symbolic, 189
see also Communication, Speech
Latency, 44, 80, 210, 216, 222
Learning, 22, 76-77, 121, 161-162, 166, 168, 219-220, 246-247, 254-256, 291, 393
theory, 349
Libido, 6, 87, 284, 309
and sublimation (neutralization), 163, 213, 216-219, 226, 236
concept, 325, 344
development of, 40, 104-105, 108, 121, 210, 319; and physical growth, 40, 104, 168
genital, 237
narcissistic, 126-129, 231, 285; *see also* Object libido
pregenital, 237
theory, 156, 288, 396
withdrawal, 128-130, 191-197, 200-203
see also Cathexis, Instinctual drives, Object libido, Psychic energy, Sexuality
Life instinct, 72
Literature, 269
Love
man's need for, 22
relation, 21-22

Manic-depressive psychosis, 443
Market research, 32
Masochism, moral, 27, 228
Mass methods, 10
Maturation, xi, 22-23, 35, 40-41
and development, 40-41, 60, 102-109, 121-122, 212, 229, 307

and learning, 83-84
correcting early unsatisfactory situa-tions, 163
in ego development, 40-41, 121, 167-169, 329
influence on conflict solution, 102, 123
Meaning, psychoanalytic approach to, 264-265, 400
Medical psychology, 421-423
Memory, 151, 166-167, 190, 246, 273, 329
development, 174
disorder, in Korsakoff psychosis, 353-368
of completed and uncompleted tasks, 404-418
traces, preconscious, 118, 121
Menschenkenntnis, see Knowledge of others
Mental apparatus
ego part of, 282
energies of, 327
equilibrium, 291
growth and development, 40
physiologic concepts of, 323
stability, 40
Mental connections, theory of (Jaspers), causal and directly experienced, 377-387
Mental functioning
causal vs. understandable relationship, 369-403
dynamics of, 384
instability of, 57
psychoanalytic view of, 374-375, 383-385, 390-393, 396-400
sociocultural influences, 329-330
see also Primary process, Secondary process
Metapsychology, 173, 182-206, 218, 224, 239, 249, 289, 294, 324-325, 328, 335; *see also* Psychoanalytic theory
Methods
correlating physiological and psycho-analytic data, 205
critique of understanding, 369-403
essential, of applied psychoanalysis, 92-98
experimental, 116, 355-368, 404-418
implies selection of data, 100, 349
knowledge of field to which psycho-analysis applied essential, 95-96

Methods—*Continued*
of psychoanalysis, 247-248, 302, 307, 317-319, 336, 343
psychoanalytic, compared to others, 100-102
reconstructive and observation, 99-112; *see also* Direct observation, Reconstruction
use of life history in sociology, 29
see also Psychoanalysis, as a scientific theory; Psychoanalysis, scientific aspect
Money, attitudes to, 440-443
Moods, 392-393
Morale, 19
Morality, sexualization of, 27
Mother
and concept of reality, 245
role in development, 162-163
Motility, 114, 123, 160, 166-167, 246
congenital equipment, 121
Motivation, 241-242, 316, 340
and social action, 90-94
classification of, 75
hierarchy and interrelation of, xi-xii, 135-136
of action, 38-42
psychoanalysis as psychology of, 324-326
theory, 159
unconscious, 35, 336, 400
Mourning, 64, 397-398
Myths, 32, 95

Narcissism
defined, 192, 287-288
in schizophrenia, 186-191
primary, 165, 186, 255
theory of, xii, 126-129, 203, 215-216, 220, 231, 285-287
Narcohypnosis, 359
National character, 97
Neurosis
adulterates inner reality, 201
and character, 424, 438-445
and concept of health, 13-14
and defense, 225-226
and prepsychotic phase, 435
avoidance of recognition of one's own, 6
changes in form of, 26
compared to psychosis, 182-185, 201

etiologic role of aggression, 134
etiology of, 26, 135, 145-146, 156, 182-184, 208-214, 286, 293, 325, 342, 398-399, 438, 445
in child and adult, differences, 209-210
in twins, 436-445
infantile, *see* Infantile neurosis
influence of sociocultural factors, 26-27, 30
predisposition to, 28; *see also* Conflict
reality testing in, 201
secondary gain, 55
variations in identical twins, 435-438
Neutralization
a continuous process, 130, 171, 194, 224
and countercathexis, 171-172, 175-176, 203-206, 228-229, 239
and ego functions, 170-171, 233, 236; *see also* Ego, Sublimation
and ego interest, 137
and object constancy, 163, 238
and object relations, 171, 199-200, 222-223, 238
and secondary process, 171-172
concept, 170-171, 227
defined, 227
degrees of, xiii, 129-132, 171-172, 223-224, 228-230, 238; *see also* Psychic energy, instinctual vs. neutralized, and gradations between
development, 218-222, 229, 237-238
impaired in schizophrenia, 175, 192-197, 203, 233
maximum not always correlated with optimum functioning, xiii, 171
of aggression, *see* Aggression, neutralization of; Self-destruction
of instinctual energies, xii-xiii, 128-134, 164; *see also* Aggression, Libido
of libido and aggression, differences, 213
of pregenital and genital libido, 237
relation to defense, *see* Defense
see also Deaggressivization, Deinstinctualization, Deneutralization, Sublimation
Nirvana principle, 84, 243
Normality, 14-16, 21, 43-45, 177-178, 185, 200, 225, 293; *see also* Conflict, Development, Health

Object
 impact on child's learning about reality, 255-258
 importance to infant, 22, 73, 81, 161, 255, 292, 330
 inanimate, 173
 need-satisfying, 163-187
 recognition of, 22
Object cathexis, xii, 127-128, 188, 287-288
 and reality, 202
 constancy, 173
Object choice, 5, 392
Object constancy, 163, 171-173, 187, 223, 238, 255
Object libido, 126-129, 185, 231, 237
Object relations
 and defense, 199
 and development of instinctual drives, 73-74
 and narcissism, 186
 and neutralization, *see* Neutralization
 and relation to reality, 200-203
 and sociology, 20-21
 clinging to and going in search of mother, 186
 development, 21-22, 93, 104-105, 111, 161-165, 183, 187-188, 193-194, 204, 208-210, 246-247, 292
 disturbances of early, 185-186
 ego's contribution to, 191
 in psychosis, 186
 nonanalytic view, 173
 satisfactory, 162-163
 see also Development, mutual interaction of ego and object relations; Ego development, and development of object relations; Reality
Object representation, 127, 188, 231
Objectivation, 39, 150, 176, 187-188, 245-247, 251, 309-310, 338
Obsessive-compulsive neurosis, *see* Obsessional neurosis
Obsessional neurosis, 11, 31, 60, 316, 438
 precocious ego development, 107-108, 125
 recall of completed and uncompleted tasks in, 404-418
Oedipal phase, 111, 222
Oedipus complex, 31, 159, 207, 211-212
Omnipotence of thought, 417
Ontogenesis, 120, 166-167, 229, 240, 392
Oral phase, 110, 203

Orderliness, 440-443
Organization, concept of, 62-63
Orgasm, inability to achieve, 11
Overdetermination, 41-42, 92, 326, 337

Paranoia, 183
Parapraxes, 336
 in Korsakoff psychosis, 353-368
Pedantry, 5
Perception, 39, 114-115, 160, 166-167, 173, 188, 190, 201, 246-247, 256, 263, 273, 279, 315-316, 329
 and recall, 407-409
 development, 122-123
 influence of needs on, 338
Personal equation, 101, 337-339
Personality
 demarcation of structures geared to typical conflicts, 325, 331
 development, 93, 419-445
 environmental factors, 425-432
 influence of social factors on, 23-28, 31, 36
 motivation of, 90-91
 narcissistic, 126
 of twins, 419-445
 residual, in schizophrenia, 190
 stratification, 146-147
 structure, 114; and action, 38-41; and social structure, 32-34, 93-95
 "theories of reduction," 112
 types, 27, 94-97, 112, 382-383
 unconscious segment, 383-384
Perversion, 225
 cultural factors in, 30
Phallic phase, 108-110, 207
Phase specificity, 74, 109-111, 207, 210-212
Phenomenological psychology, 373, 376, 379
Phenomenology, 373-376
Phenotype, 425-427, 444
Philosophy, 43, 63, 79, 150, 156, 241, 257, 274, 282, 318, 421
Phobia, 26, 31
Phylogenesis, 120, 166-167, 248
Physiology, 39-40, 73, 79, 104, 110, 121, 130, 168-170, 205, 236, 262-263, 272, 276, 291-293, 373, 390-393, 396; *see also* Brain physiology
Play, 223, 410
 psychoanalytic and biological theory of, 89

Pleasure
  and rhythmical activity, 213
  in functioning, 83-84, 119, 244-245
  possibilities, and developing ego functions, 83-84, 119, 252
  postponement of, *see* Reality principle, postponement of discharge
  pride in foregoing, 252
  search for, 39, 410
  -unpleasure balance, 251
  vs. motivating force, 241-242
Pleasure ego, 165, 241
Pleasure principle, 22, 39-40, 161-162, 241-252, 328-329, 412
  and ego, 292
  and instinct, 70, 78
  and instinctual drives, 70-71
  and play, 89
  and self-preservation, 82-85, 250, 254
  modification of, 248-252
  secondarily invested with important reality functions, 250
Political leaders, 29-30, 53-55
Preconscious (processes), 10-11, 34, 136-137, 146, 149, 166, 174, 189, 254, 262, 327, 331
Prediction, 34-35, 104-105, 157, 179, 307, 312-313, 337, 348
  "of the past," 306, 337
Preoedipal phase, 165
Prevention, 102, 105, 111-112, 158
Preverbal stage, 102-103, 118, 158, 306-307
Primary ego energy, xiv, 227, 236, 240
Primary process, 48, 124, 172, 188, 190, 249, 273, 315
  and sublimation (neutralization), 131, 218-219, 229, 233
  concept, 327
  transition to secondary process, xiii, 131, 192
"Principle of multiple appeal," 153-154
"Principle of multiple function," 41-42, 326
Problem solving, 41, 56-57, 73
Projection, 6, 93, 160, 185, 263, 325
  precursor of, 186
Propaganda, 19, 53
Protective barrier against stimuli, 106, 115, 125, 204, 410
Psychiatry, 19, 37, 369, 389, 395
Psychic energy
  and action, 41

  and automatized behavior, 56-57
  and ego strength, 139-141
  bound vs. free, 197, 233
  changes in aims and mode of, 174-176, 223, 229
  concept, 74, 236
  discharge and structuralization, 203-204
  displacement, 203
  flux, 230
  indifferent, xiii, 227
  inhibition of discharge, 171-172, 235
  instinctual vs. neutralized, and gradations between, 164, 171-172, 192, 213, 223-224, 228
  libidinal vs. aggressive, 192
  neutralization of, *see* Aggression, Libido, Neutralization
  sources, 327
  see also Aggression, Instinctual drives, Libido, Primary ego energy, Sexualization
Psychic systems
  and action, 42-45
  and energies, 41, 80
  and personality structure, 156
  and pleasure principle, 249
  and social action, 90-91
  balance between, 62-63
  changes of, in psychoanalytic therapy, 66-68
  defined by their functions, 38-39, 114, 118, 147, 322, 325
  pleasure potential, 213
  see also sub specific systems
Psychoanalysis
  a general pychology, x, 21, 37, 74, 100, 105, 116, 146, 158, 180, 289, 293-294, 300, 343
  a natural science, 375, 400-401
  an inductive science, 383, 401
  and field concept, 153
  application to sociology, problems of, 19-20, 29-36, 90-98, 116-117
  applications of, 301
  as a scientific theory, 318-350
  as psychology of motivation, 324-326
  behavioral and introspective aspects, 335-336
  biological and sociological point of view, 22-23
  biological conceptions, 421-428

Psychoanalysis—*Continued*
  biological foundation, 117, 383, 396, 399
  clinical and theoretical work in, 302-305
  clinical foundations, xiv, 342
  compared with *Verstehende Psychologie*, 369-403
  concern with social factors, 24-25, 329-330
  constructs in, 312-313, 344-345
  correlation of data obtained by other methods, xv, 179; *see also* Direct observation
  development of, 37-38, 79-80, 113-117, 120, 146-147, 268-296, 320, 339; *see also* Psychoanalysis, history of
  dispositional concepts, 345
  exposing of pseudo connections, 381-384
  fixation to single phases in development of, 269
  function of theory in, 179-181
  genetic turn, 156
  history of, 181-184, 215-216, 268-296, 320; *see also* Psychoanalysis, development of
  integration of clinical, technical, and theoretical aspects, 142-143, 148-149, 157, 213-214, 302-304, 319
  interdependence of clinical data and theory, 180-181, 276, 289, 302-305, 335, 339-343
  interdependence of theory and technique, 142-143, 153-154
  its function in regard to biological problems, 88-89
  levels of explanation, 303, 308-309
  observation and hypothesis formation, 276-277, 302-315, 324, 331, 339-345
  origins of, 20-21, 37, 320
  prehistory of, 271-272
  quantification problems, 313-315, 327
  reasons for rejection of, 384
  remoteness from descriptive level, 309
  role of clinical setting, 340-342
  scientific aspects of, 297-317
  study of reality inherent in, 29-30
  subject matter of, x, 375
  use of signs, 342-343

  see also Psychoanalytic technique, Psychoanalytic theory, Psychoanalytic training
Psychoanalytic situation
  a real life situation, 100, 340-341
  constancy of variables, 336-337
Psychoanalytic technique
  a method of investigation, 319, 336-337
  and concept of health, 3, 145
  and "historical" stratification of personality, 147-148
  behavior oriented to particular environment, 30
  flexible, 144
  goals of, 7-9, 15, 59, 66-67, 142, 147-149
  influence of ego psychology on, 117, 288
  influencing id, 25, 159
  intrasystemic approach, 145-146, 151-152
  knowledge of current milieu, 93
  meaning of ego strengthening, 145-146
  pathological reactions as means to attaining cure, 7
  prediction essential aspect in, 307, 312
  rational planning and unconscious elements, 144, 151
  reality aspects of patient's behavior, 144
  structural point of view vs. stratification concept, 146-148
  termination, 3
  theory of, 142-154
  use of irrational elements for cure, 66-67
  See also Psychoanalytic theory
Psychoanalytic theory, 325-326, 329
  advanced by new observations, 340
  and developmental psychology, 99-112, 207-214
  comprehensiveness of Freud's formulations, 179
  development of, 155-159, 241-267, 268-296, 396-399
  dynamic formulations, *see* Dynamic point of view
  empirical vs. speculative, 294-295, 301
  energy aspects, *see* Economic point of view
  experimental testing of hypothesis, 298, 315-316, 332, 347-348

Psychoanalytic theory—*Continued*
  fundamentals of, 319-331
  genetic hypothesis, 158-159, 306, 324;
    see also Genetic point of view
  hierarchy of hypotheses, 269, 320
  levels of, 294-295, 301, 308-310
  newness and scope of, 332-335
  physical and physiological models,
    322-323, 328
  principles of organization and struc-
    ture, 153
  reformulations, ix-x, 135, 215-216,
    224-225, 268-270, 285-296, 301,
    315-316
  relation between observer and ob-
    served, 336-337
  scientific goals of, 299, 323, 377, 389,
    401
  simplifications ("theories by reduc-
    tion"), 112
  structural approach, *see* Structural
    point of view
  systematization and clarification, 308,
    317-320, 349
  validation, 303, 312, 315-317, 337,
    346-350
  see also Ego, Psychoanalysis, Psychol-
    ogy
Psychoanalytic training
  curriculum, 269
  supervision, 144
  teaching of psychoanalysis, 70, 144,
    269, 347
  see also Psychoanalyst, personal analy-
    sis
Psychoanalyst
  "passivity" of, 336
  personal analysis, 144, 317, 338, 385
Psychology, 38, 150, 173, 179, 273-274
  analytic approach to, 158
  and social science, 19-20, 25, 29-32
  concept of drives, 70-75
  explanatory and descriptive, 373-379;
    see also Explanation
  intuitive, 381-382
  see also Developmental psychology,
    Phenomenological psychology, *Ver-
    stehende Psychologie*
Psychosis, 43-45, 157, 177, 233, 288,
  292, 315, 343
  and fixation, 211, 214
  and increased knowledge of early
    childhood, 161, 182-183, 187

  in child, 183-186, 190
  in twins, 435-438, 443
  organic, 190, 393
  study of, 182-183, 389
  see also Schizophrenia
Psychosomatic disorders, 211
Psychotherapist, "activity of," 336
Punishment, expectation of, 27

Quasi needs (K. Lewin), 418
Quantification, problems in analysis, 313-
  315, 327

Rat Man, 284
Rational, definition, 45-51
Rational action, 37-68, 90, 138
  and acting out, 27-28
  defined, 49-50
Rational behavior, 9-11, 13, 17, 21, 34,
  37-68
Rationalism, psychological, 388-389
Rationality, 46-48
  and adaptation, 56-61
  and health, 9-10
  overreliance on, 64-65
Rationalization, 25, 52-55, 139, 335
Reaction formation, 25, 109, 284, 377
  and sublimation (neutralization), 216,
    232
  and substitution of traits, 442-444
Realism, 257
Reality
  acceptance, 119, 251, 254, 266
  and action, interdependent relation, 39
  and change of function, 33
  and detour activity, 12
  and ego drives, 285
  and expression of aggression, 87
  and object relations, 200-203, 255-257
  clinging to, 202
  concept of, 245
  in psychosis, 183-184, 193-194, 200-
    203, 267
  inner and outer, 64-66, 185, 199-203,
    253, 264-267
  knowledge of, 39, 139, 253-260
  loss in psychosis, 193-194, 200-203
  recognition of and adaptation to, 8-9,
    14-17, 252-253
  relation to, xi, 14-17, 43, 63, 114-
    115, 137-138, 245, 252; and ob-
    ject relations, 200-203, 255-257
  social, 27-30, 92-93

Reality—*Continued*
    structure of, 47-49, 92-93
    study of structure of, inherent in psychoanalysis, 29-30, 92-93
    syntonic, objectively vs. subjectively, 50-51, 55, 92; *see also* Behavior, Thinking
    two concepts of, 259-260
    two concepts of "our real world," 261-264
    use of, in conflict solution, 27-28, 39
    ways of acquiring knowledge about, unavoidably lead to distortion of, 254-257
    withdrawal from, 12-13, 183-184, 193-194; *see also* Libido, withdrawal
Reality ego, 122, 165-167, 241
Reality principle, 63, 204, 241-267, 325, 328-329
    an ego principle, 244
    and autonomy, xiii, 260
    and ego functions, 84, 250-252, 260, 292
    and neutralization, xiii, 235
    and postponement of discharge, xi, 39-41, 58, 115, 119, 125, 244, 247, 251-252
    and self-preservation, 84
    complexity in man, 247
    development, 187-188, 244-247, 250-253, 266
    ego contribution to development of, 187-188, 244
    regulating function, 85-86, 243-244
    two meanings, 244-245
Reality testing, 48, 115, 201-203, 236, 263, 338
    development of, 183, 188
    in neurosis and psychosis, 201
    inner vs. outer, 201-202, 253, 256, 266
    see also Behavior, reality-syntonic
Reason
    and unreason, 16
    definition, 45-46, 63
    ideal of, 9-10
Rebelliousness, 258
Recall
    and tension discharge, 410-418
    in Korsakoff psychosis, 353-368
Reconstruction, 99-109, 121, 158, 162, 168, 178, 209, 307, 324, 343
Recording of interviews, 347
Reduction, theories by, 112

Regression, xi, 398
    and adaptation, 59-60
    and creativity, 13
    and group formation, 51-54
    and instinctualization, 192
    and neutralization, 130
    and sexualization, 122
    controlled, 234
    in child, 117, 190, 219
    in obsessional neurosis, 418
    in psychosis, 161, 183, 191, 195
    in the service of the ego, 60, 177
    narcissistic, 192
    partial, 10
    resistivity to, 177, 190, 218-219, 229
Regulatory principles, 84-86, 135, 138, 243-244, 315; *see also* Pleasure principle, Reality principle
Religion, 30, 53, 136, 217, 239
Repetition compulsion, 84, 89, 410
    and obsessional neurosis, 411-418
Repression, 216, 245, 249, 286, 325, 377
    and aggression, 417
    and countercathexis, 185, 197
    and denial, 201
    and ego elaboration, 211-212
    and neutralization, 196, 232, 235
    and persistence of symptoms, 366
    and resistance, 314
    counterpart in organic disorders, 353-368
    deficiency in schizophrenia, 184-185
    development of concept, 292
    id aspect, 159
    role of superego, 176, 198-199
    "sexualization," 245, 288
    superego-ego-id relation, 198
Research, clinical, 302, 307, 336, 342
Resistance, 133-134, 157, 288
    analysis of, 143-144, 148-152
    genetic aspects, 151
    relation to defense, *see* Defense
    stratification, 147
    strength of, 314
    unconscious, 293
Resonance effect, 153
Respiration, 71
Restitution, 191
Reversal, 185
Rhythmical activities, 213

Science, 217, 257, 261-262
Scientific production, 13-14, 60

Schizophrenia, 175, 262, 284, 443
  ego-superego relation in, 196
  metapsychology of, 180-206
  predisposition to, 194, 200, 203-206
  see also Psychosis
Schreber case, 182, 193, 284
Secondary process, 118, 172, 190-194, 218, 273
  and drive discharge, 249, 252
  and neutralization, 131, 229, 233
  characteristics, 174
  concept, 327
  development, 166
Secondary revision, 280
Self
  and aims, 136
  and world, fusion, 185
  cathexis of, xii, 127-129, 192-193, 287-288
  distinguished from ego, 127-128, 279, 287-288
Self-analysis, 339
Self-criticism, 114
Self-deception, 256, 266, 335
Self-destruction, 61, 87, 195, 198, 226
  neutralized aggression as alternative to, xiii, 87, 226
Self-image, xii, 192, 231; *see also* Self-representation
Self-knowledge (understanding)
  and knowledge (understanding) of others, 370-371, 383-386
  limitations, 373, 384-386, 392-394
Self-observation, 310-311, 338
Self-perception, an ego function, 114-115
Self-preservation, xiii, 15, 61, 70, 82-86, 119, 135, 226, 250, 254, 326
  an ego function, 84-85, 168, 226, 243, 247, 295
  and instinctual drives, 86-88
  and neutralization, 226, 235-236
  and pleasure principle, 82, 161-162, 250, 254
Self-punishment, 370
Self-representation
  and ego function, 226, 231, 235-236
  and object representation, *see* Object representation
  vs. cathexis of ego, xii, 127-129, 231
Sexuality, 283, 294, 327
  aims of, 87
  and aggression, 86-87

and sublimation, 216-217, 236-237
  infantile, 326, 398-399
  parents' handling of child's, 36
  plasticity of, 71
  role in development, 105, 121
  see also Libido
Sexualization, xiii, 122, 134, 164, 170, 178, 190-193, 200-203, 213, 229-230, 245
  and sublimation, 217-220, 223
Sign
  as signal and expression, 371-372
  role in clinical work, 342-343
  see also Behavior
Silence, 336
Sleep, 177
  and dream, 405-406
  falling asleep, 161
Social action
  and prediction, 90-91
  theory of, 91
Social class, 26-28, 36
Social compliance, 27-29, 94-95
Social institutions, psychoanalytic study of, 32-33, 94-96
Social psychology, 21
Social relations, x, 19-36
Social sciences, 31, 36-38, 63, 73, 101, 117, 135, 269, 318, 334
  application of psychoanalytic concepts to, 90-98; *see also* Psychoanalysis; Sociology, and psychoanalysis
  see also Anthropology, Sociology
Social structures, meaning of, 93-94
Society
  and concept of health, 14
  forms of, 26-29
  not unconscious fantasy, 93
  selective influence on psychic structures, 25-29
  structure of, 93
  useful function of neurotic in, 6
Sociology, 38, 388
  and psychoanalysis, 19-36, 51, 90-98
  use of psychological concepts, 19-20, 29-36
Somatic compliance, 27, 94
Somatic intrusion, 389, 392-396
Speech, 149-150, 154, 219; *see also* Communication, Language
Sphincters, growth of, 40, 104, 168
Stimulus barrier, *see* Protective barrier against stimuli

Stress, 205
Structural point of view, ix, xii, 63-66, 94-95, 100, 106, 114, 126-128, 135, 179, 182, 186-187, 215, 222, 225, 289-293, 328-331, 344
and instinctual drives, 79-86
and psychoanalytic technique, 146-154, 293
compared with topographic, 331
distinction between function and genesis, 221-222, 324, 330
ego in, 328-331
ego-id differentiation in man basis for differences between instinct and instinctual drives, 77-79, 162, 295
implications, xii, 325
integration with genetic, 222, 289
Stubbornness, 440-443
Sublimation, 40, 128-129, 160, 171, 192-194, 212, 284, 442
a continuous process, 224
and libidinal cathexis, 219
capacity, 219, 222-224, 238-240
content, 221-222
definitions of, 216-217
factors promoting and interfering with, 222
genesis and function, 221
in build-up of ego functions, 216, 221, 225, 228
pregenital, 60, 327
process, 220-224
relation to defense, 171, 234-235
social factors, 25-28
see also Neutralization
Substitution of character traits, 443-444
Superego
aims, 136
and action, 42-45
and aggression, 31, 87, 130, 198, 289
and cultural factors, 25-26
and ego interests, 65-66, 135-137
and external world, 24-26
and free aggression, 198
and group formation, 51-53
and internalization, 41
and neutralization, 87, 238
and neutralized aggression, 87
and reality testing, 256-257
and repression, 176, 198-199
and self-preservation, 84
and social behavior, 21
and typologies, 95

biological roots, 325, 330
cathexis of, xii
concept, 330-331
development of, 7, 31, 44, 65
functions of, 111, 114; autonomy, 177
in obsessional neurosis, 418
in schizophrenia, 195-196, 199
modification, 24
splitting of ("cleavage"), 51-53
structures in, xii
use of aggressive energy, 176
Symbol
collective, 32
formation and ego development, 172
relation to symbolized, 189, 342-343, 372-373
understanding of, 395
verbal, 149
Symbolism, 372-373, 398
Symbolization, 216, 220
Symptom
and sublimation, 216
evaluation of, 5, 369
formation, 26, 216, 319, 397, 418
freedom from, not a criterion of health, 5-7
Synthetic function, *see* Ego functions

Tachistoscopic experiments, 407-409
Talents, 35, 438-439, 443
Technology, 10, 33
Teeth, 40, 104, 168
Temperament, in twins, 424-445
Temperature orientation, 186
Tension systems (K. Lewin), 409-418
Thanatos, 295
Thinking
a detour activity, 261
a trial action, 41, 115, 261
causal, 264
creative, 311; *see also* Creativity
egocentric, 255
prescientific, 382-383, 397
reality-syntonic, two aspects, 253
scientific, 253, 261
symbolic, 365-368
see also Thought processes
Thought processes
and repression, 13
disturbances in schizophrenia, 188-190, 193
hypercathexis, 418
in obsessional neurosis, 316, 411-418

Thought processes—*Continued*
  magic, 193
  of child, 255-256
  precocious development, 60
  replacing hallucination, 166
  see also Primary process, Secondary
    process, Thinking
Time perception, 115
Toilet training, 36
Topographic point of view, 126-128, 146,
    225, 272, 278, 289, 293, 331, 338
Totalitarian system, 33, 51-55, 96
Totemism, 31
Training analysis, *see* Psychoanalyst
Transference, negative, 133
Trauma
  and symptom formation, 398-399, 418
  early, 209-212
Traumatic neurois, 410
Trieb, see Instinctual drives
Tropism, 76
Truth, 257-258
Turning against the self, 185
Twilight states, 354, 367
Twins, identical, 419-445
Typologies, 422-423
  genetic, 103
  psychoanalytic, 94-95, 103
  see also Personality types

Unconscious (processes), 32, 156, 254,
    277-278, 281-283, 288, 293, 305,
    309, 325, 370, 373
  and preconscious, 137, 147
  and understanding, 383-386, 389-400
  Freud's concept, 320-321, 327
  implications, 323
  making conscious, 147-148, 383-384

  psychoanalysis as psychology of, 21,
    381
Unconscious (system), 146, 331, 344
Understanding (*Verstehende Pycholo-
    gie*), 369-403
  genetic, 376-377, 382
  rational, 370, 395
  static, 376
  sympathetic, 370-371, 377, 385-394
Undoing, 325, 417
Unpleasure tolerance, 108, 140
Unreason, 46

Validation, *see* Psychoanalytic theory
Values
  agglutination of, 47-48
  and concept of health, 5, 8, 14
  and definition of concepts, 217-219
  and meaning, 264-265, 395
  and rationality, 65
  and validation, 257-258
  irradiation of, 47-48
  of superego, taken over by ego, 136
Vanity, 440-443
Variables, independent, interdependent,
    and intervening, distinction, 332,
    345-346
Verstehende Psychologie, 369-403, 422,
    443; *see also* Explanation, Under-
    standing
Visual imagery, 60
Vocational choice, 36

Walking, 121
War, 24, 30, 34
Weaning, 36
Wolf Man, 210